BOATBUILDING
IN YOUR OWN
BACKYARD

Paul, Johnnie and a shipway in the author's own back yard.

BOATBUILDING IN YOUR OWN BACKYARD

by S. S. RABL

CMP

SECOND EDITION

CORNELL MARITIME PRESS

CAMBRIDGE   MARYLAND

ISBN 0-87033-009-8
Library of Congress Catalog Card Number : 57-11361
Manufactured in the United States of America

DEDICATION

To Paul and Johnnie, the workmen on the shipways of my own back yard: One of them is now a
sailor, the other a shipbuilder—the very things that
I had repeatedly told them they would never be.

S. S. R.

PREFACE

In which the author tells why and how the book was written and many other things not found in an ordinary foreword.

In many books the preface has turned out to be nothing more than the author's excuse for writing them. Sometimes this excuse is very subtle, but a continued search through the wording will invariably reveal it. This book shall be no different except that the excuse will not be subtle. Very few people know how a book comes into being. I'll tell you.

The actual beginning of this book was more years ago than I care to reveal. It began as a resolve to myself that some day I would write a book. This was a big resolve for a youngster who then was hardly dry behind the ears, but when Youth is angry it often makes resolutions that are very hard to keep in later years. When I made that resolution I was mad. I devoured article after article in the boating magazines on boatbuilding. I had read book after book on the subject. All of them had the same fault. They were written by men who were professional boatbuilders. I got mad. "Why in hell do those guys write of this sort of framing or that sort of joint which is far beyond the capabilities of us kids?" I thought this and many other things that were not in the least complimentary to the authors of that day. Years passed and the resolution was forgotten for the time being.

In addition to the reading of books I haunted the boatyards. The big yards were busy and the workmen were making the same sort of joints that I had read about. Well they could; they had machinery to do that sort of work. I visited the smaller yards and found men who were building boats that anyone capable of wielding hand tools could build. Here there were men who would stop work at the least provocation to sit and spin yarns to a likely youngster of how a boat should be built "proper like." Here

were men whose boats were out on the bay working for the fishermen and crabbers. These boats stood storm and waves as well as, if not better than, the best of the highly painted yachts. "Why," I asked myself, "should these boats not make good yachts?" I have never found a single reason why they shouldn't.

I sat at the feet of old Till Price and learned how a keel should be cut; and from Uncle Gabe Moses, an old darky who built skiffs over in Bodkin Creek, I learned that the best way to allow a calking seam was to lay a saw in the joints as the planks were fitted. These men were humble and if they did not agree with your opinion (and what youngster doesn't have opinions), they told you in a nice way that you were wrong. The professional yacht builders would have no patience with you and more than once threatened to kick you from the yard.

I was then an apprentice draftsman and had started to design my own boats along the lines of the fishermen. Once I mustered nerve enough to write a short article on a "simple-to-build" small boat for one of the yachting magazines. Only those who have experienced it can ever know the thrill of seeing their first effort in print. Judged in the light of my later experiences, the boat was lousy, but I received encouraging letters from others who were looking for this sort of craft to build. Little by little my boats designed along the lines of the fishing craft were taking on a more yachty appearance. I began to preach the gospel of simplified construction to such an extent that Chas. Hall, who was then editor of *Motorboat*, coined an appropriate name for it, "Construction a la Maryland."

As the years rolled by, these articles of mine became more and more in demand. Others besides myself were taking up the fight for the boat that any man could build, notable among them my old friend Westy Farmer.

Westy was then editor of *Modern Mechanics* (now *Mechanix Illustrated*) and was designing boats much on the order of mine. A beautiful friendship was formed because years prior to this I had designed *Picaroon* for myself, and Chas. Hall had made her famous. Westy admired her (along with a thousand others) and we redesigned her for his magazine. Hundreds were built and Hank Hemingway sailed one of them that he had called *Hawkshaw* across the Gulf of Mexico to further glory. I then remembered the resolve I had made, many years before, to write the book on boatbuilding for the amateur. The book was started but the yearly demands on my spare time for the Fawcett *How to Build Twenty Boats* became so great that it was laid aside and forgotten.

In the Fall of 1945 I was visiting the office of the Cornell Maritime Press in reference to some other matters when Felix looked across the desk at me and said, "Sam, how about doing a boatbuilding book for us?" I remembered the unfinished manuscript and replied, "O.K., Felix, I will"—just like that. In the discussion of the pros and cons of full-page cuts vs. folded plates and other such weighty matters, I plumb forgot to ask Felix when he wanted the book.

The Spring of 1946 rolled around and I was idly gazing out of the window dreaming of the time when the white perch would start biting down on the bar when the telephone rang. It was a long distance call from New York and Felix was at the other end of the line. "When am I gonna get my book?" he pleaded. "Aw hell, Felix," I entreated, "ya know dam well that I gotta fix up my boat and I wanna build another. Besides this the fish are starting to bite, and you know I never write when fish are biting."

"T'hell with that," said Felix and added other persuasive language that only those who know Felix can appreciate. In the end Felix won and that is why this book was written.

A stupendous job lay ahead. The old manuscript, now ten years behind the times, had to be modernized. Since it had been started originally, many new materials that are a boon to the amateur builder had come into being. Notable among these are the new waterproof plywoods and sealing compounds; not to mention the new resin glues that have made the lot of the back-yard builder much easier. New designs had to be prepared to take advantage of the lessons learned in the war. Old and tried ideas had to be incorporated in new materials. The materials themselves had to be investigated and, not until I was firmly convinced with an actual working proof, were they accepted.

In writing all my boatbuilding articles I have always remembered how, as a kid, I saw friends putting their money into designs that were drawn by men who dreamed them from the safe confines of a rocking chair. The boats that were built from these designs plainly showed their origin after they were finished. My earliest resolve was that this would be one of the sins that I would never commit. This resolution was carried over into the policy of *How to Build Twenty Boats* and it has been built into the very heart of this book.

The designer of any boat for amateur builders carries on his shoulders a grave responsibility. Many of the boats he designs will be built by youngsters. They will save their pennies and deny themselves many things to build their dream boat. No designer can afford to let them down. The man who disillusions these kids with extravagant claims for his design which cannot be fulfilled will end his days as a coal passer on the ferry boat that crosses the River Styx.

The builder of the boat, on the other hand, has a certain responsibility to the designer. The builder must remember that the designer has spent hours of intensive thought in planning the boat. He has arrived at certain decisions for certain reasons that were dictated by long years of experience. He has determined the size and shape of every member because experience had dictated that this and that should be so and so.

The author has received many letters from amateur builders crying the blues because their boats will not work as they had been planned. If the boat was close enough for a visit, I have gone to it. The sight that invariably met my eyes has more than once brought moisture to them. "My Gawd!" I would exclaim through the tears. "Did I design that boat?"

"You sure did," the builder would answer. "I made her jest like the book sez."

Out would come my trusty pocket rule and the story of why the boat looked as it did would unfold. An uncle of the builder, who was a retired sailor or something else, had said the design was all wrong and had suggested certain changes that the builder had followed. That was when the author would throw his hat on the ground and jump on it. That was when the air around him would turn blue with words that had been learned in a lifetime around the waterfront and shipyards. Michael Angelo had once thrown a last at a shoemaker and told him to stick to it.

The builder of any small boat will be pestered by a host of well-meaning but misinformed people. There will be hordes of others who will try to show their superior intelligence by suggesting certain changes in the boat. Heed them not!

There will be others who will tell the builder that he is all wrong and that Kris Kraft, Micherson or Podge build their boats a certain way, and that the construction that the builder is using is all wrong. Chase them away!

Let the builder stop for a minute to consider the case himself. Can anyone in five minutes' inspection of a boat weigh the various merits of a thousand and one odd thoughts that go into the design? Is he as qualified to design the boat as someone who has lived with this sort of thing for over half a lifetime? "The defense rests."

Again there will be the builder himself who will want to make certain changes in the design. Let him go ahead and make them if he knows what he is doing. I am not so high-minded as to think that I own the very soul of every man who builds from my designs. I am still an iconoclast, but—the builder who makes any change whatsoever in the design of the boat accepts the responsibility of that change. This is only as it should be—I will be blamed for enough of the atrocities in this book as it is.

Still another type of pest will bother the builder in the construction of any small boat. This termite will hang around the boat evening after evening. His smiling face will appear above the sheer-strake looking down on you as you work inside the boat. When you ask him to help lift the motor in tomorrow evening he will be so sorry that he has made a previous engagement, but he is anxious to help with all the easy jobs on the boat. Beware of him. Just as he has haunted the boat in her building, so will he haunt her afloat and he will be on the dock at just those inopportune times when his presence may be wholly undesirable. In justice to him you feel obligated to take him along in return for the labor he spent on the boat, and this is just the very thing he counted on when he helped. He was subtly banking his labor in return for anticipated pleasures after the boat was afloat.

The financing of the construction of a small boat is another thing to be considered before her keel is laid. Be sure that you have enough money to purchase at least one-half of the material before any work is done. There is a very sound reason behind this statement.

Lumber purchased in large lots is quite a bit cheaper than when bought piece by piece. The lumber dealer will charge you just as much to deliver one piece of two-by-four as he will a truckload. These hidden bits of overhead expense do not appear itemized on your bill but are added, nevertheless, in the cost of the material. The labor of handling this material from his racks to the truck is also treated this way. You will, in all probability, spend next to your last penny on materials when you purchase them, and if there isn't sufficient material on hand to last you until you have saved enough to finish another item of construction, there will be a long agonizing wait during which construction is at a dead halt. For those whose money "burns a hole in their pockets," the purchase of material in small lots is preferable for in this manner they are investing their funds in the boat, even though it is an expensive way to do banking.

In the purchase of material, buy the best that your money can secure. No material in this world is too good for a boat and time alone will prove this to you. Cheap materials will give you many headaches with replacements and repairs in later years and they may weaken at times when you are depending on them to hold. Makeshift articles are more expensive than those designed for a specific purpose. Be sure that good marine fittings are secured. Many neat little fittings can be purchased at the dime stores and at the cheap auto accessory shops. These will look good on a boat for several months and then break out with a smallpox of rust spots, or disintegrate in the weather. This does not mean that such stores are to be shunned entirely. Many small articles and fittings can be found on their counters which may be used to good advantage on a boat. For example, the regular auto dome light may be purchased at a fraction of the cost of a practically identical fitting sold for marine use. However, be sure that the article you purchase will be suitable. For outside use, time has proven that hot-dipped galvanized iron and good bronze are the only types of fittings which will stand the test of years of exposure to the consuming elements of the sun and the sea.

Beware of partnerships in boatbuilding. As a general rule they will, at some time or other, come to grief. I have seen friendships destroyed by a partnership in a boat. A partnership of three has a much better chance of surviving than a dual one. This is due to the fact that generally two of the partners will agree and overrule the third.

In the selection of a boat design be sure that it will fill your needs. Many a man has deluded himself into believing that he wanted a hardy seagoing packet because of its romantic appointments, only to discover that his available sailing time was limited to short weekend trips. This dawns upon him later when he realizes that on the same size boat the space occupied by large water tankage and stores might have been used to better advantage in a more spacious cabin. Many men build pretty little sailboats (which have much less cabin room than a motorboat of the same size) and then motor them around, seldom taking the covers off the sails. Several hours of serious contemplation and a truthful analysis of your own situation will save a lot of disillusionment later. It is easy to be carried away by romancing in a boat of given design, but her beautiful sheer and snappy seagoing appearance will never compensate for hours of discomfort aboard her after she is in use. Before you build, be doubly sure that the boat will fit your ideas of comfort, your available time and, most of all, your pocketbook.

The adage, "It isn't the initial cost but the upkeep," is very well applied to any boat.

In the construction of any of the boats in this book, be sure that all of your joints are as good as your ability permits. Tight joints insure strength as well as watertightness. Many a sloppy joint has given endless hours of worry over a leak that could have been prevented by fifteen minutes more of effort. In shaping a particular part always bear in mind the function for which that part is intended. The bit of prose included below is more truth than poetry, as many have discovered to their sorrow.

"The sea will always be wild and untamed. A mother to those who earn their bread upon her bosom. A sweetheart to those who love her. An avenging angel to those who hold her in contempt."

S. S. RABL

Preface to Second Edition

It seems but yesterday that I wrote the preface to the first edition of this book. Ten years later, in reading it over, I would not change a single comma. This period of time has seen a remarkable change in the boating picture of this country. Many new materials for boatbuilding have entered the field. The very habits of the boating enthusiasts have changed. Today one may find a new boat being built in a back yard hundreds of miles from the nearest water in which it may be used. The trailer behind the family car is responsible for this. The number of small boat sailors has quadrupled in the last five years. The outboard motor has become a thing of reliability to such an extent that the number manufactured far exceeds that of the permanent inboard propulsion plant.

A new generation of boatbuilders has been sired. We of yesteryears are very willing to tell them of how things were done in "The Good Old Days". We cannot stomach their dreams of atomic or solar power. We become impatient with their ideas for improvement. We feel sorry for them because they do not have what we had, little realizing that the new generation is enjoying now "The Good Old Days" of which they will tell their own children.

In spite of all the dire predictions and the old expression that even the Greek civilization had— "What is the world coming to?"—I can see no dire moments in my crystal ball for them. Somehow or other there is a sneaking suspicion in the back of my mind that they will work it all out for themselves just as my own generation did.

S. S. R.

ACKNOWLEDGEMENTS

No book is ever the product of any one man. Even though its author be a hermit in the center of a vast desert, there are still other men who are responsible in a great measure for its being. In the formative period of any writer's career there is the influence of those who have gone before him. In my case there was C. G. Davis. Charlie Davis wrote prolifically and wrote in the language of the ordinary man. Thomas Fleming Day, poet and sailor, cannot be neglected among the writers of that time, nor can Thomas Clapham. There was also C. D. Mower and a host of others.

Marching shoulder to shoulder with me (a buck private in the rear rank) were such sterling souls as Billy Atkin, Jerry White, Jack Hanna and Westy Farmer, and I must not forget my old friend Chas. Hall; all of them champions of the cause of the home-made boat.

There were others who stood on the side lines cheering these soldiers on. Herb Stone, the Skipper of *Yachting*. The late Bill Nutting of *Motorboat* and a score of others whose encouragement tided over the dark days. All of these men contributed more to this book than mere encouragement—they made it.

In the actual process of getting the book together there were others whom I must thank: the Clemenses, Lou and "Mom," who typed the author's badly scrawled manuscript, and the boys who traced the designs. Not an iota of these people's work can be overlooked.

To Ed LeBrun, doughty skipper of the good ship *Barnacle*, must go the credit for reading the finished manuscript and for his helpful suggestions.

To *Mechanix Illustrated*, the publishers of *How to Build Twenty Boats*, and to my old friend Felix Cornell (who, we all know, published the *American Merchant Seaman's Manual*) go the author's extreme thanks for permission to use material from their publications.

Second Edition

To all the backyard builders, world wide, for their many letters. To Oscar Thomas and Don Baker, Andy Harthousen, Rog. Bollman, Eric Duffy and John Durnin for the insight they gave in the problems of the backyard builder in this mechanized age. To Mr. B. Cobb, Jr., of the Textile Products Division of the Owens Corning Fiberglas Corp., for his invaluable help and data on the use of this new material. Mr. George Bell, of Winterport, Maine, sent many helpful suggestions and photos on strip planking.

To my gal, Marian (Mrs. Oscar Thomas), who bore the brunt of the typing and gave an insight into the woes of the distaff side of the backyard boatbuilding. May she now be forever free to hang her wash in HER own back yard. Mary-Ellen Guthrie must also be remembered for her similar work. To J. Haney for his sketch of his "Haneykar" and to "Commodore" Roy Fowler for his comments, verse and adverse, on outboard boating. My extreme thanks go to all and sundry who contributed but just a mite to the making of this second edition.

CONTENTS

LIST OF BOAT PLANS

CHAPTER I

BOATBUILDING WOODS

As all of the boats in this book are to be constructed of wood, it is wise to devote some of our time to the study of this important material. We often speak of the various ages in man's development as the Stone Age, the Bronze Age, etc., and measure his advance in civilization by his discovery and application of various materials. Wood has always been one of the most important instruments of his self-expression and it has truly been the material from which the ladder in his upward climb was constructed. Wood is ageless. When the forests pass from the face of the earth man is also very likely to pass. The writer can rhapsodize over a beautiful stick of timber and wax poetic over a beautiful show of grain. To those who have worked in wood there exists no other medium like it. I have heard some men deplore the passing of wood in shipbuilding and other men deplore its passing in the construction of airplanes. I have heard the old shipbuilders tell with pride of the days when they laid a schooner's margin plank from the stem to the foremast when flitch oak came into the yards in pieces wide enough to do so. I have also listened to airplane builders speak of the beautiful Sitka spruce wing beams that went from root to tip in one piece and how these trees were carefully lowered to the ground so that the fall might produce no harmful cracks or shakes. There is something inexpressibly fascinating in the working of wood that seems to get under your skin—to stay there until you die.

TEAK, of all woods used in boatbuilding, is the finest. It is usually sold either as Borneo or Rangoon teak. The Borneo teak is darker and harder. Teak is very expensive and few of us can afford it in a boat. If we could it would be wonderful because teak is practically everlasting. An example of its durability is the old convict ship *Success* that was raised after being sunk in Sydney harbor in Australia for nearly a century, and is still sailing the seas as a floating museum. Teak can often be obtained around shipyards in the form of scrap torn off vessels under repair. This material resawed to smaller pieces will often find use in small boat construction.

MAHOGANY, either Honduras or Philippine, is an excellent wood for boat construction. It does not swell or absorb water to any great extent and is used for planking, joiner-work, and for framing in some small boats. Reddish in color, it produces a pleasing appearance when finished natural. Mahogany is widely used for trim and is the only wood which will give a boat that desirable yachty appearance. Too much mahogany finished bright will, on the other hand, tend to make most boats look over-decorated. Most mahogany sold for boatbuilding purposes is Philippine mahogany, which is not true mahogany but a type of tropical cedar. There are two grades, Lauan and Batan. The Lauan has a beautiful ribbon grain which at times tends to become fuzzy and hard to finish. The Batan runs in even grain and is best for planking. Both types do not absorb water readily, hold their fastenings well and are ideal for all parts of any boat. Both are adaptable to framing for small boats where expense is not great. Bay Wood or Honduras-Mahogany is hard and stringy and makes excellent material for transoms, rails and guards. It is hard to work but takes a beautiful finish.

WHITE OAK is the favorite wood for the keel and framing of any boat. It is tough and durable but is rather hard to work, and large timbers for keels or stems are best when cut from timber that has been water-seasoned or kept immersed in water from the time it is cut. In recent years good white oak has become very scarce.

RED OAK, PIN OAK and SWAMP OAK are the common types of oak in this country. They are used mainly for interior trim of a boat or at such places

1

where great strength is not required. Red oak is likely to rot quickly when used in damp places.

LONG-LEAF PINE is the equal of white oak for strength, life and durability. It is not quite as tough as white oak, and is likely to split if fastening holes are not drilled. It can be used for frames, keels and, if of selected material, for stems in larger boats. It is unexcelled for heavy planking and has a very long life when submerged. I have dug up long-leaf pine logs that had been submerged for 40 years in the mud and found them in almost perfect condition.

SHORT-LEAF PINE is sometimes sold as Virgin or Virginia pine and is soft and knotty. It has little use in boatbuilding but, because it is cheap. it can be used to advantage for temporary framing and shoring during construction. It is sometimes called bull pine.

OREGON PINE, also known as Douglas fir, is an excellent material for boatbuilding. It is easily worked, has a clear, straight grain and is durable. It has the same tendency to split as long-leaf pine and holes should be drilled for all fastenings. It is widely used for planking, decking and for spars. When used for planking or decking, it should be ordered as vertical grain stock. Oregon pine is rather soft and scars easily. The vertical grain is less subject to this fault than the flat grain stock. The vertical grain material is easier to finish; the flat grain stock has a tendency to lift up in slivers. It can be purchased in very long lengths and may be used for chines, clamps, keel aprons and sheer-strakes for any boat in this book.

WHITE PINE, SUGAR PINE and PONDEROSA PINE are suitable for interior joiner-work. They are soft and easy to work. True white pine is an excellent material for decks and planking but it is scarce today and, if the purchaser does not know this material, he is advised to confine the pines sold today as white pine to interior work, for they will rot quickly when exposed to the elements. I have seen some of this material disintegrate after two seasons of exposure to the weather.

SPRUCE has the quality of possessing the least weight on the greatest strength. It is used for framing in light boats, for seats and for joiner-work. It is an unexcelled material for spars. Sitka spruce is undoubtedly the finest material that can be secured for the manufacture of spars. It was highly prized in airplane construction where great strength must be secured on light weight. Sitka spruce is quite expensive but can be secured in long lengths.

CYPRESS has been called the "wood eternal" and is used for planking and on almost every other part of a boat where great strength is not required. It is soft, easily worked and takes on a fine finish when finished natural for it has a beautiful grain. It has poor holding power for nails and when two pieces of cypress are fastened together, screws should be used to make the joint. It should never be used where it will be subject to considerable wear, i.e., where ropes or chains constantly pass over it. In some of our southern states spars are made from cypress for the forests produce long timbers. The best grades of cypress are sold as Gulf cypress and the ends of most of the reputable cypress marketed are stamped with various trade-marks. Beware of sapwood cypress because it rots quickly.

REDWOOD is a product of the giant redwood trees of our western coast and is similar to Oregon pine in a lot of respects. It has a finer grain than Oregon pine and a greater tendency to split. It can be secured in long lengths and large widths and has a pleasing red color in most cases. It takes a fine varnish finish, making it suitable for interior trim and joinerwork. When in direct contact with water it has a large percentage of expansion or swell and must be worked in narrow widths if used for planking. Redwood is soft and should not be used where it will be subjected to wear. It also has a tendency to check and crack when exposed to rain and sun.

JUNIPER, sometimes known as Southern Cedar, is an aromatic wood with excellent properties. It is similar to cypress, being light in color, and will not swell to any great extent in contact with water. It has few competitors when used as planking and is generally sold in flitch boards. A flitch board (Fig. 1) is a

A FLITCH BOARD

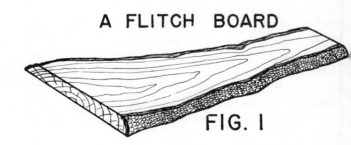

FIG. I

board that has been ripped from the tree, leaving the bark on the edges. The width is not parallel throughout the length. This is an advantage where boat planks must be tapered and curved for it eliminates waste. If parallel-edge timber were used for this purpose, there would be double waste. The waste would occur once in edging the flitch and again in cutting the curve from the edged board. In buying a flitch, the width is measured at the center of the length.

WHITE ASH is somewhat similar to oak. and can be substituted for oak in places where it is not continually moist. Its real advantage will emerge in places where continual walking will wear paint or varnish. White ash can be scrubbed. It will show clean and white when dry, making a very nice appearance. A galley table made from this material will be as inviting as one with a cloth on it after it has been scrubbed several times. White ash makes excellent drainboards around the galley sink and is unexcelled as a material for gratings over small hatches. Oars and cleats, as well as the shells of blocks, are often made from this material. It can also be used as framing in small boats.

PORT ORFORD CEDAR is without a peer in the planking of small boats. It is soft, easily worked and does not swell or shrink to any great extent when exposed to the action of wave or wind. It is rapidly becoming scarce and is rather expensive.

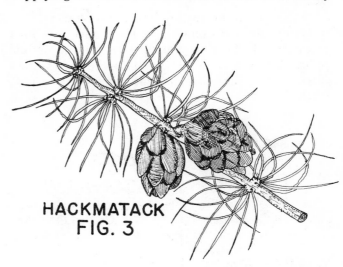

FIG. 2
LOCUST

LOCUST is an extremely hard, tough, close-grained wood that is ideal for mooring bitts, rudder stocks, cleats and other small parts that get heavy strain or rough wear. It is not commonly found in lumber yards so be on the lookout for a stick of seasoned locust timber from one of your country cousins.

OSAGE ORANGE is in the same category as locust and must be secured in the same way.

For anyone contemplating the construction of a small boat at any time, a collection of locust or Osage orange will come in very handy. Above the rafters of my shop are stored odds and ends of this sort of timber that have many times been worth their weight in gold when needed.

HACKMATACK has never been satisfactorily replaced by any other wood for its specific purpose in boatbuilding. Its peculiar growth makes it ideally suited for knees or brackets and in the old days of wooden shipbuilding there was a thriving industry supplying this article of the trade to builders. Today

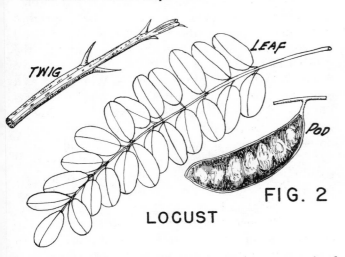

HACKMATACK
FIG. 3

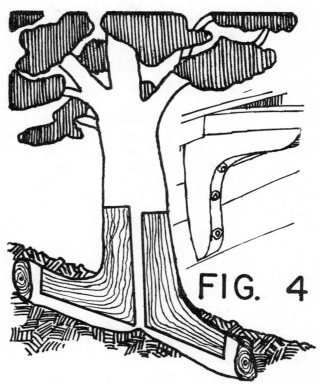

FIG. 4

WHERE BOAT KNEES
COME FROM

these knees can be bought only in the large sizes and usually to special order only. If the amateur uses this wood he must go to the forest to obtain it. In some localities it is known as larch, and in others as tamarack. It grows in moist places and on hillsides near swamps.

While we are on the subject of forest trees, it is well to pause and examine the tree to see just what makes it tick. Year by year the tree sends up its sap in the spring and this layer of sap forms the new wood around the outer circumference of the trunk.

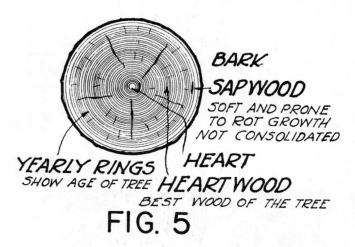

BARK

SAPWOOD
SOFT AND PRONE
TO ROT GROWTH
NOT CONSOLIDATED

YEARLY RINGS
SHOW AGE OF TREE

HEART
HEARTWOOD
BEST WOOD OF THE TREE

FIG. 5

(Fig. 5.) It takes years for this sapwood to consolidate and become firm, before which it is soft and punky and apt to rot. Some boards may have firm wood on one edge and sap on the other. Watch for this condition and examine the end grain of every board that goes into your planking. The heart wood of any tree is the place from which the prime lumber comes, but in some types of lumber the fast growth of the tree in its infancy will make the very heart of the tree unsuitable.

In most cases, the type of wood to be used for the designs in this book is specified, but there may be a time when you want to substitute another wood for the one specified. A suitability table is included for this purpose. (See Fig. 6.)

DOUGLAS FIR PLYWOOD (*Exterior Type*).—The sterling qualities of Douglas fir have not been overlooked by technicians and recent years have seen a new boatbuilding material evolve from it. This material fulfills the dream of every boatbuilder who wishes to cover the surfaces of his craft with one big sheet free of seams and their attendant leaks. In selecting plywood for the craft in this book we must

be sure that it is of the waterproof type and that it has a reliable brand marked on its edges. The manufacturers of this product have banded together in an association to protect the quality and standards of their product. Your lumber dealer will be glad to give you a booklet describing the properties and manufacture of plywood.

SYNTHETIC WOODS.—Celotex, Prestwood and Masonite are synthetic woods. Most of these woods are constructed from sugar cane by-products and are entirely reliable for marine use. Celotex will come in handy for insulation, soundproofing, and in bulkheads and partitions which are not subjected to strain. The pressed woods can be used for almost anything around the boat. The tempered variety has even been successfully used for planking in many small craft but has the disadvantage of great weight. The advantage of this material is that it can be used as covering for companionways, hatches and cabin tops. As a cabin top strong enough to bear a man's weight, it should never be used in a thickness less than one-quarter inch; for other tops it may be one-eighth inch thick. The real advantage of this material will become evident in painting when one finds that the brush will really cover and the paint will not have to be worked into any vees or beads. When used as a cabin top it need not be canvased, thereby eliminating this expense and, in some measure, reducing its cost when compared to a wooden top. Wherever exposed to weather the tempered variety should be used and, if used as decking, the rough side of the material should be placed upward so that it forms a more sure footing than a smooth finished surface.

HOW TO ORDER LUMBER.—To the beginner the purchase of lumber, the designations of finish and the charge for thicknesses are somewhat puzzling. In different localities, there seem to be various designations but, on the whole, rough lumber is cut in quarter-inch thickness and designated by the number of quarter inches in this thickness. For instance, one-inch stock would be called four-quarter, one-and-a-quarter-inch stock, five-quarter, and so on up the scale. When this is to be finished or dressed, it again receives another designation. The surfacing is designated by the number of surfaces to be run through the planer. The usual one-inch board that we buy at any lumber mill is designated as four-quarter, S-4-S. Translated into terms that we can understand, this designation denotes that it was one-inch stock, surfaced on four sides. If we measure this stock, we will find that it has lost at least an eighth in surfacing and a quarter in edging. A one-inch by six-inch board will come to us, at the most, seven-eighths by five and three-quarter inches. Regardless of how thick this lumber is ordered below one inch in thickness, we will pay for a four-quarter board, unless we order sufficient stock that it will pay our lumber dealer to re-saw larger stock and dress it down to the thickness we desire.

All lumber is sold by the board-foot. That is, we pay for a square foot of lumber one inch thick or fractions of this unit. Flooring and other tongue-and-groove lumber are sold in most localities by the square foot laid, i.e., by the amount of surface the material will cover after the tongue has been deducted. When ordering lumber from a dealer, it is safer to designate it by ordering the rough size and stating the width and thickness it is to be surfaced to, and which edges are to be surfaced. For example, if we want strips for decking, we will order 1¼″ x 2″, S-4-S to 1⅛″ x 1¾″. When ordering members for frames which must be beveled, we should specify the material S-2-S. In this case, the lumberman will surface a wide board and run it through his ripsaw, sawing it to the required widths. It will then come to us with the sides finished but the edges will show saw marks. Usually, it is wise to visit your lumber dealer and explain to him just what special sizes you require. He may try to persuade you to take something else in stock, but stick by your guns. Even though he raises "Holy Ned" in language peculiar to all lumber dealers, tell him that's what the book specifies and that's what you want.

OAK VS. YELLOW PINE.—The days when one could buy the good old *white* oak on the lumber dealers say-so, that it was *white* oak, are gone. Most lumber dealers today are purely merchants, passing the stuff that they sell through their racks as any other tradesman would his own particular line of merchandise. I have seen quite a bit of our present day oak disintegrate in a matter of three years. It takes an expert to tell *white* oak from some of the other thousand and one varieties. *Red* and *chestnut* oak have a distinctive color, you can spot them right off without a lot of training. Some dealers may act in all good faith in selling you what they firmly believe to be white oak. The odds are against it being such. Then again when you get white oak there are grades and grades of the stuff and some of them not so good as others. In big timbers it can be secured if cut from still standing stock but then you must take it green. This is not a detriment if you store it for a while and

thoroughly oil it all over before you do. Where oak is specified and not available the answer is yellow pine.

If you will look up yellow pine properties in any engineering manual you will find that it rates next to oak. The U.S. Forestry Laboratory reports are available to any one who wishes to compare the tested results from both of these woods. The best of the yellow pines is the long leaf variety. Originally cut from the bayous of Mississippi and Louisiana it was the best shipbuilding wood obtainable. Today very few of these giants rear their heads above their fellows and then, in some isolated place, where the lumbermen found it too difficult to fell. Today your best bet in buying yellow pine is to specify *Select North Carolina, grade "B" or better,* then be sure to insist that it is good close grained stock without defects.

Twenty years ago when I built my twenty-six foot cutter, *Star of the Sea,* the price difference between oak and yellow pine was such that it was frame with yellow pine or await a better fortune. I had an old Scotch-Irish friend in the lumber business and he (*Jimmy McDougal*) picked out the material piece by piece. The pine was of that variety that the smell of

	Keel	Stem	Stern Post	Deadwood	Apron	Floors	Frames Sawed	Frames Bent	Chines	Clamps	Deck Beams	Planking	Sheer Strake	Decking Bare	Deck Canvased	Transom	Cabin Stills	Cabin Sides	Cabin Top Cvd	Guards	Joiner Work	Spars
Teak			1				1				1	1	1			1	1		1			
Mahogany							2					1	2	2		1		1			1	
Live Oak	1	1	1	1	1	1	1	1	1	1	1		1			1	1	3	1			
White Oak	1	1	1	1	1	1	1	1	1	1	1	2	1			1	1	2	1			
Red Oak						3				2			3					3		2		
Elm	2	2	2	2		1	2			2												
Ash									3	3	3	3				3						3
Pine, long leaf	2	2	2	2	2	2	1	2	2	2	2	2				3	2		2			
Pine, short leaf	4					4							3					3				
Pine, Oregon	4		3	3	3		3			2	3	3		1		3	3					2
Cedar, white											2			2			2					
Cedar, Southern											2		1				2					
Cedar, Western											2		2	1			2					
Cypress											3		1				1			3		3
Redwood											4		3	2			2		3			
White Pine											2		2	1			1			2	3	
Sugar Pine												2				2		4				
Ponderosa Pine											3					4		4	4			
Silver Spruce									3			2										2
Sitka Spruce									2			2										1
Fir, common	4		4	4	3	4		4			4	4	4	4		4						4
Apatong	3	2	2	2	2	3		2	1		2	2				2			3			
Acacia	2	1	1	1	1	2		2			1	2				1						
Camphor Wood	2		2	1	1	2		2		1	1	1	1	1		1	1	2			1	
Green Heart	1	1	1	1	1	1		2	1	1	1		1			2		1		1		
Dogwood	1	3		2	2	1	2	1	1		1	1				1						
Madiera	3		3	2	2	2		1	2		2	2	1	2			2	2	3		2	

Fig. 6. Wood Selection Table. Numbers indicate order of choice.

pine resin lingered for months in the shop. When it was cut, a handful of the sawdust squeezed together would adhere in a lump. Last year the boat was inspected for a general overhaul. The only material renewed was two pieces of oak in her transom. Another boat now almost nine years old was built from standard lumber yard stock of sized *North Carolina* and was treated with *Cuprinol*. That boat today is as sound as the day she was built.

LAMINATES.—The scarcity of good timber in large sizes, the improvement in water-proof glues and the search for greater strength combined with lighter weight has produced a new type of wood construction called laminates. During the last war this system was used extensively for small boat construction and developed to its present state during that period. Large timbers are hard to work and have the ever present tendency to crack and check in the drying process. For the back yard builder their thickness, beyond the range of his power tools, means a lot of laborious hand work scarphing and bolting them together. By combining a number of thinner pieces into one integrated whole, a better assembly and much stronger construction is assured. Plywood is one outstanding example of modern lamination.

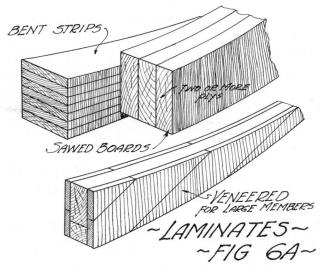

~LAMINATES~
~FIG 6A~

No laminate is any better than the glue that binds its plies. For this reason only *rescorcinal* resin glues or *epoxy* resins should be used. Where the laminate does not come continuously in contact with water, the urea glues will suffice. Good smooth wood to wood joints are important along with good clamping to hold them tight until the glue sets. Amateur builders seldom have enough clamps on hand so the thinner plies of a laminate may be held together with gal-

vanized wire nails to provide the necessary clamping action. Patent nails have little value in this sort of work as the glue bond is the main source of strength. The nails are allowed to remain in the laminate, care being taken to keep them well away from any future cuts. Where it is desirable to withdraw the nails at some later date, small squares of scrap plywood with a hole drilled in them are slipped over the nail before driving them. These allow the nail to be set up tight without scarring the wood and make for easy removal later. In glueing up the separate pieces, glue should be applied to both surfaces and the wood slid backward and forward several times to evenly distribute the glue before setting in the final location.

Some laminates are made up with a heavy center and a diagonal veneer on both sides. This method eliminates all the fancy scarph work and the tedious drilling of bolt holes. The inner core may be made of a cheaper grade of timber (structural fir will even suffice), the oak veneer supplies the necessary strength and wearing qualities required. During the assembly, *Stanley* corrugated fasteners are driven across the joints to hold the heavy timbers put. The veneer is applied to one side and after the glue has set, the assembly is turned over and the reverse side is completed.

Where extreme curvature exists lamination comes into its own particular place. Stems that formerly required accurate scarphing and bolting may now be laminated. Two methods of doing this are in vogue. The stem may be made of three or more thickness of board stock with their butts spaced well apart or they may be built up of thin strips bent around a temporary form. The former method is the most simple, the latter the stronger and has the advantage of not having any cross angle grain. This feature can be appreciated when cutting the bevel on its forward edge. In the manufacture of deck beams, strips assembled and bent over a form are far stronger than the sawed type and are made without the attendant waste of the old method. Thin strips need not be used in this method. Strips thick enough to bend easily (generally square in cross section) may be employed. In this case the use of the *urea* resin glues will suffice. Weldwood is excellent for this purpose. Chine and sheer stringers that would require excessive bend in either direction may be laminated from two or more thicknesses. They may be assembled directly on the frame from straight edged thin boards and after the glue has set may be removed from the frame and sawed to the required curvature. Figures 6A shows various types of laminates.

CHAPTER II

TOOLS AND THEIR USES

When the first settlers of the Chesapeake Bay region reached these shores, they found a boatbuilding industry established. The Indians were already at work building the log dugouts that have evolved into the graceful log-canoes on the waters of the Bay today. The settlers brought with them the white man's tools to supplant the crude implements of the Indian. The aborigines of this region slowly burned a log, controlling the extent of the fire with wet mud then laboriously scraped the charred wood away with an oyster shell until the outside was shaped to their liking. The inside was hollowed to stow themselves and their belongings during their winding travels up and down the Bay. What a blessing the adz and broadaxe have been since they were brought over on the *Ark* and the *Dove* by the settlers.

HAND TOOLS

We will assume that the reader has a working knowledge of the more commonly known carpentry tools. His tool-box should include two saws, a ripsaw and a crosscut saw. A compass or keyhole saw, and a small coping or scroll saw are handy additions to this list. A claw hammer and a good hatchet are necessities, as are two planes, a jack plane and a block plane. In the old days the smoothing plane and the jack plane had little in common but, with the adjustments possible on the modern planes, their best features have been combined into one good tool. A drawknife and a spokeshave complete the shaving tools. While on the subject of spokeshaves, I prefer the old-fashioned type with wooden handles to the more modern kind. An assortment of augerbits with a good ratchet brace will complete the boring department. As adjuncts to the brace, an assortment of screw-driving bits and a countersinking tool will be handy A small hand-drill with an assortment of bits will be

convenient for drilling for fastenings, and several sizes of screwdrivers will be a distinct advantage. A steel square, several sizes of nail sets, and a carpenter's awl.

An assortment of chisels and gouges kept in a canvas roll or in a separate box are a necessity. The minimum of these handy tools will be one-inch and one half-inch face butt chisels. Faces from one-quarter inch to an inch and a half will come in handy for various jobs around the boat so get them if you can. Gouges of various sizes, while not absolutely necessary, will be useful if scrolls are to be carved in the sheer or transom.

From the foregoing list, the reader is likely to believe that it takes a raft of tools to build a boat. This is absolutely not the case. There is an old saying that "a good man can work with a minimum of tools." To this saying I always like to add "if they are sharp." There is no doubt that the more tools one possesses, the easier the job becomes. But I have seen one of the small boats described in this book turned out by a youngster with a crosscut saw, a hatchet, a brace and three bits, a screwdriver and an old-fashioned wooden plane. The finished job would have been a credit to any professional builder and was done so well because what the boy lacked in tools he supplied in ingenuity. The clamps that he contrived from pieces of wood and rope and some of the tricks he did with his hatchet and that old wooden plane would have put many a master-mind to shame. To add to the fact that he was short on tools, his available cash was in the same condition, and the woods in the boat were a heterogeneous collection gathered here and there.

THE HATCHET.—The house carpenter generally looks down on the wielder of a hatchet. The lowest classified type of carpenters on any construction job are the *hatchet-and-saw* men, but around a boat a man who can wield a good sharp hatchet with a sure stroke can do a wonderful job. It is, in effect, a small broad-axe. The hatchet should be of good steel and always kept as sharp as possible. It will be of use in shaping up the heavy timbers of the keel and stem when the builder does not have an adz. The small type of hatchet used by lathers, called a lather's hatchet, will be useful in tight places.

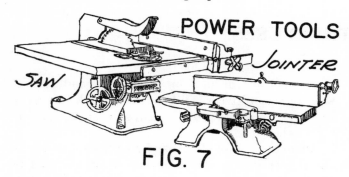

FIG. 7

POWER TOOLS.—Modern, small power tools (Fig. 7) are a boon to the amateur boatbuilder, and he is indeed lucky if he possesses any of these tools. The table saw can be used for ripping and crosscutting and produces a job with which no hand-cut work can compare. The ordinary circular saw can be made to cut quite a curve if the teeth of the blade are given an excess of set. I have used this method to cut a curvature in one-and-an-eighth-inch deck beams which amounted to three inches in seven feet. The spindle shaper or jointer will save much handwork when used to cut all the bevels on your frames, both inside and out, before they are assembled. The spindle shaper, or shaper tools in a power drill press, will produce on short notice any type of moulding required.

The band saw offers unlimited possibilities and you will find one in every well-equipped professional shop. If you intend to purchase one, it is wise to get the largest diameter obtainable. While the small-diameter saws do perfect work, they are expensive to operate because broken bands often have to be replaced. Ruptures occur when the metal of the saws becomes fatigued in bending around the small wheels.

POWER JIG SAWS VS BAND SAWS

The larger size power jig saws have a bit of advantage over the band saw. While the thickness which they will cut is limited by the blade travel, they have a good feature that offsets this. The blades in these machines are readily interchangeable and will cut a much smaller radius than the band saw. Another feature is that they will readily cut inside holes. The larger types may be altered for saber sawing and in this operation their scope is limited only by the area of the building in which they are installed. The writer has a large *Delta* machine of this type which at times has cut three inch oak and ¼" steel plate. It is universal in its application and is used on metal as much as it is on wood. A number of the boat's fittings may be sawed from brass or aluminum plate.

NEW POWER TOOLS

Since the writing of the first edition we have seen the advent of the "do it yourselfer" and home workshops, replete with new power tools that have had a distinct effect on the nation's economy. Power tools which may be transported directly to the work save endless steps and in many ways are better than those confined to a fixed location.

One "must" around every home today is an electric drill. On a boat it does in a second what it took the old hand drill a minute to accomplish. Multiply this saving by the thousand holes one must drill on a small boat and the saving of time becomes tremendous. Today, it is possible to secure bitts which at one operation will drill a hole and properly countersink it for any given size and length of screw. A quarter inch electric drill with the new wood boring bitts will drill holes in hard oak up to ¾". Strange as it may seem the cutting ends of these bitts are identical to those used by hand before the screw point auger was invented.

Many other attachments have been gimmicked to fit an electric drill. The four inch saws are a God-send in cutting plywood up to ½" thick. On one occasion the writer used a 4" *Arco* saw in a ¼" *Craftsman* drill to saw the entire length of a sheet of ¾" plywood. It went slow, to be sure, but still it was a lot less laborious than cutting the sheet with a hand saw. Sanding heads are made to fit these drills also. Do not get one that requires the drill to be vertical to the plane of the wood. These are hard to manage and are a makeshift at the best. Both *Sears Roebuck* and *Montgomery Ward* supply angle head sanders which are excellent. Recently there has appeared a jig sawing attachment for a drill that if it will hold up in service appears to have great merit.

Nothing can surpass a tool designed for a specific purpose and if your budget allows, buy one rather than a drill attachment. Stick to reputable makes like *Black & Decker, Skill-Drill* or *Porter-Cable*. They are worth the difference in price. In all cases you get just what you pay for.

In addition to saws, planers and sanders, a self contained portable jig saw has appeared. To economically cut up a plywood sheet on which a lot of pieces have been nested, this tool is a "must". On the boat it can cut holes in plywood and do other jobs that no other tool will do half as well.

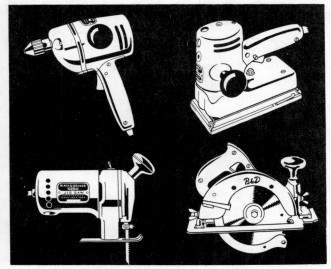

Fig. 7A. Power Tools. (Top left) Drill. (Top right) Sander. (Bottom left) Jig Saw. (Bottom right) Hand Saw. *(Courtesy of Black & Decker.)*

One big factor in the ruination of portable power tools is their overloading (Yes, even I do it!). Do not wait for a power tool to fry your hands but allow it to cool the minute it becomes hotter than usual. One last warning! Do not use power tools while standing in water or on wet ground. I know of two men who are now plunking harps in Heaven through this very act. If the tool has a grounding jumper use it at all times.

Some portable power tools have a stand which enables them to be used stationary. If well made, these stands are a big advantage. Another last warning! The medical profession is growing rich from the careless handling of power tools by the "do it yourselfers"!

SPECIAL TOOLS

In addition to the foregoing tools there are a number that are used almost exclusively in the boatbuilding trade.

THE ADZ.—For the working of the heavy timbers of the stem and keel there is no hand-tool that will excel the adz. (See Fig. 8.)

The illustration describes it better than all written words. This tool has been used in woodworking from the dawn of civilization in almost the same form in which it exists today. The hand adz or cooper's adz is a small edition of the larger tool and is handy in tight places. Not only is it the most handy tool around the boat, but also it is the most dangerous in the hands of a careless workman. To this day I can well remember the instructions that were given me at the tender age of fourteen when I first learned to use an adz, much against my father's orders. My tutor on the adz was a giant Bahama negro employed by my dad and his words still remain fresh in my memory In an accent quite different than our Maryland negroes. Bob told me. "Boy, when de day come dat you no longer be afeered of datair aides, dats de day when it's gonna bite yuh." While the adz is one of my favorite tools, I am still afraid of it and, as yet, haven't ever been "bit."

Just as in the game of golf we employ certain stances and swings, so it is in handling the adz. First of all the body is always held rigid from the feet up to the arm joints at the shoulders. This poise fixes the

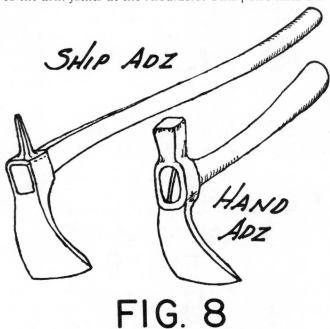

SHIP ADZ

HAND ADZ

FIG. 8

swing of the adz because the arc of the cut is always swung from the upper joint of the arms. A little stoop or side movement while it is swinging will throw the adz off the cut. For rough cutting, the arms are held rigid at the elbows throughout the last half of the stroke, bending only slightly in the first half of the swing and the last half of the return stroke. The feet are held far apart, straddling the cut, so that if the adz goes wild it will swing harmlessly between your legs. If a chip appears on the cutting edge of the adz at any time, stop at once and remove it. This is the cause of ninety percent of the accidents with an adz. Once the cutting edge of the tool is shrouded with a chip, it will skid on the timber like a stroke of lightning and is apt to swing wild and draw blood. While working any piece of wood always be sure that you have a firm footing and that the wood you are cutting is set firmly.

Practice in working unfamiliar tools will produce efficiency and it is always good practice in working the adz to nail a board to the floor and draw a pencil line on it. Follow the board with the adz, taking off a very thin chip as equally as possible on both sides of the line. When you can gauge the cut of an adz perfectly you will barely remove the line from the board. It is good practice to lay lines a half inch from the corners of a 2″ x 4″ scantling and cut away the edge until you can produce a perfect chamfer. In removing large areas of wood with the adz, it is well to saw a kerf in the piece of wood to the desired depth so that the kerfs will be about six inches apart.

A good adzeman can finish the surface of a cut so smoothly that very little planing is necessary to complete the job. The adz will be invaluable in making round spars if you become expert in chamfering corners.

THE SCRIEVE KNIFE.—Long before lead pencils were in use, carpenters used a peculiar tool to mark off the lumber to be cut. This tool is still used in the

SCRIEVE KNIFE
FIG. 9

boatbuilding trade and is called a scrieve or race-knife. (See Fig. 9.) It consists of a blade with a curled edge which, when scraped along a piece of wood, will cut a shallow groove about an eighth of an inch wide. This tool will be invaluable in marking off large timbers blackened by the weather, because the line will show clearly white, whereas a pencil line would be barely visible. A scrieve mark will be in the

wood at any time that it is desired to pick it out, and the positions of all frames and important lines on all timbers needed for future reference should always be scrieved in. It will also be a valuable aid in painting if water lines and tops of the boot-topping are scrieved in the planking, for it is easy to follow the line and make a clean-cut job.

THE BAREFOOT AUGER.—For boring long holes, the boatbuilder has his own type of auger. The customary screw point of the modern bit is lacking for a good reason. This screw point is apt to follow the soft

BAREFOOT AUGER FIG. 10

grain of the wood and throw the hole out of line. For this work the boatbuilder uses an auger without the screw or cutting lips, a tool which is usually referred to as a "barefoot" auger. (See Fig. 10.) When it is necessary to bore a long hole, as for a propeller shaft, the auger can be easily extended by cutting the shank and having a piece of rod welded into it. The barefoot auger is generally used in a hole which has been previously started with the screw type of bit. When it is desired to bore a hole absolutely straight, it is necessary to build a simple jig or guide to keep the auger in line. This generally consists of a straight piece of wood on each side of the member to be bored, and a block of wood between the boards to keep the shank of the bit in line. On long holes, it is best to bore from both sides wherever possible. When a hole goes out of line, it can be straightened easily by cutting the end of a piece of iron pipe of suitable size in the form of saw-teeth, giving the alternate teeth a little set, out and in, to give the pipe clearance as it goes in the hole. Another way to straighten a hole in an emergency is to drive a red-hot iron rod of the proper size through the hole.

FOSTNER BIT.—In boring for plugs over fastenings, a Fostner bit will come in handy because this type of bit cuts a clean hole and the depth of the cutting head will control the depth of the hole exactly. When boring with the regular screw-pointed bit the depth of the hole can be controlled by counting the number of turns of the brace handle *after* the cutting lips touch the wood. A piece of pipe slipped over the bit is another way of controlling the depth of the hole.

THE WOOD RASP.—One of the tools very seldom listed as that of the boatbuilder is the wood rasp. Fig. 10A. These are made in various shapes and sizes. They have the property of tearing wood away without splitting it and where bevels have to be cut on the job are far faster than any plane or chisel. A 12″ or 16″ coarse rasp with one side flat and the other rounded is a murderous tool in taking off wood surfaces and no matter which way the grain runs they work equally well. In using a rasp provide a good wooden handle for the tang and wrap an inch or so of the tip with friction tape to save the palms of your hands; using both hands you can certainly make wood dust fly.

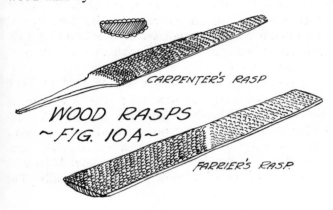

WOOD RASPS ~FIG. 10A~

There is another type of rasp which at one time was called a *Farrier's* rasp because it found use in trimming off the horse's hoof after the shoe was fitted. These are straight with parallel edges and are not fitted with handles. One side is flat, the other slightly rounded and each side is divided in half, each having coarse and fine teeth. Coarse half-round bastard and round rat-tail files will often come in

Fig. 10B. The Stanley Surform.

handy in working the wood off where the curves are sharp and the grain runs haywire.

THE SURFORM.—The old adage that "There is nothing new under the sun" has been exploded. Just recently the *Stanley Co.* has marketed a gimmick that will act as either a plane or a rasp depending in which handle the blade is inserted. It will cut with the grain as well as across it and take off wood almost as fast as a very coarse rasp. The blade consists of about 500 razor sharp cutting edges with a perforation ahead of them to relieve the chips. It leaves a very smooth cut in any direction and is available at most neighborhood hardware stores.

CARE OF TOOLS

Dull tools are a worry to any workman and no one can do a good job with them. If power tools are available, a small grinding wheel will save a lot of "elbow grease" on an oilstone or grindstone. A good oilstone, however, will be used in whetting up the tools after the power grinder has done the rough work. One of the slickest tricks I have ever seen in whetting up edged tools was to finally finish off the edges on a power-buffing wheel. These edges were always sharp enough to shave with. The test of a sharp edge is to wet the hairs of your arm and if the cutting edge will shave them off, it is really sharp. While space will not permit complete directions on sharpening every tool in your kit, it will not be wasted time to read up on this subject in some other book devoted to tools and their uses.

The edges of all sharp tools should be protected when not in use. I recall an old joiner in a boatyard who had a piece of carpet tacked to the end of his bench on which he always set his planes and chisels when they were not in use. A good motto to paste up in your shop and ponder on, is this one: The man who lends tools is out!

HOMEMADE TOOLS

By using a little ingenuity the amateur can save money if he will take the time to construct some of the simple tools described here.

BOAT CLAMPS.—In construction of any boat, even in a professional yard, there has never been a time when I have seen an oversupply of clamps. To purchase all the necessary clamps for the construction of one boat would make the job rather expensive. From time to time I have seen many ingenious homemade substitutes answer the purpose admirably. The most common of these are the small duckbill clamps cut from some hardwood. (See Fig. 11.) A carriage bolt, a wing-nut and a little spare time will make a simple small clamp that will do its work to perfection. A post clamp, similar to this but with a larger range, is shown also in Fig. 11. The carriage bolt in this clamp may be substituted with a threaded steel rod with two nuts on either end. Simple wing nuts can be made easily by welding two pieces of steel rod to a square or hex nut with a torch or electric arc as illustrated. This type of wing nut will be handy in all of the larger clamps to be described.

In spanning several planks or long spaces, it is necessary to have a clamp that can be adjusted over a long range. This is simply a bar of wood, several plates of metal and a couple of common bolts. Assembled, it is termed a bar clamp and Fig. 11 shows how simple it is to make. Where the bar clamp is short or where the curvature does not permit the use of the straight clamp, the chain clamp will come into use. This type of clamp may be purchased but is rather expensive. It can be made easily if the builder has access to a blacksmith's forge. Bars of steel are bent as shown in Fig. 11, nuts are welded on and other simple attachments made as shown. A length of chain completes the clamp which can be adjusted within

very close limits. In line with clamps and other pulling arrangements, wonders can be performed with a piece of stout rope and a stick forming a tourniquet. Often when planking is to be applied, two planks may be set on opposite sides of the boat, the rope rove between them and the stick twisted around and around until the rope is twisted so taut that the planks come up tight against the frames. In fitting a single plank on one side of the boat, the rope can be rove around a frame on the opposite side. Many other odd jobs around the boat can be done in the same manner with a small set of blocks and a fall, in nautical language called a tackle and always pronounced "taykle."

In pulling the apron down on the keel or keel horse, several turns of wire rope with a couple of wedges inserted under them will be helpful. The wedge is one of the most powerful of prime movers and can exert enormous force when properly handled. Two pieces of hardwood and two long bolts with plenty of thread will also do this job admirably. The

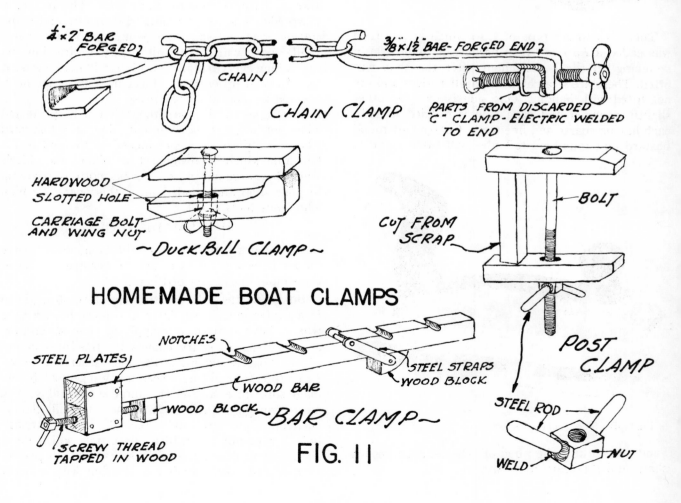

HOMEMADE BOAT CLAMPS

FIG. 11

principle of the lever should not be forgotten in the erection of a boat. With intelligent use, this tool will exert all the force that is necessary around a small boat. A piece of two-by-four timber with a proper fulcrum can often be used to pull a contrary plank into shape. The end of the timber may, on many jobs, be tied down with a rope lashing to exert the force in the proper direction.

PLANE.—Special planes can be made to cut various grooves and beads and their cutting bits ground out of old flat files. Rabbeting and beading planes may be constructed from small files and spar and hollowing planes from the larger sizes. Steel bits used in the old-style wooden planes are still sold in some hardware stores. There was a time when all workmen made their own planes, the bits being the only part that could be purchased. Maple is the best wood from which to make these wooden planes and, while not wanting to appear old-fashioned, it is my firm belief that nothing can equal them in cutting ability if they

are made properly. I have made many of them for special jobs with marked success. This reminds me of a plane I now possess. I came across the bit of an old plane of Sheffield steel and, knowing the excellence of this steel, I wanted a plane made from it. I had used the old square-edged wooden planes with sore hands resulting from the sharp edges and was determined that this new plane should possess none of these faults. When the plane was finished, one of the old German workmen in the wood shop of a large airplane plant exclaimed: "Ach, das iss a shtream-lined hovel!" The rounded edges and sloping back instead of the regular handle really gave it a stream-lined appearance, and *streamlined hovel* it remains to this day. Figure 12 shows this type of plane as well as the method of making these tools from two pieces of wood rather than laboriously digging the well out of a solid block. It is important that the angles of the bits be held exact, as this is the proper cutting angle.

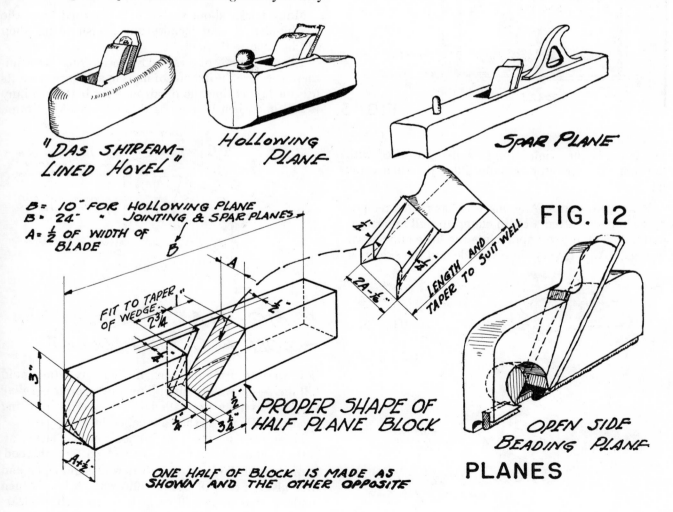

"DAS SHTREAM-LINED HOVEL"

HOLLOWING PLANE

SPAR PLANE

B = 10" FOR HOLLOWING PLANE
B = 24" " JOINTING & SPAR PLANES
A = ½ OF WIDTH OF BLADE

FIT TO TAPER OF WEDGE

LENGTH AND TAPER TO SUIT WELL

FIG. 12

PROPER SHAPE OF HALF PLANE BLOCK

OPEN SIDE BEADING PLANE

ONE HALF OF BLOCK IS MADE AS SHOWN AND THE OTHER OPPOSITE

PLANES

SWEDISH BAND SAW.—For ripping down planking and cutting the curves in heavy timbers too thick for a compass saw, an old discarded band-saw blade can be used to make a *Swedish* band saw. (Fig. 13.) This

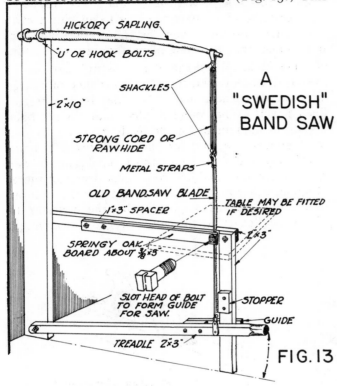

HICKORY SAPLING

"U" OR HOOK BOLTS

SHACKLES

2"x10"

STRONG CORD OR RAWHIDE

METAL STRAPS

OLD BANDSAW BLADE

1"x3" SPACER

SPRINGY OAK BOARD ABOUT ⅜"x3"

SLOT HEAD OF BOLT TO FORM GUIDE FOR SAW.

TREADLE 2"x3"

A "SWEDISH" BAND SAW

TABLE MAY BE FITTED IF DESIRED

2"x3"

STOPPER

GUIDE

FIG. 13

saw is really the original jig saw, being worked with the foot (the operator actually did a jig when using it).

PLANKING CLIP.—Any one who has rigged temporary shores or fitted a chain clamp to pull an ornery plank down tight will appreciate the little clip shown in Fig. 13A. It is very simply made and the sketch is

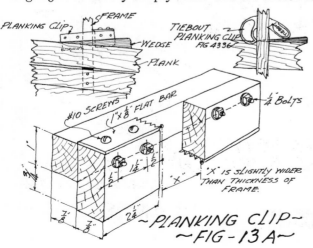

PLANKING CLIP

FRAME

TIEBOUT PLANKING CLIP FIG 4336

WEDGE

PLANK

#10 SCREWS

1"x⅛" FLAT BAR

¼" BOLTS

"X" IS SLIGHTLY WIDER THAN THICKNESS OF FRAME

~PLANKING CLIP~
~FIG-13A~

self explanatory. Ralph Mattox used a similar clip in constructing his twenty-six foot power cruiser with great success.

A "store boughten" gimmick to do the same work may be purchased from the *Tiebout Company* in New York. It is the Tiebout Planking clip and is listed in their catalogue as Figure 4336.

BEVEL GAUGE.—There will be times when a larger bevel square than those on the market will be needed around the boat. Figure 14 shows how one of these may be made with three thin pieces of wood and a bolt with a wing nut.

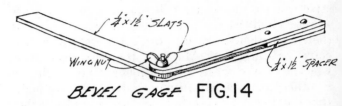

¼"x1½" SLATS

WING NUT

¼"x1½" SPACER

BEVEL GAGE   FIG. 14

Many tricks about tools can be learned from the boatbuilder in your locality and a visit to his shop will be time well spent.

HOME MADE DUCKS.—The occasions are numerous where the driving of nails in a floor prevent its use for laying down and fairing with battens. Many is the time when I have heard this expression, "Man,

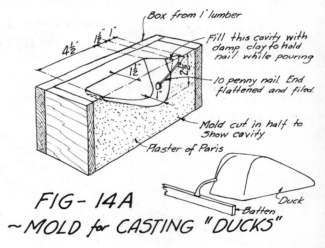

Box from 1" lumber

Fill this cavity with damp clay to hold nail while pouring

10 penny nail. End flattened and filed.

Mold cut in half to show cavity

Plaster of Paris

Batten

Duck

FIG-14A
~MOLD for CASTING "DUCKS"

if I were to drive nails in our floor my wife would kill me."—So would mine! The only answer is *spline weights,* as they are called in engineering drafting rooms, or *Ducks* as they are called in a shipyard.

These may be made at home from a Plaster of Paris mold as shown in Fig. 14A. A pattern of wood is made first. This is smoothed with sandpaper and then given a coat of hot paraffin wax. A box is then made so that there will be at least an inch of clearance all around the pattern. On a good flat surface lay down a piece of wax lunch paper. Set the pattern on it and the box around the pattern. Pour plaster of Paris or patching plaster inside the box around the pattern. When this has hardened remove the pattern. Be sure in making the pattern that the cavity for the clay to hold the nails is also included.

Fig. 14B. Sam Rabl using home-made "ducks".

After the plaster has thoroughly hardened for at least a week the mold is ready for casting. With some moist clay (not wet) fix one of the ten-penny nails, which has been previously flattened and filed in the cavity and secure it with the clay.

Any scrap lead may be melted in a fruit juice can over the family gas stove. Battery lead presents a hazard in its poisonous fumes. Do not melt it in the house. Melt only enough lead at one time to make one casting, plus a little over.

Pour the lead carefully to within an eighth inch of the top of the mold which should be set level. As it cools add more to make up shrinkage and when the top has been reached and just before the lead is finally jelled slick the dross off the top with the edge of a flat board. In this case the top of the casting will be the bottom of the the duck. Some powdered sal-ammoniac on top of the molten lead will help in separating the dross from the lead. If two pourings are required, sal-ammoniac or powdered resin will help the bond. Some block tin or bar solder in the bottom of the melting pot will hasten matters a bit.

At least six ducks will be necessary for the average small boat. You will never have enough. Where the ducks are widely spaced, hold the batten down with a finger as you draw the lines.

During the construction of *Fish Hawk,* I purchased both the Stanley Surform plane and rasp. Perhaps I am old-fashioned but I still prefer the old-fashioned plane, and a wood one at that. As to the rasp—it cannot be excelled in producing smooth work, especially so across end grain.

PORTABLE JIG SAW.—The wonder tool, as far as the work on *Fish Hawk* is concerned, is the *Black & Decker* portable jig saw. This little tool has more than paid for itself already in the amount of labor it has saved. Working single-handed, it beats a bandsaw all hollow. The work is not taken to the bandsaw table but the saw is taken to the work laying on trestles and you sit across most of the boards you are sawing. The garboard edges were sawed after the planks were glued and battened, something that would have been very difficult on a bandsaw without several extra hands to help. A lot of the deck plywood was sawed right on the job. It will cut as little as an eighth of an inch off the edge of the plywood deck, trimming it flush with the sheer stringer. This operation heretofore called for the laborious job of pushing a plane. With it, the frames have been beveled, the ¾″ plywood transom cut out, all of the curves in the standing top as well as its beams and coaming and all the openings and curved edges of the cockpit floor, many of these at a bevel.

CHAPTER III

FASTENINGS

Ever since man constructed the first boat in primitive times, he has had the problem of fastening timbers together. The early Egyptian in the valley of the Nile held the planking in shape by passing ropes around the outside of the boat and used an elaborate system of posts to make the ropes form a truss which gave longitudinal strength to the structure. The Norsemen built beautiful clinker-planked hulls with a lacing of rawhide strips rove through holes in the planks. These strips were so effective that the *long ships* are reputed to have reached the shores of this country. The Romans, expert in the working of bronze and copper, fastened the timbers of their galleys with these metals. Few metals or alloys have been found that will surpass bronze in resisting the corrosive effect of sea water.

TREENAILS.—The old ships that made history from the thirteenth century until their passing, were usually made of wood and fastened with pins, today called treenails (Fig. 15) or, as the shipbuilder pronounces it, *trunnels*. These pins are used in many fastenings in boats, both large and small, and nothing can equal the hard wood of the locust tree for this purpose. It takes a lot of force to draw these wooden nails, especially if their ends are split with a saw-cut and a wedge driven in each end. These are hard to procure in small sizes, but I have cut them from locust sticks that were ripped square from a board and rounded with a dowel cutter. Never attempt to use maple dowels as treenails, for maple does not resist the action of water and dampness and will soon rot away.

DRIFT BOLTS.—The next advance in fastenings were drift bolts. These were rounded iron rods, slightly pointed and driven into a hole of a smaller diameter than the rod. (See Fig. 16.) In the driving

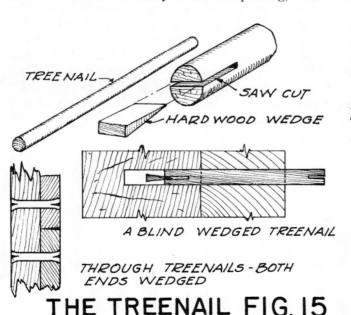

TREENAIL

SAW CUT

HARDWOOD WEDGE

A BLIND WEDGED TREENAIL

THROUGH TREENAILS - BOTH ENDS WEDGED

THE TREENAIL FIG. 15

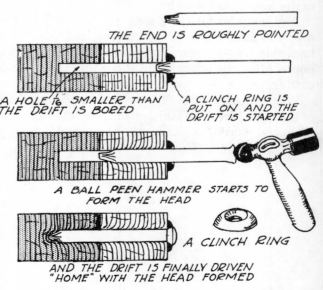

THE END IS ROUGHLY POINTED

A HOLE 1/16 SMALLER THAN THE DRIFT IS BORED

A CLINCH RING IS PUT ON AND THE DRIFT IS STARTED

A BALL PEEN HAMMER STARTS TO FORM THE HEAD

A CLINCH RING

AND THE DRIFT IS FINALLY DRIVEN "HOME" WITH THE HEAD FORMED

THE DRIFT BOLT   FIG. 16

process a small head is formed on the rod. To make them draw the timbers tight, rings of rod of a smaller diameter were forged and slipped over the rod so that when the formed head came down close to the top timber it was prevented from entering by the ring and drew the two or more timbers tightly together. Galvanized rods can be bought today in almost any size and clinch-rings have progressed to a kind of washer that fits the driven head perfectly. Drift bolts can be used to good advantage in fastening heavy timbers of the keel and stem. Their application is not complex. Drill a hole one-sixteenth of an inch smaller than the rod. Measure the depth of the hole and cut a rod slightly longer than the depth with a hacksaw and pound a slight point on one end. This is done cold, on a heavy block of iron, so that the galvanizing of the rod is scored as little as possible. Next, insert the rod into the hole and give it a couple of taps before you slip the clinch-ring over the rod and drive it home. In driving the rod it is well to hammer on the outer edges in order to form a flat rivet head.

THE BOAT-SPIKE.—A favorite fastening for heavy timbers is the boat-spike. (See Fig. 17.) This is a large square nail. The end is chisel-pointed and the head is in the shape of a truncated pyramid. In light timbers, a hole is drilled the diameter of the side of the square spike and about three-quarters of the length of the spike in depth. The edge of the chisel point should be driven so that it is across the grain. In some boatyards a clinch-ring or washer is slipped under the head of the spike to prevent it from being driven down into the wood and to make it draw tighter. Usually, a boat-spike is driven until the top of the head is flush with the surface of the wood. Care should be exercised in doing this, to prevent cracking of the wood.

THE THROUGH-RIVET.—The through-rivet is simply an iron rod driven through two or more pieces of wood in the same manner as a drift bolt, except that the projecting end is cut off and another clinch-ring is headed up on this end. This type of fastening may be used on rods as small as a quarter inch in diameter, using ordinary flat washers to head them. Brass or copper rods will find favor in the smaller sizes where the expense is not so great.

THE BOLT.—Modern machinery has produced an inexpensive fastening which is my favorite type wherever it can be employed. This is the through-bolt and nut, or, in more simple language, a bolt. (See Fig. 17.) It can be secured in any type of metal, from bronze to the lowly iron bolt purchased at the corner

hardware store. Galvanized bolts and washers should be used on any boat job. When the builders of horse-drawn carriages started business on a production basis, presaging the modern automobile factory, they invented a fastening for their wooden vehicles which could be inserted by one man without a helper. These are marketed today as carriage bolts and are neat fastenings that will hold in wood much better than the ordinary bolt and are more convenient to apply. They are made especially for use in wood and should be used wherever the head will be exposed.

The LAG-SCREW, shown in Fig. 17, is sometimes called a lag-bolt or a lag. This is a large wood screw having a bolt head which can be turned with a wrench. It is inserted in a hole from a sixteenth to an eighth of an inch smaller than its diameter. A washer should always be used under its head. Many builders make the mistake of driving this type of fastening almost home before the wrench is used. It is perfectly permissible to drive a lag, but never any more than the distance equal to the smooth part of the shank.

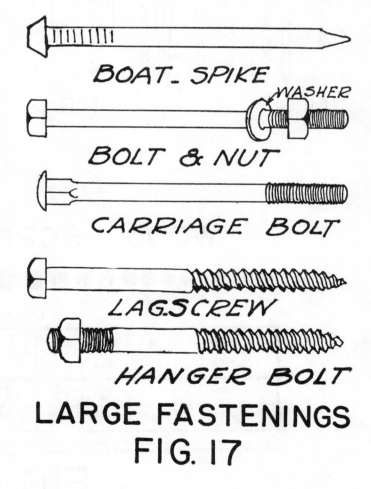

BOAT-SPIKE

BOLT & NUT

CARRIAGE BOLT

LAG SCREW

HANGER BOLT

LARGE FASTENINGS
FIG. 17

In driving a galvanized lag, be sure that the wrench fits the head snugly. A loose wrench will mar the galvanizing and produce a good place for rust to start, eventually destroying the lag.

THE HANGER BOLT, also shown in Fig. 17, is simply a lag-screw with a thread and nut on the end where the head is ordinarily found. Its advantage is that the nut can be removed, making it possible to release the object which it is holding. Its greatest use is in holding down an engine or other mechanical apparatus which must be removed for periodic overhauling.

NAILS.—There are several types of nails. (See Fig. 18.) The wire nail and the cut nail need no description here as they are common and are used extensively in all types of construction. They can be secured at any marine hardware store in both plain and galvanized types. The boat nail is used in much the same manner as the boat-spike. When driven home, the head is set down flush with the surface of the wood, leaving a depression all around the nail which will securely hold putty. It is best, however, to set these nails slightly deeper with a nail set so that the wood can be planed later and to avoid "monkey faces," a term boatbuilders apply to hammer marks on the surface of planking or decks. To avoid splitting in hard woods, a hole smaller than the nail should be drilled for all nails. Boat and cut nails should always be driven with the long part of the point across the grain.

SCREWS

WOOD SCREWS (Fig. 19) are used extensively in the construction of small boats. They have round, flat or oval heads and are made from galvanized iron and from copper alloys. Brass and Everdur are the favorite alloys. The round and oval heads will find

NAILS   FIG. 18

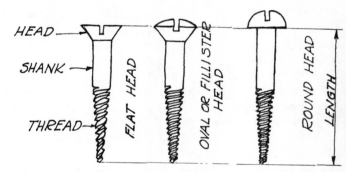

WOOD   SCREWS FIG. 19

WOOD   SCREW   SIZES

SCREW GAUGES

LENGTH	$\frac{1}{4}''$	$\frac{3}{8}''$	$\frac{1}{2}''$	$\frac{5}{8}''$	$\frac{3}{4}''$	$\frac{7}{8}''$	$1''$	$1\frac{1}{4}''$	$1\frac{3}{4}''$
GAUGES	0–4	0–8	1–10	2–12	2–14	3–14	3–16	4–18	6–20
LENGTH	$2''$	$2\frac{1}{4}''$	$2\frac{1}{2}''$	$2\frac{3}{4}''$	$3''$	$3\frac{1}{2}''$	$4''$	$4\frac{1}{2}''$	$5''$
GAUGES	6–20	6–20	6–20	8–20	8–24	10–24	12–24	14–24	14–24

Black circles give exact size of shank; gauge is term used to specify this diameter, taken just under screw head. Table indicates what screw gauges are standard for different lengths of screws. 1½″ screws are available in gauges 4 to 18.

FIG. 20

their greatest use in trim and joiner work. The flat head is used where the fastening is to be concealed, as in planking and decks. Holes should be drilled for all screws. There was a time when the boatbuilder would frown whenever a galvanized screw was mentioned. In the old days of hot-dipped galvanizing, the zinc of the galvanizing bath was of such a consistency that it filled all the threads of the screw, making it almost worthless. Electro-galvanizing of screws was tried and found unsatisfactory because it would not resist corrosion. Today we can buy hot-dipped galvanized screws which have perfect threads and open slots. The Navy and Coast Guard builders are using these screws with increasing satisfaction. Not satisfied with this fact, I exposed this new type of screw to the action of salt-spray in an airplane-testing laboratory for a period of a year and the screw showed no signs of deterioration. I highly recommend them for fastening the planking and decks of any of the boats in this book. Galvanized screws are preferable to nails because of their great holding power, and brass screws often wring off their heads when driven in hard wood. Beeswax, soap or tallow rubbed on all wood screws makes them enter the wood easier. Wood screw sizes are shown in Fig. 20.

If nails are substituted for screws in the planking, the ends and butts of the planks should be screwed. It is my practice to screw the side planking completely, screw the ends of the bottom planking at the chines and keel, and then nail them where they cross frames or stringers. The margin plank should be screwed to the sheer-strake and at its butts and the fastenings should be plugged if the deck is not to be canvased. Plugging will be discussed later. Strip-decking should be screwed at its ends but may be boat-nailed where it crosses the beams. The boat nails should be plugged if no canvas is used.

Copper Nails and Tacks.—In smaller boats, where clinker planking is used, another type of fastening is employed: copper nails which are riveted over burrs, or copper tacks, hook-clinched. To fasten with a copper nail, a hole slightly smaller than the nail is drilled and the nail is driven through the planks until the head comes flush outside. (See Fig. 21). Next, a burr or copper washer with a hole slightly smaller than the nail is driven over the nail until it comes flush with the inside of the planking. A short length of $\frac{1}{8}$" iron gas pipe is an excellent tool for driving the burr over the nail and setting it down. After the burr is set, the nail is cut off just above the burr and riveted over. A heavy iron rod or dolly

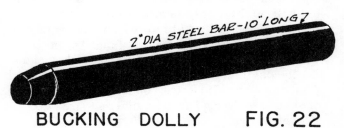

2" DIA STEEL BAR - 10" LONG

BUCKING DOLLY FIG. 22

(Fig. 22) is held against the head of the nail while the point is being "headed up." When copper tacks are used, the process is simpler. A small hole is drilled and the dolly is held against the inside of the planking opposite the hole. The tack is driven in from the outside and it starts to turn when it strikes the dolly, thus forming a hook which will defy removal without splitting the plank. At one time, I owned an old Rushton canoe fastened in this manner, whose fastenings were as strong after fifteen years' use as the day they were driven. Rushton canoes are in existence today, though their manufacture was discontinued two decades ago.

Nails riveted over burrs are used only on planking that is lapped or clinkered and three-quarter-inch plank is about the limit for this work. Three-eighth-inch planking is the limit for tacks, and the tacks should always be ordered a quarter-inch longer than the total thickness of the two planks they will be required to join. Both of these types of fastenings may be used on the smaller boats. Care should be

BURR

THE NAIL IS DRIVEN THRU THE WOOD

THE BURR IS DRIVEN ON

THE POINT IS CUT OFF

AND RIVETED

RIVETED COPPER NAILS
FIG. 21

used in driving any fastening and, to avoid a split piece of timber, every one should be drilled for.

RIVETS.—The rivet is the old and time-tested method of fastening one piece of metal to another. The small tinner's rivet (Fig. 23) is the most popular one for light metal. This is inserted in a hole which is drilled or punched in the metal. A tinner's rivet set is used for setting the metal down around the rivet and forming the head.

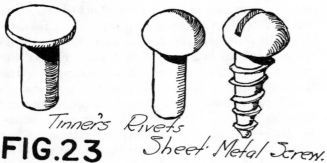

FIG. 23   *Tinner's Rivets*   *Sheet Metal Screw.*

SOLDER.—Solder is a metal adhesive. The old half-and-half solder is my favorite. For a flux I like a mixture of muriatic acid into which zinc chips have been thrown until they cease boiling. Do not use a small soldering iron as it will cool too quickly, and do like the old time tinners do: tin your iron on a block of sal-ammoniac. If electric connections are available, an electric soldering iron with different sized tips is a convenient tool.

SHEET METAL SCREWS.—Sheet metal screws are handy fastenings. They are simple and quick because all you have to do is drill a hole and start the screw in; it will cut its own threads as it goes.

METAL FASTENINGS.—Although the boats described in this book are composed of wood, there will be some metal parts. Therefore, we must give some thought to metal fastenings.

A new type of nail has appeared on the market which is rapidly gaining favor with boatbuilders and in many cases is replacing screws. Fig. 23A. This is the *Stronghold* or *Anchorfast* nail manufactured by the *Independent Nail and Packing Co.* of *Bridgewater, Mass.* The makers of these nails publish an interesting little booklet which is an education to boatbuilders in itself, *Building a Boat With Nails.* It is yours for the asking if you mention this book.

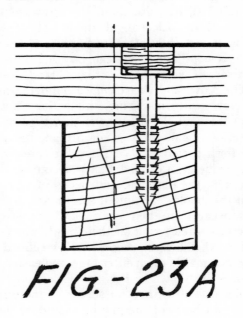

FIG. - 23A

Just as this book goes to press, an outstanding glue has appeared. It is the Miracle Adhesives Corporation N.P. 428. It is much better than the resorcinal resin glues and is not critical to temperature. It may be used in sub-freezing weather without impairing the bond. This is an epoxy resin glue and equal proportions of resin and catalyst are used, eliminating all fussy mixing of the two components.

It will bond metals as well as wood and shear tests up to 5,000 P.S.I. have been recorded. This is an excellent resin to use with Fiberglas where it gives above average results. Manufactured by the Miracle Adhesives Corp., New Philadelphia, Ohio.

CHAPTER IV

LAYING DOWN AND TAKING OFF

When the boatbuilder draws the shape of the hull on the floor from the architect's plans, he calls the process *laying down*. When he has the lines on the floor and starts to make the templates and layouts for the shape, he calls this process *taking off*. The architect depicts the shape of the hull on a drawing which he calls the *lines*, or the *lines of form*. In the old days this drawing was termed the *sheer draft*. It shows the shape of the hull as viewed from three different directions. (See Fig. 24.) The drawing, or blueprint,

represents the views of the hull as we would see them without perspective (that property of optics which makes things seem smaller the farther they are away from us). The blueprint is divided into three views, or three projections: the *profile*, the *plan* and the *body plan*. The profile shows all the lengths and heights in their true measurements with all widths foreshortened. The plan shows all the lengths and the widths in true measurement with the heights foreshortened. The body plan shows the boat as viewed

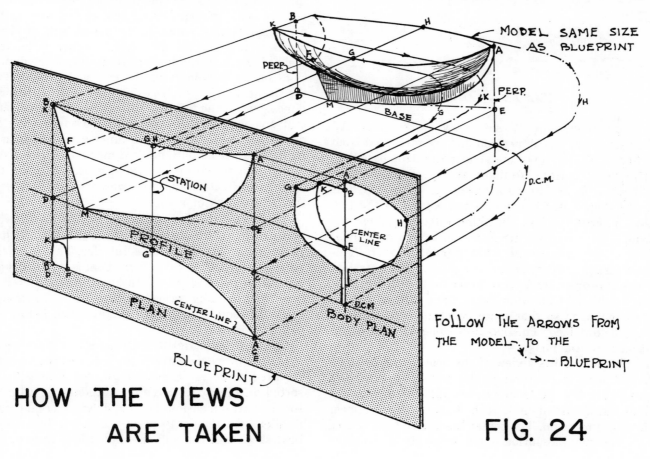

HOW THE VIEWS ARE TAKEN

FIG. 24

from the ends with all widths and heights true but with the lengths foreshortened.

In measuring these views, there must be some common line from which all measurements are taken. To fix the length, the architect generally draws two *perpendiculars* (called perps) at the ends of the drawing and measures the length between them. In all the designs in this book the perpendiculars were selected as occurring at the point where the sheer line cuts the rabbet at the stem and where it crosses the after-face of the transom at the stern. The distance between these end perpendiculars is further divided by other perpendiculars at which measurements for height and width are taken and these are called *station lines*. The station lines naturally will be the same in the profile and the plan. In the body plan they appear as cross sections through the boat.

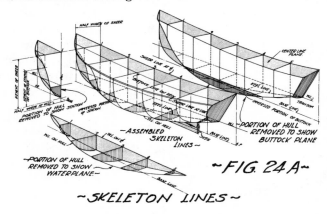

~FIG. 24.A~

~SKELETON LINES~

The profile shows a side view of the boat. All heights are in true dimension and are measured from a line at the bottom of the view, termed the base line. The measurements are taken at the station lines. In this view the architect shows how he wants the sheer to be shaped, the contour of the bottom of the hull and its keel and how the chine will sweep from the bow to the stern. The transom in this view appears as a line only because its width cannot be seen. This holds true for every frame or station. Where straight lines appear on the keel or other parts of the profile, the architect will often carry them out to an end perpendicular so that more accurate measurements may be obtained. This has been done on most of the designs in this book.

The plan shows a view of the boat as a fish would see it looking up through the water, or as a bird would see it if he looked down. Here all widths (or half widths, as only half of the boat is drawn) appear in true dimension. The center line of the boat is used as a common measuring point for all the dimensions

in this view. In this plan the transom appears as a shape, though foreshortened, because we cannot see its entire length.

If we look at a boat from its ends, we can see no farther than its widest point. If we look from the bow, the curvature beyond the widest point is hidden from view. The same is true of a view from the stern. The architect overcomes this difficulty in the *body plan*. This is actually two views combined in one. The half sections from the stem to the widest point are drawn on one side of a common center line, while the half sections from the stern to the widest point are shown on the other side of this center line. The body plan shows all the half widths and heights in their true dimensions. The lengths appear contracted, just as they would appear on the actual boat without the effect of perspective. In some of the smaller boats in this book, no lines are given, because the whole shape of the frames is detailed. As these boats are more conveniently built upside down, the floor line is used as a base line.

LAYING DOWN.—When the architect plans the shape of his hull, he does so on a piece of paper thumb-tacked to a drawing board. He uses some convenient scale of reduction, such as an inch on his drawing equaling a foot on the actual hull, or if the hull is a big one, he may use a smaller scale. If a scale of one inch equaling one foot is used, the dimensions on his drawing must be enlarged twelve times the size to which they are drawn to meet the required dimensions of the finished hull. It can be seen clearly that any mistake the architect makes in scaling his drawing is multiplied twelve times when the boat is built. Thus, if he only made a mistake of one sixty-fourth of an inch on his drawing, the error on the completed boat would be twelve sixty-fourths or three-sixteenths of an inch.

To correct the errors on the architect's drawing and develop sections and bevels in most boats, it is necessary to lay out the lines full size. This is usually done on a smooth floor or, if the boat is small enough, on a large piece of paper. In large shipyards this is done in a building termed the mold loft. In smaller shops it is done right on the building floor before the boat is erected.

CONTRACTED FAIRING.—Often where floor space is limited or where extreme accuracy of the lines are required a process called *Contracted Fairing* is resorted to. (Fig. 25.) Here the stations and all other fore and aft dimensions are laid down at a scale much smaller than they will be on the actual boat. Most boat shops will use half the dimensions because the feet, inches and fractions are easier to divide this way. For instance if the actual dimension is 2'–6¼" it is laid down as being fifteen and one eighth inches. The stations being much closer together and the lines of greater curvature, small errors are greatly multiplied and a much fairer boat results from this process. In Figure 25 note how all of the three views are laid down atop each other. This is resorted to even though the boat is not contracted. If you are afraid of confusion of lines a different colored pencil may be used for all three views. It might be well also to note that with the contracted process, the bevels will not show true nor will the slope of the transom show in its true length for development.

If the boat is to be laid down on a floor it is best prepared by painting it a light gray color. As space is usually limited in boat shops, it is the usual practice to lay the plan on top of the profile, using the base line of the profile as the center line of the plan. This also enables the use of common lines for the station lines of each view. As the base line and the center line are coincident and we must measure all dimensions from them, this is the first line laid down on the floor. With a chalk line long enough to go a couple of feet past the end perpendiculars, a line is "snapped" down on the floor. (See Fig. 26.) The perpendiculars are erected at the given length, as shown in the illustration. These "perps" are checked and rechecked. It is important that they be correct in every respect for all other measurements will depend on them to a great extent. At some convenient identical dimension on each "perp," a spot is laid off. The loftsman calls each point of measurement that he puts on the floor a "spot," pricking it in the floor with the point of a carpenter's awl. He will invariably draw a circle around all spots of half-breadth, and a square around

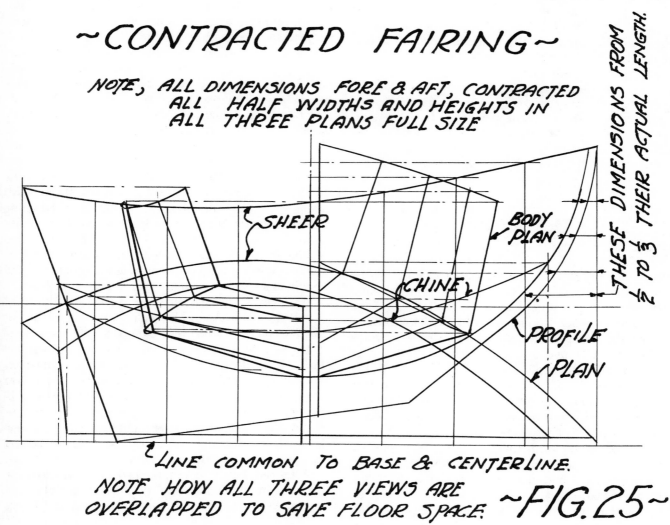

~CONTRACTED FAIRING~

NOTE, ALL DIMENSIONS FORE & AFT, CONTRACTED
ALL HALF WIDTHS AND HEIGHTS IN
ALL THREE PLANS FULL SIZE

THESE DIMENSIONS FROM ½ TO ⅓ THEIR ACTUAL LENGTH.

SHEER

BODY PLAN

CHINE

PROFILE PLAN

LINE COMMON TO BASE & CENTERLINE.
NOTE HOW ALL THREE VIEWS ARE
OVERLAPPED TO SAVE FLOOR SPACE. ~FIG.25~

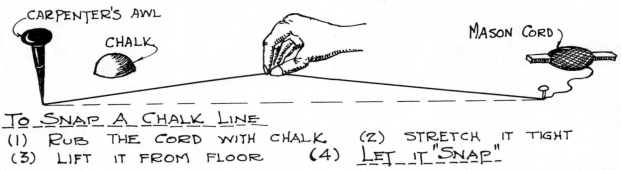

To Snap a Chalk Line
(1) Rub the cord with chalk   (2) Stretch it tight
(3) Lift it from floor   (4) Let it "Snap"

HOW TO SNAP A CHALK LINE   FIG. 26

the spots of height (Fig.27) so that he may distinguish them when they are close to one another. He will mark all important points with a crow's foot.

Between the spots on the end "perps," another line is snapped to lay off the station lines. This line must be checked to see that it is parallel to the base line laid down previously. The spacing of the stations is then laid down both on the base line and on the line parallel to it. After these points are checked, lines are snapped between the two lines which form the station lines. After making sure that all lines are correct, they are penciled or scratched in on the floor or paper.

Dimensions for all of the straight lines of the hull, such as the keel lines and the transom lines are now laid down as indicated on the plan of the lines. After these are snapped down they are also penciled in. By

HALF WIDTH SPOT   HEIGHT SPOT   CROW'S FOOT

THE FLOOR SPOTS FIG. 27

this time you will have become rather tired of setting the end of your rule on the base line each time and will wish for some other way of fixing this end of the rule. The loftsman who knows all the tricks will nail a small square stick or batten along his base on which to butt his rule and measuring sticks. In the large lofts, every stick is called a *batten*. This is probably derived from the French word *baton*. Another batten long enough to go the entire length of the boat is now secured. If it cannot be found in one piece of wood, it is glue-spliced. I have seen Oregon pine battens in the large steel shipyards that were sixty feet in length and one continuous piece of wood. Sometimes it is possible to use a batten in two sweeps, but this is not recommended.

Now that we have the necessary tools to do our lofting, we begin by laying down the sheer from the

architect's figures, or *offsets*. As the closest scaling that the architect can do on his small drawing is an eighth of an inch, he gives his offsets to the nearest eighth of an inch on his scale. His dimensions on the offset table are given in feet, inches and eighths of an inch. He will specify a dimension to be five-seven-three, and this will mean that he wants that dimension to be five feet, seven and three-eighths inches. He will write every fractional part of the inch in eighths and, even though an offset ends in four, it will still be a half inch. Three quarters will be six and so on. When all the offsets are laid down for the *sheer*, the batten is tacked alongside them. The caution to *never* drive a nail through a batten is not an idle one. A hole through your batten will mean a break when you try to bend a sharp curve. Drive the nails *alongside* the batten. (See Fig. 28.) When the batten is finally down on the floor and set on every mark, sight along it from all directions. If an unsightly hump or hollow appears in the line, withdraw the nails at the point where the hump occurs and let the batten spring free. Do this all along the line wherever a hump occurs, at the same time holding as many of the architect's spots as possible to produce a fair line.

FAIRING.—The process of smoothing up the lines is called fairing. An old loftsman, who is now fairing his lines on a floor of fleecy clouds, taught me a trick for detecting unfair spots in a line that has never failed. Old George Horney would put his hands on his knees, turn his back to one end of the line, stoop over and look at it between his legs. The reason this method is more accurate than others is because in this position your head is brought closer to the floor than in any other and the line will be more contracted in its perspective, thus accentuating the unfairness.

After the sheer is faired, the process is repeated for the keel and chine and then the lines of the plan are faired. When all lines are fair and true, the intermediate frame lines are laid in between the station

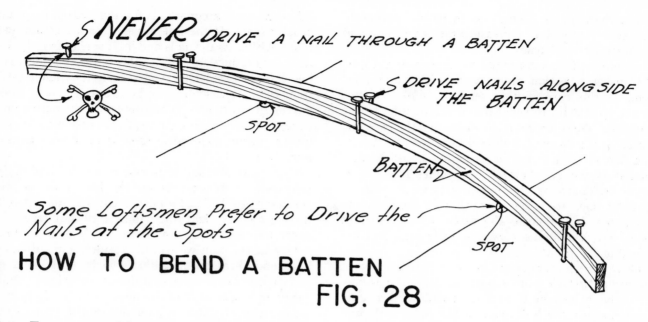

NEVER DRIVE A NAIL THROUGH A BATTEN

DRIVE NAILS ALONGSIDE THE BATTEN

SPOT

BATTEN

SPOT

Some Loftsmen Prefer to Drive the Nails at the Spots

HOW TO BEND A BATTEN
FIG. 28

lines. Two square sticks are prepared and these are butted against the base batten, the various heights on all the frame lines are marked on one stick and the half widths on the other. At some logical point on the floor a line is laid down to act as the center line of the body plan. The center station line, or midship line as it frequently is called, is often used as the center line of the body plan. If this line is selected, the base batten will be convenient for laying down. If the boat is to be constructed in the shop where the lines are laid down, it will be well to put the body plan at some point where the boat will not cover it, as the body plan will be a good reference drawing while the boat is being built.

A square stick is tacked along one side of the center line of the body plan to act in the same manner as the base batten on the plan and profile and the sticks are used to lay off the height and half-width of the various points of sheer, chine and keel. With the sticks butted against the base and center-line battens and held at right angles to them, the crossing of the sticks should be made at the point at which the half-breadth and the height of any given point coincide. This point is pricked in the floor and marked for future reference with the number of the frame it represents. When all spots are drawn in, they are connected to form the body plan and the process of laying down is completed. There is still considerable work to be done in the way of drawing lines on the floor but this is development work and comes under the heading of "taking off."

LAYING DOWN ROUND HULLED BOATS.—So far we have dealt with the Vee bottom hulls. Those which

have full rounded contours demand a slightly different treatment. Some method must be employed to measure and lay down their surfaces. If we were to cut the hull transversely at any point, we would get a surface very similar to the frame of a V bottom boat. This surface would be bounded by the frame and the deck beam. A series of these cuts if marked out on their proper positions on the floor would form the *body plan*.

If a cut were taken transversely through the hull at every individual frame it would show the form to which that particular frame would have to be shaped so that in conjunction with the other frames it would give the proper longitudinal curvature to the hull.

To properly dimension a curve we must set up a series of ordinates or parallel lines. To dimension the frames or moulds on a rounded hull we first set up a series of level planes parallel to the base line. (See Fig. 24A). If we were to float the hull at any particular draft parallel to the base line and could cut it through at this plane we could measure the width of every frame at this level. If we do this operation at equally spaced intervals throughout the depth of the hull we have a series of measurements by which these planes form ordinates for the curve of the frame. As each one of these levels of flotation is bounded by a curve, the designers term this curved edge of the plane a *water line* and to properly dimension the frame they give a dimension for each level which is listed in the offset table as the *half width* on that one level. Thus through a series of water lines (which appear as straight lines in the *body plan* and *profile* and in the plan as *curves*) we have the necessary ordinates from which to measure the center line and so dimension the frame.

Sometimes it is impossible to dimension a frame or transverse section properly through water lines alone. In this case another series of similar planes are set up which are vertical and are parallel to the centerline. These are called *buttocks* and the base line is used as the datum for their measurements. A buttock line 12″ out from the centerline would be designated as the 12″ *buttock,* sometimes this line is simply designated as "12″ out". As the measurements for these lines are taken upward from the base line they appear in the offset table as *heights.* These lines appear straight in the *plan* and *body plan* and are curved in the *profile.*

There are some instances in which neither a *water line* nor a *buttock* will properly dimension a frame. As we have seen both horizontal and vertical cuts taken through the hull, we can also take a sloping cut. These appear in the *body plan* as diagonal lines and are called *diagonals.* Their measurements are taken along the diagonal and away from the center line. Any convenient line parallel to the base on the centerline may be used as their datum in laying down.

Quite often the diagonals will be shown on a lines plan and no dimensions given for them. The architect in these cases uses the diagonals to study the water flow around a sailing hull when she is heeled. One of my early mentors, old *Tom Clapham,* used to say: "Fair the sailing lines (the diagonals) to the sweep of a white pine batten and let the *so called* water lines take care of themselves." The foregoing is the case in *Picaroon II* so when you see these do not be like my little Indian friend, Gordon Adams, who, when building *Ocean Place,* went into a dither about them and then mailed his now famous postcard "HOLD EVERYTHING!!! The light has dawned."

With a knowledge of how the hull is dimensioned we are now ready to "lay it down". This process is the art of transferring the dimensions that the designer has obtained from his small scale drawing to the floor and smoothing them up or *fairing.* On large boats this is often a laborious process to bring all three series of lines into one co-ordinated whole. As most of the boats in this book were small enough to design on a large scale it will only be necessary to lay down the *body plan* and the *stem outline.* To properly draw the frame contours, first lay down the *water-lines* and *buttocks* and spot the offsets on these.

After the spots are marked off a thin batten is sprung around them. If the line appears unfair at any one point, withdraw the nails and let it spring free. If this does not produce fairness do this to the spot above or below it after replacing the batten in its original position. In some cases it may be necessary to go in or out, up or down, on several spots until the batten produces a sweet flowing curve. In no case alter a spot over a quarter inch unless there is an obvious *unfairness.*

One invaluable aid in *fairing* a rounded hull is the *intersections.* If we examine the lines plan we will see in the profile that the curved buttock lines cross or *intersect* the straight water lines until they reach the sheer where they also intersect that line. If we take a look at the plan we will also see the curved water lines and sheer crossing the straight buttock lines. It soon becomes evident that this crossing is an identical point in all views of the hull. In the body plan if we can conceive it as a point where the lines of the water planes and those of the buttock planes cross at right angles, we can use this fact to an advantage.

As an example let us say that the straight 24″ buttock line intersects the curved L.W.L., 16½″ ahead of frame No. 6 in the plan view. If the lines are fair then the curved 24″ buttock line should intersect the straight L.W.L. 16½″ ahead of frame No. 6 in the profile. Thus after we have laid down the water lines in the plan view, if we measure the intersections and transfer them to the profile we have an additional series of spots beside those on the frames through which to draw the line. If the resultant line will not fair, something is wrong.

Some of the boats in this new edition have been so thoroughly detailed that it is only necessary to lay down the body plan which often may be done on some of the plywood ordered as planking for the hull. In some cases where heavy timbers are involved in the construction, they have been detailed so that they may be laid down on building paper and this used as a pattern or on the very wood itself. In laying down the body plan for any boat it is best to lay out each frame in full both sides of the centerline. To avoid confusion between the sections forward and aft of midship it is well to use two different colors of pencils to draw the lines. As a general rule red or blue is used for the aft sections and black for the forward ones. In the offsets for the new designs the old system of feet, inches and eighths has been abandoned and the actual feet and inch fractions are substitutes to avoid confusion. As your rule will in all probability read in inches it is also well to reduce all offsets to inches before you start to lay down to avoid mistakes.

CONVERTING FEET TO INCHES.—All dimensions given on the details will be in feet, inches and fractions. This is done because engineering scales read this way, and to give them thus, eliminated one chance of error. Your six foot rule will probably read in inches. Here is a table of conversion to save you the mental effort.

CONVERSION TABLE
Feet to Inches

	2 Ft.	3 Ft.	4 Ft.	5 Ft.	6 Ft.
0″	24″	36″	48″	60″	72″
1″	25	37	49	61	
2″	26	38	50	62	
3″	27	39	51	63	
4″	28	40	52	64	
5″	29	41	53	65	
6″	30	42	54	66	
7″	31	43	55	67	
8″	32	44	56	68	
9″	33	45	57	69	
10″	34	46	58	70	
11″	35	47	59	71	

TAKING OFF.—We will assume that the lumber for our keel is in the shop and we are anxious to *take it off* for cutting. There are many ways of securing the shape of the timbers from the lines on the floor. The safest and most accurate way is to make a template or pattern from one-eighth inch basswood, lay this on the timber and mark it off. Another accurate method is to lay thin, transparent drafting paper over the lines on the floor, trace the outline of the keel timber on it and then transfer it to the lumber. Some builders set tacks on the line with their points up (Fig. 29) and then carefully lower the timber down on the tacks so that their points will enter the wood, then wood is tamped down on the floor so that the tacks will penetrate and stay there when the wood is lifted. Another method is to drive a line of tacks along the line to be transferred. These tacks are not driven in the usual manner but their heads are driven sideways into the floor along the line. The timber is then lowered to the floor and pounded until the heads of the tacks produce an impression in the timber. All of the profile timbers are treated in a similar manner and are checked by laying them down on the lines after they are cut. An assembly of these timbers over the entire layout will be a good check for alignment before and after the holes are drilled for the fastenings. See Fig. D—Chap. XV for a take off batten

PROJECTION.—Neither the *plan,* the *profile* nor the *body plan* shows the transom in its true shape. The profile shows its length as being true, and the plan shows its widths as being true. To obtain the real or true shape in all directions, we must develop the transom as a *true plane.* We see in this process the art of projection in use. (See Fig. 30.) Projection is the carrying of a point off in space. We may project any point in any convenient direction. The plan of the transom is simply the projection of the points in the profile down to show the true widths. If we project these same points at right angles to the length, as shown in the profile, and apply the half widths as shown in the plan, we obtain its true shape. We have combined two views both of which show their respective dimensions as being true.

With all the members of the backbone of the hull out of the way, we turn our attention to the frames. When the architect designs the boat he usually makes his drawing to the outside of the plank. This is done so that the thickness of the planking will not throw a large error in his displacement calculation, as every square foot of one-inch planking below the water line will add five pounds to the displacement. If this were not taken into consideration, the boat would float somewhat higher than was intended. Since most of the frames in the boats in this book are straight, we can take off the plank by simply nailing a square stick the thickness of the plank on the *inside* of the frame lines of the body plan and build the frame against this. Most boats in this book are lined to the inside of planking.

The frames are joined together by a floor timber on the center line and by knees at the chine. The frames are built on the floor with the station side of the frame toward the floor. In other words, after the timber is laid on the floor, no part should be wider than the line which represents it in the body plan. The face of the frame away from the floor is the face to which the floor timber and the knees are fastened. This gives one face perfectly smooth and another encumbered with the floor and knees. The face to the floor is called the smooth face and the face away from it the rough face. The smooth face is always set on the station line. The rough face goes forward of the station in the forward part of the boat and aft in the aft part of the boat. This is done so that the bevel may always be cut away from the stock as fitted to the line on the floor. Figure 31 shows how the knees are laid out to obtain the maximum length from the width of stock specified.

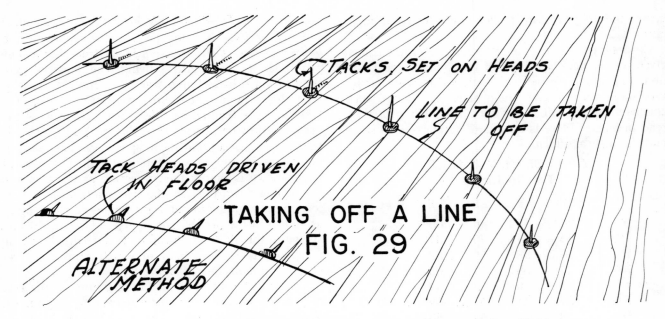

TAKING OFF A LINE
FIG. 29

ALTERNATE METHOD

TACK HEADS DRIVEN IN FLOOR

TACKS SET ON HEADS

LINE TO BE TAKEN OFF

PROJECTING THE TRANSOM

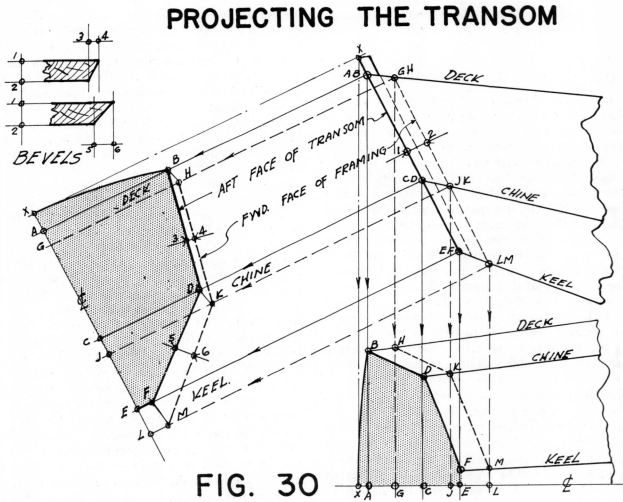

BEVELS

FIG. 30

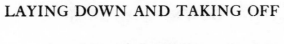

MOLDING THE
FRAME KNEE
FIG. 31

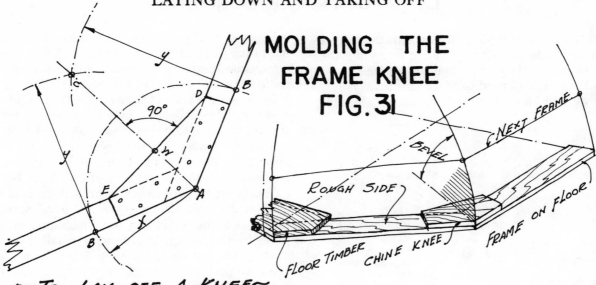

90°

NEXT FRAME

BEVEL

ROUGH SIDE

FLOOR TIMBER   CHINE KNEE   FRAME ON FLOOR

~To Lay Off A Knee~

"1." FROM CHINE POINT "A" DRAW ARC TO ANY CONVENIENT RADIUS-"X"

"2" FROM POINTS "B" DRAW ARCS TO RADIUS "Y" (greater than x)

"3" DRAW LINE A-C TO INTERSECTION OF ARCS "Y"

"4" ALONG THIS LINE LAY OFF A-W WHICH IS WIDTH OF KNEE STOCK

"5" DRAW LINE SQUARE TO A-C AND EXTEND TO INSIDE OF FRAME-D & E.

"6" SQUARE OFF TO FRAME AND THE RESULT IS THE KNEE SHAPE

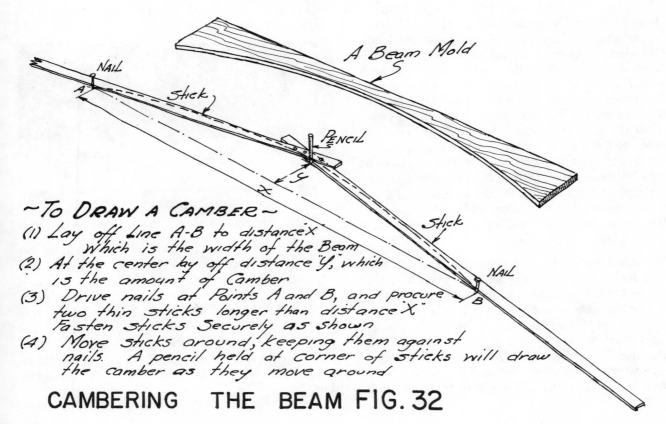

NAIL

A

Stick

A Beam Mold

PENCIL

X   Y

Stick

NAIL

B

~To Draw A Camber~

(1) Lay off Line A-B to distance "X"
    Which is the width of the Beam

(2) At the center lay off distance "Y", which
    is the amount of Camber

(3) Drive nails at Points A and B, and procure
    two thin sticks longer than distance "X".
    Fasten sticks securely as shown

(4) Move sticks around, keeping them against
    nails. A pencil held at corner of sticks will draw
    the camber as they move around

CAMBERING THE BEAM FIG. 32

Forward of a certain point in the boat, the frames must be curved to allow the planking to go into the curved rabbet without the hollows which would result if they were allowed to remain straight.

Since ancient times the deck beams of all ships

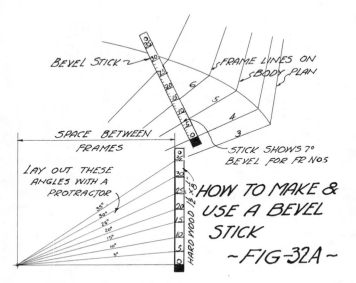

SPACE BETWEEN FRAMES

LAY OUT THESE ANGLES WITH A PROTRACTOR

HOW TO MAKE & USE A BEVEL STICK ~FIG-32A~

STICK SHOWS 7° BEVEL FOR FR NO5

have had a curvature, termed the *round-up* or *camber*. The theory that this shape adds strength to them has been proved a fallacy because the sides of a boat are a yielding medium and will not resist the load. The camber, however, does allow the water to run off more easily and gives the deck a neater appearance, so it is one of the traditions of the sea that can well be incorporated in modern design. To my knowledge, there are five different ways of drawing a camber, but the simplest is the one described here. All cambers of the deck are more or less an arc of some circle, and the simplest way to draw this arc is with two sticks, two nails and a pencil, as show in Fig. 32. The template for marking off the beams should be made in the reverse or hollow and at least a foot wider than the boat for it will be used for other purposes than laying out the beams.

MEASURING AND CUTTING FRAME BEVELS.—If you have a tilting table on your band saw, much of the bevel on frames and other members may be cut as you saw out these members. Where frames are widely spaced this angle can only be determined at the point where a waterline or other nearly horizontal member crosses the frame station. A bevel square is used to pick up the angle from the lines. Remember in applying this angle to the wood that

it is not normal or square to the curve of the frame but in the plane of the *waterline*. Mark the waterline on the wood and hold the shank of the square parallel to this line. Cut a couple of inches at this bevel. Now hold the square normal to the edge of the frame and re-set it. Measure this angle on a protractor and this is the angle to which your table must be set. In sawing, remember that the bevel will almost invariably under-cut the line. It is for this reason that frames are set in the direction of the closed bevel.

Where frames are closely spaced there is another method, and this one gives you the bevel normal to the curve of the frame. Lay out a measurement equal to the frame spacing. At one end of this distance draw another line perpendicular to it. From the end away from the perpendicular take a protractor and lay off every five degrees up to thirty-five. Extend these marks to the perpendicular. Now, divide the distance between the marks into five equal spaces. Mark off these divisions on a stick about ⅛″ x 1½″ and number them for ready reference. By holding the zero mark on one frame line and the stick normal to the line, the approximate amount of bevel to the next frame forward or aft of it can be read directly off the stick. Always measure in the direction of the frame thickness, for forward frames, forward—for aft frames, aft. Fig. 32A.

Fig. 32B.   An impromptu mold loft on the basement floor.

Where there is no adjustment in the tilt of the table as the work passes the saw, it is generally customary to set the saw to the least amount of bevel and cut the whole length of the cut to this angle, afterward finishing the bevel by hand or readjusting the table for short increments of the greater bevel along the frame as the angle becomes sharper.

For a complete treatise on Fairing—See *Ship and Aircraft Fairing and Development* by the same author.

CHAPTER V

FRAMING THE BOAT

The framing of a boat is, in reality, its skeleton—the bones on which the skin or planking is fastened. The keel forms the backbone of the boat and the frames form the ribs. The frames of a round-bottom boat are often called ribs. In the system of construction used in the larger boats described in this book there are two types of frames, the *main* and the *intermediates*. The main frames shape the boat and the intermediates supply the extra strength needed between them.

In all the boats to be described later, the construction should be done with the boat upside down. The framing has been designed with this in view. It is much easier to plank a boat's bottom in this position and, when facilities are available for turning over larger craft, it is highly recommended for them also.

All frames, except those which are steam bent, should be constructed flat on the floor over a full-sized drawing of their shape. To do this, secure one or more sheets of cheap plywood (good one side) and draw the body plan on this. The frames should be drawn in full on both sides of the center line. Both the forward and the after frames may be drawn from a common center line and base line. To avoid confusion, use red and blue pencils for the separate bodies.

The frame stock is cut and laid accurately to the lines, fastening them temporarily to the plywood with small nails. The chine knees and floor timbers (Fig. 33) then are screwed to the frame or holes for the bolts or rivets are bored while they are in this position. At the same time, the deck beam or a temporary spall is fitted across their top to hold their shape during the erection. After one frame is complete, it is laid aside and another started.

When all members of the frame are completed, a berth must be prepared on which to erect it. In the case of the rowboats or *Teal*, nothing more than a pair of sawhorses is required for support. For the small boats built upside down on a floor, no more is

required than some wooden cleats which are nailed to the floor and to which the frames are nailed.

FOUNDATION.—Where the boats are constructed upside down in the open, or where a concrete floor is

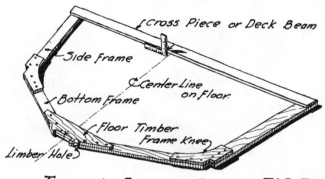

~TYPICAL BUILT-UP FRAME~ FIG.33

used, a foundation is necessary. (See Fig. 34.) This consists of two pieces of 2″ x 4″ rough stock for the small boats to 2″ x 12″ for the larger ones. These

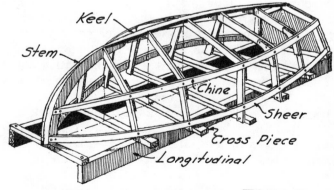

~BUILDING BERTH~ FIG. 34

pieces should be about two feet longer than the boat and spaced one-half the boat's beam apart. Their top edges should be truly level and, if in the open, they should be firmly anchored to the ground with stakes. Be sure that the tops of both the longitudinal and crosspieces are parallel and level. On a concrete floor, the berth should be anchored with angle iron clips and expansion bolts. On the smaller boats the longitudinal members should be made heavy enough to take the spring of the keel so that the berth may be set on sawhorses to raise the work to a convenient height. This allows the boat to be moved around in the shop and is much more convenient than a fixed berth.

Sometimes the larger boats are constructed on a keel-horse or large timbers supported on stakes

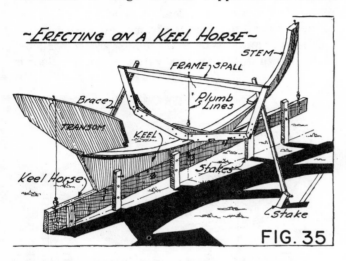

~ ERECTING ON A KEEL HORSE ~

FIG. 35

driven in the ground. (See Fig. 35.) In this case, the horse is set to the slope of the keel so that the frames may be plumbed during the erection.

In starting the erection, the frame station lines are marked on the berth or the horse. At this point, note which way the frame lies in reference to the station. For all boats in this book, the cross-spalls of the berth at the forward frames should be set on the aft side of the station line, and those for the aft frames should be set on the forward side of the station line. The midship frame, in all cases, has the spawl set aft of the station. This throws the rough faces of all frames toward the ends and allows for their bevel. Be sure that all spalls are set square to the center line, which should be accurately marked with a saw cut both on the frame-spalls and the spalls of the berth.

The midship frame is erected first, making sure that it is square to the center line and plumb to the base. Temporary braces are run to the berth or ground and nailed to hold the frame in its true position. The nails should be driven securely home but their heads should be allowed to project enough so

that they may be withdrawn later. When the boat is built on the ground, stakes should be driven to hold the braces or, as they are sometimes called, shores.

The frame next to midship, either forward or aft, is then erected, plumbed, squared and securely braced. This process is continued until all frames are set. They should now be checked for alignment before any further work is undertaken.

When the boat is built upside down, the stem and transom are erected and set to square and plumb lines. Next, the keel is bent around all members and fastened in. At this point, be sure that the berth has not warped or been distorted by the pull of the keel.

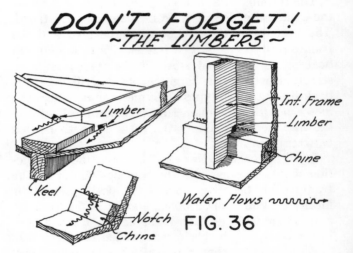

DON'T FORGET!
~ THE LIMBERS ~

FIG. 36

Also check to see if all the limber holes are cut. (See Fig. 36.) They drain the water along the boat to the pump and should never be less than ½" square holes in small boats, to ¾" square holes in the larger ones. Actually, the limbers are not holes but notches in the frame and do not become holes until the planking is fitted.

After the keel is in place, the chines are fitted into the notches which have been cut for them. They should be fastened securely to the keel and stem forward, and worked aft, fastening, bending and twisting as you go. To make the chines bend easier, sometimes they have to be soaked overboard for several days or wrapped in rags soaked with boiling water.

The sheer stringers are now bent in, similar to the chines. Where both of these members meet the transom, the transom planking may have to be relieved to allow them to enter. The same may be true at the keel. For this reason, some builders prefer to plank the transom after all stringers have been fitted.

If there are any intermediate frames, they are now fitted between the chine and the sheer. They are not beveled but are set square to the planking line. Forward where they take a bit of curvature, they will have to wait until the stem is rabbeted later to get their shape. As a rule, the first two panels aft of the stem will require curved frames. Where straight stems are fitted, no curved frames are required.

In spacing the intermediate frames, the distance along the chine and along the sheer stringer is divided into one more space than there are frames to be fitted. For example, if there are two intermediate frames in the space, then three spaces are required; if three frames are fitted, four spaces are required and so on.

Between the first frame and the stem and the last frame and the transom the same spacing as in the panel next to them is carried on. After the intermediate frames are fitted, little notches should be cut at the bottoms of all frames to allow the water to drain off the chine, as shown in Fig. 36. Be sure to cut these notches now because it will be almost impossible to cut them after the boat is planked. Another notch should be cut at the lowest point of the chine to allow the water to drain to the bilge.

The bottom stringers are now laid in and their crossings marked off on the frames if they have not been cut previously. These are notched and the stringers are fastened in.

FRAMING DETAILS

STRIP-BUILT BOATS.—If the boat is a strip-planked one, the hull is planked over the molds first. When all planking is completed, the boat is turned right side up without removing the molds. The frame stock is put in the steam box and the steaming process started. When by trial it is found that the frame is pliable enough to bend, it is placed in the boat and a nail, previously driven, is partly set in the keel to prevent the frame from moving. While an assistant pushes on the upper end of the frame, inside the boat the builder pushes the hot frame down against the planking with his foot. Occasionally, a block of wood is placed at the sheer to produce more bend than is actually needed. This aids the closer fit of the frame after the fastenings are driven. (See Fig. 37).

Frame after frame is inserted in the boat in this manner until all are in place. After bending a few frames, the novice will learn to handle these hot timbers with a dry rag between his hands and the steaming wood. Where excessive bevel occurs, he will learn also to put a clamp at the head of the frame and twist it as the frame is bent so that it will automatically follow the inner surface of the planking. Some builders prefer to allow the frame to follow the inner

surface without twist. This method has no objectionable feature other than the fact that the frames will not lie in a straight line across the boat but will be more or less at right angles to the deck line. So what?

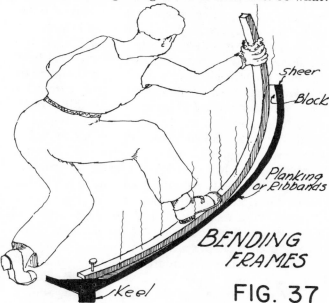

BENDING FRAMES
FIG. 37

In olden times the builders made the cant frames at the bow where excessive curvature existed and Columbus and many other men gained fame by sailing across oceans in these ships. One precaution should be taken, however, in fitting frames this way. Be sure that the heads meet the sheer where deck beams are to be fitted. This method makes the fitting of floor frames a bit tedious but it has its merits.

After all frames are bent, the hull is braced with cross-spalls across the sheer-line and the molds are removed. Care should be taken, however, that all frames are fastened securely to the planking. Make it a rule to drive all frame fastenings and fit as many floors as possible before removing the molds. After the hull is bare of molds, the sheer-clamps should be fastened below the sheer, allowing enough distance below the top of the sheer-strake so that the deck beams may be properly fitted. It is a good practice to set the sheer-clamp a bit higher than necessary and to notch the deck beam or the clamp until the top of the beam comes even with the top of the sheer-strake. When the sheer-clamp is finally fitted, the bilge stringer is bent in. Great care need not be exercised in fitting this member for an inch or two out of correct position will not seriously weaken the boat. If the bilge stringer is to be used in conjunction with some other framing, such as the cockpit beams, then it must be accurate. It is much better to fit an auxiliary stringer to take these beams.

NEW METHODS OF STRIP BUILDING.—The advent of the resorcinal resin glues has altered the process of strip building. Today, these glued boats are so stiff that they need very little framing. As a general rule, the molds have been eliminated and functional bulkheads take their place. Where these bulkheads are widely spaced, or where greater strength than the hull alone would be required, then frames are bent in against the stripping of the hull. Steam bending of the frames has been eliminated to a great extent by fitting frames composed of layers of wood thin enough so that they do not need steaming. When these laminated frames are nailed to the hull, each lamination nailed to its neighbor, and resin glue used to bind the whole assembly, the result is a frame far stronger than the old steam-bent one. See Chapter VII for further description of strip built boats.

CARVEL-PLANKED BOATS.—Where the boat is carvel-planked in the regular way, some builders prefer to make their molds in a different manner. They are made to the inside of inside ribbands. In doing this the thickness of the plank is first taken off. This is added to the thickness of the frames and the sum of the two added to the thickness of the ribbands. The sum of the whole is then deducted from the line of the outside of the planking and the molds built to this. (See Fig. 38.)

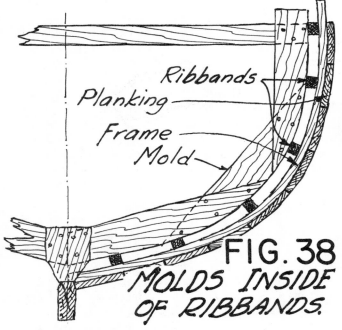

FIG. 38
MOLDS INSIDE OF RIBBANDS.

Ribbands
Planking
Frame
Mold

In this method the frames are bent outside the ribbands and this is the easiest of all methods. Being bent on the outside of the form, the frames may be definitely forced against a convex surface instead of a concave one. The planking is then applied over the frames. The boat is turned over and the molds removed. From here on, the procedure is the same as for the strip-built boats.

STEAM BENDING.—Wood in the natural state, as it grows in a tree, is composed of numerous small fibers clustered around microscopic cells. In the seasoning process, these fibers lose their natural flexibility and become somewhat brittle. Where seasoned wood is required to take an excessive bend the flexibility must be restored and this is done by steaming. While all of the boats described in this book were designed to eliminate steam bending, a description of how this is done will be an aid to any amateur builder.

The simplest way to restore flexibility to wood fiber is by getting moisture into the fiber. This may be done by soaking the wood in water for a period of time, but hot water or hot moisture is a surer method. The professional boatbuilder does this by steaming in a large box supplied with steam from a boiler. The amateur builder does it in the same way on a smaller scale.

The steam box and boiler may be reduced to one

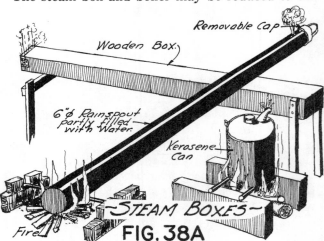

Removable Cap
Wooden Box.
6"ϕ Rainspout partly filled with Water.
Kerosene Can
STEAM BOXES
FIG. 38A
Fire

simple element by soldering an end on a length of 6" galvanized rainspout. A cap is made to fit the other end, Fig. 38A. The pipe is set on a slope and partially filled with water. Heat from a gas flame or wood fire is applied to the water-filled end and the material to be steamed is placed inside the pipe. The upper end of the pipe is capped and the lumber allowed to remain in the hot steam until pliant.

Another arrangement is a wooden box set on permanent supports. A five-gallon kerosene can forms the boiler. Many other variations of the steam box will suggest themselves to the ingenious backyard boatbuilder.

CHAPTER VI

MAKING THE FITS

After the framing of the boat is complete we must turn our attention to the covering or planking. This will require some fitting and if the back-yard boatbuilder does not have some experience in this, it will be well to learn. If he does, it will be wise to review the process.

In the simple boats of the chine variety there is little fitting to be done, but before the planking is applied we must *bevel* the stem and the chines as well as the keel to allow the planking to lie flat on them and prevent the entrance of water.

To bevel the chines the keel must also be leveled, for they lie in a straight line. We secure a straightedge

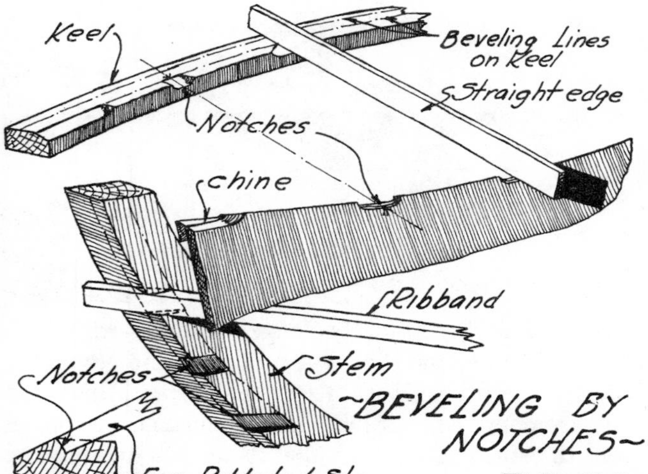

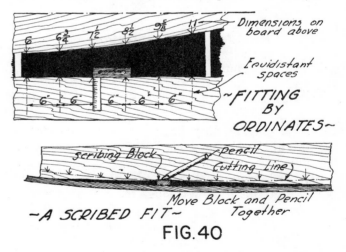

~BEVELING BY NOTCHES~

FIG. 39

long enough to reach across the gap between them. Starting somewhere near midship, we notch down on both chine and keel until the straightedge lies flat at the bottom of the notch. (See Fig. 39.) After cutting a series of these notches about a foot apart on both sides of the boat, we finally join them into one continuous surface.

The *stem rabbet*, or *bevel* if it is a split stem, is

done in a similar manner. A ribband or batten the same thickness as the intended planking is secured. An assistant holds this along at least three frames behind the stem while the builder cuts a notch deep enough to allow the batten to come flush with the stem at the rabbet line. The end of the batten is placed on the rabbet line if the stem is a rabbeted one, or allowed to run through if it is a split one, as shown in Fig. 39.

Often where it is necessary to fit a board, such as in the planking, the one edge may be bounded by a straight line while the other is a curve. It is an easy matter to take ordinates to accomplish this fit. (See

FIG. 40

Fig. 40.) *Ordinates* are lines from which a curve is measured. On the straightedged plank or board we mark off these ordinates square to the straightedge at equidistant points. If the curve is a sharp one they may be spaced at six-inch intervals or, if it is a long fair one, they may be as much as eighteen inches apart. The ordinate lines are marked in pencil on the lower board, as shown in Fig. 40. The space between the planks is then measured with a rule held along the ordinate line and the resulting figure is chalked on the board above. This is done for all ordinates.

The board which is intended to fill the gap is laid off with ordinates square to one of its straight sides. The figures chalked on the hull are now laid off on their corresponding ordinates on the board. When all of these are complete, they are connected with a batten and the cutting line is secured.

Where the curve is long and it is possible to lay the board to be fit to it, the fit may be made by *scribing*. This is done by setting up the board to be fit in its proper position. A block of wood is secured so that its height is just enough to come a bit above the largest part of the gap, as shown in Fig. 40. The block and pencil are now moved together to draw the cutting line. Caution: Never use this method where a great amount of curve is present. (See wrong method, Fig. 41.)

Now we come to the method of securing a fit that

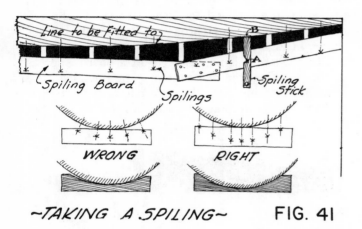

~TAKING A SPILING~   FIG. 41

all other boatbuilding books seem to consider a mystic rite. Years ago when I saw professionals take a spiling, I stood enthralled. I had read how you use a pair of dividers set to an exact distance. The writers stressed that *exact* as though the entire success of the boat depended on it. I did not discover that this was a lot of "malarky" until some time later when I found old Uncle Gabe taking a spiling. "Don't you use dividers?" I asked Uncle Gabe. "What is dey?" he asked in return.

I found that Uncle Gabe didn't even have a pair in his tool-box but he got accurate spilings just the same. He used a notched stick. He took a couple of thin boards and nailed them together to conform, as close as straight lines would, to his curve. Holding the spiling stick in the same direction all the time, Uncle Gabe took his pencil from the woolly white

hair behind his ear and made his spiling marks by placing his pencil in the notch at *A* (Fig. 41), while he held the end of the stick, *B*, on the plank to which another must be fitted.

Uncle Gabe then took off his spiling board and fastened it in the proper position on the flat plank to be fitted. He set the notch on the spilings and marked the board to be cut with the end of the spiling stick. When he was finished with his stick and board he hung them on nails in his shop. Old Gabe never tacked his spiling boards to the work; he always held them with a gadget resembling an enlarged clothespin which he had cut from hickory saplings. Even after I saw his method, I stuck to my dividers for a while —it took a long time for me to learn that every time you drop them they change their measurement.

In spiling a sharp curve it is important always to hold the spiling in one direction and do not follow normal to the curve. The right and wrong methods are shown in Fig. 41.

BACK-MEASURING.—Another method of fitting similar to spiling is back-measuring. (See Fig. 42.) A board is laid in position to transfer the measure-

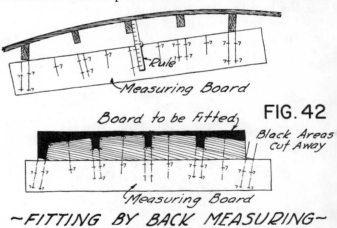

~FITTING BY BACK MEASURING~

ments in any direction. The edge of the board is generally laid in a line that will represent the edge of a board to be fitted. With a rule and pencil, lines and measurements are drawn on the measuring board from the surface to which the fit must be made. The lines drawn on the measuring board are drawn in the direction of frame faces and other objects that must be fitted around. If possible. the same back-measurement is used for all marks (in Fig. 42 it happens to be 7″), but any random dimension may be used as long as its line and the measurement are marked on the measuring board.

After the measuring board has been checked on the boat to make sure that no dimensions have been missed, it is removed and laid alongside the board to be fitted. Following the direction of the pencil lines, the measurements are now transferred to the board to be fitted. Note in Fig. 42 how the inside and outside edges of the frames lie along the same line at numerous places and two measurements are given for the points.

TEMPLATE.—Where the piece to be fitted is rather large, as in the case of plywood, a template is constructed. This is a frame of light strips that is built to the existing edges of the place in which the fit is to be made. This may be as complex as it is possible for an object to be, but a template may still be made to fit it. (See Fig. 43.) One good feature of the template is that if it cannot be removed through the openings in the boat, a plywood sheet of the same size cut to fit will not be able to be set in place for it will not enter any opening through which the template will not come out.

The builder's ingenuity will often suggest combinations of template and fitting boards that will save hours in making the various fits. I have seen the country builders use such unconventional methods as bending a piece of copper tubing to get a template for a hard-to-spile curve. In making any fit by other than the conventional methods, one must always keep in mind the fact that the fit is no more accurate than

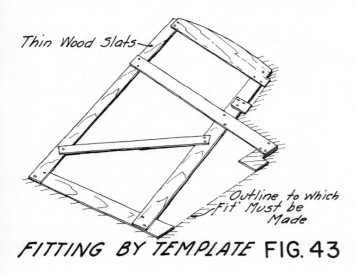

FITTING BY TEMPLATE FIG. 43

the pattern. In the professional boatbuilding shops, there is a saying that in winter the chunk stove is fed on mistakes.

BEVELS AND ANGULAR CUTS.—In measuring cuts across wood that are not square, some standard must be set up to accomplish this. If we remember our high school geometry, we will know that these measure-

ments are given in *degrees*. The circle is divided into 360 parts, each one of which is a degree. If we look at the mariner's compass, we may see this clearly. Starting at NORTH, we see the starting point as zero and the ending as 360. Going one quarter around the circle to EAST, we see 90. As this is a *right* or square angle, we begin to recognize the carpenter's

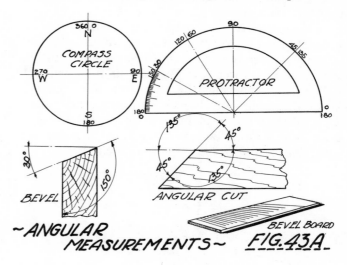

~ANGULAR MEASUREMENTS~ FIG.43A

square. By going back half way, we see NE or 45° and recognize the miter by which we cut two pieces of wood to form a square joint. We have *halved* the angle. Again going around in the same direction from E to S we see 180°, and that the line between NS and the center point of the compass will be a straight one. For all mechanical work we need go no further, for 180° is all we ever need.

We must have some sort of rule, or scale, to measure these angles and this rule is called a *protractor*. These may be purchased in many forms and if you have a power saw you will already have one on the guide for making angular cuts. You will also note that this is similar to your bevel square and, in many cases, may be used as such, having the advantage that it may be pre-set from its own protractor. Some machinist's squares have a similar arrangement.

Often it is inconvenient to measure an angle of the figure given. The difference between the angle and 180° is called its *complement*. Thus, to mark off a 45° angle we might set our bevel square either to 45° or 135° and mark it off.

Bevels are generally given in the *Amount of Material To Be Taken Off*, thus if we have a 30° bevel, we cut the wood away until the remaining sharp angle would measure 60°. This is not the *complement* but the angle of the wood still standing, as we have worked off a square or 90° corner.

The amount of degrees is generally shown on plans with a number and a small circle to the right and above it. A bevel of less than 90° is often designated as a *closed* bevel and one more than that amount is called an *open* one. The angle and its complement are often confusing and it is good practice to mark off the bevel in pencil and check it before cutting as "putting back on machines" is difficult. Early boat builders measured their angles and marked them on a bevel board for ready reference. This is still good practice. Watch the angles particularly while cutting with a tilting power saw. As most of these will tilt only to 45°, they must be set to the difference between this and ninety to make the cuts greater than 45° and the work turned 90° to its normal position. Make sure that the table is set right in the beginning and then cut a piece of scrap wood to check it.

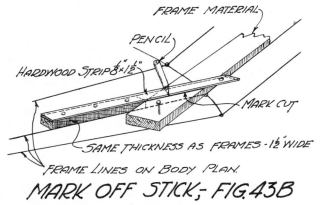

MARK OFF STICK; FIG.43B

MARK-OFF STICK.—To any one who has laboriously measured the angular cuts of a frame on a body plan with a protractor and then transferred it to the wood, a little gimmick called a mark-off stick will be a boon. These are so simple to make that the time consumed in their construction will be repaid a thousand times in their use. Rip off a piece of your frame material about 1½" wide and 1' long. On the top of this tack a hardwood stick the same width and twice as long. (See Fig. 43 B.)

To mark off a piece of frame material, it is set to its line on the body plan and temporarily nailed in position. The mark-off stick is placed against the other line of the frame and it's up to you to push the pencil.

NEW WRINKLES IN MAKING FITS.—Several clever tricks on making fits have been developed since our first edition. They are worth while, so we'll pass them along.

It is no longer necessary to use tacks or other means of picking up the shape from the body plan. Go to some engineering or art supply store and purchase several yards of cheap draftsman's tracing paper. Lay this over the layout and, in pencil, trace the outlines of the pieces to be cut. The tracing may be done freehand. Do not try to take the entire sweep of the curves in one stroke of the pencil but follow the line in short, sketchy, overlapping strokes. The pattern is carried to the wood to be cut and pricked through the paper with an awl or pointed nail. The tracing wheels used by tailors and seamstresses are excellent for this work. They can be purchased at the notion counters of most department stores. Once a pattern has been pricked through, it may be used again by dabbing the outlines with a small cloth bag of powdered chalk or talcum powder.

If the body plan is laid out on this paper, it may be reproduced also by the Ozalid process which is done by the blueprinting companies in most large cities. This process has practically no shrinkage and for all practical purposes is safe to use for boats up to 9' of beam. In boats of larger sizes, the 30" or 36" widths of paper are overlapped, being registered in position with match marks so that they may be assembled again in their proper positions. By having one set printed right side up and another reversed, it is only necessary to lay out one side of the boat. When the prints are properly assembled, the outline of the frames on both sides of centerline are available. Join the various sheets with Scotch tape or rubber cement. Glue will wrinkle the paper.

As the plywood sheets at the chine approach the bow, they become difficult to mark off because the angle becomes too flat to properly insert a pencil. Another clever trick has been devised to do this marking. Before the sheets are clamped for marking, drill on the corner of the chine a series of one-eighth diameter holes about 6" apart. Drill these clear through the chine stringer. After the sheet has been marked off as far as you can go, enter the inside of the boat and drive six-penny finishing nails through the holes into the plywood. When the sheet is removed for sawing, the nails or their impressions will give a series of spots through which a line may be drawn. The same holes may be used for top and bottom sheets.

CHAPTER VII

PLANKING AND DECKING

The earliest boats were hollowed from solid logs. There were no problems of framing or planking, for the shell of the log combined the two. Primitive man later found that he could make his craft lighter if he allowed the interior to be thicker in some spots, thus contributing to the strength of the craft, while the parts not needing the strength could be cut away. This was the primitive separation of the framing and the planking. As his craft became larger and the trees could not be secured large enough to construct them, parts of various trees were joined to accomplish this. It was found, through centuries of building, that the boat (now it had become a ship) would be less laborious to build if a frame were set up and covered with sheets of wood. Here, at last, was the entire separation of framing and planking.

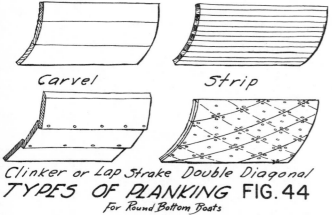

TYPES OF PLANKING FIG. 44
For Round Bottom Boats

DOUBLE-DIAGONAL PLANKING.—Every shipwright has dreamed of producing a planking that combined the greatest strength on the least amount of weight. The acme of this, so far, is double-diagonal planking. Two or three (sometimes four) layers of planking are applied to the hull and between each is placed a layer of muslin or light canvas soaked in marine glue. The planking is laid in thin strips diagonally across

the hull. Sometimes these strips are less than an eighth of an inch in thickness and are joined at their intersections with clinched copper tacks. I have seen the wooden floats of the early Navy patrol planes which were built in this manner take repeated landing impacts without leaking. The new moulded plywood boats now appearing on the market are made in a similar way—a cold or hot setting plastic taking the place of the canvas and marine glue between the various layers.

STRIP-PLANKING.—When I was just old enough to sit up and take notice of the things around me, the fishermen in the town of Hamden, Maine, were turning out a distinctive type of boat, later known as the Hamden Boat. The outstanding feature of these craft was their planking. The banks of the Penobscot River

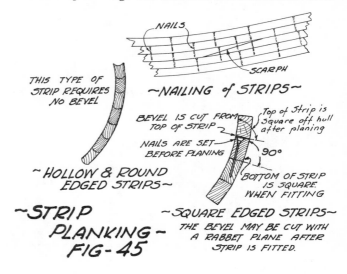

~STRIP PLANKING~ FIG-45

were lined with box factories turning out boxes from the white pine forests of that state. From the cull of making boxes there came many long, thin strips which could be purchased for little or nothing. Fishermen, besides being poor folk, are often ingenious

39

and they made use of these strips in planking the boats that they used in their daily work. I constructed one of these boats from cypress strips and it proved a success.

The strips are edge-nailed as you go, using a nail set to flush the heads. The nails used should always be galvanized finishing nails and six-penny nails are about right for all ordinary work. They should be toed, as shown, to increased their holding power. When the going gets tight, where the planks go together, they should be placed close to the edge of the plank and toed inboard. The nailheads near the outside of the plank should be set in far enough to escape the blade of your plane when the hull is finished.

The butts of the strips should be made in a long scarph. A box similar to a miter box is made to do this, Fig. 45, so that all butts will have the same angle. In arranging the butts, try to have them fall at least two feet apart in adjacent planks and spread out well all over the boat.

For the amateur builder strip-planking has the following advantages:

The tedious spiling for every plank is eliminated and the hollowing of wide planks on the sharp turns of frames is entirely absent.

No ribbands are necessary over the molds, thus saving this material.

No caulking is necessary and the boat stays tighter when stored out of water over the winter.

The same care applied to the fitting of strip-planking will give a much smoother hull than the ordinary method and the seams do not drop their putty as the boat grows old.

MODERN STRIP-BUILT BOATS.—When the old boys of Hamden, Maine, built their first boats from strips of native wood, they little dreamed that some day the system they were using would become the amateur's answer to the dream of beautiful rounded hulls without the necessity of spiled planks of steam-bent frames. When the chemists of the Borden Co. produced their first resorcinal resin glue, Cascophen (now Elmer's Glue), they knew they had something good but I doubt if even they had the backyard builder in mind. The combination of a planking system of thin strips and something to bind these separate strips into one homogeneous fabric became possible only in the last decade. Where the old Hamden boats required frames to be bent in to them and temporary molds to shape them, the glued strips are so strong that little, if any, framing is required. Always having been a lazy cuss, I could never entirely see the waste of good labor when the molds of any boat were torn out of her

after she was framed. Today, everything must be "functional". Well! There must be frames and there must be molds. The mold spacing is about the same distance as would be required for the frames. Let's make the molds function as frames or the frames function as molds and there you have functional spelled with a capital *eff*. Modern strip planking is far easier, labor but not timewise, than plywood. While it is true that one sheet of plywood covers a large area, it is also true that it takes a lot of labor to achieve the result. A sheet of 4ft. by 8ft. plywood is heavy and awkward and a flock of clamps are required to hold it down. I have fitted plywood sheets alone, wishing all the time that I had six extra hands and was twins to boot.

Strip planking on the other hand may be bent around the hull with very little effort. It it best for the man who works solo. There are several gimmicks which, if you will make them before you start stripping the hull, will provide helpers which will never argue with you or feel that the boat is half theirs after it is finished.

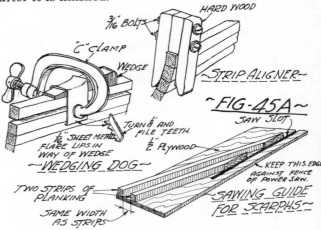

In the same type of wood we will find two different pieces that will refuse to bend to the exact same curve. While it is easy to hold two strips co-incident at the molds, varying grain sometimes will throw them off between these points. A few "aligners" on the job will hold the strips to their designated curve until the nails take over. These are made of pieces of hardwood as shown in Fig. 45A. Driven over the strips they hold them in line and release your hands for the important job of driving the nails. Make three or four of these.

Sometimes the curvature becomes such that the nails alone will not pull the strips tight. Wedging dogs will come in handy here. These are made as per the sketch in Fig. 45A, and one or two of them should be made.

Where a power saw is available, a guide to cut the scarphs is a whole lot faster than the old miter-box idea. The slope of the cut is 1″ in 8″. Figure 45A shows how this is made.

The glue spreading problem is a messy one. Once either the resorcinal or fiberglas resins or weldwood glue have *set* in a brush it is worthless. Brushes may be cleaned after use but how often do we forget this out of weariness in the late hours when we knock off. Some time ago I decided to do something about this problem. Lying in one corner of the shop was a short length of ¾″ manila rope. I served this every four inches and then cut it close to the serving. After separating the fibers it produced a very good brush. Tying these to a stick proved unsatisfactory so an old tomato can, plus a short length of broom stick, produced the handle shown in the sketch, Fig. 98, Chapter XIV. Dipping the served end in diluted shellac will eliminate the shedding of some of the fibers, but if these are not too numerous they will not harm the glue joint. Several 2″ or 3″ widths of sheet rubber nailed to the end of a stick will also make a good spreader. Some of the larger boat yards and commercial plants doing a lot of glue work use a mechanical glue spreader. This is simply an adaption of the moisteners that you see in many stores used in connection with their gummed wrapping tape. It consists of a roller and a pan to hold the glue, the strip being pulled over the roller which picks up the glue from the pan and applies it to the wood. As the glue level drops one end of the pan is blocked up to raise the level at the roller end. It is good practice to cover the roller with masking tape which is removed at the end of the day, leaving the roller clean.

Just another thing about glueing. Wear the oldest shirt and trousers you possess. The glue is just what the manufacturers say it is, *waterproof,* and it will not wash out. If you can do this operation without getting any glue in your eyebrows let me know how you do it. Some builders wear rubber gloves to keep the glue off their hands.

One of the new inventions that no one will condemn you for using is paper towels. Have a roll of these on hand. Use them to wipe away the glue runs which later will set up as hard as glass. Do this the minute a run starts and you save hours of work later. Wax lunch paper or *Reynold's Wrap,* held on with masking tape, will protect any surface that you do not want glue to stick to. Do not wash your hands or brushes in hot water; this sets the glue hard. A chemical sold as *MEK* will dissolve most of the epoxy resins before they set. Continued use of this on the hands is injurious.

Now that we are ready to apply the strips, let's investigate them. These may be made from any material that is fairly straight grained and not prone to split easily when nailed. Mahogany, either Philippine or African soft, is best. Next in order comes Southern cedar or Juniper (if it is free of knots), Port Oxford Cedar, Cypress, White Pine or Douglas Fir. This material may be purchased finished to size or in boards and ripped in your own shop. The ripping should be done with a special saw blade. These blades are sold under various designations such as *planer, variety,* or *combination* saws. They can be distinguished from the others in that they have one

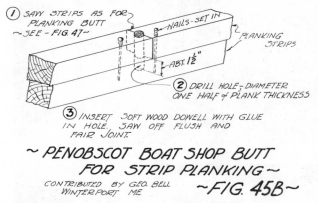

① SAW STRIPS AS FOR PLANKING BUTT ~ SEE - FIG. 47 ~
NAILS - SET IN
PLANKING STRIPS
ABT. 1½″
② DRILL HOLE - DIAMETER ONE HALF of PLANK THICKNESS
③ INSERT SOFT WOOD DOWELL WITH GLUE IN HOLE. SAW OFF FLUSH AND FAIR JOINT.

~ PENOBSCOT BOAT SHOP BUTT FOR STRIP PLANKING ~
CONTRIBUTED BY GEO. BELL WINTERPORT ME.
~ FIG. 45B ~

deep-cut large tooth followed by a series of smaller ones. They leave a remarkably smooth cut that a little sanding will finish off. The hollow ground blades are best.

Even though you buy your boards dressed, the ripped sides cannot compare to those finished on a planer. As our 1″ material will be $1\frac{3}{16}$″ thick when you get it, you must rip it either to the width or thickness of the strips. In the larger boats such as *Picaroon* where the strips are $1\frac{3}{16}$″ square you have the option of putting the dressed sides inside and out and glueing the sawed edges. On *Titmouse* and *Osprey* where the thickness is ⅝″ and the width $1\frac{3}{16}$″ there is no choice. If you are real persnickety and want the inside of the boat absolutely smooth you will have to plane or joint one edge and then rip the other. There is no point to a planed finish on the outside of the boat as this is sanded smooth in the final operation.

At such points where excessive flare or tumble-home occur either the inner or outer edge will take a bevel. This will not be serious. A block plane set rather coarse will cut all that is needed for the bevel very easily. The strip is tacked temporarily at its end and beveled as it is bent in. It is far easier to bevel only the top edge allowing the bottom one to remain

Fig. 45C. Progressive steps in strip planking a *Harbor Gull*, designed by R. D. Carlson in the Penobscot Boat Shop at Winterport, Me. (Top left) Molds erected; (Top right) Hull partly stripped; (Bottom left) Interior view, showing frames; (Bottom right) Outside of hull after filling and sanding.

square. In this way you are planing the edge that you see and its correctness of bevel can always be tested by a short length of square-edged strip applied at every frame. A little practice will give you a sense of bevel so that eventually you will know just how much to take off a strip without even measuring it. Some types of rabbet planes which will cut out to their sides are also a big help in beveling, because when using these the bevel may be cut after the strip is nailed.

The old idea of having the strips follow the sheer has been discarded and most builders today start at the bottom and work up, leaving the strips run off the sheer where they will. If the planking is to be finished natural and you want the strips to follow the sheer, the best way to do this is to set one strip an equal distance below the sheer all along the boat and work the bottom planking up to this, fitting them to the guide strip. After the bottom is all filled in the topside strips are carried above the guide strip in the regular manner until the sheer is reached.

Sometimes the strips will start to climb sharply at the ends, making the bend difficult at some one frame. In this case it is better to start tapering them. This can be done in several ways. The easier method is to rip alternate strips with a long taper, down to no width at all at their ends, keeping, of course, their thickness constant. The other method is to pack out the curve with *stealers* tapered at both ends until the hollow is packed out sufficiently to allow the parallel stripping to proceed again. Your own judgment, coupled with a little trial and error fitting, will decide this matter best. Where the strips start to get thin use smaller headed nails to set up the thinner ends.

On some boats, such as the round bottom *Picaroon* and *Fish Hawk*, if we were to start the strips at the keel and run parallel we would get into a mess at the stem. On boats such as these it is best to fit a wide garboard strake or a flat bottom the same thickness as the strips and work up from this. An 8″ board is spiled to fit against the keel. After the fit has been made if any width is remaining at the ends it is tapered down to a sharp point from the midship width. On *Fish Hawk* a planked flat bottom has been fitted—no hollow curves will appear when stripping.

In nailing the strips, common six-penny, hot-dipped, galvanized nails are used. These are spaced about six inches apart. Do not drive the nails completely home as hammer blows on the planking will mar it. Drive the nail to within a quarter inch of the strip and set it flush with a large cup-pointed nail set. Nothing mars a boat more than nails which peep out. First of all learn to drive the nail true. The angle at which it is started determines all of this. In spite of all precautions that you may take, adverse grain may sometimes deflect a nail. Learn to grip the planking between your fingers where the nail is being driven. If it is going to come out you will feel a bulge starting. Withdraw the nail at once and start it again a quarter inch away.

The best advice I can give on strip planking is not to be afraid of the job before you start. Familiarity, I know, breeds contempt and I have seen a lot of this sort of work done. On the other hand, if you do not have confidence you will never start it. Don't be "chicken." The old adage about practice making perfection still works. Perhaps your first stripping job is not all that is to be desired and if you are ashamed of it after you have finished, a coating of fiberglas will come in handy.

CANVAS AND PAPER PLANKING.—Many boats are lightly planked and then covered with canvas. In building a boat by this method, a form is prepared and the molds set up. These are made to the inside of the ribbands (see Fig. 38, p. 34) and the ribbands bent around them. The thin frames (as in a canoe) are bent over these ribbands and the thin planking is applied haphazardly over them and fastened with copper tacks clenched on the inside of the boat. The whole hull is then covered with canvas and rendered watertight by filling and painting.

Some craft, such as kayaks, are framed on molds and ribbands which form a part of the permanent structure. No planking is applied, but the frame is covered with canvas and rendered watertight. In some cases, these craft are actually double-diagonal planked with paper. The paper used is heavy kraft or brown wrapping paper in commercial use. The roll of paper is put on a bandsaw and cut into four-inch lengths. Starting diagonally, this is applied to the hull, glued to the molds and ribbands with *Weldwood* glue or some other waterproof cement. The paper is then allowed to set firm and another layer is applied. running diagonally in the opposite direction and fastened to the under layer in its entirety with cement or glue. Layer after layer is built up in this manner until the skin is about three thirty-seconds of an inch in thickness.

A slower method but one rendering the paper more waterproof is to apply each layer with varnish as the adhesive. Three weeks should be allowed for each layer to dry. Some of these craft have been constructed with heated rosin to which a small amount of linseed oil has been added. I used such a craft for several years and its only disadvantage was that it punctured easily upon rough handling.

CARVEL-PLANKING.—Through the ages many types of planking have been developed. Earliest records of the Egyptian craft on the Nile show that they were carvel-planked. Carvel-planking has received its name from a distinctive type of boat, called a carvel, the origin of which has been lost in antiquity. In this type of planking, wide strips of wood are used to cover the hull and these are butted edge-to-edge. (See Fig. 44.) While we may term each individual board of a boat's covering a plank, they are collectively called *strakes* when considered for the full length of the boat. Each strake may consist of one or more planks.

Carvel-planking a la Maryland is somewhat different than in other parts of this country. The topsides of the boat and its bottom separated to form two distinct divisions of the boat's skin joined at the chine. The topsides may be made like the barrel staves even though they have no transverse curvature. This is considered a waste of time in this part of the country and in most cases the plank widths are run in parallel widths. The bottom is a heresy in most boatbuilding circles; the planking does not follow the accepted practice of other parts of the country but is placed diagonally across the bottom in much the same way as in the ordinary flat-bottom rowboat. This planking is not caulked until the boat becomes so old that this is necessary and then only light caulking is resorted

Fig. 45D. A small centerboarder with "a la Maryland" planking.

to. In the new boat, the planking is allowed to swell tight like barrel staves.

Two schools of thought exist regarding the planking of a boat. One of these holds that the surface of the hull should be divided in such a manner so that an equal number of plank widths should be placed at any transverse station, Fig. 46. This requires that

the planking gradually diminishes in width toward the ends of the boat like the staves of a barrel.

The other school holds to the tenet that when the boat is finally finished, the surface should be so finished that no seam will be visible. It is often possible to plank a boat, such as those shown in this book, with parallel planks, thus eliminating the wasted material and the extra labor of diminished planking.

Somewhere on the boat, parallel planking will run out to a very sharp end which will be hard to fasten

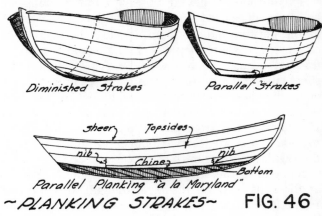

Diminished Strakes   Parallel Strakes

Parallel Planking "a la Maryland"

~PLANKING STRAKES~   FIG. 46

and hold in place. This is eliminated by a nib, Fig. 46. Often the ends of some boats will have wider plank widths than at midship (on a dory, for instance) and several nibbed planks will be necessary in this case.

Few boats are planked with lumber the full length of the boat. Often it is not an economical method, so the planks are joined or butted. It can be readily seen that if all planks were butted at the same point completely around the boat, a weak spot would develop there. To eliminate this condition the butts are staggered, that is, they are so divided as to eliminate the possibility of a large number of them falling in any one frame space. Some rule must be set up to govern the spacing of butts and this is a good one to follow: *Never space butts in adjacent planks without having at least four frame spaces between them. Never place butts in the same frame space without having at least three planks between them.*

Some boatbuilders will butt planks on a frame. This is poor construction, false economy and actually harder work than a proper workmanlike job. The proper way to butt a plank is by the use of a butt block, Fig. 47. To fit a butt block, the planks are allowed to overlap and a saw-cut is made through the two planks. This saw-cut should not be made directly square to the planks but at a slight angle favoring the outer plank. Thus, when the butt is pulled tight, the joint will close. Often it is necessary to make another saw-cut through the joint so that it will close properly, but a tight butt will result.

The ends of the butted planking are secured to a block by screws or rivets. These should be of oak or other hardwood and generously smeared with white lead or other waterstopping material before fitting. To facilitate caulking, an *outgauge* should be planed on the edge of all planks, Fig. 47. Submerged planking should be fitted so that one-sixteenth of an inch

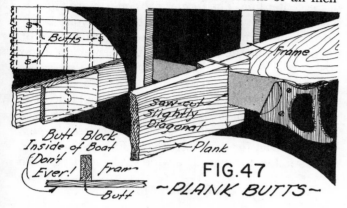

FIG. 47
~PLANK BUTTS~

remains open between the planks to allow for swelling. No plank below the water should be over six times its thickness in width. Planks between wind and water (the topsides) should be fitted tight.

Diagonal bottom planking should never be caulked until the boat reaches an age where caulking compounds are useless but they should be *outgauged* to make a tighter fight when they swell together.

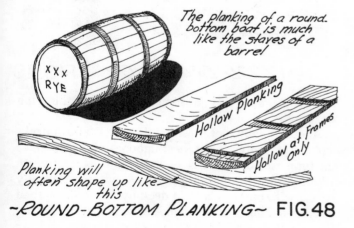

~ROUND-BOTTOM PLANKING~ FIG. 48

Before a plank is finally fitted in place, paint should be applied to all surfaces that cannot be reached with a brush after the plank is set.

ROUND-BOTTOM CARVEL-PLANKING.—If we examine the staves of a barrel, Fig. 48, we will find that they have two things in common with the planking of a round-bottom boat. First, they diminish in width

as they approach the heads of the barrel much as the planking of a boat diminishes as it approaches the ends, Fig. 48. Secondly, the staves have a concave and a convex side to them, the concave side being on the inside of the barrel. Where the planks of a round-bottom boat turn the sharp curve of the bilge they also must have a concavity to fit against the frames.

The hollowing of boat planking is tedious work and must be done with a hollowing plane. (See Fig. 12, p. 10.) The plank used in making this strake must be thicker than necessary, as shown in Fig. 48. A substitute for hollowing the whole plank is to hollow it in way of the frames only. Professional builders frown on this method but I have never seen a single disadvantage in it other than the small bit of weight added to the boat. On the other hand, the small amount of extra planking between the frames adds extra strength to the boat at the turn of the bilge where it is most needed.

Diminished planking on a small boat will often take a noticeable *sny*, as illustrated in Fig. 48. Where a large amount of sny is present, watch that the grain will not cross the plank end, as shown at the right-hand end of the plank in the illustration. It is better to insert another butt to eliminate this condition.

In fitting the diminished planking, the sheer-strake and the garboard (the one next to the keel) are fitted first. The distance between them is equally spaced at a number of points along the hull. A spiling is taken for every plank and the frames marked. Next, the distances are picked up from the hull and the line faired on the plank. This forms the spiling edge for the next plank. The planks are applied up from the garboard and down from the sheer. The last plank to be fitted is called the shutter and this plank will call upon all the builder's ingenuity to hold it while being fastened, as there is no opening through which to insert a clamp.

The planks around the bilge are often made two-thirds or half the width of the rest of the planking to avoid thicker stock from which to make them. This practice often results in thinner planks on the turn of the bilge where thickness is most needed.

CLINKER-PLANKING.—Somewhat later than carvel-planking and yet so early that its origin is unknown, another type of planking was developed that has found favor in small boat construction. This is lap-strake or clinker-planking. In this method, the individual strakes are overlapped and fastened together. On small boats and canoes, clinched copper tacks may be used for this operation on the thinner thickness of wood but where the thickness reaches a half-inch or over, the riveted fastening using copper nails is preferred. (See Fig. 21, p. 19.) The old Viking long boats were clinker-planked and the individual planks were held together with leather lacings. In clinker-planking, the secret of a tight boat is to make the faying surface a perfect fit where the two planks overlap and have the fastenings in the seam sufficiently close to prevent leakage between them. The disadvantages of clinker-planking are the difficulty in repairing a damaged plank and the tendency of the nails to enlarge their holes as the boat warps and twists in a seaway. This is noticeable in old clinker boats and at this stage they are termed "nail sick." Sometimes a complete re-riveting of all fastenings will cure this malady. The main advantage of clinker-planking is its lightness and boats constructed in this manner do not need preliminary swelling to become watertight.

FINISHING THE PLANKING.—Regardless of how close the ordered planking has been planed to one even thickness, some planks will protrude farther than others when the boat is finished. Everyone is interested in getting his planking as smooth as possible. In the old days this was done by a laborious process of planing. A jack-plane set to a fine cut was run across the surface of the hull in a diagonal direction until the whole hull was planed. Then it was run in the opposite direction. A smoothing out was taken in the run of the planks and, after that, several sandings with varying coarsenesses of sandpaper were given. (Plywood is a blessing.)

The advent of the electric sander has changed all of this. A rough paper is put in the sander and the hull dressed down. A fine paper in the sander finishes the job. The old method of diagonal strokes across the hull still holds for the rough cut. The direction of the smooth cut should follow the grain of the wood.

DECKING

Decking is, in reality, just another type of planking; it is the roof covering of the hull. Due to the greater chance of leakage from shrinking and swelling, deck planks are run in narrow widths as compared to hull planking. A bare wood deck is a rarity these days and well it might be. Without a doubt, they are the best looking decks and if tradition is carried out in laying them, they are the most romantic, making the little boat look like a real ship. Romance is for the young and there was a time when I thought there was nothing like a real wood deck with its strakes properly laid, plugged and finished natural. It took years of being disturbed in my sleep to get to the point where I threw romance overboard and canvased

my own decks. There will be some youngsters, however, who will read this book and will want a bright deck in spite of my warning. Here goes but, remember, you were warned!

Around the sheer of boats that have bright decks it is proper to fit a margin plank first. Sometimes this is called the covering board. There are two ways of running our decking, Fig. 49. The strips either may follow the margin plank or they may be laid parallel to the center line. The former method is more difficult but some claim that it looks better. Everyone is entitled to his own opinion. I like to see the strakes of the deck follow the center line, but, then again, I am lazy.

STRIP DECKING.—If you decide to lay a strip deck in spite of all the former warning, it should be done properly. The ends should be nibbed as they have been on seagoing packets since *Hector was a pup.* This is shown for both methods in Fig. 49. When the planks follow the margin, a wide strake is fitted down

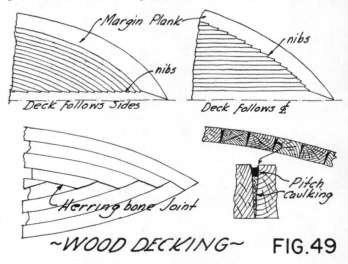

~WOOD DECKING~   FIG.49

the center and this is sometimes called the king strake.

Another method of finishing the latter type of decking at the center is the herringbone joint similar to the type used on the bilge of strip-built boats, Fig. 49. While we are on the subject, I see nothing radically wrong with building a strip deck by the same method of edge-nailing and Weldwood glue as one would use for a hull. We might even go a step further and lay the deck with mahogany strips, inserting between them a thin strip of ash, not over a sixteenth of an inch thick. This type of deck, finished to a smooth surface and varnished, would be a wow! Warning: If you fit this type of deck, do not try to use a stained filler. The white of the ash will take the stain.

The builders of some of the modern speedboats snitch a bit on the foregoing method of natural decks and lay them in wide boards. At intervals down the length of these boards, they cut a series of grooves that are as far apart as the usual narrow strips of decking would be. These are filled with white cement and the casual observer cannot tell the difference. A seam batten is fitted under the joints of the wide deck boards. There is nothing radically wrong with this method because it has been time-tested.

CANVAS-COVERED DECK.—The only sure non-leak deck that has stood the test of time is the canvas-covered type. If you don't want to be bothered with rain dripping your neck, use this method. The wood is laid with tongue-and-groove material and all the high spots of the joints between the individual boards are planed down. Then the surface is covered with white lead or liquid marine glue and the canvas rolled down into it. The edges of the canvas should be turned up in the way of all deck erections and down along the sides. Allow at least two inches when trimming off your canvas before it is tacked. You can always trim a second time but you can never put the canvas back after it is cut. In turning down the canvas at the sides of the boat be sure that there is enough material so that the tacks will come in the sheer-strake rather than in the edge of the decking. This prevents the entrance of rain water that lays behind the guards if they are not properly bedded in

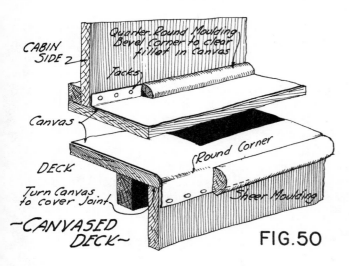

CABIN SIDE

Quarter-Round Moulding
Bevel Corner to clear
filler in Canvas

Tacks

Canvas

DECK

Round Corner

Turn Canvas
to cover Joint

Sheer Moulding

~CANVASED DECK~

FIG. 50

sealing compound. Figure 50 shows the proper method of fitting canvas.

Always try to get your canvas wide enough to go entirely across the cabin top. If this is impossible and a joint or a series of joints must be made, make the

joints athwartships and lap the canvas down from the high side. If there is sheer forward, start from midship and work forward so that water running along the canvas will run over the joint rather than under it. Space the tacks about an inch apart along the edges and one-half an inch at the joints.

Finishing of the canvas after it is laid is a source of argument. Some authorities advocate wetting the canvas before it is painted, others recommend a liberal soaking of linseed oil. I have tried every known method—all ended in cracked paint after a period of years. My advice is to select the method that looks best to you, lay your canvas and pray. A pair of duck-billed pliers will be helpful in stretching the canvas.

What appears to be an everlasting deck is frequently laid on some of the larger yachts. The deck is laid and canvased in the usual manner and over this is laid a bare wood deck with the planks well-bedded in marine glue. Then, the seams are caulked and payed with pitch or marine glue as a precaution against leakage.

PLYWOOD DECKING.—Plywood seems to be the answer to the dream of a deck that will never leak. If the seams are well-battened and the deck made tight at these points and at the sheer, there is no cause for a leak. However, plywood does have a disadvantage for decking. When laid flat and exposed to the sun, the best of the fir plywoods will develop fine hair cracks in time, and no amount of painting will eradicate them. The manufacturers of the waterproof plywood, Super Harbord, have recently developed a plywood that promises to overcome this difficulty. This material is called Super Harborite and it is ordinary waterproof plywood covered with a fibrous material similar to paper. This material is impregnated with the same phenolic resin that forms the waterproof binder between the layers. It has a smooth surface and the grain is entirely hidden below this surface.

PLYWOOD PLANKING AND DECKING

Plywood may be applied as planking to any surface of the hull on which a piece of paper may be laid without wrinkling. Where any great curvature exists in two directions, Fig. 51, the plywood cannot be forced down on its edges or, if the surface is hollow, it cannot be forced down in the center. The plywood will compress or stretch a little so that the double curvature of a deck often will plank well with plywood. Frequently a single seam in plywood will facilitate its being fitted to a slight double-curved surface.

The easiest way to fit plywood to any surface is by making first a pattern of heavy brown wrapping paper or building paper. In the beginning, it is well to cut the paper to the exact size of the plywood sheet. Then this is adjusted to the boat in the most economical position to use the sheet of plywood. Holes are cut through the paper at convenient points and the paper is stuck down to the frame with adhesive masking tape such as that used by painters.

After the paper is in place, the edges of the finished sheet are marked. This is done best by using a piece of blue keel or crayon or a carpenter's pencil sharpened to a long point. The pencil or crayon is rubbed along the edges of the wood beneath the pattern, leaving a mark on the paper. Do not trim your plywood to the exact line before trying it on the boat.

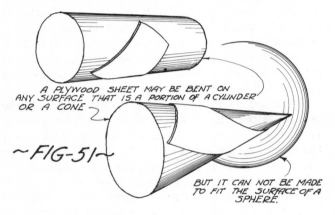

A PLYWOOD SHEET MAY BE BENT ON ANY SURFACE THAT IS A PORTION OF A CYLINDER OR A CONE

~FIG-51~

BUT IT CAN NOT BE MADE TO FIT THE SURFACE OF A SPHERE.

Always check patterns from port to starboard, as the two sides of the boat may be slightly different. Wherever possible, lay out in pattern form the full length of the boat so that the separate sheets of plywood may be laid down with their straight ends butting, thus ensuring accurate fits at the joint.

In the absence of paper, patterns may be made from thin strips of wood or laths (see Fig. 43, page 37). It is good practice to template the location of all frames and stringers below the plywood to aid in locating the fastenings at a later date.

Under certain conditions plywood may be laid or clamped directly on the surface of the hull that it is to cover. The edges may be marked directly from the members to which it fastens. While it is in this position, do this: Mark both edges of all stringers and frames with a pencil! By doing this, the plywood sheet can be laid flat on the shop floor and all spacing of the screws which are to secure it may be laid off. This eliminates the tedious feeling under the sheet for security when it is in place. After the spacing of the fastenings is laid off, the holes for them should be

drilled in the sheet *from the inside of the sheet outward*. This eliminates the risk of the fastenings missing the wood beneath them, as well as the collection of drill chips that accumulate under the hole after it is bored. Countersinking of the holes may be done before the sheet is erected or later. In driving screws through a plywood sheet, two braces, one with a screwdriver bit and the other with a countersink, will save a lot of changing from one to another if only one brace were on the job. Automatic screwdrivers can leave ugly scars on the face of fir plywood!

The time will come in the planking of a boat when all surfaces are covered to the extent that a clamp cannot be inserted around the edge of the sheet to hold it. At this time, thin strips of sheet iron banded around the boat and pulled tight with a turnbuckle will be handy. At other times a small hole through the plywood (which can be plugged later) will be useful to hook a wire secured around a stick and passed through the sheet. A turnbuckle at the other end of this wire will perform wonders in pulling the sheet down into position.

After you have marked the location of all stringers on the inside of your plywood sheet and bored all of the holes, it would be wise to give these surfaces a couple of coats of paint, just as you did the frame before you put that sheet in place. How about it?

Watch the surface of your plywood on excessive bends. Pick those sheets that are free of brash grain. Do not point the uprising grain in the direction of the bend. Sometimes it will leave the ply below it.

Save the sheets with the most uniform grain and the least patches for the parts that you want to finish natural. A sheet with fine grain will make quite a unique finish for your interior panels when heavily scorched with a blowtorch and the scorching removed with a wire brush. Try it.

WHAT HAS BEEN LEARNED ABOUT PLYWOOD.— From time and experience considerable knowledge has accumulated on the use of plywood in boats. The old idea that it would not rot is just so much malarky. Very little rot has been experienced in the hull proper; most of it occurs in the cabins and deck edges. Raw plywood edges absorb water. Rain water often carries the spores or seed of the rot down where these edges can soak them up. Rot is actually caused by a fungus, second cousin to the mushroom and common mold. It takes its nourishment from the wood fibers. Like a plant, to which family it belongs, it flourishes where there is an excess of moisture and no ventilation, for it needs little oxygen to survive. Often it may be detected by a musty odor and in extreme cases by a white vein-like structure on the surface of the wood. The answer to this problem is to seal all raw edges of the plywood with a good sealer or wood preservative after the final fit has been made. Joints of the plywood laid up in epoxy resin glue or resorcinal glue should be reasonably safe.

Some sheets of plywood have a bad habit of checking, others very little. Bad checking occurs mostly on the flat surfaces of floors and decks. The only answer to this problem is to cover them with canvas or fiberglas. The *Harbor Plywood Corporation* sells a product which it calls *Harborite* whose surfaces are covered with a thin layer of plastic paper and which is free from checking. By the time this appears in print there may be more sources for this material.

There is a mistaken idea that only *marine* plywood can be used in boats. Actually this material is only a very good grade of *exterior* plywood having the same wood and glue. *Exterior* is sold in several grades. Common usage divides this into two, *good one side* and *good both sides*. *Good one side* allows small, open knotholes and blemishes on one side of the sheet. Where expense is an extreme factor, the cheaper grade may be used, the knots and blemishes being turned to the interior of the boat. Where the hull is to be fiberglased, the good side is turned in and the defects on the exterior filled out with Famowood or some other type of plastic putty before the glass is applied.

In plywood boats that are to be fiberglased it is perfectly safe and advisable to reduce the specified thickness ⅛″.

Since the great shortages of all materials in this country began, plywood manufactured in foreign countries is appearing on the markets. Investigate this thoroughly before you buy. There are many American plywoods today which do not bear the stamp of the D.F.P.A. Some of these are good. Their exterior variety is marked with red dye on one of the edges. In the long run the old reliable grades of *Weldwood* and *Super Hardboard* are the safest.

While we are on the subject of sheet material the new type of perforated *Masonite* works well in interiors, having a pleasing appearance and supplying much-needed ventilation to the closed spaces.

LAMINATED VENEER CONSTRUCTION.—Laminated veneer construction is not properly *planking* or *decking* alone. It is a *method* but is not applicable to a standard frame and is so new that the designers are still fluid on their thoughts about it. Unquestionably it turns out a beautiful rounded hull as witness the many molded plywood hulls produced commercially.

Laminated veneer is not truly molded plywood which is produced over a form that is used over and over again. Laminated veneer is very much like double diagonal planking except that it is tripled and the three layers are bound with resorcinal resin glue. While some of the smaller boats may be built without a single frame except their keels and stems, it is well to frame those over 20′ in length.

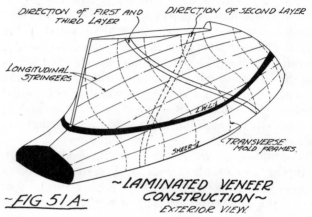

~FIG 51A~

~LAMINATED VENEER CONSTRUCTION~
EXTERIOR VIEW.

The frames may be set at intervals as great as the molds of an ordinary boat and they may be made at the same time as bulkheads and may be spaced to suit the bulkhead locations. These mold frames are built up in futtocks of two timbers with their joints staggered and the whole assembly glued and nailed with patent nails. Where a bulkhead occurs it is made

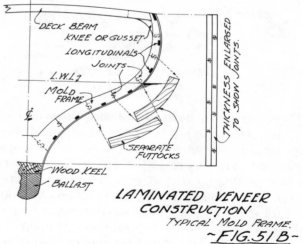

LAMINATED VENEER
CONSTRUCTION
TYPICAL MOLD FRAME.
~FIG. 51B~

from plywood with a wood facing strip fastened to its edge. In another method of construction the boat is planked over temporary molds and stringers which are removed later. Where any frames are needed in this method they are laminated from thin strips of wood much in the same manner that the old steam bent frames were put in the strip built boats. My own preference would be the frames built in the hull permanently and longitudinal stringers built around them. It is not much more work to make the permanent frames than it is to build molds and they add immensely to the strength of the boat.

In fastening the layers of veneer it is necessary to nail or staple them to the stringers. It is the very devil of a job to clench all of the protruding points if the molds and stringers are removed. After the frame is completed it is most generally erected upside down. The first layer of veneer is applied diagonally, working from right to left, fitting one edge and allowing the left hand edge to remain straight. The rough fitting is done with a sharp knife and as the veneer is about $3/32''$ thick this is not difficult. The final fit is made with a small block plane of the type that can be held in the palm of the hand. This veneer is generally of mahogany and comes in widths from $3''$ to $4''$. If it is not procurable in your locality, the Williamson Veneer Co. in Cockeysville, Md. makes a specialty of furnishing veneer for this type of work.

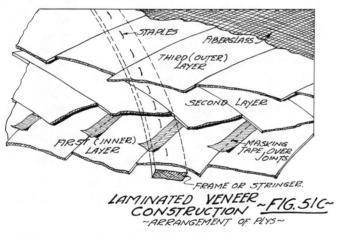

LAMINATED VENEER CONSTRUCTION ~FIG. 51C~
~ARRANGEMENT OF PLYS~

There are two methods of fastening the veneer to the frame. One is to use $1/2''$ brass-head nails driven with an ordinary hammer. The other is to use a stapler or tacker very much the same as the ones you see men putting up posters with. There are several types of these gimmicks. The *Markwell* people make one with which all you do is squeeze the handle and it drives a staple into the hardest wood. It is sold as the *Markwell* L4 Tacker and the staples to fit it are the *Markwell* rustproof-type RBTC with a $5/16''$ leg.

After the first layer of veneer is applied all over the hull it is generally customary, if you want a clean inside of the hull, to strip each seam with $3/4''$ masking

tape to prevent glue penetration. It is also good practice to mark the positions of all frames and stringers on the outer surface of the first veneer layer with chalk so that there is a guide for driving the staples for the second layer. The glue for the first layer is applied to frames and stringers as each strip goes on. The glue for the second and third layers is applied under and to the underside of each strip after it has been fitted. A good planking job may be finished natural if it is so desired. The best job in any case is to fiberglas the entire hull after it is finished. Figures 51A, 51B and 51C show this method of construction.

METAL BOATS.—Often I receive inquiries as to whether a certain boat can be built of metal. The first reaction is to say "Don't do it." In spite of this, there are still those who are persistent and will build a metal boat regardless of what other people say about them. If your inclinations and abilities run to metal working, there is no reason why the boat *cannot* be built. There are quite a number of reasons why they *should not* be built.

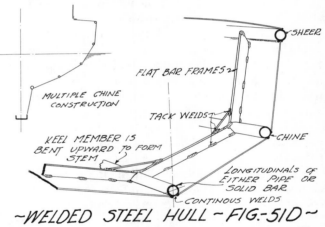

~WELDED STEEL HULL ~FIG.-51D~

The first reason is that the average back yard builder does not possess the required equipment. As a matter of fact, a steel boat can be built with hardly anything more than an arc welding machine and an acetylene torch with an assortment of hammers thrown in for good measure, and believe me, when the boats are finished they look it. Unless you are an expert in welding light metal and know the theory of sequence welding, the boat will end up with more wrinkles than a dried prune. While the larger boats may be built of metal at a weight less than that of a wooden one of equivalent size this is not true of the smaller ones.

Corrosion is the one big factor in steel construction. You will probably point to the fact that large ships are built of steel. Sure they are, and there is a crew aboard them continually fighting rust with a full time job of scaling the rust away and repainting. On a large ship a plate ½" thick has an active life of twenty years. The surface corrosion on any steel plate is the same regardless of its thickness, thus, even though you build your boat of ⅛" plate, its active life would be five years. If five years of use is worth all the labor you will put into a boat, then do not let this fact deter you. Fig. 51 D.

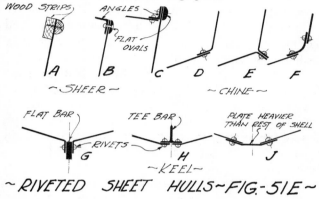

~ RIVETED SHEET HULLS ~ FIG. 51 E ~

There are methods of delaying the corrosive action. Hot dip galvanizing, zinc spraying and some of the new anti-corrosion paints are all good but they cost money and are not entirely positive.

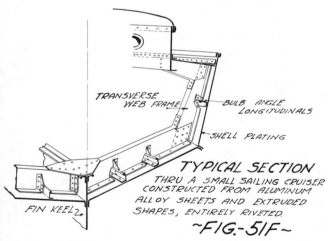

TYPICAL SECTION

THRU A SMALL SAILING CRUISER CONSTRUCTED FROM ALUMINUM ALLOY SHEETS AND EXTRUDED SHAPES, ENTIRELY RIVETED.

~ FIG. 51 F ~

Weight is another factor in the small steel boat. One inch wood planking will weigh approximately 2¾ pounds per square foot. Steel of equivalent weight will have to be ¹/₁₆" thick or #16 gauge to weigh the same and this, even though galvanized, has a very short life. I have seen men who have gone to elaborate pains to convert metallic ships' lifeboats. These boats were designed to spend their active life hung in davits. Overboard they hardly last over three

seasons. I remember well one of these jobs with an elaborate mahogany cabin rusting away in a local boat yard after a life of two years.

Aluminum boats are another matter. There are alloys on the market today which are practically non-corrosive. The structure on these boats should either be *Heli-arc* welded or riveted. The ordinary torch weld does not seem to possess the necessary strength. In the riveted seams, Figs. 51 E & 51 F, watertightness is secured either with flannel soaked in soy-bean oil or with some of the new rubber compounds. If you are contemplating an aluminum boat, consult with the *Alcoa* or *Reynolds* representative in your district as to the proper alloy to use.

Electrolysis is one big enemy of metallic hulls. It has more corrosive effect than just the water action on the hull. Various different metals will set up an action similar to an electric battery and eat away one or the other. This subject cannot be covered thoroughly in a book of this sort. Read up on it before you build a metal boat, or a wooden one for that matter.

FIBERGLAS FOR BOATS

For years on end men who build boats have been searching for a material that would not rot.

From the time before the Christian Era when man first made glass, he had the material but it was only recently that he learned to use it. When the *Owens Corning Co.* first formed this material into hair-like fibers, they opened a new field in boatbuilding. For their weight, these fibers are stronger than steel and can be formed into mats resembling loose felt or may be spun into threads from which cloth may be woven. Very appropriately this rot-proof, non-burning material is called "Fiberglas."

Fiberglas in itself was not the entire answer. Marching along with the glass makers, our industrial chemists were inventing plastics which were as clear as glass and still flexible such as Plexiglas, Lucite, and a host of other allied materials. Some of these are heat hardened while others are hardened by an activator mixed with various types of gunk just before use.

Combined with Fiberglas, these resins made the ideal boat building material. There are many types now on the market. Most of them are good.

Actually, the finished Fiberglas boat or any other product made from these materials can be compared to a reinforced concrete structure. The resin forms the cement, the glass fibers the steel reinforcing. The activated type of resin is the best for the amateur boat builder as the facilities for heat hardening are not always at hand and curing temperatures are critical.

Fiberglas not only lends its versatility to the hull of the boat, but fuel tanks, battery boxes, hollow spars, canopies and a hundred other odd items of marine equipment have been molded from it.

We are deeply indebted to the *Owens-Corning FIBERGLAS Corporation; Plastics Reinforcement Division,* for their kind permission to re-publish the following information.

HOW TO MOLD A SMALL FIBERGLAS BOAT

So many hundreds of people have asked us how to mold their own Fiberglas-reinforced plastic boats at home that we have written this short manual on the subject. The instructions are general and directive, intended to give the hobbyist a better picture of the project he faces.

Procedures and suggestions given here are by no means the final word. While sound and supported by first-hand experience with reinforced plastics and by discussions with experienced engineers, remember . . . this is a field of rapid change. In this fast-growing industry, new products, new processes, new ways of handling accepted materials come along every day.

The most difficult advice for us to give the inexperienced individual is whether he can build a small boat which will do credit to his efforts and to the materials he is using. Quite frankly, we do not believe every hobbyist can do a successful job. Certainly, it's easy enough to build a hull which floats and demonstrates the basic virtues of Fiberglas. But whether the product of your labor will be what you expected at the start or what you have been able to do in wood or metals is quite another story.

We find many people who are misled by publicity which gives an over-simplified picture. They rush into the project too eagerly—without adequate evaluation of their abilities or preparatory experiments. Their eagerness is soon cooled by the results they get.

On the credit side is the fact that America is blessed with a host of enormously resourceful and ingenious amateur craftsmen. Indeed, many of the great contributions to our mechanical age have come from basement and backyard shops. In the field of Fiber-glas-reinforced plastics particularly, we can point to hundreds of sports car bodies, boats and other items made by amateurs and exhibiting amazing quality and ingenuity. Polyester resin with Fiberglas reinforcement and other similar resins produce a new alloy which in turn is opening vast new areas to the home craftsman. With cheap molds, or forms, you can mold articles which are strong, yet light, corrosion-resistant and impact-resistant—and in shapes impossible or impractical in other materials. But remember, these new materials are still expensive compared to wood, and there are acquired skills and methods of handling the glass and resin which may spell the difference between success and failure.

Do this before embarking on your boat project: Try several small jobs, such as a hatch cover or an engine housing, to get the "feel" of the materials. In this way you will be able to determine whether you should tackle the bigger job. Remember that you will be spending a sizable amount of money for glass and resin. You don't want it to be money thrown out.

In concluding these introductory remarks, let us point out that the method of molding outlined in these pages lends itself only to small boats not longer than about 16 feet. There are several reasons for our opinion but most important are:

1. Critical design factors encountered in molding larger hulls. Design data is most limited and the lack of this data can lead to costly errors.
2. The need for more expensive equipment and well engineered molds to do the bigger job adequately.

DESIGN CONSIDERATIONS.—Of the many thousands of small Fiberglas boats in service today, most have been copied from wooden craft designs. Methods of joinery and thickness of hulls have been arrived at by a combination of trail and error, builders' experience and the small store of engineering data available. This lack of design data is a serious obstacle for the home builder who wishes to attempt a hull greater than about 16 feet, but it should not present too great a problem to the hobbyist who wishes to construct a small dinghy or runabout.

Let us consider the unique features of Fiberglas construction. How does it differ from wood . . . and how do these differences affect the boat design?

Perhaps the most distinctive design feature is the ability of this material to be formed to shapes impossible or impractical in wood. Curves actually lend themselves better to Fiberglas construction than flat or straight lines, so the round bilge wooden boat is a "natural". Limits to the shapes which can be imparted to hulls are dictated largely by mold engineering and the problem of removing undercut shapes from the mold.

Your Fiberglas Reinforced Plastic boat should be far lighter and stronger than its wooden counterpart. But light weight cannot be achieved unless the design takes into consideration certain properties.

Since the material basically is very flexible, special provision must be made to provide the needed rigidity. Many of the small plastic boats are disappointingly heavy because stiffness was built into the hull by adding layer upon layer of glass and plastic. There are more efficient ways of solving the problem. Use wood strips or light synthetic core materials molded into the hull. In some flat plastic hulls, flutes or corrugations can be molded into the hull itself to give longitudinal stiffness. In still other cases, air tank seats molded into the hull do the trick. Thwarts, gunwales, keel and decking all contribute towards strength and rigidity. When designing for F-R-P remember to consider the total boat in all its parts. Remember . . .

- round curves impart greater strength and rigidity than flats.
- a rounded bilge displacement hull will, as a rule, have more rigidity because of its curves.
- planing hulls need their flat areas stiffened by one of the aforementioned methods.
- sharp corners commonly found in wooden boats should be avoided with Fiberglas construction. Such corners will be structurally weak and subject to crushing and chipping.
- flotation units are necessary. They can be obtained by molding air cells integrally with the hull or by fitting in blocks of light foam material.
- brackets for thwarts, oar locks, etc. may be cast independently, then cemented to the hull with glass and plastic.
- wooden gunwales, rub rails, thwarts and brackets should not be attached with screw fasteners that hold in the plastic. Either bolt through, using broad flange washers or cheats, or mold the wooden members into the plastic. When working with Fiberglas construction, it is important that you *distribute loads over a wider area than you would in wood or metal.* This principle applies to joints as well as fastenings.

(a) Air tank seats, provide strength, rigidity and safety. It is advisable to insert expansion relief plug in each tank.

(b) Wooden stiffeners molded into bottom.
(c) Wooden rub rail fastened with screws from inside.
(d) Conventional wooden thwart.
(e) Fiberglas bracket molded to hull and screw fastened to thwart.
(f) Skeg-wood core molded in place with glass mat and cloth. Note rounded corners at transom. Do not mold corners with less than 1/4" radius.

THE MOLD.—*Procuring A Suitable Mold.*

There are three ways to obtain a mold for your Fiberglas-Reinforced Plastic boat:

1. Use a wooden boat as your "male" mold. Many boats have been made successfully this labor-saving way. The wooden hull is cleaned, and a parting agent applied as described in succeeding paragraphs.
2. Take the lines of a wooden boat and transfer them to a mold. Suggestions for modifying these lines follow.
3. You may feel qualified to design your own original boat, but judging by the many odd-looking craft on the waters now-a-days, it really is best in the long run to buy a good basic design from an experienced naval architect, and then modify the lines according to the properties of Fiberglas.

Making Your Mold. While there are a variety of mold techniques used in commercial production, we feel that there are only two choices open to the amateur interested in building one or two hulls.

If you are going to produce one or two boats, use a male mold. If you build more than two, or are particularly concerned about a perfect outside finish on the hull, use a female mold. Since a female mold is most commonly formed from a male plug, you can readily see that many extra mold operations are required.

Technique #1—Building the Mold. Since mold construction is somewhat a separate skill and a subject unto itself, we do not intend to deal with it at any great length in this short manual. It is sufficient to say that you should familiarize yourself with the various techniques. Some references on the subject are given in the appendix. Here are the basic steps:

1. Construct a wooden framework.
2. Cover with wire cloth or chicken wire, forming it to the approximate inside dimensions of the hull.

3. Apply plaster which has been reinforced with jute fiber.
4. Smooth and even the plaster with a flexible straight edge.
5. Bring out the final contours with more plaster and careful sanding.
6. Treat the mold with a sealer hardener.
7. Apply several coats of carnauba paste wax.
8. Apply parting agent.

Technique #2—Use Another Boat as Your Mold. This method probably is the most popular, because so much of the hard work already is done.

1. Find a boat to your liking. Remember that a round bilge boat will lend itself better to plastic construction. A hard chine hull may be used if proper measures are taken to stiffen the hull.
2. If the boat to be used as a mold has reverse curves, realize that you will have problems releasing it from the mold.

   a. If the reverse curves are confined to the stern section, it has been found practical to leave off the transom and pull the hull shell forward off the mold. The transom would be attached after removal from the mold.
   b. If the wooden boat with reverse curves is old and not worth keeping, it can be disassembled partially to detach it from the plastic hull shell.
   c. Canoes customarily have reverse curves along most of their length. Those who have used an old canoe as a male mold find it best to make the Fiberglas shell in two halves split down the keel. By butt jointing at the keel with resin as a cement, a good, strong joint is obtained. A strip or two of cloth or mat bridging the joint on the inside and outside over the keel insures the bond.

LAY-UP MATERIALS

There are four basic materials recommended for this project: 1. Fiberglas Cloth; 2. Fiberglas Woven Roving; 3. Fiberglas Chopped Strand Mat; 4. Polyester Resin.

Fiberglas Cloth suggested for this purpose is an open, square-weave fabric about .013″ to .015″ thick, weighing about 10 oz. per square yard. It comes in standard widths of 38″, 44″, 50″ and 72″, and in varying roll lengths (usually about 120 yards per roll.) Be sure to obtain cloth with Owens-Corning Finish #114 or equivalent, or failure of the laminate may result.

Fiberglas Woven Roving is a coarse, square-weave fabric made from 12 to 60 untwisted strands of glass. A commonly used type weighs about 26 oz. per square yard and is approximately .036″ thick. Widths vary from 42″ up to 80″, in roll lengths of 50 to 100 yards. One layer of this 26 oz. woven roving would be roughly equivalent in strength to three layers of the 10 oz. cloth recommended.

Fiberglas Chopped Strand Mat is composed of a random pattern of 2″ fibers loosely bonded together with a high-solubility polyester binder. The specific Owens Corning product to use is Treatment #216 in either 1-½ oz. or 2 oz. per square foot weights. The mat comes in widths of 38″ and 76″. Roll length for 2 oz. is 150′, for 1-½ oz. is 200′.

Resin to use is a polyester type which hardens without pressure at room temperature. It is light amber in color and has the consistency of honey. The resin must be activated or hardened by chemical promoters—a catalyst and an accelerator. With certain resins, the accelerator is pre-mixed and you add only the catalyst. The pot life (gel time) of the resin may be varied from a few minutes to several hours according to the amount of promoter used and the temperature during application. Ultimate hardness is not reached for several days. Color may be incorporated right into the resin. The color may be fairly permanent, but remember that any pigment is subject to fading.

What Combinations of Glass Materials to Use. A boat can be built using any one of the three glass materials exclusively. But a combination yields the best results. Considering the proposed molding technique, probably a sandwich of one layer of woven roving between two layers of cloth will satisfy most small boat requirements. Mat can be used between the cloth, but woven roving is relatively easier to handle and will give a more uniform surface with the male mold technique.

Relative Merits of the Three Glass Materials. The glass cloth lies flat, conforms very well to compound curves, and gives strengths roughly 40% greater than mat. It has the disadvantages of high cost, and low shear strengths between multiple layers.

Mat is at least 40% cheaper than cloth, gives bulk for rigidity and locks or integrates well in multiple layers. However, it is not as strong as cloth, soaks up a great deal of resin, and must be tailored on sharp curves. On a male mold, mat may give a slightly lumpy, non-uniform surface.

Woven roving has strengths approaching those of cloth at a price slightly higher than mat. It has the uniform, formable characteristics of cloth, but must be combined with cloth as a surfacing agent so that the coarse pattern does not show through.

How to Determine the Cost of Your Boat. It is difficult if not impossible to tell you precisely how much your boat will cost. Prices of materials on a retail, small quantity basis vary widely. However, we asked several people who molded prams eight feet and longer what they paid for glass and resin at retail prices. The figures ranged between $50 and $70. The costs did not include mold or finishing trim on the boat.

The following suggestions will help you determine your costs fairly accurately.

1. After estimating the number of plys of cloth, mat and woven roving needed in the boat, multiply the square footage or pounds times the unit price quoted to you on the glass materials.
2. By using the following glass-to-resin weight relationships found in different types of laminates, you can roughly determine the pounds of resin needed.

a. A mat laminate will yield...25%–30% weight of glass, 70%–75% weight of resin
b. A cloth laminate will yield...45%–50% weight of glass, 50%–55% weight of resin
c. A woven roving laminate will yield...55%–60% weight of glass, 40%–45% weight of resin

Small quantities of resin are sold in quarts or gallons. One quart of resin weighs about 2¼ pounds.

DESIGN DATA.—Engineering data on required hull thicknesses is extremely limited. Also, since we are talking about small boats for a variety of conditions and purposes, we cannot be too specific in our advice. As a guide, however, it is safe to say that any given hull thickness in plastic reinforced with Fiberglas cloth or woven roving will have more than twice the strength of the same thickness in conventional wood. In other words, if your boat in wood is designed for ¼-inch plywood, ⅛-inch of glass cloth and plastic will be more than adequate. It is true that the stiffness of the ⅛-inch wall may not be sufficient, and that ribs might be necessary where they would not be required in the wood construction.

In determining the thickness of your hull, you should think more in terms of the number of layers of material than the precise thickness that results. The reason for this is that thickness will vary a good deal according to the viscosity of the resin and how

the resin is brushed out on the fabric. The following relationships will serve as a guide.

In the case of multiple layers of woven roving or cloth, you can expect the resin to increase the thickness of each layer of fabric 40% or more. That is, one fully saturated layer of .013″ fabric will result in a laminate .018″ or .020″ thick.

In the case of mat, the problem is more difficult because of the varying, bulky nature of the material. Mat is specified according to its weight in ounces-per-square-foot (1 ½ oz., 2 oz. or 3 oz.). Under the contact molding conditions described in this manual, you can estimate a thickness of approximately .030″ to .040″ for each ounce of impregnated mat.

Before starting to lay up your boat, before you order any material, we strongly recommend you make several square-foot test panels representing minimum hull thickness. With these panels, you will better be able to estimate the amount of strength and rigidity which will be needed in the hull.

Remember, after the basic shell of the hull is finished and pulled from the mold, you can test it for weakness and add additional layers of glass on the inside. Adding new material to a cured surface is quite practical, and the lap joints can be sanded down flush with the old surface.

While it is preferable to lay up the hull in one continuous operation with the resin not completely hardened, it is almost never practical. Optimum strengths would be achieved if such a time schedule were used, but a perfectly sound laminate can be obtained by adding to cured surfaces.

Some Advice On Core Materials Used For Stiffening. In the average small boat not too many stiffening members will be required, but there are so many choices of materials that you should be informed of what is available and suitable.

Wood. Many different kinds of wood have been successfully employed as stiffening members in Fiberglas boats. Plywood probably is the best, for if water ever gets through a rupture in the plastic, the plywood will not warp or swell badly. Where extreme lightness is important, balsa is very popular.

Foamed Styrene. This material probably cannot be employed too successfully since it dissolves readily when it comes in contact with the styrene component in the polyester resin. However, it is good, relatively cheap flotation material.

Foamed Acetate. Foamed Acetate (trade name of Strux) is employed widely as a core material and for flotation. It is more expensive than foamed styrene, but it does not dissolve in the polyester resin.

As in the case of all foams, it can be carved easily and shaped with hand tools.

Paper Honeycomb. Honeycomb is available on the market made from paper, aluminum, cotton duck and Fiberglas. Phenolic treated paper honeycomb is cheap and the most satisfactory for a small boat. It usually is incorporated where a double bottom or large area needs bulk for stiffness. Ordinarily it is not used in strips. Before using it extensively, make a variety of test panels to determine its peculiarities. The phenolic treatment on the paper affords some stiffness and prevents deterioration from water in case of penetration.

Hollow Tubing. Soft aluminum tubing or polyvinyl chloride tubing can be pressed to the shape of the hull contour, then molded in place with glass fabric.

THE LAY-UP PROCESS—BASIC STEPS AND SUGGESTIONS.—

1. Get the "feel" of the materials by laying up some test panels.
2. Procure your mold. If the mold is plaster, seal it properly. Next apply several coats of liquid paste or floor wax, and then several coats of parting agent.
3. Pre-cut and tailor your materials to the approximate shape and size of your mold. Set them aside in layers in the order in which they will be applied.
4. Roll or brush a base coat of resin on the mold.
5. Lay the fabric on the wet surface. If the panels to be handled are large, an assistant will be helpful. It also may be useful to first wrap the fabric around a mailing tube, and then unroll it on the mold.
6. Work resin into the glass thoroughly before it gels so that no white spots are evident.
7. Do not activate too much resin at a time, or it will gel before you have used it. Gel time under average conditions will be about ½ hour @ 70°. Start out by catalyzing no more than one quart of resin at a time. If the work progresses rapidly, you can always increase this amount.
8. Supplementary heat often can be used to good advantage in the home shop. Several cheap infra red bulbs will help harden local areas. If the work room is too cold (around 45 to 50 degrees), you may be able to raise the temperature of the mold by placing an electric heater underneath the mold.

9. With your fingers, brush or roller, work out all wrinkles and air bubbles as they appear. Some people work very effectively with a squeegee. Try it.
10. Do not try to lay up the laminations too fast; permit the glass to wet out thoroughly. Too rapid a lay-up may generate so much chemical heat that blisters will occur.
11. In general, apply resin to the top of the hull working down, and from the middle of an area working out toward the edges. This minimizes wrinkling and permits air and excess resin to escape.
12. If color is to be incorporated into the laminate, there are several caution points.

    a. Certain pigments, like black and red, slow down the resin cure, requiring a higher concentration of catalyst.
    b. Certain pale colors, white in particular, must be introduced early in the final laminations or insufficient color density will be noted.
    c. Since the clear resin permits you to see voids or dry spots, it is desirable not to add color until the final lamination.
    d. You should determine the importance of the above points by making small test panels.

13. Until recently, many resins were subject to annoying pin holes as they cured. This problem has been overcome largely in the new resin formulations. The tiny holes usually are caused by surface tension or shrinkage of the resin. You should take care to see that they are eliminated by re-brushing the uncured resin, or if they persist in hardened surface fill with pulverized glass and resin.
14. If larger blisters or void spots are apparent in the cured laminate, cut open the pocket and fill with pulverized glass and resin.
15. Any roughness or bumps from laps, etc., can be smoothed down with coarse sand paper (4–16) or a file (an electric disk sander is almost a must for this project). Progressively finer papers should be used for finishing
16. There are a few tricks in sanding. One common problem is how to avoid clogging of the paper.

    a. For extensive removal of material, it is best done about 24 hours after lay up. At this time, the laminate has not reached its ultimate hardness and can be cut down fast without gumming up the paper.

b. Don't try to sand immediately after the resin has hardened or your sand paper will become impossibly clogged.

c. Resin filled sanding disks can often be cleaned in acetone if the resin is not completely hardened.

17. Remember that the quality of your outside surface finish is proportionate to the care with which the resin is applied and the amount of sanding you are willing to do. The final coat or coats of resin should be smoothed on with a brush or squeegee. The roller, while it applies resin quickly and evenly, tends to leave a finely dimpled surface. A mirror smooth finish may be obtained by wet sanding with fine paper and rubbing with a pumice or rotten stone mix. Needless to say, this operation entails a great deal of work, but the results make it worthwhile.

18. At this point in the operation, the boat should be ready to remove from the mold. You may first want to trim off the excess flash on the gunwale along the shear line. This can be done with a hack saw or similar fine tooth instrument. The hull shell should be tapped fairly vigorously with a soft head mallet to loosen the bond. Flat pry bars can be inserted to lever the hull loose from the mold.

If you run into serious trouble in removing the boat from the mold, here is a trick which has proved successful. Insert several tire valves through the hull, possibly along the keel or garboard, and force air in with a bicycle pump. The holes made by the valves can easily be plugged up later.

19. Check the strength and rigidity of the hull by applying pressure amidship at the top of the gun'l, the turn of the bilge and the midpoint of the keel. Test the transom carefully. Bear in mind that a Fiberglas-reinforced plastic hull is more flexible than a wooden hull, but returns to its original shape even after extreme deformation. If you feel the hull needs beefing up, here are some suggestions.

20. If your boat is to be powered by an outboard motor, reinforce the transom by molding in a piece of fir plywood ¾" or thicker. Cut a piece which covers the complete width and depth on the inside, and mold in place with several layers of cloth. In all post-joining operations, be sure the surface is free of any parting agent residue, and roughen the surface with a coarse disk sander to insure a good bond. Lacquer thinner will cut the wax film successfully, but a brisk sanding is also advisable.

21. Many small boats require additional stiffness along the bottom, between the garboard and the turn of the bilge. With a generously curved round bilge dink, the curvature alone provides great rigidity. But an outboard runabout, where you have a flat planing bottom, often requires stiffening members, especially to operate at high speeds. To solve this problem, mold in several light wooden strips, such as pine, fir or balsa, from the stern all the way forward to the chine. These wooden strips can be sprung into position by temporary props or weights. Mold sufficient layers of material around the core strips, because the layers of Fiberglas will be taking the strain, not the core material.

22. There are two ways to add a deck section to your boat. Make a reinforced plastic deck in a female mold, and then join it to the hull. Or, for an easier way, one layer of glass cloth and resin laid over plywood will make a very strong, weather resistant deck.

23. To install row locks, attach the base of the row lock to a block of wood 1" thick, 6" long and 6" high. Then mold it into the side of the boat, making at least an eight-inch overlap with several layers of cloth.

24. For seat supports or brackets, you can mold the brackets independently with about five layers of cloth or two layers of mat. Cement the brackets into the proper points on the hull with scrap pieces of glass mat or cloth and fasten the wooden seats to them with screws. Or more simply, some builders will fit the wooden thwart tightly in place against the hull and mold it in place with strips of mat and cloth.

Seats can be molded in Fiberglas and joined to the hull in the same fashion. But wooden seats are probably quicker and easier to make.

25. For flotation units, two methods are common. Attach blocks of foamed styrene or acetate under the seats. Or wall off the stern and bow seat or tumble home sectons. Fiber board or heavy cardboard covered with two layers of cloth and resin make a good bulkhead.

26. Your Fiberglas boat can be painted with any good grade of alkyd base marine paint, but sand the surface slightly beforehand and use a recommended Fiberglas primer surfacer.

Antifouling paint is required if the boat is to be used in salt water—not for protection, but to prevent barnacles and other marine growth from attaching to the hull.

Female Mold Procedure. In using this technique, the same basic steps are involved, but there are some differences to be noted.

1. A female shell or mold must be cast from the male form.
2. A female mold is best made by first laying up a layer of cloth over the male form and then a layer or two of 2 oz. mat. The cloth will provide a uniform void free surface. The mat will build up bulk for rigidity.

3. After the female mold has been properly prepared with wax and parting agent, you will want to apply a resin "gel-coat." A "gel-coat" is a thick layer of white or colored resin which is brushed onto the female mold up to a thickness of $3/64''$. This layer completely hides the fiber pattern and provides the smooth outside hull surface. Since a "gel-coat" is unreinforced this resin is specially formulated to resist cracking and to absorb impact blows. While a standard, boat laminating resin can be used by the home builder for this purpose, there are some specially prepared "gel-coats" available.
4. While the "gel-coat" is still tacky proceed to lay up the glass laminations as previously described.

CHAPTER VIII

INSTALLING THE MOTOR

DETERMINING THE POSITION OF THE SHAFT HOLE. —When the lines of the boat are not laid down on the floor or when the location of the propeller shaft hole is hard to determine, one more trick is available to the boatbuilder. A 12″ board is procured long enough to reach from the proposed location of the flywheel to a distance of a foot over the stern. This is supported at the point of the motor flywheel by a piece of rough

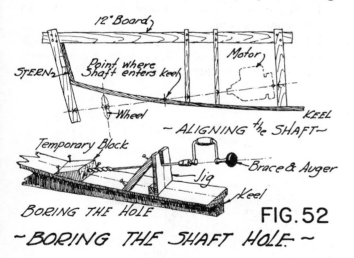

BORING THE HOLE   FIG.52

~BORING THE SHAFT HOLE~

lumber, Fig. 52. Over the stern another piece is fitted in such a manner that it will extend below the bottom of the hull far enough so that the bottom of the board is at least 6″ more than one-half the propeller diameter. Several more boards are now extended below the 12″ one so that they will display the curvature of the top of the keel. The stern board should have several blocks attached so that it may be fixed to the transom in its original position at some future time. After the entire rig is securely fastened together, it is removed from the boat and laid flat on the floor or ground.

A string is now stretched across the rig to represent the center line of the shaft. Care must be taken in

running the string so that it is the proper distance above the bottom of the boat to clear both the flywheel of the motor and its crankcase. The same precaution is necessary under the keel aft to give propeller clearance.

After the line is determined, it is accurately marked on all boards and the rig is replaced in the boat. From the marks on the boards the line can be extended now to any point desired for building the motor beds and boring the shaft hole.

BORING THE SHAFT HOLE.—Once the line of the propeller shaft is determined, the hole through which it passes must be bored in the hull. A bit an eighth of an inch larger than the shaft is needed. The ordinary wood bit would be too short and the type that carpenters use has a screw point which will follow soft grain in the wood and cause the bit to go out of line. The bit used to drill the shaft hole must be a barefoot auger (see Fig. 10, p 10) with an extension welded to its shaft.

The line of the shaft is set up with a string either from the inside or from the outside of the hull. A jig is set up to guide the bit (see Fig. 52). The jig has a hole the exact size of the shank of the bit. Next, a block of wood is fixed to the keel and in its end a shallow hole the size of the barefoot bit is bored. Then the barefoot bit is placed in the jig and from there on it's just hard work.

Often, in spite of every precaution, the hole runs out slightly. In this case it can be straightened by the primitive method of heating a bar of iron red hot and burning the hole in the proper direction.

BUILDING THE MOTOR BED.—It is wise to defer building the motor bed on a small boat until the shaft hole is bored. By this method, any small misalignment of the hole can be corrected in the bed. A string is stretched through the shaft hole along its exact center. This is the working line of the bed and should be set up so that it can be refitted in case of breakage.

Usually, a stick is nailed securely in place at each end and the point at which the string passes these points is marked with a pencil or a sawcut.

Once the line is run, the line of the top of the stringers of the bed must be determined. Most motor manufacturers supply an installation diagram with their motors showing the distance of the mounting lugs or the bedplate flange from the center of the shaft. Set the top of the bed stringers a half-inch below the mounting flanges to allow for shims later. The depth of the bed stringers also must be determined.

When the depth of the stringers is at hand, the location of the tops of the cross timbers or motor floors can be determined. Usually the stringers are mortised to the motor floors and an allowance should be made for this in setting the tops of the floors. The tops of all motor floors are the same distance below the center of the shaft except when in so doing the floor becomes too shallow for sufficient strength.

The boat should be level and this should be checked before proceeding with the beds. The floor timbers

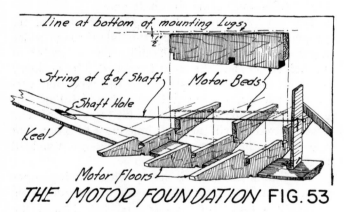

THE MOTOR FOUNDATION FIG. 53

are fitted with their tops level, Fig. 53, and, after this is complete, the stringers are set at the proper distance on each side of the string to accommodate the mounting bolts. The stringers are properly notched over the floors and their joints drift-bolted together. Care should be taken that no drift bolt comes in the way of an engine holding down bolt.

STUFFING BOXES.—The function of the stuffing box is to prevent the entrance of water to the hull where the propeller shaft passes through it. It is a packing gland containing flax or lampwick packing and compressed tight enough around the shaft to prevent the entrance of water but loose enough to allow the shaft to turn, Fig. 54.

There are many types of stuffing boxes. The modern self-aligning types are the most popular. These

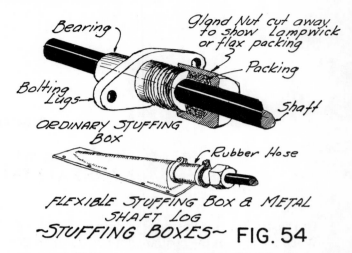

STUFFING BOXES~ FIG. 54

are generally constructed with a length of heavy hose which will bend to the required shaft angle, as illustrated.

When the difference in shaft angle is too great ior the stuffing box to accommodate, a tapered shim is placed under the casting.

Stuffing boxes are used also where rudder stocks pass through the hull.

THE PROPELLER.—The propeller of a boat is often called the screw. Actually, that is what it is—a screw boring through the water and pulling the boat ahead

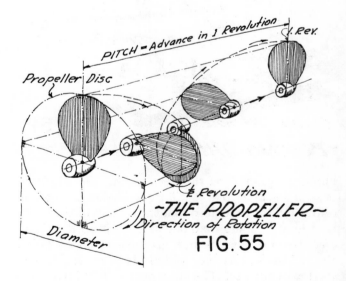

~THE PROPELLER~
FIG. 55

as it does so. Certain propeller terms should be understood before proceeding.

The *diameter* is the distance across the circle swept by the blades, Fig. 55, or twice the distance from the tip of any one blade to the center of the hub.

The *pitch* is the theoretical distance the propeller would travel ahead in one revolution if it were working in a solid medium. By measuring the distance a wood screw sinks into the wood in one complete turn, we obtain its pitch.

A propeller does not work in a solid medium like wood and, consequently, does not cover the full distance of its pitch in water. The difference between the distance it actually travels ahead and its pitch is called the *slip*. Slip is expressed in percentage. A propeller with 20% slip loses one-fifth of its pitch on every revolution. The slip on most motorboats will range between 20% and 30%. More than 30% slip is excessive and a new propeller with less pitch should be tried on a boat to remedy this condition.

R.P.M. is the number of revolutions that the propeller turns per minute. It is engine speed.

The following are known propeller facts:

The larger the diameter, the slow the speed, the less the slip.

The less the pitch, the faster the motor will turn, thus increasing the horsepower.

Increasing the diameter for the same speed in R.P.M. increases the efficiency and decreases the slip.

Always use the basic wheel size given by the manufacturer of the motor.

It is the usual practice to fit three blade wheels to high-speed motors and two blade wheels to the low-power, slow-turning ones. Where there is a great amount of sea grass, a "weedless" wheel is helpful but is not a cure-all.

THE SLIP OF THE WHEEL

The measure of efficiency of a boat's propeller is the actual amount that it drives the boat ahead The amount that the wheel loses in its effort to push the boat ahead (as we have noted before) is called the slip.

Efficiency of any particular wheel is measured by the amount of its slip. While a certain wheel will drive one boat at a certain speed, it may be an absolute failure on another. To know this we must determine the amount of the wheel's slip.

To calculate the slip two things must be *definitely* known.

1. The actual speed of the boat.

This can only be determined by a timed run over a measured course. To say the boat is making about fifteen knots or that the course is about a mile long is worthless. In the absence of a measured course. determine a distance between any two buoys by measuring them from the scale on a Coast and Geodetic Survey Chart. Time the run accurately between the buoys and convert either to feet per minute, mile per hour, or knots.

Very few buoys are an exact mile apart so the time of the run must be converted. As most charts give distances in yards, measure the distance between the buoys in this unit and convert as follows:

Example: Buoys 2160 yards apart

$$\frac{2160 \times 3}{* \ 5280} = 1.22 \text{ miles}$$

Now for instance let us say that the run was timed at 3 minutes and 20 seconds or 3.33 minutes. The speed in miles per hour is then as follows:

$$3.33 : 1.22 : : 60 : X$$

X being the miles per 60 minutes or 1 hour.

$$\frac{1.22 \times 60}{3.33} = 21.9 \text{ per hour}$$

* For knots use 6080

2. The actual number of revolutions that the motor is turning the wheel. Here again "about" is valueless. If the motor is not equipped with a tachometer, read the R.P.M. with a revolution counter and a watch.

TO CALCULATE SLIP OF WHEEL

88 ft. per minute = 1 mile per hour
101.6 ft. per minute = 1 knot

1. Convert miles per hour or knots (from boat's actual run over measured course) to feet per minute.
Example:

20 knots = 20 x 101.6 = 2320 ft. per minute.
16 miles per hour = 16 x 88 = 1408 ft. per minute.

2. Calculate travel of wheel pitch in one minute (in feet) by multiplying pitch in inches by R.P.M. and dividing by 12.
Example:

Pitch of wheel = 13"
R.P.M. of wheel = 1800

$$\frac{13 \times 1800}{12} = 1950 \text{ ft.}$$

Subtract the number of feet the boat actually travels (1) from the pitch travel of the wheel (2) and the result is the slip in feet per minute.
Example:

Wheel travel at 1800 R.P.M. = 1950 ft. per minute
Boat travel at 18 M.P.H.   = 1544 ft. per minute

The wheel is slipping 410 ft. per minute

3. Convert the amount of slip into a percentage of the wheel travel.
Example:

$$\frac{410}{1544} \quad \begin{array}{l} 26\% \text{ (Approximate)} \\ \text{This is excessive} \end{array}$$

If the slip is between 15 and 20% for wheels turning less than 1500 R.P.M., or between 20 and 25% for wheels turning over 1500 R.P.M., the wheel is within the practical range of efficiency. Efficiency experts may tell you different, but experienced men do not strive for peak performance, they are content to let well enough alone. If the slip falls below the accepted standard—wonderful! But if it exceeds it, change the wheel to one of a lower pitch. Take the present speed and calculate what the pitch should be with the normal amount of slip. This will be much lower than the pitch of the present wheel. The result will be increased R.P.M. and hence more power The ultimate is a faster moving boat. Sometimes it takes more tries than one to achieve success. For any new boat, follow the wheel size specified by the engine manufacturer.

HOISTING IN THE MOTOR.—Most small auxiliary motors are so light in weight that they can be lifted into a boat by two men. The smallest of the four-cylinder motors becomes a problem that increases in seriousness with the increase in motor size, demanding either a chain fall or some other tackle capable of lifting over 500 lbs.

If permanent structure (such as the roof rafters) above the boat is capable of suspending the load, the motor may be hauled aloft and the boat moved under it. The motor is then lowered on the beds. A similar procedure may be followed when the boat is afloat by taking her to a boatyard where a crane is available.

Failing in the two former methods, an "A" frame must be constructed to do the job. This is composed of two large timbers or saplings, as shown in Fig. 56. The tops of the timbers are lashed together and wooden cleats nailed to them to keep the tackle from

slipping. They are set up astern of the boat so that the feet are halfway between the point where the motor is to be picked up and where it is to be landed. Two guys are necessary with sufficient tackle to take the thrust when the "A" frame is inclined. The motor is hoisted and the guys are brought into action. When the motor is in position, the guys are made fast and the load is lowered away.

ALIGNING THE MOTOR.—After the motor is seated on its bed, it must be aligned to the shaft connecting it with the propeller. If the bed stringers are set a half-inch below the mounting lugs of the motor, as earlier instructed, four wedges, about six inches long, are prepared. They should be as wide as the bed and about three-eighths of an inch thick at one end and five-eighths at the other. These are placed under the mounting lugs and adjusted until the propeller shaft flanges at the rear of the motor are face-to-face all around. A feeler gauge is handy in securing perfect alignment.

When the boat is finally overboard, the wedges are adjusted again to secure perfect alignment. Then, permanent wedges are made from hardwood and the holding-down bolts are fitted.

MOTOR PIPING

Unfortunately, the fitting of a motor to a boat does not stop when it has been set in the boat. It must be piped up.

EXHAUST PIPE.—The principal pipes are the water and exhaust pipes. After they leave the engine, they become one. Years of experience with this type of piping has taught me that the easiest way to silence the exhaust and to keep it cool is to turn the discharge of the cooling water into it. There were certain

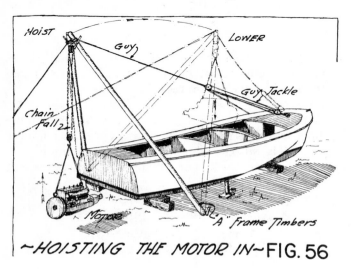

~HOISTING THE MOTOR IN~ FIG. 56

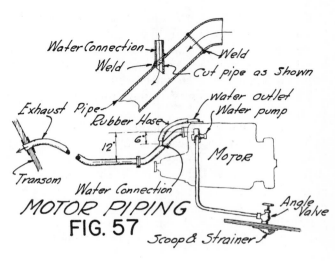

MOTOR PIPING
FIG. 57

disadvantages to this until a satisfactory method was worked out. It was found that immediately after leaving the motor, the exhaust pipe should be turned *down*. The cooling water must not enter the exhaust pipe any less than six inches below the manifold. This is necessary to prevent the back-flash of cooling water from coming in contact with hot valve stems and cracking them.

My favorite method is to weld a half-inch pipe spud into the exhaust pipe, Fig. 57, and connect this to the water outlet of the motor with rubber garden hose and hose clamps. The end of the spud should be cut off, as shown, and the opening turned with the flow of the exhaust. This helps to atomize the cooling water as it enters the exhaust and promotes the cooling of the hot exhaust gases.

At frequent intervals in the exhaust line it may be necessary to fit elbows. These should *never* be right-angle bend elbows as they would offer too much resistance to the passage of the exhaust gases. The proper fitting to use is a forty-five degree ell and, if it is necessary to make a right-angle turn, two of them should be connected with a close nipple. Cast-iron fittings should be used for all screwed and flanged fittings of the exhaust piping. There is a sound reason behind this. A fitting of cast iron is easy to break when it is necessary to replace a piece of pipe that has rusted out. Rubber steam hose has been successfully used for exhaust piping after the pipe leaves the section just aft of the manifold and water is present. Rubber exhaust pipe helps to deaden the sound of the exhaust.

WATER PIPING is our next consideration. The pump must be connected to the scoop and strainer so that it may be supplied with water from outside of the boat. This is usually ½″ piping and should be of brass. It presents no difficulties, as shown in Fig. 57. A combination scoop and strainer should be fitted outside the hull and a shutoff valve or stopcock on the inside to facilitate repairs when necessary.

WIRING OF THE MOTOR is the next operation and it is started at the battery. The battery should be placed in an easily accessible location for it will need frequent attention. Obtain Number Naught starter cable long enough to reach the motor with a little to spare. After this is cut, the battery lugs should be securely soldered to it. If you are not familiar with this operation, take the cable to a garage and have it done. A good connection on this wiring is important for it carries a heavy current and every bit of it must go through the connections. At the motor end, two copper lugs are soldered on and these are fixed, one to

the starting relay and the other under some convenient bolt on the motor to ground it. Figure 58 shows the wiring of an ordinary four-cylinder motor. This will familiarize you with the wiring system. Motors

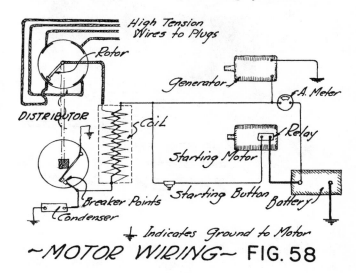

~MOTOR WIRING~ FIG. 58

are accompanied by a wiring diagram when shipped from the factory.

THE FUEL PIPING demands our attention next. Government regulations on construction of the tank are stringent. So many gas tanks have exploded on motorboats and so many people exclaimed, "There oughta be a law!" that finally one was passed. The law requires the fill pipe to extend within an inch of the bottom of the tank. Should a spark ignite the gas in the tank, it can ignite only that within the pipe and there is not enough volume there to do any damage. For your own protection, obey this law.

THE GAS TANK.—In constructing your gas tank Fig. 59 be sure that there are sufficient swash plates within it to prevent the swash of the fuel when the boat rolls. These add immeasurably to the strength of the tank. Be sure to fit the vent also required by law. The outlet to the tank has not been subject to legislation as yet but there are certain things about it that should be known. After a time, gasoline is liable to scale the tank's interior. This scale and muck, as well as water from condensation, collects on the bottom of the tank. It is not long before this finds its way into the fuel line. Result: a choked pipe. To prevent this, it is good practice to extend the outlet connection an inch up inside the tank. This prevents scale from entering. A drain connection also should be fitted to the lowest point in the tank. While on the subject of tanks, it is well to explain how to repair a tank that has held gasoline. The fumes of

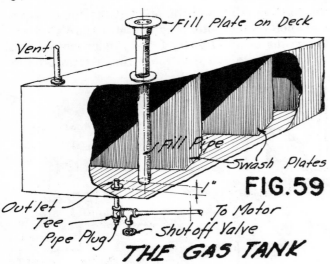

Vent — Fill Plate on Deck

Fill Pipe

Swash Plates

FIG. 59

Outlet
Tee
Pipe Plug
Shutoff Valve
To Motor
1"

THE GAS TANK

gasoline remaining in the tank are very explosive, as many angels have discovered. *Don't* heat or solder such a tank until the fumes are removed by either steaming the tank out or dropping small pieces of dry ice in the fill pipe and waiting until the CO_2 gas from their evaporation starts to come out of the vent.

It has been my practice to dispense with the ordinary copper tube fuel line until the motor is almost reached. Quarter-inch brass pipe is fitted with the joints soldered after they are screwed up. At every turn, tees are used instead of ells and a pipe plug screwed in shellac at their idle end. By doing this, the line may be cleaned out at any time. Use this scheme at the bottom of the tank, if at no other place.

MOTORBOAT REGULATIONS

Disasters have produced laws for the protection of human life. Motorboatmen became lax in their handling of explosive gasoline and laws were necessary to protect them from themselves. These are Federal laws and if you violate them, you have Uncle Sam to to reckon with. The enforcement of these laws pertaining to safety of motorboats is now in the hands of the U. S. Coast Guard and those boys "ain't foolin'."

The laws have become more stringent in recent years simply because the public must be protected from their carelessness. Every requirement of the U. S. Coast Guard is reasonable and behind them all

there is only one thought—safety. The requirements are simple and must be incorporated in every pleasure boat. We will deal with them separately.

THE FUEL TANK.—The filling opening of a gas tank must be outside the cockpit or any enclosed space of the boat. Often a tank is filled beyond its capacity and runs over. The fill should be in such a position that no fuel will run inside the boat and cause a fire or explosion hazard.

The filling pipe must be extended to within an inch of the bottom of the tank. The vapor fumes contained in a fuel tank are explosive. The extended pipe prevents flame from contacting this vapor. In this type of installation you can drop a lighted match down the fill pipe and only that vapor contained in the pipe will flash.

When a gas tank is filled, the explosive vapor contained in it must leave the tank to make room for the gasoline. The law requires that the tank be equipped with a vent pipe to prevent the escape of this vapor to the inside of the boat. It is good practice to lead this pipe out through the hull at a point lower than the fill opening. By so doing, any overflow from the tank runs overboard. The end of the vent should be so constructed as to exclude rain and spray from going back into the tank.

An efficient shutoff valve should be fitted directly at the tank so that the motor fuel line may be shut off in case of accidental damage.

THE BACKFIRE TRAP.—The law requires that an efficient backfire trip be fitted to the motor so that, in case of a backfire, the flame coming from the motor will not ignite explosive gases in the boat. Most modern motors are equipped with this device. One can be made for an old motor by constructing a funnel to fit the air intake of the carburetor. The diameter at the intake of the carburetor should be made to fit that opening and the funnel air opening should be twice that size. Three layers of 16-mesh copper screen, spaced 1/16" apart, should be fixed securely in the air opening of the funnel.

Automobile motors equipped with an air filter will pass the law.

VENTILATION OF THE MOTOR COMPARTMENT.— Explosive gases lurk in closed motor compartments and the law requires that these be ventilated. This may be done either with a forced draft blower or by the use of vent cowls.

CHAPTER IX

THE CABIN

The old order of scads and scads of mahogany is passing fast. Today we maintain that a cabin should be light and airy. The advent of the gals aboard our boats has led to this. It is one of the changes that I do not regret. The style today is flat panels of waterproof plywood and anyone who has tried to paint the old tongue-and-groove and beaded interiors of yesterday will welcome the change Large, light-painted areas give the cabin the appearance of being more roomy than it actually is. To take advantage of the white or tinted interiors, they must be broken with a contrasting color and that is where natural wood comes into play. This should be varnished and, since the cabin must be refinished occasionally, it should be made of removable strips. It may be any kind of wood, though we still hold to mahogany for trim. Redwood varnished natural answers the purpose well. A study of the modern interiors that appear in various boating magazines will be helpful in planning your own.

ARRANGEMENT.—Seldom will the amateur builder follow the exact cabin layout that the designer has specified for the boat. I have spent hours in planning the layout of some particular small cabin, only to discover when the boat was completed that the builder had ideas of his own that were more pleasing to him. Finally, I came to the conclusion that it was a waste of time to design someone else's cabin arrangement for him. The owner of a boat has the right to arrange his own cabin. He has to live in it and, as he makes his bed, so must he lie in it. Cabin arrangements will be discussed in general and the builder of all the craft in this book will be allowed to arrange his own.

DIMENSIONS.—There are certain definite rules that have been formulated through years of experience with small boats. The builder will do well to study these in arranging his cabin:

If full standing height is required in a cabin, it should be no less than 6'3" from the top of the floor to the under side of the deck beams. Some builders will snitch on this a bit and allow 6'0" for the same dimension.

The minimum possible headroom for any cabin is 4'0", to maintain sitting headroom on a 12" seat.

The minimum headroom over any seat is 3'0". This is measured from the top of the cushions.

The height of any seat from top of cushion to floor is maximum 19", usual 16" and minimum 12".

The minimum width of any seat should be 12", the usual is 16".

The usual comfortable dimensions for seats to sleep on or for berths are 78" in length (6'6") and 30" in width (2'6"). The minimum is 6'0" for length and 21" for width. A person of average size can sleep on a 69" berth and on one where he has a minimum of 18" at his shoulders and 10" at his feet. Men experienced in cruising aboard small boats will endure all sorts of discomforts for other arrangements but will insist on comfortable berths, for it is here that they seek rest for the rigors of the following day.

FURNITURE.—Where space is at a premium, as in the cabins of small motorboats or auto trailers, the furniture must be designed to take up the least possible space as well as serve to maximum advantage. The furniture, about to be described, was designed for this specific purpose and, while dimensions are given for the various parts, they serve only as a guide. The finished size of the various units will have to be made to suit the individual conditions.

A combination of seats and tables, similar to the familiar home breakfast nook, Fig. 60, can be made to serve as a bed at night. The space between the seat must be made the same width as the table. At night, when the berth is made up, the table is lowered and the back seat cushions are laid on top of the table, thus forming a continuous mattress. The seat ends, seats and back are constructed of ¾" plywood to the approximate dimensions shown. Sliding bolts, such as those used to secure cupboard doors, are fitted beneath the table and slide into holes in the upright at the front end of the seats. The table is hooked to sockets in the wall when in use and removed from these sockets when used in forming the berth. A support is arranged at the front of the table to hold it

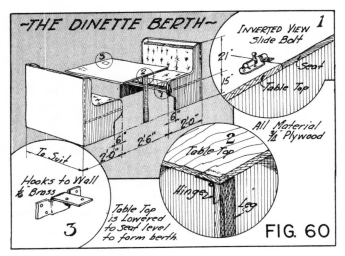

FIG. 60

level when it is in use. The support is folded up underneath the table when it is lowered.

Thirty inches is considered a minimum width for a single berth of this type while 54 inches is the minimum for a double berth and this distance must be maintained between the seat ends and the wall. The cushions may be covered with any material that the builder desires and the filling may be of horsehair, cotton, or kapok. Kapok is recommended for marine use due to its freedom from mildew as well as its buoyant qualities. Cotton filling, obtained from discarded mattresses, may be used. The cushions should be at least three inches thick and tufted.

All edges of the plywood should be neatly rounded and large surfaces well reinforced with battens screwed on. As the unit is intended for marine use, all glued joints should be made with Cascomite waterproof glue. Brass or galvanized screws should be used for assembling. Where the surfaces are to be finished natural, the screw heads should be let in and plugged. A natty finish can be obtained if the edges of the plywood are painted with a band about two inches wide and the rest of the wood either varnished natural or stained with transparent stain of any preferred color. The grain of most plywood provides a beautiful contrast to the rest of the furniture which is painted a solid color.

Many difficulties of sleeping comfort may be solved by the use of a pipe berth (Fig. 61). This can be made to any dimension and folded against the side of the boat when not in use. While those of you who traveled to Europe or Tarawa aboard transports may not

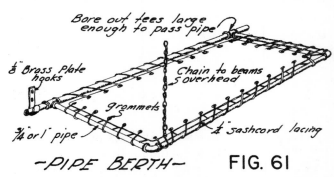

—PIPE BERTH—   FIG. 61

believe it, they can be made very comfortable. The trick is to allow the lacings to be slack.

GALLEY.—While headroom and sleeping accommodations are paramount aboard a small boat, her crew, like an army, travels on its stomach—galley arrangements are important. Most important to any galley is its stove for, even though the crew lives on canned foods, it is important that they be warmed. For the small boat, the stove of the canned heat type is best. Next in preference is a stove of the primus type, burning either alcohol or kerosene. The usual type of stove sold for auto camping is a hazard aboard the boat and anyone who has used them will tell you they were invented by the devil. Where there is room to install a permanent stove, any of the excellent alcohol stoves sold for marine use will answer the purpose.

One of the best little stoves that the writer has encountered in recent years is the Coleman Stove issued to our armed forces. It is generally referred to as "The G. I. *Coleman* Stove". It will burn almost any type of gasoline but the unleaded type is better. The casing around the whole outfit forms two pots ready for use any time the stove is. The wrench which fits all of its parts forms a portable handle for either of the pots. An attachment below the burner will clean the orifice with one complete turn. The whole stove is made of non-corrosive parts which makes it excellent for marine use. Note how this same stove forms a part of the portable galley of *Picaroon* later on.

On the larger boats, a galley sink should be installed especially if the mate wears skirts, slacks, or shorts and bra; for the girls go for this sort of thing. The most practical thing to replace the sink is a dishpan, one of the old-fashioned tin kind. Even this is a piece of extra baggage when you consider that one has the whole ocean to wash dishes in.

CROCKERY AND DISHES should be given some consideration and kept at a minimum. Chinaware is neat and easy to keep clean but has a bad habit of breaking when dropped or tossed around in a seaway. Beetleware or plastic crockery is the most practical and, next to this, I prefer the good old enamelware. Every galley of any size should have its dishrack to lend a seagoing atmosphere to the boat. Several types of these, as well as a glass rack, are show in Fig. 62.

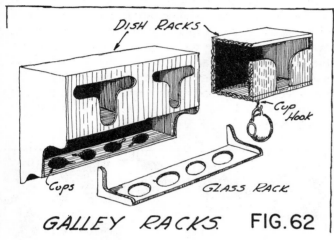

GALLEY RACKS. FIG. 62

On small boats where space is at a minimum or in open boats where cooking facilities are only used on an all-day trip, it is good practice to make a self-contained galley box in which a small sterno stove is fitted, Fig. 63. This can be made to contain the necessary table ware and, when in use, the open lid protects the stove from the breeze. See also portable galley of *Picaroon*.

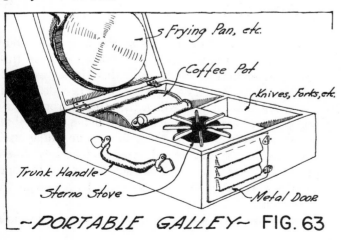

~PORTABLE GALLEY~ FIG. 63

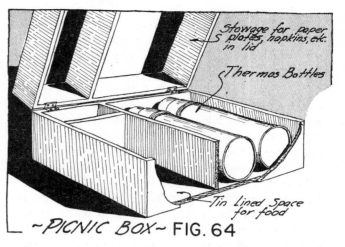

~PICNIC BOX~ FIG. 64

Where cooking facilities are not required, a picnic box, Fig. 64, will answer the purpose nicely. Space for thermos bottles carrying hot soup and coffee are shown.

THE REFRIGERATOR.—The most practical refrigerator for the small boat is the kind sold for auto camping trips. A box built of plywood and insulated with 1″ of fiberglass or celotex will keep ice and food longer but is more expensive even though you build it yourself. The box should be constructed as shown in Fig. 65. A removable watertight box should be

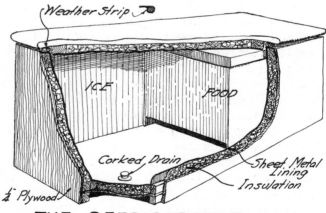

~THE REFRIGERATOR~ FIG. 65

made to fit inside the main box. Food which you do not want to come in direct contact with the ice may be stored in this box.

Built-in refrigerators are an abomination in any boat. I have seen more dry rot start in the areas behind these boxes than in any other part of the boat. If you must have a built-in refrigerator, make it so that it can be removed as a unit and the area behind it inspected and painted occasionally.

STOWAGE SPACES.—There is never enough space aboard the small boat to carry all of the necessary cruising equipment, no matter how carefully one tries to condense it. Never have I wanted a chart in a hurry without having to move a carload of suitcases, blankets and extra grub to get at it. Years of experience have taught cruising men that the best way to cruise is to take plenty of everything but reduce it to a minimum. The use of every cubic inch of available space in the boat is, therefore, imperative.

The space under seats and berths is often neglected as stowage space. In the old days we fit drawers under them. Invariably someone would leave a drawer open for the next fellow to stumble over when he entered the cabin in the dark. The advent of waterproof plywood for berth fronts has solved all of this. You simply cut a hole in the front and reach in through it, Figs. 66 and 68. The type of nets that are fitted to Pullman berths are excellent for the stowage of clothes and blankets. While on the subject of lockers, it is well to mention that the wise cruising man generally fits the bottom of lockers near the bilge water with watertight bottoms and sides made of soldered galvanized iron. In spite of all efforts, the lockers generally become a Hurrah's Nest, a place where all the junk aboard the boat finds a permanent resting place; a place for everything and nothing in its place.

VENTILATION OF CUPBOARDS AND LOCKERS.—Any confined space aboard the small boat is subject to becoming musty. There is only one cure for this—ventilation. A small amount of air admitted to any of these spaces will eliminate mold and mustiness to a great extent. Ordinarily, this is accomplished by holes or lattices in the door. The perennial shapes for holes generally are copies from the symbols of playing cards, spades and clubs being in great favor, followed by hearts for those of a romantic nature.

There are unconventional silhouettes which may be cut in door panels, Fig. 66. Many will lend an air to the boat in keeping with the boat's name or her owner's ruling passion. Basket-weave latticework is another favorite. To make the strips, mahogany, or some other wood that will make a pleasing appearance when finished natural, is ripped into thin strips about the thickness of a ripsaw in a saw table. The strips are then woven in the same manner as a slat basket, leaving space between them equal to the thickness of the strips. A frame is constructed large enough to enclose the lattice. A saw-cut is made on its inside edge and the lattice slats are inserted. Often small holes are drilled through frame and lattice and

toothpicks are driven in the holes to retain the strips.

STOWAGE OF FOOD.—While not quite within the province of this book, food must be stored on the small boat and the stowage is the responsibility of the builder. While the perishable food may be stored in the ice-box, many foods are subject to spoilage from dampness. These are not convenient to carry ashore at the end of every voyage. Coffee, sugar, salt and pepper are the common things which need attention. Crackers and other salty foods readily absorb the moisture aboard the boat. Long ago I found the answer to all of these problems in the rubber-sealed screw-top Mason jar. Placed in these containers and screwed tight, the substances are free from the effects of moisture. A small quantity of silica gel placed in every jar will absorb moisture. A simple stowage for these jars can be made from two pieces of plywood with three- or four-inch spacers between them. The top piece of plywood is cut with holes just large enough to hold the jars. This will keep them safe when the boat is rolling in a seaway.

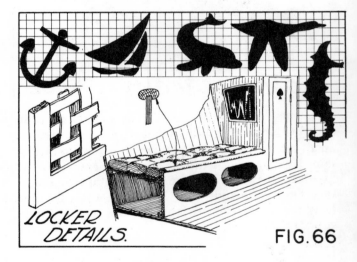

LOCKER DETAILS.　　　　FIG. 66

STOWAGE OF WATER.—Formerly we stowed our water aboard small boats in wooden casks or tin-lined copper tanks. The taste of this after a week of hot weather still lingers. Today there is a dearth of one-gallon glass jugs in which such things from cleaning fluids to cider are packaged. I have found that water will keep better in these than in anything else. Chlorinated city water will keep indefinitely when placed in these containers. A rack similar to the one described here for Mason jars should be made to hold them.

Every boat of any size should have a separate

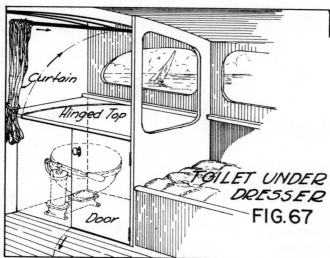

Curtain

Hinged Top

Door

TOILET UNDER DRESSER
FIG.67

concealed under a seat, Fig. 68.

On boats with a cabin large enough, a separate toilet compartment should be carefully arranged. The toilet room with washbasin, bowl, mirror and linen shelves or lockers is important. Plan it well; taking advantage of every cubic foot of space.

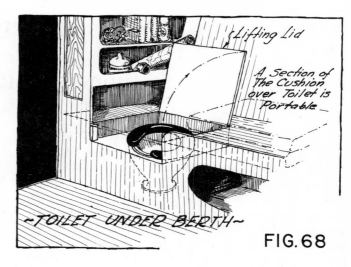

Lifting Lid

A Section of The Cushion over Toilet is Portable

~TOILET UNDER BERTH~

FIG.68

toilet room. In the small boat, we have to resort to subterfuge to obtain it. In some boats, the toilet stands out in the cabin, unashamed. One scheme ingeniously conceals the toilet under a dresser whose top folds to a vertical position closing the front and a curtain closes the sides, Fig. 67. In others it is

CHAPTER X

JOINER WORK DETAILS

The interior of a small boat cabin is not just a place to sleep in or stow all the miscellaneous junk aboard the boat. It is one part of the little ship in which you will want to live. Here you exercise all the ability of your craftsmanship in joinery. If we examine the numerous stock boats appearing on the market, we will find a tendency to simplify the joinerwork. It is a trend for the better, though the reason behind it is that the men who built beautiful joinery by hand have joined the ranks of the dodo bird.

While it is possible to create good joinery entirely with hand tools, a small power unit can add immeasurably to the appearance of the joinery and, at the same time, save the builder hours in the eventual completion of his boat. To this end, the details shown in Figs. 69 to 74 have been devised.

Plywood has entered the field of joinery material with a gusto. All bulkheads, dresser tops and faces, berth boards and the hundred other details of the interior may employ it. Fir plywood does not lend itself readily to a natural finish and mahogany-faced plywood is expensive and contributes a dark aspect to the cabin interior. Painted surfaces are fast supplanting the solid mahogany interiors of the boat of our fathers. A full-painted interior looks glaring unless relieved with bits of natural wood or gleaming metal. A thorough study of the interior should be made to distribute the relief effectively.

Where openings through plywood are necessary, a small amount of natural trim around them often imparts just that touch that is needed to make them change from a plain hole to something that is a part of the interior. The framing of natural wood can be made of strips, Fig. 69. It is often difficult to make strips of an even thickness match up properly. For this reason, the top and bottom of the opening is framed with a slightly thicker face than the sides. The tops are also allowed to extend past the greatest

width of the sides. The bottoms are given a similar treatment.

Doors through plywood present no great difficulty if the method followed in Fig. 69 is used. Here the

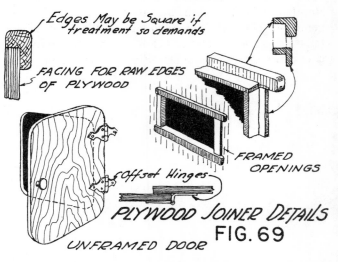

PLYWOOD JOINER DETAILS
FIG. 69

opening is cut about a half or three-quarters of an inch less all around than the actual door. Offset hinges of the type purchased for kitchen cabinets are used to swing the door. Even very large doors of plywood may be made with this sort of construction. Usually, it is impossible to secure screws short enough to seat within the thickness of the plywood. In this case, the regular length screws are inserted and the projections through the plywood are filed or ground away.

Fit chromium-plated hardware and then remove it until after all painting and varnishing is done. Thus, the care that must be exercised to keep paint or varnish away from the hardware is dispensed with. This applies also to the separation of painted grounds and varnished trim. The plywood panels are installed and varnished joint strips are placed over them. In this way, all of the poor joints in the plywood are hidden. If the panels appear too large, false joint strips may be installed. It is advisable to make all joint strips removable to facilitate painting. Chromium-plated washers such as those in buses and station wagons are useful, Fig. 70.

LINOLEUM.—The addition of linoleum and the new types of tile board made from pressed wood can add that snappy look so much desired around the galley. All wood furniture is made from plywood,

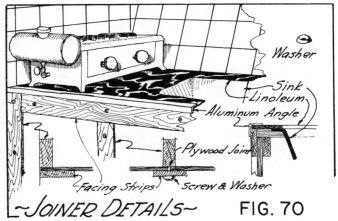

~JOINER DETAILS~   FIG. 70

Fig. 70, and the tops are covered with linoleum. This is applied to the face of the plywood with linoleum cement and care should be taken in planning the installation so that the edges of the linoleum are set down watertight. The linoleum should always overlap the sink edge to prevent water from running under it. It is often necessary to sink the edges of the metal lip around the sink down into the plywood dresser top.

All linoleum and tile board edges look better if they are dressed up a bit with the aluminum moldings that can be purchased for this purpose. Around salt water these moldings have a tendency to gather a white corrosion. The metal should be cleaned occasionally with steel wool and covered with floor wax.

CONVENTIONAL WINDOWS AND DOORS pose a problem for the amateur builder. I worried with these for years until the simple method shown in Fig. 71 was used. A real joiner would call this a shoemaker's job. Perhaps it seems to be, but with the advent of waterproof glues it has become one of the most satisfactory methods for the amateur. The edges of the sash or door frame are overlapped, screwed and glued. In making this type of sash or door, a frame of 3/4″ or 7/8″ material is made. The depth of the saw-cut on the table saw is set so that it is *exactly* one-half the thickness of the material. Do not trust your rule for

this but take a sample piece of the material. Make a saw-cut and turn the material over. The two cuts should leave just a tissue-paper thin piece of wood between them. Once the depth of the cut is made, all rabbets and overlaps should be cut. The easiest way

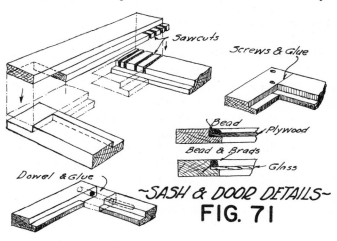

~SASH & DOOR DETAILS~
FIG. 71

to be certain that the overlaps are correct is to take a series of close saw-cuts in the way of the lap and cut the material away between them. Warning: Be sure that the correct face of the material is put down on the table. You probably will ruin as much material as I did before this lesson is properly absorbed.

While on the subject of joiner work, we must consider interior and exterior shaped moldings. Where the shape of the molding is such that a natural bend would exert excessive strain on the wood, it is best to

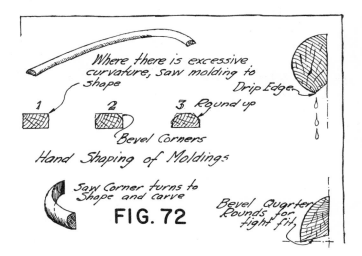

FIG. 72

saw it to shape, Fig. 72. Where a slight curvature exists in one plane and an excessive one in the other plane of the molding, it can be a combination of sawed and bent job. The particular molding location will determine this.

After the molding is sawed to shape, the corners are first beveled with a spoke shave or rasp. The corners of these beveled edges are again removed and this process repeated until the molding can be finished round with sandpaper.

There is nothing so messy as a painted cabin that shows streaks of dirt where a molding spills drainage on its side. This can be eliminated to a great extent by beveling away the underside of the molding, Fig. 72. The water then drips off the sharp edge and does not stream down the side of the cabin.

Deck moldings that are to fit tight may be beveled on their undersides to a point where only the outer edge bears, as shown in Fig. 72. If these moldings are set in a light bedding cement or white lead, a truly watertight joint is assured.

THE COMPANIONWAY and its slide, by which the cabins of small boats are entered and locked, always have been the source of much discussion. The type that I have found most successful is shown in Figs. 73 and 74. The door (or the way) is made of several boards sliding in a groove in the jamb. The jamb and sills are made of one piece of material and an inner strip fitted to retain the boards. Thus, the cabin cannot be entered by removing a door strip. Note how the U-bolt hasp is secured on the inside of the slide to prevent its removal. Nothing but the absolute wrecking of the slide will gain entrance without removing the lock. Some of my friends contend that the locks are only to keep honest people out. Therefore, they make a flimsy lock that can easily be broken, thus saving their boats from being wrecked by an intruder.

The slide of the companionway is made as shown in Fig. 74. The slide timbers are slotted and a brass strip is placed on the slide so that it tracks in the slot. Often another strip is added on the top of the slide timbers to reduce the friction. Small brass pads are placed under the slide to ride on the upper strip. The tops of the slides may be either flat or cambered and here, too, plywood makes construction easy and strong.

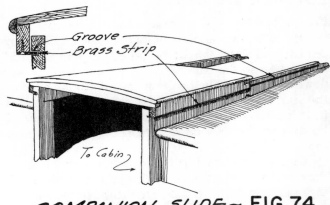

~COMPANIONWAY~   FIG. 73

~COMPANION SLIDE~   FIG. 74

CHAPTER XI

PLUMBING

Under the head of plumbing may be classed such things as wash basins, sinks and, of course, the Johnny. This may range from the great outdoors typified either by sensitive human flesh exposed to the elements over a coaming rail or a yawl's bumkins. The acme of these things is the electric operated, plastic and chromium trimmed thunder mugs as are now displayed in the ads of the best yachting magazines. Each type has its advantages and disadvantages and a few words about them may not be amiss.

TOILETS

COMMODE TYPE.—This type is still in use on quite a number of small yachts in England and other European countries. It may consist of a simple galvanized utility bucket over which a comfortable removable plywood sheet has been fitted, or it may be one of the conventional china bowls stowed beneath a berth as is done under the bed at home. In very small boats where space is at a premium, the crew may much prefer the great outdoors if they be of the masculine gender but when the mate goes cruising with the skipper nothing is too good for her. Often a board with the conventional Chic Sales hole cut through it and placed over the galvanized wash down bucket will be all that is needed.

PUMP TYPE.—This type may be purchased at almost any marine supply store and consists of a china bowl, a more or less comfortable seat and a hand operated pump. The pump is a double acting one which at one stroke picks up the necessary water from outside of the hull to flush the bowl, and at the other stroke expels the soil. Where electric current is available, from the starting battery, the pump may be operated from this. One of the disadvantages of the pump type toilet is their bad habit of choking up at the critical moment when strangers come aboard the boat. Match sticks, cigar butts and other foreign sub-stances that will pass the ordinary toilet at home will stick in the pump valves of a boat toilet, causing the owner much embarrassment and giving him a good working knowledge of a plumber's life when the contraption is taken apart.

STRAIGHT THROUGH TYPE.—This type is best from an operational standpoint. No pump is required and it will pass anything which would not obstruct a home toilet. It flushes continually while the boat is under way and keeps as clean as one of these things can be expected to. They are impossible in sailboats where the heeling in a fresh breeze would cause them to overflow. They have the disadvantage of freezing when the boat is left overboard in the winter but the party fishing boats on the Chesapeake Bay solve this difficulty by filling them up with hard grease, thus expelling the water from them. The grease is removed when the boat is again put in operation. In connection with this, in laying up the pump type toilet, some owners fill the bowl with kerosene and work it through the pipes and valves.

The straight through type may be home made. The party fishermen on the Bay do this in a very simple and satisfactory manner. They secure a hopper-type toilet bowl similar to Crane Co., Figure C.M. 12-043. This is a cast iron bowl, porcelain enameled inside, which is about 16″ high and often can be obtained secondhand. This is set on a board. (See Fig. 75.) The fishermen cut a hole through the board large enough to take a piece of 4″ lead pipe and through the hull directly below this they cut another hole. They pass the lead pipe through the board and cut it about a half-inch above it. This half-inch projection is carefully beaten down flat until it forms a tight-fitting flange against the board. The flange is then secured to the board with copper tacks.

The pipe projecting through the hull is cut off ¾″ from the hull. This is wrapped with lampwick packing

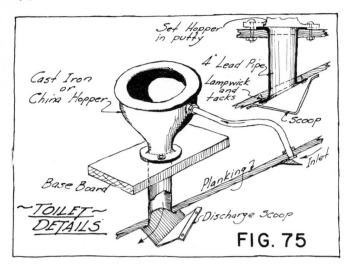

Set Hopper in putty

4" Lead Pipe

Cast Iron or China Hopper

Lampwick and tacks

Scoop

Inlet

Base Board

Planking

~TOILET DETAILS~

Discharge Scoop

FIG. 75

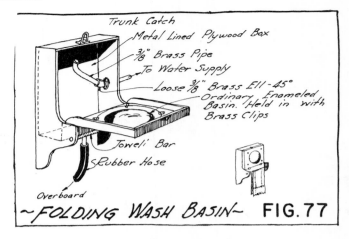

Trunk Catch

Metal Lined Plywood Box

3/8" Brass Pipe

To Water Supply

Loose 3/8" Brass Ell-45°

Ordinary Enameled Basin. Held in with Brass Clips

Towel Bar

Rubber Hose

Overboard

~FOLDING WASH BASIN~   FIG. 77

soaked in white lead and flanged over the same as the inside end and secured with copper tacks. Then the toilet bowl is set in white lead putty and lampwick packing and bolted to the board.

A piece of $\frac{1}{16}$" brass sheet is bent, as show in Fig. 76, and screwed to the hull with the large end aft. A water scoop is made from another piece of brass and a pipe connection inserted through the hull, as shown. A piece of garden hose connecting this scoop to the toilet rim completes the outfit.

The toilet flushes continually while the boat is under way and it is always clean. It will work in a slight tideway and even the rolling of the boat will remove soil from it. This type of toilet will pass anything not too large to go through the bottom opening. The author has found a toilet of this same type installed in his own boat a very convenient place through which water bailed from the boat may be disposed of.

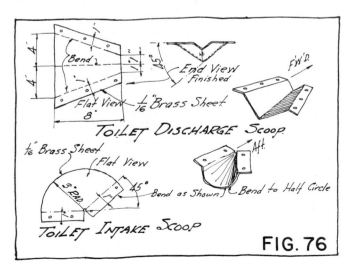

Bend

End View Finished

FW'D

Flat View

1/16" Brass Sheet

TOILET DISCHARGE SCOOP

1/16" Brass Sheet

Flat View

Aft.

45°

Bend as Shown

Bend to Half Circle

TOILET INTAKE SCOOP

FIG. 76

LAVATORIES

Like toilets these may range from a simple enameled basin such as one might buy at a dime store to those of gleaming white with dazzling trim that attract the girl friend in the ads of the boating magazines. Almost any type to suit the space or fancy may be purchased. There are those that fold into a very small space to ones that will fit in an unused corner of the toilet space. Most of these basins are supplied either by a gravity tank or a small hand operated pump drawing from the boat's fresh water tank.

Just as the toilet was improvised, so may the lavatory be. An ordinary enameled wash-basin is fitted in a plywood box. (See Fig. 77.) The interior of the box is lined with metal and soldered watertight. A drain connection may be fitted also. The projections of the box hold the basin lid when it is in use and may be utilized to hold a towel bar, as shown in Fig. 77.

In some cases the lavatory may consist of a simple metal ring installed in the toilet or some other convenient space. The ring is arranged to fold against a bulkhead when the basin is not in use, and an ordinary enameled basin is fitted within the ring when the urge comes to pretty up. The basin is emptied by the simple expedient of dumping it in the toilet or overboard.

SINKS

These like the lavatories may be purchased or be home made and may range from gleaming stainless steel to simple galvanized iron sheet. If you are unable to work a pair of tin snips and a solding iron, your local tinsmith may be called upon to make the sink to any dimensions that you may give him.

BILGE PUMPS

While these very necessary fittings aboard a boat cannot be classed along with the plumbing, they do handle water and so I will insert them here.

The oldest and by far the most satisfactory type of bilge pump I have ever had experience with is the old-fashioned tin pipe pump with a bell top and a wooden stick handle. These will handle more water per stroke than any other type. If there is room aboard the boat to stow one, never be without it regardless of how many new-fangled brass contraptions that have now been invented to replace it. The next best type is the built in pump with a large brass barrel and a fairly long stroke. These are piped permanently to the bilge and the discharge is led over the side with fairly large piping. They may be procured from any marine supply house. Small double acting force pumps with ball check valves and rubber hose may also be purchased to pump your bilges. These stow in a small space but are almost useless to combat an accidental leak.

PIPING

Plumbing takes its name from the Latin word for lead. This type of piping was used extensively both at sea and ashore in the days gone by and even today some boat owners prefer their plumbing to be fitted up with this material. It takes an expert to properly wipe a lead joint and for this reason it is fast becoming obsolete. Where long runs of piping is needed copper tubing with simple swage fittings at its terminals will be found to be the best. For discharge lines, rubber hose will be found to be the most convenient as it is easily bent and may be just as easily removed for cleaning when it becomes clogged.

Such a wide variety of through-hull connections, valves and other plumbing fittings may be purchased at your local marine hardware dealer that it will be of little value to enumerate them all. They may be purchased to take lead or copper piper or rubber hose as the builder desires. Often with a little ingenuity an ordinary brass gate valve may be adapted to make a good sea-cock. Other through-hull connections may be made with a brass pipe nipple fitted with a pair of lock nuts on each side of the hull planking. The thread of the nipple may be cut to any length necessary to pass through the hull and at the same time take the locknuts.

CHAPTER XII

SAILS AND RIGGING

Ages before James Watt began dreaming of the steam engine, one of our lazy ancestors noticed that the wind blew objects across the lake on which he fished from his crude craft. Paddling that raft from place to place had been work. A great light began to dawn in his brain. "Why not let the wind move this daggone raft for me," he said to himself. From that time on, the sail began to develop. From a crude piece of fabric, it advanced until today we have, perhaps, a beautiful expanse of nylon which is aerodynamically correct and will move our boats against the wind as well as with it. Sail will eventually disappear from our commercial craft but sailing, rather than horse-racing, is the sport of kings and we will continue to sail as long as it remains a sport.

The modern sailing rig has developed from a perfectly square piece of cloth set across the boat to catch the wind going in the direction that the boat wanted to go, to a series of sails set so as to swing across the boat and make the boat actually move in a series of zig-zag darts in the direction from which the wind is blowing. The various combinations of sails aboard a boat have been given distinctive names and one may see many variations of the four shown in Fig. 78.

SAIL NAMES

Generally, the sails take their name from the mast on which they are set. Starting from the bow of the boat there is the jib. In some rigs there may be two or three of these, but for the boats in this book we will consider only one. The next sail aft set on the mast is usually called the mainsail and in salty language it is pronounced "mains'l." Should the boat be rigged as a schooner, this sail will be the foresail (this is shortened to "fores'l"). For a better understanding of sail names, refer to Fig. 78.

SLOOP RIG.—This is a single-masted rig, having a jib and mains'l. It is the most popular of small boat rigs. Today, it is very hard to distinguish between a sloop and a cutter, another single-masted rig. The cutter has the mast stepped farther aft than the sloop but where the cutter starts and where the sloop ends is anybody's guess. *Titmouse*, whose construction is described in Chapter XVI, is a sloop. *Pelican* might be called a ketch.

YAWL RIG.—The yawl is a sloop with a small sail added aft of its mains'l. It has the advantage of being able to sail in a blow without reefing. The mains'l is furled and the boat proceeds under jib and mizzen (the smaller sail). The rig should be designed to do the foregoing and the proportions of area to do this should be in the order of 1-3-1. As a general rule, the mizzenmast of the yawl is set aft of the rudder

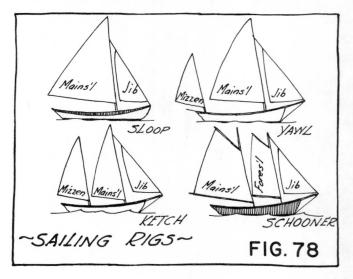

~SAILING RIGS~   FIG. 78

post.

KETCH RIG.—The ketch is a boat similar to the yawl with the sails named the same—jib, main and mizzen. In the ketch, the mizzen is invariably stepped forward of the rudder post and often they, too, are designed to handle under jib and mizzen alone.

SCHOONER RIG.—The schooner is a typically American rig and the sails are named jib, fores'l and mains'l. The masts are foremast and mainmast. In this rig we see a sail of a different type than those described previously. The fores'l carries a gaff. This is an old-style sail which preceded our modern "Jib-headed" ones. While some schooners are built, as depicted, with both sails gaff-headed, they are more often rigged with a gaff-headed foresail and a jib-headed mainsail.

CAT RIG.—This is a single-sail rig in which the mast is stepped far forward, or "in the eyes" of the boat. At one time it was quite a popular small boat rig but lately has been superseded by the conventional jib and mains'l rig. Not every single-masted rig may be called a cat, however, for there are many rigs that carry only one mast and one sail.

SAILS AND THEIR CONSTRUCTION

Sails are made of a number of small pieces of sailcloth sewn together. These pieces are called the cloths. The joints between them are called the seams.

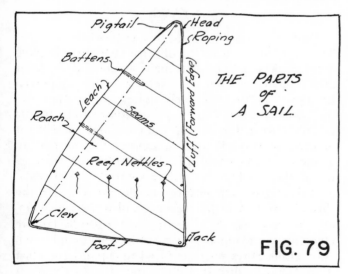

THE PARTS of A SAIL.

FIG. 79

(See Fig. 79.) Modern practice demands that the seams run across the sail in the direction of the air flow. Sails thus constructed are termed "crosscut" sails. There are three edges in modern sails. The edge leading into the air is termed the luff; the edge from which the air leaves the sail is called the leach. The base of the sail is termed its foot and the top of the sail terminating in a point or an edge laced along a gaff is called the head. Frequently, for better aero-

dynamic effect, the edges of the sails are given a curvature. This usually is found in the leach. The curvature is called the roach. To strengthen a sail a rope edge is applied to the luff and foot and, if gaff headed, to that edge also. This rope is sewed either inside the cloth or to its edge This is called the roping. Sometimes it is referred to as the boltrope The lower corners of the sail are given distinctive names. The forward corner is called the tack; the after corner is called the clew. To keep the roached edge of a sail extended in a smooth surface, small wood or plastic strips are installed in pockets sewed to the leach of the sail. These are called battens. Often, in a heavy blow it is necessary to reduce the sail area. This is accomplished by gathering the foot of the sail into folds and tying them securely around the boom by small ropes fastened to the sail. These ropes are called reef nettles. Sometimes they are referred to as reef points.

SPARS

Poles of various sizes are needed to support the sails in their working position. Collectively, these are called spars. Individually, they all have names, sometimes confusing, but each for a specific purpose.

MAST.—The main spar which supports the sail in its vertical position is called the mast. This is stepped upright in the boat. The lower end of the mast is called the heel; its upper end is called the head. Generally, the lower end of the mast terminates in some sort of a tenon and this fits into a mortise in a block of wood termed the step. We say that a mast is stepped so far aft of a certain point to describe its position. Heavy reinforcement is generally fitted where the mast penetrates the deck, for here a great amount of strain is developed. This reinforcement is called the partners.

BOOMS.—To extend the foot of most sails, another spar is used. This spar is called the boom. While a mast may be shaped so that its greatest diameter is at the partners, the boom generally has its greatest section at its midlength. While most of the boats in this book have only a boom to extend the foot of their sails, a gaff-headed sail has another spar at its head. This is called the gaff. The ends of a gaff are designated by the end of the sail to which they are fastened. The lower and most forward end of the gaff is termed the throat end and the opposite one is called the peak.

Booms and gaffs are fastened to the mast in many ways. These may run from a simple rope lashing to a complicated metal fitting called a goose-neck. Gaffs are held to the mast by either wood or metal jaws and in the more complicated rigs, by a sliding goose-neck

Booms are sometimes used on *jibs* to extend them to the wind. They may be pivoted on the deck or lashed directly to the foot of the sail. Often the distance along the foot of a jib is longer than the distance from its clew to the nearest point on the stay to which it is hooked. When this is the case, the spar along the foot of the jib must either be made short enough to allow the jib to come down or it must be detachable. On small boats, where it is only necessary to extend the jib occasionally, this is done by a light pole fastened temporarily to the mast and running from it to the jib clew. This is termed a *whisker pole*.

Sometimes the jib tack is set ahead of the stem head and a permanent spar is used to accomplish this. This spar is called the bowsprit and often is referred to erroneously as the jib boom. Boats lacking bowsprits are often termed knockabouts. Frequently, we hear such terms as knockabout sloop or knockabout schooner.

CARE OF SAILS

Sails are fastened to the booms and masts in a number of ways. In the old days they were left on the spars for indefinite periods. In that case, they were laced to the booms and gaffs and were attached to hoops on the mast. When the day's sail was over, the sails were neatly folded on the spars (furled was the right word for it) and a watertight cover put over them. The covers or jackets were supposed to be watertight but a hard rain would invariably find its way under the cover. The result was a mildewed spot on the sail. Today we take all small sails off the boat and stow them in a dry place in the cabin or ashore. At such times the sails are stowed in containers or waterproof canvas sail bags.

REMOVING SAILS.—Many methods have been devised for easy removal of sails. So far, the best is the metal track and slide idea extensively used on all modern sailing craft. (See Fig. 80.) These may be bought at any marine hardware store handling boat fittings. They are made of brass or other non-corrosive metals and, considering the ease with which a sail can be removed with them, they are inexpensive. Another method is the use of a wooden track and cast metal slides, shown in Fig. 80. The slides are fastened permanently to the sail and the tracks are attached to the spars.

There are some sailors who must be scientifically correct and who will not allow a bit of air to leak

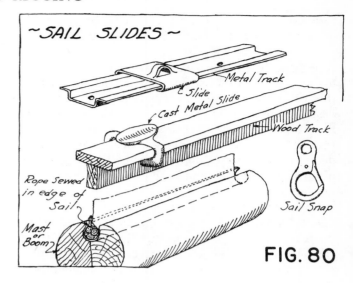

FIG. 80

from the pressure side of their sails around to the suction side. These men cut a hollow groove in their spars and slide the roped edge of the sail in it. This sort of construction of the mast or boom requires the spar to be made in two pieces. The slot is cut before the two pieces are glued together.

STAYS

Modern masts are stayed to prevent their bending. This is done by a series of wire ropes which have different designations. The main supports of the mast take their name from the hemp ropes that supported the masts of the old wood sailing ships—they are the *shrouds*. (See Fig. 81.) Sometimes the shrouds go only part of the way up the mast and another set of wires or stays is used to support the mast head. These are termed *topstays*. To increase the angularity of the topstays for better support of the mast, auxiliary struts are inserted at the point where the shrouds are fastened. These are called the *spreaders*, also shown in Fig. 81. The stays described heretofore give the mast support in an athwartship direction only. Other stays must be fitted to support the mast in the opposite direction (fore and aft). At the point where the shrouds are hooked, a stay generally is run to the stem head or the forward end of the bowsprit. This is called the *forestay*. To support the mast head, another stay is carried forward; this is called the *foretopstay*. When it is necessary to support the mast against the push of a sail, another stay often is run aft. This stay is called the *backstay*. Frequently, this stay is called a *preventer*. The various stays take their names from the mast that they support such as *foreshrouds* and *main* or *mizzen shrouds*. Collectively,

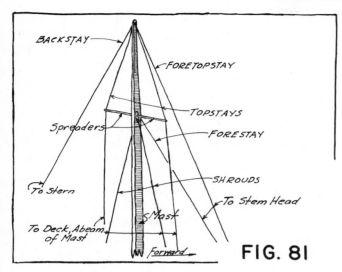

FIG. 81

these permanent ropes of a boat's rigging are called *standing rigging*.

RUNNING RIGGING

Ropes are needed to work the sails, to hoist them aloft and to trim them to the wind. This collection of ropes aboard a small boat is called the *running rigging*. (See Fig. 82.) Each rope of the running rigging serves a definite purpose. Ropes that hoist a sail are called *halyards*. In the old square rig the halyards hoisted the spars aloft; our modern designation is a corruption of the words *haul yard*. They take their

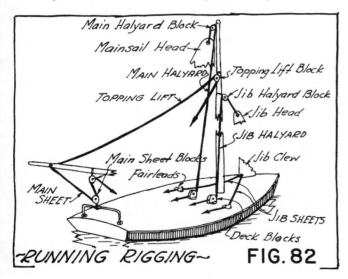

RUNNING RIGGING~ FIG. 82

designation from the sail which they service, such as *main halyard, jib halyard*, etc. *Gaff-headed* sails have two halyards aloft—the *peak* and *throat* halyards. To trim the sail to the wind, another set of ropes is used.

These are called the sheets (a sail is never called a *sheet*). These also take their designation from their sails, such as *main sheet* and *jib sheet*. Often where the jib overlaps the mast, as it does in many modern designs, the jib sheet is made double so as to relieve the necessity of moving it around the mast every time the sail is trimmed to the opposite side. Often, to lead the mainsheet across the tiller on a boat fitted with an outboard rudder, an iron bar is used, called a *traveler*. Sometimes these are used on jib sheets, also. Often it is desirable to hoist the boom above the boat when headroom is needed or for other purposes. In this case, another piece of rigging is fitted. This is the *topping lift*.

ROPE AND RIGGING

Commonly, two types of ropes are in use on small boats—fiber and wire

FIBER ROPE.—Fiber ropes are made from the fibers of jute, sisal, hemp or abaca. They usually are composed of three main strands and they, in turn, are composed of numerous strands of fiber. (See Fig. 83.) Fiber ropes are easily knotted or spliced.

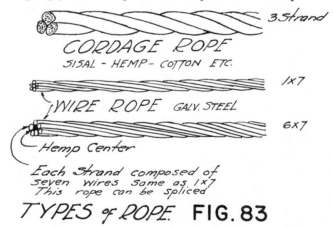

TYPES of ROPE. FIG. 83

Fiber rope is easier to work than other types when wet. Among the fiber ropes, jute is the softer but is not looked on with favor by sailors. It is cheap and was used extensively during the war as a substitute for the scarce Manila rope.

NYLON is now being made into rope and promises to fulfill the sailor's dream of the ideal cordage. When bleached white, cotton rope makes a dressy job but is expensive and hard to work when wet. Braided sash cord is frowned on by most sailors except for tiller ropes.

WIRE ROPE.—Many types of wire rope are marketed and are constructed for marine use from galvanized steel, stainless steel and bronze.

Wire rope is designated by numbers which denote its construction by strands. For instance, six by seven designates that the rope is composed of six main strands, each composed of seven separate wires. Usually, this is written 6 x 7. Likewise, 1 x 7 is a rope composed of one strand with seven wires. (See Fig. 83.) The diameter of wire rope is first given, next the construction and then the material; thus, "1/4" diameter 6 x 7 galvanized wire rope." In some extreme cases, where flexibility is paramount, a finer type of stranding will be given, as in 6 x 19 or 6 x 37. Most ropes of this type have a hemp center to aid in flexibility and contain oil to lubricate the rope.

Never use the ordinary aircraft cable aboard a boat. It rusts easily. Some small boats use a 1/8" diameter solid wire for riggings and make twisted eyes. This wire kinks easily and is not *yachty*. The eyes in 1 x 7 are easily worked by unstranding a wire at a time and wrapping it around the remaining wires. You may see this on telegraph pole guys but it also is not considered yachty.

EYE ENDS FOR WIRE ROPE.—Three types of eyes may be formed in the ends of wire rope. The simplest

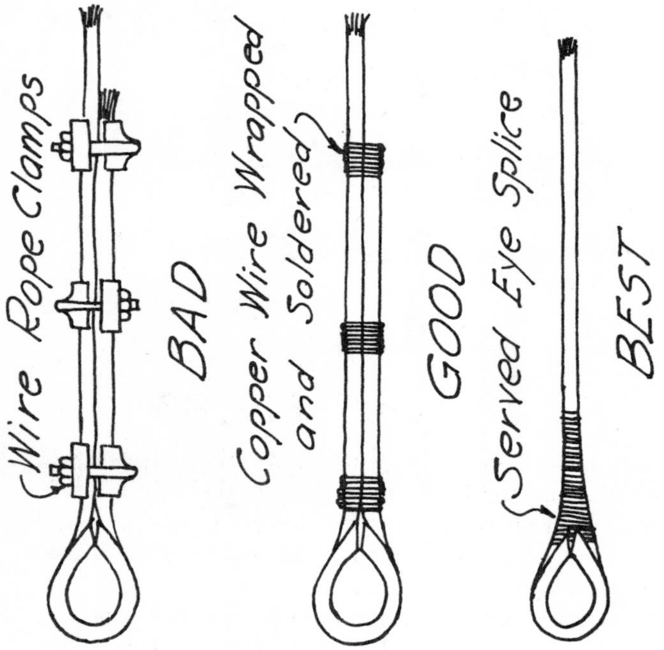

WIRE ROPE EYES
FIG. 84

from the standpoint of labor, yet the most expensive in the cost of material, is the type using wire rope

clamps. The rope is doubed back on itself around a thimble at least thirty times its diameter and the clamps are applied, as shown. While this type of eye can be recommended for temporary work aboard a boat, it is never seen on first-class jobs because of its clumsy and unshiplike appearance.

Similar to the clamped eye is the type in which the clamps are replaced with wrappings of copper wire. These are neatly wrapped and soldered after being carefully hammered into place between the two lines of rope.

The best of all eyes is the one in which the rope is spliced around the thimble and the splice then served with yacht marlin and varnished or shellacked. (See Fig. 84.)

Eyes are worked in Manila and other rope similar to the eyesplice in the wire rope but with a lot less effort. The art of working rope has been dealt with so many times in other books by experts on this subject that it would be a waste of good space to go into that art in this book. Get several of these books and study them if you intend to sail.

BLOCKS.—Certain fittings are necessary to properly work the ropes of the rigging. Some means must be employed to eliminate the friction of a running rope where it is required to turn a corner. For this purpose a block is employed. (See Fig. 85.) These

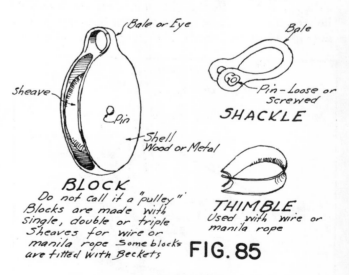

FIG. 85

are made in many forms and with several sheaves as occasion demands. They are attached at their eyes by a *shackle* passed through the eye at the head of the block. Several kinds of shackles are used. The regular shackle has its pin passed through the eye of the block. In other locations it is required that an *upset* shackle block be employed. Here the bale of the shackle is passed through the eye of the block. In other places it is required that the block be able to *swivel* or turn. Swivel blocks are also made in regular or upset shackles. Many other types of blocks are manufactured but none other than the regular shackle type will be employed in the boats described in this book. Whenever it is necessary to attach one end of a tackle to a block another fitting is employed at the end of the block opposite the eye. This is called the *becket* and in most blocks is only another eye at the bottom end of the block.

Where it is necessary to fasten one end of a rope permanently, that end is eyespliced around a *thimble* (Fig. 85), and a shackle is rove through this thimble. Often it is required to open the thimble before splicing so that the shackle may be inserted.

EYE LOOPS AND TANGS.—Some method of fastening wire rope to the boat is necessary. Aloft on the mast this is done by either of two methods, eye loops or tangs. (See Fig. 86.) The former is the simpler

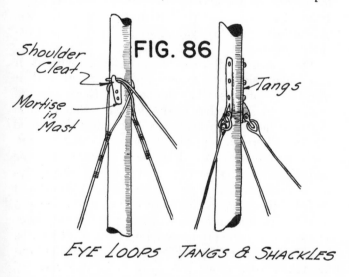

and a sure-fire method—it is the one I prefer. The attachment of blocks to the mast may also be made by this method. In doing this, a wire rope is spliced with two eyes, a large one served with marlin of the yacht type to go around the mast and a small one around a thimble to receive the shackle of the block. Where tangs are used, the wires are attached to the tangs by an eye splice and shackle.

TURNBUCKLES.—Some means of keeping wire rope rigging tight must be employed. A turnbuckle is best for this purpose. There are many types of turnbuckles. One with two jaw ends may be used or one with a jaw and eye will answer the purpose. (See Fig. 87.) The turnbuckles are held to the hull by the use

of a metal strip called the *chain-plate*. Note: Where wire rope rigging is fitted, be sure that a copper strip is carried down from one of the chain-plates to below the water line. One of my boats had her planking severely damaged by a lightning stroke coming down

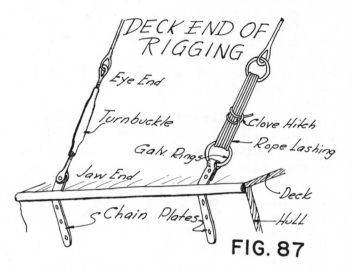

the rigging and going through her planks to reach the water. If the lightning wants to come down your shrouds, furnish it a path to travel easily.

THE LANYARD.—Our great-grandfathers used the lanyard to set up their hemp rigging as a substitute for turnbuckles. It will never bind due to corrosion and is convenient to use where masts must be removed often. The lanyard, shown also in Fig. 87, is so simple that a youngster can reeve it.

A NOTE ABOUT SPARS.—Here, as in everything else aboard the boat, the old order of things is passing. Years ago we laboriously tapered our spars, keeping all edges square. Then we carefully worked out the exact amount to take off each edge to make them octagonal. In some of the big spars, this was repeated again to make them sixteen-sided. Then we rounded them. (See Fig. 88.) Shades of Don McKay and George Steers come back to witness the degradation of the boatbuilder. Today he makes many of his spars square!

While it is possible that our forefathers would deplore the fact that the spars of today are not round, they would not be able to say that we fail to produce spars that are just as strong and much lighter. A city block away from your boat a person cannot tell whether your spars are round or square, so why worry! Once I broke a main boom on one of my boats. It was a beautiful spruce spar, sixteen feet long. The break was such that a repair was impossible. I did not want to lay the boat up while a new spar was being made so I purchased a straight-grained piece of 2" x 4" fir. Dividing this in third lengths, I tapered only one edge and left the top straight to install a sail track. For better appearance, the edges were rounded to a three-quarter-inch radius. The results were pleasing to the eye and the spar answered its purpose so well that the boat still carries it. After this the handy two-by-fours and two-by-threes were pressed into service to make masts as well as booms to the saving of hours of expensive labor.

Some spars, such as small boat booms, are made of two pieces in a "tee" shape. Screws and Weldwood glue or Cascophen are employed to make the joint between the two pieces.

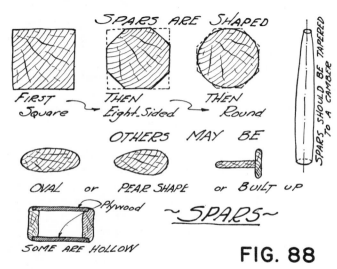

FIG. 88

Hollow spars are lighter and equally strong if properly designed. The fancy way of making them is shown in Fig. 88. However, if a proper glue joint is made, there is no reason why the plywood cannot overlap the thicker material entirely. In making these spars, solid bulkheads should be placed in between the thick material to properly space it. Where the spar goes through the deck and where spreaders or other fittings are fastened, a length of solid material should be inserted also. The thick pieces in the ordinary small boat spar need not exceed 1" nor the plywood 1/4".

BUYING SAILS.—After several sorry experiences I am dead against amateur-made sails. Sailmaking is an art. I have heard it called a black art with some justification but nevertheless no one can make a sail like a sailmaker. There are so many new fabrics on the market today that I will leave the selection of

the proper weight to the sailmaker's experience and the builder's purse.

The sailmaker needs the sail dimensions to work to. For estimating purposes all he needs is the size of the boundary edges. For actual manufacture he should have a sketch of the sail plan. If you are not capable of making a copy from this book have it photostated.

BUILD UP SPARS.—Most of the boats in this book have hollow spars constructed of solid wood and plywood sheet. Any one who has worked down a solid stick of wood to its proper diameters and taper will at once see the tremendous saving of labor involved in their making, not to mention the difficulty of securing good wood of the proper size which, in most parts of this country, is fast becoming non-existent. Aerodynamically, the spars as designed are not as good as a round- or pear-shaped one, but on the other hand not a single one of the boats using them was designed for racing. As for appearances, a hundred feet away from the boat no one will detect the difference. Strengthwise, for equivalent weight they have a decided advantage.

The spars in all cases were designed with their fore and aft sides of solid wood when vertical, or their tops and bottoms when horizontal. Regardless of their length, spacer blocks should be inserted between the wood faces at intervals of 4' to employ 8' plywood sheets. Where the splices of the wood faces occur, the spacer blocks should be made at least 24" long and the faces glued and screwed to them. Where plywood butts occur they should be 12" long, glued and nailed. Other spacers should be no less in their length than the greatest dimension of the spar. These spacer blocks are designed to be glued up from short lengths of the same material used for the solid faces. As lumber today loses about 3/16" in dressing the faces, 1" lumber becomes 13/16". Two-inch lumber dressed four sides will measure only 1 5/8" wide and three-inch, 2 5/8" wide hence the odd dimensions of the spar faces. Plywood sheets should be cut to exact parallel widths on a table saw to match the exact dimensions of the assembled wood. Plywood and wood splices should be at least 4' apart.

There is no way to assemble a spar of this kind straight and true other than to make a jig to hold it thus. Even though your material is as straight as a die it is limber until assembled. From one sorry experience of my own, when in a hurry, I learned this fact the hard way. The jig is simple, consisting of scrap pieces of two-by-four nailed to a level floor or a large bench. As one side of the spars has always been designed as a straight line the jig blocks are aligned to this by stretching a piece of fish line between the end blocks and setting all others to this. It is always well to also stretch this line very tight and see that the floor or bench is an equal distance below the line at every block. If any discrepancies occur back up the blocks at these points. (See Fig. 88A).

It is well to glue and nail all the spacer blocks against the straight side of the spar before it goes in the jig. The other side is glued in the jig. The jig blocks should be made slightly wider than the spar, allowing the spar to be wedged tight and thus eliminating a clamp at every spacer block.

Both the plywood sheets and the solid parts of the spar are glue coated before assembly. Urea glues such as *Weldwood* work well in this type of construction. Nail the plywood to the solids with four-penny galvanized-head nails or patent nails of equivalent

size. These should be driven on centers not to exceed the largest sectional dimension of the spar. The heads of the nails should be set and puttied. After one plywood side of the spar is in place it may be removed from the jig and reversed.

Several things should be observed with this type of spar. Where bolts go through the spar for rigging fittings the spacer blocks should be of hard wood. The bottom of all masts should be capped with $\frac{1}{16}''$ sheet lead set in sealing compound to a distance of 6'' above the step to prevent moisture absorption. Fiberglas is also excellent for this. Braided or solid antenna wire run inside the mast before assembly will give you a moisture free antenna for your radio that will lead into the cabin without the use of waterproof lead-in insulators. A strip of $\frac{3}{8}'' \times 1\frac{3}{16}''$ wood under the sail tracks will do away with the necessity of removing the track whenever the spar is painted.

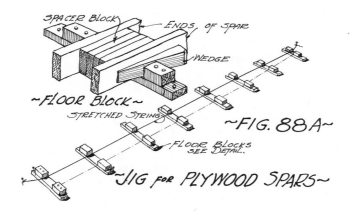

~FIG. 88A~

~JIG for PLYWOOD SPARS~

CHAPTER XIII

CAULKING AND PAINTING

The mere mention of caulking or painting never fails to bring thoughts of springtime to my mind. There is no more romance around the boatyard than the measured tick of the caulker's beetle working along with such regularity that you can match it with the second-hand of your watch. The smell of fresh paint wafted across the yard means more than an odor. It means that the new cruiser over in the boat shed is nearing completion. It means that the boats up on the skids will soon be back in the water and going their joyous way.

COTTON.—For caulking small boats, cotton is purchased in hanks. To save yourself a lot of trouble afterwards, treat the hank as follows as soon as you break its paper covering.

Unroll the cotton to its full extent. You will find that there are numerous lengths of it.

If the diameter of the separate strands is any thicker than your thumb, they should be split in half. This is easily done by starting at one end of the strand and pulling it apart.

When the hank is separated into its various strands and split, roll each strand into a separate ball. Take care that the cotton does not pick up shavings from the floor as you roll it.

The cotton is now ready for use.

CAULKING.—To caulk a seam, the cotton is first lightly shoved in the end of the seam with a jack-knife or caulking iron. With a twisting motion of the iron, the cotton is loosely inserted in the seam in a series of small tufts. This is called *tufting*. (See Fig. 89.) The cotton is now ready for *setting home*. This may be done with a caulking iron or a wheel. If the iron is used, the cotton is driven to the bottom of the seam with light taps on the head of the iron. If a seam is too tight to receive the cotton, it should be opened with a *dumb* iron, which is similar to a caulking iron except that the edge is sharper and the taper

is greater. A wide wood chisel will often substitute for a dumb iron. Where seams are extremely tight, it is good practice to split the cotton strand to avoid forcing the cotton into the seam.

CAULKING WHEEL.—My favorite caulking method is the use of the wheel. These cannot be purchased.

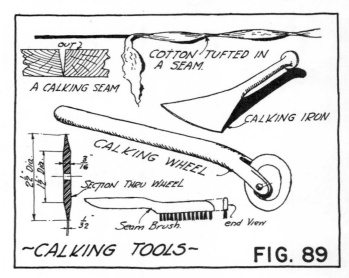

~CALKING TOOLS~ FIG. 89

If the reader wants to continue building boats for a hobby he will be wise to have one made. A disc of 3/16" steel is placed in a lathe and the edges chamfered down to a thickness of a thirty-second of an inch, as shown in Fig. 89. A slotted handle of hardwood, about a foot long and an inch square, is made to receive the wheel. A bolt through the wheel and handle completes the tool.

After the cotton is tufted in the seam, the wheel is applied to it and with a firm pressing motion and the cotton is rolled down with a to-and-fro motion until it will set no deeper.

PRIMING THE SEAM.—The seam must be primed before the putty is applied. Here the art of the painter comes into play. A peculiar type of brush is used to prime a seam. These brushes are sold in paint stores as *striping brushes* and are used by painters in Baltimore to stripe the brick lines of painted brick houses. The bristles are rather stiff and their width is just right to enter a seam.

APPLYING PUTTY.—A light coat of thick paint is applied to the seam over the cotton and, when this is dry, the seam is puttied with a good commercial caulking compound or a homemade variety made by mixing whiting with white lead to the consistency of putty. A small amount of engine lubricating oil is added to this to prevent hardening.

The compound is worked in the seams with a putty knife, an art which all written instructions can never teach you. Actual experience is the best teacher. The above-mentioned compounds should be used to putty the nail and screw heads throughout the boat.

PAINTS AND THEIR USE ON BOATS

The use of paints for marine work differs in many respects from house work, though their object is the same, the preservation of the wood by the exclusion of all moisture, and the beautifying of the surface over which the paint is applied. Boats would be sorry-looking objects, indeed, if they were not painted. The different colored streaks of wood and innumerable little plugs would make them look like the proverbial spotted pig.

RED LEAD.—When the boat is planked it is a good scheme to apply a coat of red lead paint to the inside of the planking, at least as far up as the turn of the bilge. This coat of paint should be renewed every spring, for it will keep a lot of water from soaking into the planking.

BOTTOM PAINT.—The outside, below the load water line, should be given a coat of copper bottom paint unless the bottom is to be painted with copper bronze. In the latter case, give the wood one or two coats of lead-colored paint first, forming a body on which to lay the copper bronze.

FINAL COATS.—The topsides should be given one coat of paint as soon as it is smoothed off and sandpapered and another coat when the seams have all been payed and puttied. Then it is wise to use the boat for some time and allow this paint to wear off, receiving all the knocks and scratches a boat is apt to get when first put in use, and give her the last finishing coat of paint a couple of weeks later. The first coat of paint that goes on the planking acts only as a filler, for most of it soaks into the wood. This filling coat should be thoroughly sandpapered before the application of the second coat; in fact, every coat of paint should have the body prepared by carefully washing off any grease and rubbing down any unevenness that may show with sandpaper.

WHITE PAINT.—White topsides, the color now used by nine boats out of ten, is a better color for wear than black and when worked in combination with a bright green boot-top it is as handsome. White lead mixed with oil, turps and a little dryer gives a dull white paint, rather chalky in composition, which can be retouched without showing ugly scars when it wears away in any particular spot. This is its principal advantage over the high-finish colors for they are more difficult to retouch without showing where a spot has been repainted. As to whether it preserves the wood any better than the lead paint, there is little choice between the two. However, one thing to be carefully avoided is the introduction of too much zinc into the white paint. Zinc makes a hard, brittle paint, whereas the pure lead is more flexible and less liable to chip, blister, or crack.

COLORS.—There are a number of firms today which make a specialty of manufacturing good paints, not only in the black and whites for yacht exteriors, but also any shade of color an owner may desire, and the use of colors is becoming more popular. We see boats with their topsides painted a bright green, brown or red but the principal difficulty of these colors is their liability to turn black from the gases which arise from the water near our big cities. Under these conditions, boats have been known to turn from a bright vermilion to a bilious pink overnight and take on the appearance of having been painted with a tar brush.

ZINC.—The disadvantage of using zinc in the paint for a boat's topside will be apparent when you start to scrape off the paint. The zinc becomes so hard that it almost will turn the edge of a boat-scraper. Since a boat should be painted from one to three times a season, if you want it to look presentable, you can readily see that the burning off has to take place at least once in every two or three years.

GOLD STRIPE.—The proper way to paint a gold stripe line to attain the desired brilliancy is to paint the stripe with sizing and then apply gold leaf. Most of the patent liquid bronzes have a fondness for turning into a beautiful pea green from the action of salt water.

STAINS AND VARNISHES.—When a boat is to be kept bright or the outside is to remain unpainted, as in the case of cedar or mahogany, three coats of varnish, one after the other, should be laid on over a coat of wood filler. Even mahogany is treated this way sometimes. However, owing to the unevenness of the color in the different mahogany board, generally they are stained a rich, red-brown, equalizing the color throughout the boat. This is rubbed down and two or three coats of spar varnish applied.

The degree of glossiness depends upon the amount of elbow grease expended in the rubbing-down process between the various coats of varnish.

Stain, besides giving the wood its rich, red hue, acts as a filler, filling up the grain of the wood so that the first coat of varnish lays on a smooth, glasslike coat instead of drying in and forming innumerable little pit holes. This filling process is particularly desirable for treating oak, as the open grain of oak is more noticeable when it is not filled. Unless oak is protected from the weather, the tannic acid which it contains turns into an ink-like stain from the action of salt water upon it.

A good varnish is required to withstand the wear and tear a deck gets in the course of a season. We are all familiar with the varnish used in the interior of houses and know from experience how every scratch or blow produces a white mark. If this kind of varnish is used, footprints will mar the appearance of your decks. Any man who has had to get on his marrowbones and scrape off the varnish on a boat's deck will testify that the best is none too good. Do not put on a cheap varnish because its cost is cheap. In the long run it will be expensive; it will show scratches plainly and will lose its luster quickly.

For painted decks, whether the paint is applied directly to the wood or to a canvas covering over the wood (in general use on small boats today), there are regular floor paints on the market in various shades of light yellows and browns that wear well and at a short distance cannot be distinguished from a natural wood deck.

The treatment of the boat's interior depends altogether upon the kind of wood used. If it is an expensive, handsomely grained wood. the use of a varnish through which the grain of the wood can be seen is preferred. Unless the varnishing is done properly, the results will be unsatisfactory rather than improving upon the appearance of the wood. Most amateurs varnish too fast. Each coat of varnish should be allowed to dry and then rubbed down thoroughly before the next coat is applied.

A shiny, glassy interior, reflecting all the lights, distracts attention from the beauty of the wood. Therefore, it is customary to rub down the gloss to a dull finish with pumice stone.

To varnish the interior properly, the wood should be slightly warmed and the room free from dust. Don't expect to apply a coat of varnish a half hour after you have opened the cabin doors of a yacht that has lain under a canvas cover all winter. The wood is chilled and damp, which prevents the varnish from soaking into the pores properly. Here, as on the outside of the hull, when mahogany is used for bulkheads and panel work, it is customary to even the color of the wood by applying a stain at first. In fact, in treating any wood, one coat of wood filler (a colorless pigment, which simply fills the pores of the wood and gives a splendid top coat to lay the varnish onto) will not only save a couple of coats of varnish or paint, which would otherwise be absorbed by the wood, but also gives it a finer gloss.

CLEANLINESS IN PAINTING.—Cleanliness is one of the most essential points in painting. Use clean brushes and cans and be careful to prepare the wood so that it will be in proper condition to receive the paint by treating all knots to a coat of shellac. Otherwise, the sap from the knot will stain a nice white coat to a dirty yellow and will cause varnish to blister and peel. Dampness has the same effect. You cannot varnish during a rainstorm nor on woodwork that is wet, so do not blame the paints or their manufacturer if they do not give the effect you had anticipated. Usually, the painter is responsible for poor results.

ROT PREVENTION

The old adage, "Save the surface and you save all," is just so much tommy-rot. Actually, we paint to save the interior and on wood this is not done by saving the surface. There are many cases where wood has rotted under perfectly painted exteriors. The trick in wood preservation is to *penetrate* the surface.

DRY ROT.—The enemy of all wooden structures afloat or ashore, dry rot is actually a cancer working in wood like a germ, attacking and living on the cellulose of timber. It is a vegetable of the fungus class, like a mushroom, living upon the fibers of the wood in much the same way as insect termites. Under certain conditions, wood may be infected with the germ of rot from other infected pieces.

Early in shipbuilding history it was found that *sodium chloride*, the common table salt, would prevent rot. A salting board was placed between the planking and ceiling of the old ships and granulated rock salt was thrown on it periodically. This grew down inside the ship and helped to combat the germs of rot that live in humid, damp and unventilated places. On unpainted timber, dry rot will start to show in the form of white veins on the surface, looking like mould and betraying itself by a mouldy odor. *Copper sulphate* (bluestone) is another chemical that will act in the same manner as salt. Both of these chemicals are applied to the raw wood in liberal doses in a saturated solution of water and allowed to soak in.

The tidewater builders in Dixie swear by their native pine tar to preserve timber, thinning it with kerosene, turpentine or gasoline. I have never seen signs of bad decay in a piece that had been treated with pine tar. *Carbolineum* and *creosote* are even better rot preservatives, but neither these nor pine tar should be used where the wood is to be painted later. Their unpleasant odors linger in the boat, too.

Best of all surface treatments against rot is *Cuprinol*. This is a copper solution and may be obtained in green, brown or a clear color. It may be applied as a priming coat under paint or may be used as the final coat in the void spaces of the boat. The clear solutions of Cuprinol can be used for mildew-proofing canvas.

The only positive rot-proofing is *impregnation*. This is beyond the amateur builder and its description is given only as a matter of passing interest. By this method chemical solutions, such as creosote or zinc chloride, are forced into the very inner fibers of the timber under pressure, rendering it rot and vermin proof. The zinc-chloride method diminishes the danger of fire, too.

PIGMENTS

Paint is composed of two substances, the *vehicle* and the *pigment*. The vehicle is the oil, turpentine and other liquids which tend to hold the color in suspension and carry it from the can to the wood. Once on the wood, the function of the vehicle is to leave the paint by evaporation and the products that remain form into a binder, holding the minute particles of the pigment together.

RED LEAD (OXIDE OF LEAD).—Red leads come in two basic forms, reddish powder and heavy paste. Red lead, white lead, or zinc form the base of most Red lead, white lead, or zinc forms the base of most ing process. Lead melts easily at 620° F. but in this burning process the temperature is boosted to 900° to 1200° F. At this point oxygen is induced into the lead, producing an oxidizing effect, and the resultant compound is the bright reddish powder that we know as red lead.

LITHARGE.—Another form of lead oxide, litharge is made by the same process but at different tempera-

tures. Actually, the litharge forms first and, as the temperatures are raised and additional oxygen induced, red lead is produced.

FUME RED LEAD.—This is a compound of extremely fine particles developed from metallic lead by the heat and oxygen process used in making regular red lead, but it is distilled instead of burned.

Fume red lead is used when a paint pigment of extra fineness is desired, or in other words, a thinner paint film than ordinary red lead, yet having the same dense body with the same covering power. When mixing fume red lead, a greater amount of mixing oil per pound is required than for regular red lead.

In mixing red lead powder, it is advisable to mix a little linseed oil with the powder until a pliable paste is formed. Allow this paste to stand at least 24 hours (several days would be better) to give the oil time to wet all the particles of pigment completely. Anyone who has attempted to make cocoa by adding all the water at the start will appreciate this point. This is often referred to as *breaking up* the dry red lead. Add small amounts of oil to the paste, stirring well, until the proper consistency is reached.

WHITE LEAD (BASIC CARBONATE).—White lead is made by two separate processes. In the first, metallic lead is corroded by acetic acid forming white flakes, which are later ground into a fine powder. This is sold either in this form or as paste, the latter being more favored. The second process (basic sulphate) of making white leads is from lead sulphide ore (galena) by the *sublimation* process. This process resembles that of making red lead to the extent that the ore is roasted, the fumes mixing with oxygen to form the white powder we know as white lead. This process makes finer pigment particles in much the same manner as fume red lead. White lead paste is mixed like red lead paste.

ZINC OXIDE.—A compound of zinc and oxygen, this is the finest of all white pigments. Due to its extreme hardness, zinc oxide is unaffected either by change of temperature or the gases present in the atmosphere. It is used in making white enamels and may be combined with white lead or other pigments.

COLOR PIGMENTS.—Color pigments are added to the base pigment to give color to paint. They are made principally from mineral or natural earth colors and from chemical colors. The most common natural earth pigments are siennas (raw and burnt), umbers (raw and burnt), yellow ochre and various mineral blacks. The most common chemical colors are chrome yellow Prussian blue, chrome green, cobalt blue and vermilion.

CARBON BLACKS.—Lampblack, gas black and graphite are the most common carbon blacks in use aboard ship today. They are pigments of pure ingredients and, in themselves, will make a durable paint, but their best use is to tint white, red or zinc lead to obtain a desired shade. Because of their extreme opaque quality, only a small amount with leads is required to make an excellent black paint.

DRIP BLACK, BONE BLACK, IVORY BLACK and other blacks of this type are also carbonized products but, as they are made from animal and vegetable matter, they are naturally of an inferior quality and strength. Therefore, about five times greater an amount than carbon black should be used. For tinting purposes, these blacks should not be added while in their dry state but should be mixed with a small amount of linseed oil.

All carbon blacks have a non-drying tendency and more driers must be added when they are used as pure pigment.

EXTENDERS

Extenders, as the name implies, are materials used to extend or increase the pigment base. Frequently they are called auxiliary pigments or inert ingredients, having no chemical action on the compounds of paints.

Some of the more common extenders are: Silica asbestine, china clay, barytes and gypsum.

VEHICLES

LINSEED OIL.—The most common vehicle used in making paint today is linseed oil. It is obtained from crushed flaxseed and is a natural product. It is prepared in two forms for paint mixing: raw oil, the product in its original state; boiled oil, produced from the raw oil by dissolving certain drying compounds in it. These compounds may be manganese and lead oxide or cobalt and, since they are dissolved by a heat process, the term "boiled oil" has become widely used. Boiled oil is somewhat thicker and darker than raw oil and it has a quicker drying action because of oxidation in its manufacture. Therefore, when using boiled oil, the amount of driers can be reduced considerably or omitted entirely.

CHINA WOOD OIL (TUNG OIL).—This is extracted from the nut of a tree which grows along the Tung River in China. It has stronger drying properties than linseed but has a tendency to skin over in a way that prevents its use in paint. It may be heat-treated in mixtures of resin or linseed oil after which it will dry with a smooth surface. It is more water-resisting than linseed oil but less durable.

FISH OIL.—Commonly considered a non-drying oil, fish oil is seldom used as a binding agent for good paint.

In the preparation of lubricant compounds such as are used for sluicing down running rigging and hawsers, fish oil is both practical and economical.

THINNERS

Thinners are used in paint to make it thin or to "cut" the oil vehicle and make the paint easier to spread. They also speed the "setting" of the paint. Turpentines are the best and most widely used thinners. They perform a double function in paint because, being oxidizers, they hasten drying by absorbing oxygen from the air.

GUM TURPENTINE (GUM TURPS).—Gum turpentine is made from pine resin by distillation and generally is considered to be a better thinner than wood turpentine.

WOOD TURPENTINE.—This is produced by distilling the wood of the pine tree with steam. Wood turpentine is rapidly becoming the accepted equal of "gum turps."

TURPENTINE SUBSTITUTE.—A distillate of crude oil and of a cheaper grade. Turpentine substitute should not be used to thin varnishes because it has a tendency to separate the resin from the oils.

COAL TAR THINNERS.—There are a number of coal tar distillates used as thinners in some paints that are for a specific purpose. Naphtha and benzol are the most common.

DRIERS

Certain chemical compounds of a metallic nature have been found to add some drying properties to vehicle oils and thus shorten the drying time for paint.

Driers are manufactured chemical products, the most widely used being *Japan* drier.

VARNISH, SHELLAC AND LACQUER

VARNISH.—A compound of resin, boiled oil, thinners and driers. The melted resin is mixed with the boiled oil and the thinners and driers added. Turpentine is generally used as thinners for the best varnish. Oxides of lead manganese make good driers.

To prepare the surface for varnish, clean well, fill and rub down. Dust off all particles and apply varnish with a varnish brush by flowing it on in a smooth coating.

SHELLAC.—In its raw form, shellac is a flaky substance taken from a tree that grows in India. The flakes are soluble only in alcohol and, as the alcohol evaporates rapidly, the shellac soon dries to a hard, smooth surface.

There are numerous manufactured substitutes for shellac and most of them have a trade name ending in "lac."

Shellac and its substitutes are widely used as a filling coat on new wood.

LACQUER.—A compound of shellac, coloring matter and other ingredients dissolved in alcohol. Lacquer is widely used for decorative work.

PREPARED PAINTS

Ready mixed paint is probably best for the amateur boatbuilder because he will use reasonably small quantities of many kinds of paint. It will not pay to buy the many different ingredients and mix small quantities.

To prepare ready-mixed paint, pour off most of the liquid (vehicle) into another can and stir well the pasty pigment which has settled to the bottom. During the stirring process add small amounts of the liquid and continue stirring until all the liquid is used. The mixed paint should be well boxed before it is used. Boxing paint means pouring paint, back and forth, from one can to another until the mixture is smooth and free from lumps.

The following are the most common ready-mixed paints; their names, in most cases, define their use:

Hull or freeboard paint (usually black)
Inside flat paint (white & colors)
Gloss paint (inside & outside)
Inside enamel (white & colors)
Outside flat (white & colors)
Outside or cabin enamels (white & colors)
Overhead paint
Mast and spar paint
Motor paint (heat resisting)
Signal color
Hold paint
Deck paint
Deck lacquer
Boot-topping
Waterway paint
Water line paint
Spar varnish (outside)
Inside varnish
Shellacs (clear, white & orange)
The materials for mixing paint usually consist of:
White lead
White zinc
Red lead (powder or paste)
Color pigments (various)
Carbon black (usually lampblack)
Driers
Linseed oil (boiled or raw)
China wood oil
Fish oil
Turpentine (or substitute)
Alcohol

APPLYING PAINT

Never apply paint in a thick coat. It will not dry and harden but will rub off easily for days afterward and catches dirt continually. Put it on in thin coats and it will dry quickly and form a hard surface.

Never paint over a dirty surface or a rough, unprepared surface. Paint is used too frequently to save scrubbing. The surface to be painted must be cleaned and scrubbed down to a smooth surface before any paint is applied.

PRIMING COAT.—Again emphasizing the fact that the priming coat can only be put on once, it is extremely important to brush the paint into the wood if it is to take hold. Do not flow it on, brush it in.

Many compounds have been developed for the primary coat, but red lead has always been supreme in this field and is favored by marine and civil engineers all over the world.

A good red lead priming paint should contain turpentine as thinner and a good drier.

SECOND COAT.—When applying a second coat of the same color as the priming coat, it is wise to add a small amount of lampblack or some coloring to give the second coat a different tint. If this is done, missed spots or *holidays* may easily be detected.

Subsequent coats may be the same color as the priming coat or any color desired for decoration.

A new practice is to use an aluminum pigment mixed with zinc oxide and a varnish vehicle for a second coating. This is a good mixture to cover red lead because it dulls the tint and a fine white finish will take well when applied over it.

All paint should be brushed out thin, not flowed on.

BRUSHES

TYPES OF BRUSHES.—Duster brush, used in cleaning; sash trim or tool brush, used on small surfaces; varnish brushes; oval, flat or French bristle (the oval is used in rough work, the flat for medium and the French bristle for high-grade work); flat brushes, ranging in size from two to four inches; wall or surface brushes, from four to six inches; wire brushes, of various sizes, to brush blisters and rust off iron.

USE OF THE BRUSH.—The following instructions on the use of paint brushes should be helpful.

1. Hold the brush by the handle and not by the stock, otherwise the hands may become poisoned.

2. Hold the brush at right angles to the surface, with only the ends of the bristles touching and lift it clear of the surface when finishing a stroke! Otherwise the surface will be uneven and have laps and spots which give a very poor appearance.

3. Do not cover the brush with the paint; dip the ends of the bristles only. Do not repeat this until the preceding charge has been exhausted. Apply the paint with long strokes parallel to the grain of the wood. If painting along smooth surfaces, draw the brush along the entire surface, wherever possible, to reveal as few breaks as possible.

4. The successive applications should be applied systematically. On the second application be sure to cross the preceding work at right angles. In each complete application keep all strokes parallel to each other. During the crossing use a medium pressure; in the final application use a light pressure. The final application should be in the lengthwise direction of the work.

5. An overhead surface should be systematized thus: Lay off the ceiling panels fore and aft and the beams athwartship.

6. Vertical surfaces, bulkheads, etc., should be painted with the lines vertical; the boat's topsides horizontal. Each succeeding coat of paint should be laid off in the same direction; this is an exception to rules.

7. During the work keep the paint in the pot well mixed.

9. Use two coats of thin or medium paint rather than one coat of heavy because a heavy coat will show the brush marks and will give an uneven finish.

10. Wait until the preceding coat is entirely dry before applying the second coat. Paint dries after coming on contact with the air; a second coat would retard this process.

CARE OF BRUSHES.—Good painting requires good brushes and a good brush deserves good care. To clean a brush that is not to be used for an indefinite time: rinse well in kerosene, wash in warm soda water or with brown laundry soap, rinse well in clean water, shake out and hang up to dry. If the brush is to be used again within a few days, it should be kept in a *brush-keeper*, which is usually made from empty kerosene cans or such and partially filled with kerosene or water. The brush is suspended in the trough either by a wire inserted through the handle and hooked on the edge, or by a rod through the handle laid across the opening. In either case, the bristles of the brush should be kept immersed in the liquid without touching the bottom.

PAINTING WRINKLES

Handfuls of clean rope yarns make excellent "soogee" rags and will remove the most stubborn dirt from paint work.

A few turns of rags around a paint brush just above the bristles will stop the paint from working onto the handle. A half of a toy rubber ball, cut and fitted over the brush handle, is also good. Try this the next time you have to paint the overhead.

On some brushes the bristles may spread. To prevent this bind them with a soft wire or twine much like the straws of a broom are bound.

Generally, the brush is held by the handle but frequently the wrist and palm of the hand get tired and sore. In this case, experienced painters have found comfort and ease by changing for a spell and holding the brush by the *brindle*, or metal band, which allows plenty of play on the brush. Keep the *brindle* clean.

When mixing paint in more than one container, remember to *box* the contents together to get a uniform paint film. This boxing of paint is necessary especially when using colors.

Considering the prompt action of driers and turpentine in paint, it is advisable not to put these ingredients into the pigment until just before using. While paints should be mixed about 24 hours previous to their use, they should not be allowed to stand for long periods of time unless they are kept in well-sealed and airtight containers.

For a quick set and a thorough drying, it is suggested that a small amount of powdered litharge be stirred into the finishing coat. Paints containing litharge should be used within two or three days after preparation. If boiled oil or litharge is used, add only half the specified amount of driers.

Alcohol is an efficient cleaner for brushes that have been used in shellacs. After cleaning with alcohol use brown soap and warm water. Shellac brushes should never be allowed to stand long after using, as shellac has a very quick drying point.

In revarnishing a surface, a light sandpapering before applying varnish will give it an ideal finish. In new varnish work, treating the wood to a little tung or raw oil will give the varnish a good hold. Surfaces must be kept free of dust while varnishing, as this will show up in the finished surface. It is not advisable to varnish in the direct hot sun or damp weather.

Linseed oil is useful for softening brushes that have become stiff.

It is necessary to have a hard undercoat for permanence in painting and, to attain this, do not put too much oil in a priming coat.

While the addition of driers to paint is desirable, too much drier will cause too rapid top-drying resulting in a wrinkled effect.

One gallon of correctly mixed paint will cover approximately 600 square feet of wood surface.

Running, streaking and sagging may be caused by improper mixing and stirring as well as by applying the paint too thick.

A WORD ABOUT ANTI-FOULING PAINTS

I know of no superior anti-fouling paint. All of them fulfill their manufacturer's claims (more or less). The red type seems to have good qualities but the fishermen who must buy the best for the least money swear by the brown type. Green anti-fouling paint seems to be worthless here on the Chesapeake except for boot-topping. Often, when I was younger, I would try out some particular make of bottom paint. At that season's end my boat would come out of the water with scarcely any barnacles on her bottom. Eureka! I had found the ideal bottom paint. The next season the same boat would come out of the same waters covered with these pesky critters. I would be dumbfounded until I'd hear old Till Smith or Uncle Gabe exclaim, "Dem barnykills sure is bad dis year!" Some years they will and some years they won't. The reader must choose his own bottom paint.

It is best to prime the bottom of a new boat with anti-fouling paint mixed thin with turps or gasoline. At least two coats more should be applied over the priming. The last coat of bottom paint should be applied just before the boat enters the water. Where the toredo is prevalent, it is customary to haul a boat twice a season and apply the bottom paint. Boatyards in your own locality will inform you of this.

It has been ten years since the foregoing discussion on paint has been written. We have seen the advent of many new types of paint made possible by the advent of plastics. The foregoing material is time tried and positive. Some of the new paints are covered with extravagant sales talk and some of them have not lived up to their original claims. On the other hand some show wonderful promise, witness the improvement in the automotive field. Buy your paint on performance and not on manufacturers' claims.

I have often been asked to recommend paint by friends and clients and have lost both by doing so. I have seen the very best of paints and varnishes improperly applied. I have seen others thinned with liquids that were never intended for paint thinners and when the finished result was not satisfactory Sam Rabl was a heel of the first order for having even suggested that particular paint. No sir! You choose your own paint and we all will remain friends.

CHAPTER XIV

USEFUL INFORMATION

METAL WORK

Today, with an acetylene torch and electric welding machine in almost every garage, the manufacture of special fittings about the boat presents no difficulty. Many small fittings that formerly were forged at the village blacksmith shop are now welded at the garage. Electric welding may be done on all iron and steel fittings. For brass or bronze, the acetylene torch comes into use by brazing their various components.

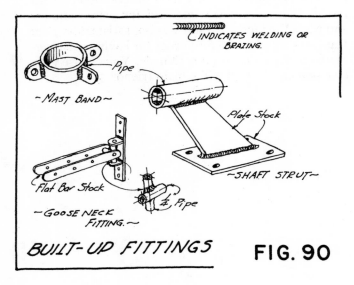

BUILT-UP FITTINGS FIG. 90

Figure 90 shows a few possibilities of the built-up fitting. Mast bands are made from ordinary water or steam pipe with lugs welded or brazed on. Struts are made from pipe and plate stock cut with a torch and welded together. The pipe is selected large enough to leave about a quarter of an inch all around the shaft and babbitt poured after the strut and shaft are fitted to the boat. The shaft is smoked with a candle to prevent the babbitt from adhering to it. No

better bearing could be desired. To fit a *Cutless* rubber bearing, the pipe should be selected from extra heavy stock and bored after welding to a loose fit around the bearing (plus five thousandths).

The welded steel fittings should be hot-dip galvanized to protect them from the effects of salt water. While this is beyond the capabilities of the average mechanic, the fittings may be sent to firms who do this sort of work. Welded steel shaft struts should not be galvanized. Salt water and the bronze wheel soon will set up enough electrolysis to destroy the galvanized coating.

Often special metal shapes are required aboard a boat, notably in propeller struts. A knowledge of casting, pattern and foundry methods will save the builder quite a bit of money and solve many construction difficulties.

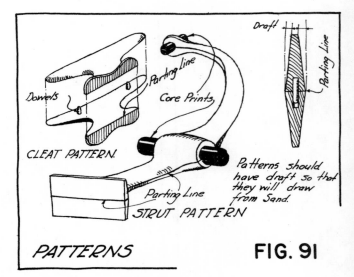

PATTERNS FIG. 91

To make a casting, the moulder in the foundry first makes an impression in sand with a pattern, Fig. 91.

Then he fills the impression with liquid metal which eventually hardens to the shape of the pattern. The sand is held in a box called a *flask*. The flask is composed of two boxes which accurately match each other when put together, Fig. 92.

Sometimes difficulties occur in removing the pattern from the sand. In this case, the impression must

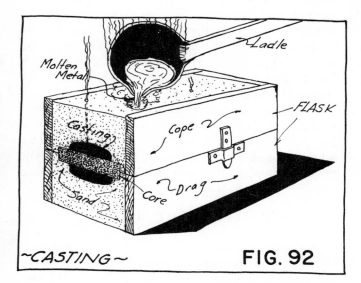

~CASTING~   **FIG. 92**

be made in the sand of both parts of the flask. The lower part of the flask is called the *drag*, the upper part the *cope*. Frequently, to facilitate removal, the pattern must be split in two parts so that it can be moulded both in the cope and the drag. Here the pattern must also be doweled so that it may be accurately fitted together again in the moulding process. Often, where a small number of castings is required from a pattern and the moulder can work it in his flask without a lot of trouble, the pattern is not split.

To prepare his mould, the moulder first places the pattern (or half-pattern) on his moulding board. He places his drag around it in an upside down position. Then he fills the drag with moulding sand, ramming and packing it tight around the pattern. After this operation is complete, he turns the drag over and places the other half of his pattern to match that in the sand of the drag. Next the cope is set on top of the drag and it is filled with sand, leaving an entrance called the *gate* and an opening called the *vent* to allow the passage of air when the molten metal is poured. The mould is now ready for casting.

Often a casting will require a hollow interior or a hole through it. To do this, a pattern of the shape of the desired opening is made from closely-packed loam

held together with an adhesive. This loam pattern is set in the sand in such a way that it stops the molten metal from flowing into the desired hollow part. This loam pattern is called the *core*. It is necessary to support the core in the sand. This is done by creating impressions in the sand alongside the pattern in which the core may lie. The depressions are moulded by placing auxiliary parts on the pattern and they are called *core* prints.

So that the pattern may be easily withdrawn from the sand, a certain amount of taper is necessary. This taper is called *drag* or *slip*. Since molten metal shrinks in the cooling process, it is necessary to allow for this shrinkage by making the pattern longer. For brass or bronze castings required for boats, three-sixteenths (3/16) of an inch should be added on the pattern for every foot of length of casting. Patterns are coated with red enamel or orange shellac. *Core prints* and the inside of *core boxes* are painted black.

MARLINSPIKE SEAMANSHIP

Most textbooks on this subject tend to confuse the reader with too many details. Although a lot of the information is of interest, a grea tdeal of it is not needed, especially by the small boatman. However, some knowledge of rope and its uses is essential.

The most commonly used ropes are Manila and wire. Manila rope may be either three or four stranded and is designated as to size by its circumference, except in the smaller sizes, which are designated by the diameter or the number of threads they contain. Manila rope is usually twisted, or layed, right-handed. It is made up of a number of yarns or threads which are twisted into strands. These strands are, in turn, twisted into rope and for very large sizes, the rope may be twisted into cable.

Before the fibres from which Manila rope is made are twisted into yarns, they are sprayed with oil, which constitutes about 12% of the weight of the finished rope. This oil acts as a lubricant, easing the strands of friction when a strain is applied and it also helps to preserve the rope.

It must be remembered that fibre ropes will shrink when wet. Therefore, the strain on any rope must be eased off in damp and rainy weather, or the line will be over-stressed and may even part. Another point to remember is that rope must be thoroughly dried to prevent rotting before being stowed away.

Sometimes linen and cotton ropes are used on yachts. The same precautions must be observed in their use. They present a fine appearance, and are used extensively for fancy work, but they do not possess the strength of Manila.

Wire rope is designated as to size by its diameter. It is further determined by the number of wires in each strand and the number of strands in the rope. It is used on small boats for guys and stays, principally, though it can be used for running rigging, such as tiller ropes and halyard pendants. It should be galvanized or stainless steel when used for standing rigging and may be further protected against weather by a coating of white lead and tallow.

A kink in wire rope will ruin it and a rope that has been kinked should only be used under greatly reduced load. Where it is to run over a sheave, the diameter of the sheave must not be less than twenty times the diameter of the wire and may be larger if the rope is stiff. The rope should be discarded when about half the thickness of the outside wires are worn through.

Wire rope may be spliced in a manner similar to

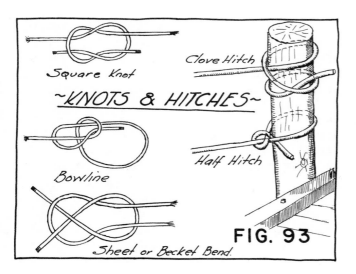

FIG. 93

fibre rope. It also can be made up by the use of sockets, the wire being secured in the throat of the socket by filling it with melted lead.

Though there are thousands of knots, most of them have limited applications and usually can be replaced by a simpler knot.

The simplest and probably the most useful is the square knot or reef knot, Fig. 93. Its only disadvantage is that it cannot be used for bending together two ropes of different size, unless the ends are stopped down.

Almost as simple, and one which may be used where the rope are of different size, is the sheet or

becket bend. It is particularly valuable with small lines, such as fish line, though, of course, it may be used with larger ropes as well.

The bowline, used for forming a loop of any size, is indispensable to the yachtsman and should be as familiar to him as knotting his tie. It is absolutely secure and will not jam or slip. It may be used for forming an eye in the end of a mooring line and experience soon will show its wide usefulness.

Besides the knots, a knowledge of one or two hitches will prove of value. The half-hitch is useful in mooring, or anywhere that a line is to be made fast to a piece of timber. Another hitch, useful for similar purposes, is the clove-hitch.

A thorough knowledge of the foregoing knots and hitches are all that the average man needs around a boat. Practice them until you are certain of them all and are able to tie them in the dark. Then you may be confident that your work is seamanlike and safe.

GET THE RIGHT MOORING

Insurance statistics of marine casualties show that over forty per cent of damages paid are caused by bad anchor devices. Many an owner will lavish money on expensive fittings for his boat and then, either through ignorance or a desire to save money on an invisible accessory will trust her future to inferior ground tackle.

There are as many kinds of anchors as there are boats; they range from the humble block of a discarded auto motor to the expensive bronze anchors of the folding type. The kedge anchor Fig. 94, is

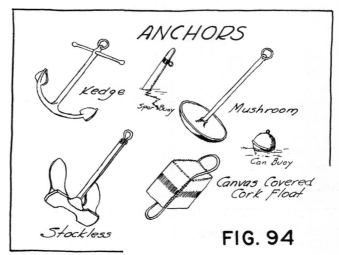

FIG. 94

the most common type, being what everyone conceives when the word anchor is mentioned. It consists of three parts: starting from the bottom, the flukes, the shank and the arms or stock. The flukes are the real holding power—their function is to dig into the mud. The stock tends to keep the anchor in a position so that the flukes will "bite." The shank forms the connecting bar between the flukes and the stock. Without a doubt, weight for weight, the kedge anchor has more holding power than any other type. It has a number of disadvantages, the greatest being its unwieldiness aboard a small boat. To overcome this difficulty the arms sometimes are made to slide through the shank so that it may be laid flat on the deck.

A further improvement on the kedge anchor is the folding kedge in which both the arms and flukes fold against the shank. This allows the anchor to be stowed in a small space. One great disadvantage of the kedge anchor is its tendency to foul on a rock bottom by having the flukes catch in a rock and stick so that the cable often has to be cut to free the vessel. Another fault is that, when the boat lies at anchor in a calm and slowly rides around the anchor, the mooring cable becomes fouled on the flukes. When this happens and a blow comes up, the pull of the cable is on the flukes and the anchor pulls out. The kedge is not recommended for a permanent mooring.

The stockless, or Navy-type anchor was invented to overcome the disadvantages of the kedge anchor. This anchor is easy to stow and is practically non-fouling. It requires about thirty per cent more weight for the same holding power and must be fitted with a slightly longer cable than the kedge. The mushroom anchor has more holding power than any other anchor in a muddy or sandy bottom and is the type that the lightships at sea use to ride out the winter gales.

A novel anchor, intended for all purposes except permanent moorings, was introduced recently. It is called a "plow" anchor because its peculiar shape resembles a plowshare. Developed originally for flying boats, it is light in weight compared to other anchors and is said to have more holding power per pound than any of the standard types. This anchor is particularly suitable for small boats having limited stowage space.

In addition to the manufactured anchors, there are other makeshift devices which will hold a small boat if they are heavy enough. An old motor block will hold any small boat up to twenty feet; a better

anchor is a flat block of concrete with a ring-bolt cast in its center. A car wheel with a bolt through the center forms another excellent anchor. All of these, of course, are for permanent moorings where the anchor does not have to be taken aboard the boat.

The anchor is connected to the boat through the mooring cable. This may be of Manila rope, chain or, in some of the more expensive outfits, stainless steel cable. Rope has the advantage of being easy to stow but when it gets old its strength is a doubtful factor and it should be renewed every season when used as a mooring cable. Chain, if galvanized, is excellent but will sometimes impose quite a strain on the mooring bit of the boat because of its inability to yield to a strain. A combination of half chain and half rope, with the rope having strength equivalent to the chain, is perhaps the best of all mooring cables. The weight of the chain keeps that portion of the cable on bottom so that the boat has to lift it in a seaway, thus eliminating any shock on the cable. The chain is at the anchor end where it also takes the wear of the cable dragging on the bottom.

Some means of marking the anchor location must be provided. This device is generaly a buoy, which may consist of any device that will float. There are three types of buoys in general use, the can, the spar and the cork float, Fig. 94. Most can buoys are manufactured and vary from a ball of metal to a cone. The spar buoys are sticks of wood attached to the anchor cable, while the cork float is exactly what its name implies. These may be constructed of cork salvaged from several old life preservers and sewed in a canvas bag which will fit tight around the cork. Ropes sewed around the bag, as illustrated, form an efficient way of picking it up. The whole assembly should be painted white so that it can be seen at night. When the skipper is ready to cast off this mooring, he attaches the float to the eye of the mooring cable and simply heaves it overboard. When ready to pick it up again, it is a simple matter to catch either the buoy or mooring eye with a boat hook and haul the cable on board. This eliminates the catching of a messy can or spar fouled with seagrass and barnacles.

Perhaps the simplest pick-up buoy is a piece of 2" x 4" plank painted white and fastened to a light line spliced into the mooring pennant. This is left permanently attached and is laid on deck or hung in the rigging when hauled aboard. Lightweight balsa pick-up buoys, serving the same purpose, are carried by most marine supply dealers and are inexpensive.

Another type of simple buoy is a beer barrel with

a bolt run through its bung and out the other side. Care should be taken that the ends of the bolt are made watertight. Like all other buoys and spars, with the exception of the pick-up, this type is secured to the mooring cable and a separate line is led from it to the boat. A simple way to anchor a small boat offshore is to place a pulley on the anchor and lead an endless line from the anchor to the shore. A tail attached to the endless line is secured to the boat so that it may be hauled in or out at will.

This idea is useful on a boat camping trip, when one wishes to sleep ashore.

The length of an anchor cable should be twenty times the depth of water.

Size of Boat		Size of Anchor		
Sheltered Harbor	Exposed	Stockless or Mushroom	Size of Rope	Size of Chain
18 Ft.—20 Ft.	14 Ft.—16 Ft.	50 lb.	3/4″ dia.	1/4″
20 Ft.—25 Ft.	16 Ft.—20 Ft.	100 lb.	7/8″ dia.	5/16″
25 Ft.—30 Ft.	20 Ft.—25 Ft.	150 lb.	1″ dia.	3/8″
30 Ft.—35 Ft.	25 Ft.—30 Ft.	200 lb.	1-1/8″ dia.	7/16″

MARINE-CONVERTING A CAR MOTOR

In a free choice between auto and marine engines, perhaps the marine is the better selection, but this should not stop auyone from putting a converted auto engine in his boat until such time as he can afford a real marine motor. Auto engines were designed for a specific purpose, just as were marine and aviation engines, but auto engines have flown and aviation engines have driven boats, so there you are!

When installing an auto engine in a boat it is wise to use as few home-made conversion parts as are necessary to make a satisfactory installation. As a rule, it is the conversion gadgets that give the most trouble. Most of the fishermen's installations use only a water pump and a universal joint. These conversions are going out daily and doing their job in a manner that disproves for all time the old bunk that an auto engine will not work in a boat. All that has been written on the subject to the contrary can be nullified by one visit to any fishing village and hearing the fishermen brag of their Fords, "Chevvys" and Buicks—and they are not talking about their cars but their boat motors.

The auto engine was designed to run on a level roadway most of the time and it should be placed in the boat in this position. The most successful installations have their beds level and the difference of angle is taken up by a universal joint, Fig. 95. This furnishes the most practical and easiest solution to the oiling problem. The auto carburetor will work

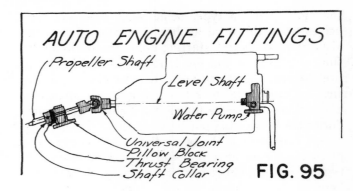

best when level, also. Regular marine carburetors are tilted to take care of the engine setting at an angle and the oiling systems also are designed for this condition.

Universal joints may be salvaged from an auto graveyard, but it is best to purchase one that is flexible as well as universal. The boat will weave and twist and auto bearings cannot be expected to take care of this condition. Be sure to align the shaft as accurately as possible after the boat is overboard. A thrust bearing should be fitted somewhere between the universal and the stuffing box. The most practical thrust assembly consists of a steel collar pinned to the propeller shaft with a ball-thrust plate between this and a pillow-block bearing, directly behind the universal joint.

Cooling is the next major problem. The water in the auto engine is cooled in the radiator because of the necessity of using the same water over and over again. This condition is not present in a boat and the radiator can be dispensed with. A water pump of at least 1/2″ discharge is fitted to the motor at the most convenient point. Sometimes the motor already has a water pump attached and this is replaced with a larger one. The most convenient point to attach the pump is to the old fan pulley shaft.

When the motor is to be used on salt water, the problem of corrosion arises, as brine will eat through thin cylinder walls which were not intended to combat this element. One of the best things to do in this case is to install a fresh-water cooling system. This may be one of two types; the keel radiator or the heat exchanger system. The keel radiator, Fig. 96, is simply a length of large-size copper tubing running outside the hull against the keel through which fresh water is circulated by the water pump. A tank inside the boat is placed so that its bottom is above the highest part of the cylinder heads and its function is to keep the system always full of water. From time

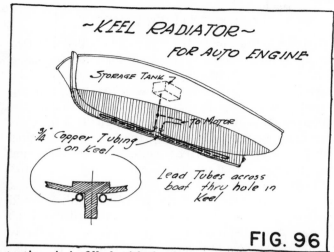

~KEEL RADIATOR~
FOR AUTO ENGINE

STORAGE TANK

TO MOTOR

¾" Copper Tubing
on Keel

Lead Tubes across
boat thru hole in
Keel

FIG. 96

to time it is filled with fresh water to replace losses in the system due to leakage and evaporation.

The heat exchanger is, in reality, a water radiator in which the warm water from the motor is cooled by cooler water from the sea without actual contact except through the heat exchanger tubes, much as in the same way the passage of cool air through the radiator in a car does the same trick.

You may find that the absence of a breeze under the crankcase of the auto engine will raise the temperature of the lubricating oil to a point where its efficiency is impaired. This difficulty can be overcome by placing coils of copper tubing in the oil pan in such a way that they will not interfere with the crankshaft. Water is taken from the outside of the boat through the coil before it reaches the pump and is delivered to the engine jacket. As for the manifold, in a boat this part also lacks the cooling air that the forward motion in a car imparts to it and, if the user is able to purchase a water-cooled manifold from one of the companies manufacturing conversion parts, all well and good. Failing this, keep all woodwork at least 15" away from the manifold and protect the wood with sheet asbestos. Do not, under any circumstances, cover the manifold with asbestos. This practice only makes the manifold burn out quicker due to the fact that the hot air surrounding it cannot escape and the manifold retains heat instead of losing it.

The use of common sense, a subject that I have often preached in connection with other boat problems, holds good in this case. Do not expect an engine that is on its last legs in a run-down auto to perform miracles in a boat. The motor should be in reasonably good condition when installed and the best motors are those that are new and have been salvaged from wrecked cars.

Auto motors present no corrosion problems in their native element so this should be taken care of by painting all the steel and iron parts below the mounting lugs with at least three coats of red lead paint. It will be impossible to get to them later. Scrape all the aluminum parts and give them three coats of a hardbody bituminous paint.

Examine all wiring in the installation. Electricity has a bad habit of leaking through water, so be sure that all starting and ignition wires are well out of the wet.

As for the transmission, it may be used as is; it may be entirely removed from the motor and a regular marine reverse gear connected; or it may be rebuilt. The rebuilding job or the marine reverse gear have the advantage of giving the propeller full motor speed in reverse. The boat can be reversed with the regular reverse in the transmission but it will be very slow. The latter method is the one generally used in the fishing boats. Most installations of a marine reverse gear are not entirely satisfactory unless both the motor and gear are connected with a steel frame of angle or channel sections and this frame, in turn, secured to the motor foundation of the boat.

CONVERSION KITS.—Nowadays it is possible to purchase conversion kits for most of the popular makes of auto engines. These include a water-cooled manifold and circulating pump as well as a conversion for the transmission so that when you are finished you have an almost-one-hundred-percent marine engine. Several companies deal in these conversions exclusively. Both the *Barr* and the *Osco* conversions are excellent.

Another factor determining the life of an auto motor in a boat is to see that the motor is not run above an economical speed. Just because the motor roars at a great clip doesn't mean that it is moving the boat along at a speed consistent with the noise. Most auto motors will turn at a higher speed than is economical for a marine propeller. Throttling the motor to a point where the boat will move along at a good rate of speed, without racing the motor, is the best practice. You would not expect the motor in a car to last long if it were pushed to the limit. Certainly it cannot be expected to give good service in a boat, under conditions for which it was not designed.

AIR COOLED MOTORS

A word about the new aircooled motors which are excellent for the small motor boats and auxiliary power for sailing craft, may not be out of place at this time.

The small aircooled motor needs no water cooling system being, as its name implies, cooled by air. Do not stick one of these motors away in an enclosed box and restrict its air circulation. If a box is needed be sure that two sides of it are open. Galvanized expanded metal or wire mesh may be used to cover the open sides of the box. Most of these little units are fitted with their own gas tank. In fitting the motor be sure there is ample room to fill the tank and room to swing the rope to start them. Both W. C. and Perko manufacture fittings for these small motors, including rudders, shafts, skegs and all the necessary stuffing boxes and bearings.

Where one of these motors is fitted as auxiliary power for a small boat it is not necessary to bore the skeg to pass the shaft. A simple method of installing the motor and shaft off center is shown in Fig. 96A.

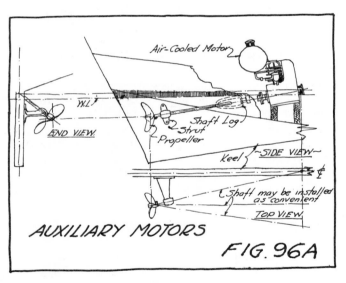

AUXILIARY MOTORS

FIG. 96A

It is not even necessary to run the shaft parallel to centerline. It may be installed so that the motor is outboard of the propeller and tucked away under a seat or it may be placed on center and the shaft offset enough to allow the propeller to clear the skeg or keel. My own *Picaroon* carried this sort of installation for years without any noticeable bad effects. In fact she sailed better and had more speed than identical motors installed in identical boats which worked their wheels on center through an aperture in the keel and rudder. The wheel working out in undisturbed water was evidently the answer to its greater efficiency.

MOTOR OPERATION

Men who own motorboats may be divided into two classes: those who strictly leave their motors alone and those who tinker. I refuse to state which of the two is the happier. Happiness often lies in doing what you like to do and if you like to tinker, the annoyance of having a motor continually out of order may be compensated by the fact that it takes tinkering to put it right again. Further tinkering again throws it out of adjustment and the cycle starts all over; it's an endless performance.

From my own experience in a boatyard, I would advise that you let your motor alone until it will no longer run satisfactorily; then, unless you absolutely know what you are doing, take it to a competent boatyard and let their mechanics have a look at it. You may have been a man who has built his own boat in a manner that excited the envy of professionals. That workmanship was the result of experience. If you have the same experience on marine motors then, by all means, fix it when it fails but don't tinker with it. I have seen men continually adjusting and grinding valves, fitting new spark plugs and keeping their motors in tip-top shape (as they thought) but the experienced ear on the dock knows full well that the motor is not working properly. It might be well to note how the motors of the fishermen will look as dirty as all get out, but will perform day by day without failure. The fishermen are too busy to tinker. Look at all the automobiles on the street running all the time and whose drivers have not the mechanical ability to drive a nail straight. They don't tinker with their motors. On the other hand, a friend of mine owns a Packard. John loves to tear that motor down. Time and again he will come to work with hands begrimed from oil and grease and barked knuckles. When the motor is working right, John will stand beside it and, with a loving expression in his voice, exclaim "Don't she sound sweet!" The next day John is tearing that motor down again to see what made it tick so well. Such is happiness!

There are other men who must have on the dashboard of their boats all the instruments and gadgets that you would find on the instrument panel of a B-29. I am one of these; perhaps I should have said "was," for I have learned that instruments can be a source of worry if you let them. It took several years of looking at a tachometer on the same engine to learn that atmospheric conditions from day to day will affect a high-speed motor to as many as three hundred revs. I no longer worry over a loss of speed after looking at the barometer. A high barometer means more air pressure at the motor and acts, in a measure, as a super-charger. A low barometer means a loss of revs. Conditions of the water in which the boat is running can also affect the cooling and make the tach drop. Forget it! On the other hand, it was noting a quick drop in the oil-pressure gauge that saved a motor when the shaft of an oil pump let go. Watch the oil pressure and charging rate!

EMERGENCY EQUIPMENT

At some time or other in a boat's life there arises an emergency. Sometimes it is small but inconvenient at other times it borders on a catastrophe. While it would be folly to carry the necessary means of combating every possible emergency there are those which can be guarded against with little effort and expense.

The most important article of emergency equipment is the first aid kit. This may range from the simple ones purchased in a dime store to the elaborate kind that are waterproof and contain all sorts of medical aids. This type may now be purchased as surplus war equipment as they were placed aboard every life boat and raft both in the Navy and Merchant Service.

Second in importance is emergency grub. This also may be purchased in sealed watertight tins that stow in a very small space and drinking water is also put up in sealed tins. Often these will be required because a breakdown keeps you away from a meal or because the grub you brought along on the trip has been spoiled or in some way has been dropped overboard. Emergency rations (as those who have *had* to eat them know) are not quite as palatable as that chicken sandwich you had in the lunch box but they are welcome in a pinch. Chlorinated city water will keep indefinitely in sealed glass bottles so be sure to have a quart tucked away somewhere on the boat. Thirst is worse than hunger to endure. Speaking of thirst, it is a good policy to keep a pint of medical brandy concealed from your guests but ready in an emergency for someone who has taken a drenching in cold water.

Money is another thing to keep tucked away in some obscure corner of the boat. Folding money in this case is useless as it moulds in the dampness. Several dollars in quarters or halves will often do more good than all the emergency rations that the boat can hold. If the gas tank runs dry in a place too far to row the boat home the man at the gas dock will

not appreciate a can of Spam in return for the product from his pump. Then again you are liable to meet some fisherman when your own catch is very small. Saint Peter himself was a fisherman and will not chalk up a mark against you in the books if you buy big ones to take home and show the folks ashore what you caught.

Motor spares may be classed as emergency equipment. These may be numerous enough to rebuild the engine if necessary but the following list will answer in almost any emergency as they are the parts that cause most of the trouble.

Spark plugs
Rotor for distributor
Set of distributor points
Condenser
Diaphragm for fuel pump
Glass and screen for strainer
A couple of feet of gas line and fittings to piece out a break.

A self igniting water light on a ring buoy is a very good safeguard to have aboard the boat. One of the worst things to have happen is for a man to go overboard from a moving boat on a dark night. Under these conditions the man disappears before the boat may be turned around to find him. The direction of sound at night is confusing and even though a tight circle is turned there is danger of running the man down. The self igniting light on the ring buoy gives a rendezvous for both the man overboard and the boat. In connection with this do not allow your guests to sleep on a cabin top or open deck. I have seen men go to their death this way when on a perfectly calm night a boat was rolled by waves from a passing steamer.

Last but not least are emergency keys. Keep one for the cabin and one for the ignition hidden away in some secret spot on the boat. I, also, have left my keys at home.

A BOAT TRAILER

We are indebted to my old friend Rog. Gintling and to *Mechanix Illustrated* for the design of the excellent trailer shown in Fig. 97. Rog. has swung the whole regatta circuit dragging his many famous Snipes and his Moth behind him like Mary's little lamb. From personal knowledge of this trailer and Rog., I can recommend none better.

A great deal more use and enjoyment can be derived from a small boat by having a trailer to carry it from place to place. A boat taken along on your vacation will increase the pleasure of your trip; more-over the boat on the trailer affords a good place to stow the equipment one needs on an extended trip. Those who have small racing boats will find a trailer indispensable for getting around to the various regattas. To a person living in a city a trailer will make a small boat feasible where it was not practical before.

The trailer shown in the photograph and detailed in the drawings will prove a good one for boats ranging from a small dinghy to an eighteen-foot sailboat. It is very easy and economical to build, and will track nicely behind a car.

The first thing to do in building the trailer is to secure a running gear. This can be made from the front wheels of almost any automobile. The lighter the wheel assembly the easier the trailer will handle. If possible it would be well to get a set of wheels without brakes. The old Ford front wheels with the cross springs, one over the other, make an excellent trailer for light boats, but with a boat over 300 pounds it sways too badly at high speeds. The wheel assembly with tires can be bought at almost any auto junk yard for very little.

On the trailer in the drawing the wheels were prevented from turning by bending the steering arm (while the wheels were straight back over the axle), then putting a bolt through the end of the arm and a hole drilled in the flange of the axle. However, this

is not necessary if an electric or acetylene welding outfit is available. In this case the spindles themselves can be welded and it will help to eliminate any play in the spindle bolts.

The next thing to do after the running gear is reconditioned is to make the frame. 2"x6" timbers

Courtesy of Mechanix Illustrated

are used for this job. Any wood will do, but a light strong wood makes the best job. This goes for all the wood on the trailer. The trailer in the drawings was made from a 1925 Reo front axle, and the frame width will probably be different for yours, so check this. Bolt in the back cross piece using the angle clip with two $\frac{3}{8}$" carriage bolts in each piece. Then cut the spreader so that the frame will set directly over top of the ends of the spring when bent to its correct

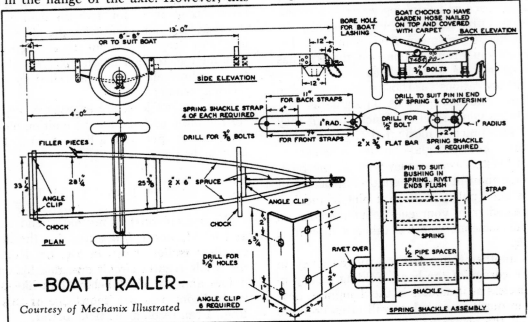

Courtesy of Mechanix Illustrated

Fig. 97.

shape. Make the tongue with its cross piece. Bolt the side pieces together through the tongue with three ⅜" bolts, and the cross piece on the inner end of the tongue using the angle clips and ⅜" bolts. This completes the frame.

You are now ready to fasten the frame to the wheels. Here it might be well to say something about the rear spring shackle. If the spring shackle and hanger of the car are in good condition they may easily be used by bolting the hanger right to the frame. This will raise the frame about three to four inches higher, allowing clearance above the wheels if the boat to be hauled is a wide flat one. If the boat will sit between the wheels it is advisable to keep the frame and boat as low as possible because of safety in turning corners and to facilitate hauling out and launching. Shown on the drawings is a safe, easily made hanger which has given excellent service. If the shackle as shown is to be used, make up the parts and assemble it on the spring. Do not draw up the lower bolt tight and be sure the pin through the spring is riveted sufficiently flush so that it will pass through the hanger straps easily. Grease the bolts and pin well before final assembly. Locate the frame over the springs and bolt on the straps with two ⅜" bolts. The after straps will have to have filler pieces under them to take up the thickness of the shackle. Be sure the wheels are straight with the frame or the trailer will run to one side.

The chocks merit a bit of consideration, for they will control the balance of the trailer. The tongue or draw bar on a trailer such as this should carry between forty and seventy-five pounds, and the boat should be located to give this correct balance. Fit the chocks neatly to the bottom of the boat and after the boat is tried on the chocks it should be marked so the correct position will be assured thereafter. Bolt the chocks to the frame with ⅜" carriage bolts. The tops of the chocks must be padded to keep the boat from being chaffed. A satisfactory padding may be made by nailing a piece of hose on top. A piece of garden hose will do but an old piece of pneumatic hose is firmer and would be better. Notch the top of the hose so the nail heads will pass through. Over this stretch a piece of old carpet folded a couple of times to form several layers and nail to each side.

It is best to buy the hitch. This may be procured at almost any auto supply store. A small ball and socket hitch can be had for less than a dollar. For a heavy boat it would be better to pay a little more and get a stronger hitch with shock springs. This should be bolted to the end of the tongue.

THE SPRING OVERHAUL

With the advent of the first housefly, or the song of the first robin, those of us who own a boat begin to get itchy fingers and soon saunter down to the boatyard "just to look her over." A casual inspection will reveal enough to get started on, but with the beginning of every season the inspection of any boat should not be "casual." There is a set system of examination that those who have owned a boat for a number of years have found to be the best and that, in the long run, will cut the time involved in the overhaul to a minimum.

The first looking-over should be for the discovery of any defects. The old-timer will get out his pocket knife and start poking into the wood to reveal any "soft spots" under the paint. Paint hides the effects of rot and the seasoned boat owner knows where to expect to find this meance if it is present. He will start poking the planking at the rabbet in the stem and follow its line from the top to the point where it joins the keel. Should the knife enter easily at any point, he will start digging away the paint to discover the reason. Let us assume, for example, that a bad spot does exist. The rotten wood must be removed and graving pieces or "dutchmen" securely fitted so that the strength of the little ship is not impaired. If many rotten areas are found, the entire member should be replaced.

Around the transom and along the keel are other likely places to look for rot. Examination should be made for damaged timbers possibly caused by that hard knock the boat got against the dock last year. When a plank is badly scarred, it is advisable to renew the affected length. Any renewed plank should extend over at least three frames and should be cut at the center of the space between the frames so that butt blocks may be fitted. Never splice in a new plank, depending on the frames alone to cover the joint, as is sometimes done in cheaply constructed boats.

Where frames have been broken, a length of new frame should be bent in alongside of the damaged ones so that it will cover at least three planks each side of the break. It should be securely fastened both to the broken frame and to the planking.

Worn and scarred places on the rails and guards should be renewed by fitting an entire new piece or by graving pieces. After all of the bad places in the hull have been repaired, another thorough inspection should be given the boat. In the meantime, if she had a winter cover, this should be aired and dried before it is stowed away for the next layup. All of the windows or cabin ports should be propped open to air the inside of the boat. The interior around the bilge should be given a thorough scrubbing and cleaning with strong soap powder and water and all old oil and grease removed from the interior below the motor. Grease and oil, besides looking messy, create a fire hazard.

After the bilges have been cleaned, they should be painted with a good, white lead paint, tinted gray. Also, they may be given a coat of pine tar oil or creosote, both of which are somewhat smelly; or they may be given a coat of whitewash which will give the boat a sweet and clean odor and protect it from dry rot to a great extent. A strong solution of salt water in all the dark places will be a good rot preservative, too. The decks and cabin top should now be inspected and any bad places repaired. If the canvas is worn and cracked in many places it is advisable to renew it. All the mouldings should be removed and the old canvas torn off. The new canvas is laid in a mixture of white lead and varnish or in liquid marine glue, made especially for this purpose. After the canvas is laid it should be primed with a thin coat of casein glue. When this is set it can be sanded to a very smooth surface.

If the canvas is bad only in spots, these can be repaired with neat squares of new canvas laid in paint or glue and their edges neatly tacked. Another good trick is to apply hard marine glue (which is sold for canoe repairs) around the edges and press it down to a thin edge with a hot iron. Leaks around the skylights or ports should be repaired with seam putty or stick marine glue. Another way to stop a deck leak is to apply some of the new elastic cement made for this purpose. This new type of cement runs like water when applied but finally hardens into a rubbery substance which is eternally elastic, resisting the twisting of the hull without breaking loose and leaking again.

When the hull is in tip-top condition, give some thought to improvements before starting to paint. For instance, it might be well to replace her old painted mouldings with new ones of mahogany or oak to give her a more snappy appearance. Nothing sets a boat off more than a little varnished wood, or "bright-work," as a yachtsman would call it. You may want to make a more weatherproof companion slide or to fit a hatch forward in the cabin that may be hinged to allow better ventilation and give access to the bow without going over the cabin top (a

hazardous undertaking in rough weather). Time and the condition of your pocketbook will determine the extent of your improvements.

Now for the painting. The one best rule in any kind of paint work is: "Start from the top and work down." First of all, no paint work should be started, other than priming coats, until all the dirty work on the hull and motor is complete. Then start with the removal of any of the cracked and blistered paint. There are any number of good paint removers of the paste or liquid type on the market, but most old-timers around the waterfront still prefer to remove their paint with a blowtorch and a putty knife. This will introduce a fire hazard to the novice. If you are inexperienced in blowtorch paint-removing, practice on old painted scraps of wood until you get the idea.

With all the old paint removed, the bright-work should be gone over, removing the old varnish with a liquid remover and finishing up with a cabinet scraper or a piece of broken glass. There are some handy little scrapers on the market that are easy to sharpen and do a better job than a piece of glass will do. The bare wood of the bright-work should then be given a coat of linseed oil and, if a darker color is desired, the oil should have a little oil stain mixed in it. After the oiling, it is sanded down smooth and the first coat of varnish applied. To preserve the finish, buy the best varnish that you can afford. The new bakelite resin types are excellent for boat work. All bright-work should be given at least four coats and thoroughly sanded with fine sandpaper after each coat. Varnishing should not be done on a damp day or when dust is flying.

With the varnishing finished, turn your attention to the painting. Start with the uppermost part and work down because you are apt to drop some paint and if this should land on a freshly painted surface below where you are working, there are messy words and paint. The best instructions for painting are issued by the paint manufacturer and generally they are printed on the can. Follow these to the letter!

At all times have a rag soaked in turpentine ready for use so that if you smear two different colors together, they can be wiped off at once. If any paint touches varnish, wipe it off at once. And don't paint around wet varnish or varnish around wet paint. Sand each coat of paint after it is dry, if you want a smooth job. Where two different colors separate it is well to cut a line with a race or scrieve knife so that the line will always be easy to follow. This should be done at the water line on the hull where the anti-fouling paint meets the topsides. Leave the anti-fouling until the very last, for you still have some work left on the bottom, which has been purposely laid aside until this time.

After all the bad places on the bottom have been repaired, the hull should be worked over with a wire brush to remove all the loose anti-fouling paint. The entire bottom up to the topsides should then be given a fresh coat of anti-fouling. Just before the boat is ready to go in the water, the second coat should be applied so that it still will be wet when the boat is floated. Seams that have opened with the drying out of the hull due to the warm and windy weather should not be caulked if they are less than a sixteenth of an inch, because the wood will go back this much when the boat gets in the water. The wider seams should be caulked cautiously and then only with a thin strand of lampwick. Before the last coat of anti-fouling paint is applied and the boat is ready to go over, putty all the open seams with a mixture of tallow and red lead. This will keep the water out until the planks have swelled and at that time it will squeeze out of the seam easily.

Have a can of dry oatmeal or sawdust on hand when the boat is launched. If the hull is leaking badly and shows no sign of lessening as the wood swells, a handful of the meal should be placed as close to the leak as possible on the outside of the boat. The water working into the leak will carry some of the flakes with it and they will jam into the hole. With the swelling of the meal or sawdust, the leak soon stops and a hauling-out is saved. Some leaks appear to originate at a spot which reason leads us to believe does not leak. The boat should be sponged and the trickle of water carefully followed. Some aluminum powder sprinkled on the water in the bottom of the boat will help to determine the direction of the flow and the leak may be traced to its source and stopped. Sometimes, carefully chinking of the leak from the inside will help a lot and last an entire season. The real cure for any leak on a boat is to fix it from the outside.

If the boat is powered, the motor should be checked for alignment by uncoupling the shaft flanges to determine if the two faces are parallel. If they are not parallel, the motor should be shimmed up on its bed until both flanges meet without any opening around their circumference. The joints of the fuel line should be gone over and checked for leaks and, if there is a strainer in the line (there should be), clean it so that all of last year's sediment

will not get back to the motor. The stuffing box should be repacked if it shows any signs of a leak and the gland should be set up again no tighter than necessary to stop the flow of water. Examine the exhaust line; scrape all badly rusted parts and give the pipe a coat of aluminum paint.

If you own a sailing craft, the spars should have been scraped and varnished when the rest of the bright-work was done. The wire-rope rigging should be examined for badly rusted spots and renewed if necessary. If the running rigging is worn at places and still looks good, it should be reversed or turned end-for-end so that the worn parts will not come in the same position as they did when last used. Spread the sails out on the lawn to air and inspect them. Rips can be mended with baseball stitches or a patch. If the sail is dirty, a good scrubbing on the dock with soap powder and a broom will work wonders. It should be rinsed overboard and, if slightly mildewed, it should be rinsed in a tub of clear water with some mild laundry bleach and hung out in the bright sunlight to dry. Be sure that it is thoroughly dry before bending it on the boat.

A hopelessly mildewed sail that I saw last spring was revived and modernized by dyeing it blue; this is the only color that will hide mildew. If you are purchasing new sails be sure to have them mildewproofed by your sailmaker before they are placed aboard.

PROPORTIONALLY INCREASING OR DECREASING A DESIGN.—The question often arises as to how a given boat design may be enlarged or decreased and still keep the same proportions. This can be done safely within 25% above or below the original if all dimensions are treated proportionally. This should not be done by anyone who is not boat wise and in so doing the designer is relieved of his responsibilities.

The formula for direct proportion is this. *A is to B as C is to X.* Don't let all of this scare you. It is only a way of representing actual figures. *A* is the length of the present boat, *B* is that of the proposed one. *C* is any individual dimension on the present boat. *X*, representing an unknown, is the value of that same dimension on the proposed boat. It is not necessary to do this for every dimension. As all dimensions are composed of units and all are proportional, let us set up a conversion factor by which we can get the dimensions of the proposed boat by simple multiplication. Let us assume that we have a boat 18' 9" which we wish to enlarge. By the 25% rule this is 18' 9" x ¼ of that length, which will be 23' 5¼".

We can now see that we will be dealing with a lot of fractions; to eliminate these let's go to the table of decimal fractions for easy work. We then have 18' 9" is to 23' 5¼" as 1 is to X (using 1 as a unit, in this case, a foot).

Thus we have: 18' 9" is to 23' 5¼" as 1 is to X

Or: 18' 9" : 23' 5¼" : : 1 : X

The time-honored rule for the solution of this is to multiply the *means* (23' 5¼" x 1) and divide by the *extreme* (18' 9"). Going to the table we find that 5¼" is .4375 and 9" is .7500, thus we have:

18.7500 : 23.4375 : : 1 : X

Solution: 23.4375 x 1 = 23.4375

23.4375 is then divided by 18.7500

```
18.7500) 23.4375 (1.25
         18.7500
         ───────
          468750
          375000
         ───────
          937500
          937500
```

Thus, we multiply all dimensions by 1.25 to increase the boat. This also proves the formula as we have increased the length of the boat one quarter or 25%. 1.25 expressed in proper fractions is 1¼.

In increasing a boat by this method, unless it be a very large one, all structural sizes such as keel, frames and planking may remain the same. In most cases, unless you are an experienced boat builder, it will pay to consult a good naval architect on this matter.

BUILD A MODEL FIRST.—If you have never built a boat, or even if you have, a construction model will be a big help if made previous to the full-size job. In doing this you will experience all the difficulties you will encounter on the real work at a smaller scale and *forewarned is forearmed*. If this practice pays off in large industrial projects and helps experienced men to anticipate trouble beforehand, it will be of far more value to you. Very seldom do I design a plywood boat these days that I do not make a model to check it.

This type of model is generally made of balsa wood which may be secured at any hobby shop along with the cement to hold it together. By making the model one-eighth full size it is easy to construct it from stock sizes of balsa. If you consider that ⅛" balsa is one inch lumber it starts to get easy. A 1" x 2" stringer is ⅛" x ¼" on the model (⅛" x 2/8"). Sheet balsa may be purchased in 6" widths which will represent a 4' sheet of plywood (⅛ of 48" = 6"). One-sixteenth inch sheet balsa will answer for ⅜", ½" or

⅝" plywood and by dividing all dimensions by eight the proper size material may be secured. For a scale you can use the *eighths* on an ordinary carpenter's rule, but it is far easier to purchase a cheap engineer's scale that has 1½" to the foot on it. This is one-eighth full size and with it you may read the fractions without a lot of mental gyrations. Do not be too fussy about exact scale sizes, the nearest quarter-inch above or below the actual framing sizes will suffice, therefore, ⅛" balsa sheet should answer for all the framing.

Fig. 97A. Study model of a plywood cruiser. Built up from Hobby Shop wood and cement.

Draw the body plan one-eighth full size. Lay it over a soft pine board and cover it with wax lunch paper. Cut all the balsa to scale width and assemble it over the body plan using ordinary dress pins to hold it temporarily until the model airplane cement you have used on the joints has hardened. A safety razor blade or a sharp *X-acto* knife cuts balsa easily.

Fig. 97B. Roland Cueva built this model of his *Benjamin Packard* and left the planking off of one side to show the interior.

Set the frames, stem and transom up on a base-board, or small keel horse, and temporarily brace them in their proper positions. Run in the various longitudinal members. Fasten all joints with model cement and *lil* pins which you can secure at the hobby shop. After the cement on the frame has hardened you can start covering it with the planking. Do not try to put the balsa on in scale size sheets. You can lay off the butts on the sheets by drawing them on with a ball-point pen. A 6″ x 36″ sheet is standard in balsa. This equals three standard plywood sheets at 1½″ to the foot. Mark off the sheets and put the whole length on. Lay it on the model and mark off the edges. Right here you will be getting a good idea of what will happen to the real sheets. Wooden spring clothes pins make excellent clamps. Cut the sheets to within an actual eighth of an inch of the marks (1″ to scale) and try them again. Continue this until you have a fit. Before finally fastening the sheet to the frame, mark its outline on a sheet of paper 6″ wide. Save this, for it will give you a good idea of just how to rough cut the actual sheet later on and with a lot of excess material removed from their edges, the plywood sheets will bend far easier. For all strip-planked boats use ⅛″ square strips. It may pay you to buy a balsa stripper at the hobby shop as saw ripping this size material creates half waste.

If you find this model beyond your capabilities then do not waste money on actual material. Fifteen-year-old kids make airplane fuselages far more complicated than a boat hull in this same manner. In addition to the experience gained, you can use the model to pick up a lot of bevels on the actual job. If it is to be used for this purpose, plank only one side.

The time consumed in making a model will be saved by experience on the actual job. Later on you may finish it completely and have it as an ornament for your den. Regardless of your experience, if you have learned not a single thing from the model's construction, then all the effort in writing this has been wasted.

KIT BOATS AND FINISHED HULLS.—For the man who does not wish to fabricate his own hull, or who has no facilities to do so, there are boats on the market today which may be purchased in prefabricated kits. Some of these are excellent; others smell to high heaven. Many are manufactured by large, reputable companies; others by fly-by-nights whose only interest is a fast buck. Before you purchase from a glamorous advertisement investigate the product by inquiring among the boatmen in your neighborhood. In some of the large boating centers there are dealers who will not only sell you the kit but will rent you building space, and the necessary tools, and who will also give you any needed advice during the construction.

There are other firms who sell their hulls in completed form, leaving the cabin and interior trim to your own devices. These types of hulls may be purchased in fabricated plywood, molded plywood and fiberglas and may range in size from a car-top dinghy to a family-size cruiser. Some dealers also have finance plans so that you may purchase your boat as you do your car or household appliances.

Just a few cardinal rules apply to the assembly of these products. Become thoroughly acquainted with all the parts before you assemble. Plan your work step by step. Most of all read the manufacturer's instructions before you start and not after the boat is finished.

PLANS AND BLUEPRINTS.—Due perhaps to the numerous give-away programs that people see on television today, they seem to think that everything in this country is for free. A naval architect, like any other professional man, is a specialist in his line. He is in business to make a living (often a very precarious one). He pays the same amount for the food he buys in the super markets as you do, so that his wife and kids may live like yours. I have seen men unhesitatingly pay a stiff doctor bill. I have seen others offer a bonus to a slick lawyer to get them out of some scrape of their own making; and I have heard these same men let out a bellow that was heard clear up to the Pearly Gates when some naval architect presented his bill.

Most of the reputable designers today belong to the *Society of Small Craft Designers* (the S.S.C.D.) and are controlled by a strict code of ethics, just as any other professional man. Believe me, they do a lot more work for what you pay them than the men in any other profession. If you want a special house you pay a civil architect a good fat fee to design it for you. Why, then, should you expect anything less from the man who designs your yacht? Quite a number of these men sell stock plans. In this way you get the services of a reputable designer at a reduced price. Remember when you buy this sort of service that the designer must pay for the blueprints, he must add a profit like any other tradesman, and in the end answer your queries after you receive the plans. His prices are not at all unreasonable.

Quite a number of magazines sell boat plans. Some of these are in booklet form. There is one catch to plans of this sort. For a lot of hobby projects there are sold what is called *full size blueprints*. These are prints of the original art used to make the reductions as they appear in the publication. Many people buying these prints for a boat envision a print large enough to use as a pattern. They are very much disappointed when they receive a print only two or three times as big as the illustration in the publication

Again there are other companies who sell boat prints, some being full size, so that you may use them as patterns. An inquiry before you buy may save you some grief.

Now about the plans in this book. They were made from reproducible tracings which can be blueprinted if necessary. I have tried to make everything so legible that prints will not be necessary. On any of the prints you will get nothing more than a reproduction which will approximate two-and-a-half times as big as the illustration. At the present cost of blueprinting and mailing, a set of prints for the simplest boat will cost you more than you paid for this book. They are not necessary but if you must have them they can be furnished.

Now about your letters. Please do not be like the man who uses a product and reads the directions later. Often I have found that if a reader had spent as much time contemplating the problem as he spent in writing the letter he would have arrived at the answer. Often he solves the case before the reply returns. I have actually seen this happen numerous times when I visited some near-by inquirer. And another thing—always include a self-addressed and stamped envelope. Often a letter will appear to be written in Hindustani; it takes hours to decipher the contents and signature. Don't make it any harder. If a letter goes astray it may be because the post office has received a version of what you have written which was figured out to the best of my ability. To be safe, print your name and address.

Often some vital information will appear in several places in this book. This is not that I am getting senile. There are a lot of people who will skip whole chapters of a book in a hurry to reach the end just to see how it all turns out.

THROW-AWAY BRUSHES FOR GLUE.—Modern glues and fiberglas resins are very rapid in setting up and ofttimes we turn around, pick up a brush and find it hard. One way of saving money on brushes is to make them yourself. They may be made as shown in Fig. 98 from manila rope, an old tin can and a piece of broom stick.

Sometimes these brushes will shed a few rope fibers but then again cheap hair brushes will shed hair, so you must take your choice.

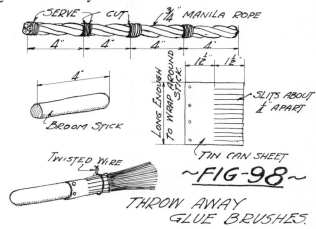

THROW AWAY GLUE BRUSHES.

HOW TO COVER YOUR BOAT WITH FIBERGLAS

Courtesy of the Owens Corning Fiberglas Corp., Plastics Reinforcement Division.

There's been a lot of talk about the best way to cover a boat with Fiberglas. Some of it has been sound; some not so accurate.

There's a little knack to covering a boat with plastic and Fiberglas, but it's not difficult if you follow the instructions with care. Once you get your boat covered, you can look forward to more sailing pleasure for years.

It's always a temptation to rush into a do-it-yourself job without giving enough thought to the basic preliminary steps. The finished results are certain to be a monument to carelessness.

On the other hand, it takes only a little longer to do the job right . . . step by step. That's why you'll find the following points so strongly emphasized.

1. Be sure your boat is structurally sound and dry, and that you have sanded off all old paint and varnish.
2. Fill all seams and bad places with a non-oil base putty.
3. Buy only good materials, from recommended kit suppliers.
4. Take your time! Don't "blitz" the job. It's *your* boat. It's not hard to do a good job if you just follow instructions.

Keep these principles always in mind as you read and work. And in case of doubt, get expert advice before going ahead.

When the first Fiberglas molded boat hulls came on the market, boat owners naturally sat up and took notice. They began to ask whether their present boats could be made leak-proof, tight and strong with the same materials.

The answer is yes. The application of woven Fiberglas fabric to wood boat hulls, decks, cabin tops, etc., is completely practical. In the past few years it has gained tremendously in popularity, and a number of good kits have come onto the market.

By this process, a permanent bond is established between the area to be covered, the Fiberglas fabric and an air-setting resin or plastic. The resulting covering is tough, smooth and highly resistant to impact. Yet, if it becomes injured, it may be repaired without great skill or cost.

Any hull that is reasonably sound structurally may be covered by this method. But it should be remembered that a wood hull is only as strong as her fastenings. If these fastenings are badly corroded and the surrounding wood is soft, "pounded out" or decayed, the hull is structurally unsound and may leak. Even though you can't slap on a little Fiberglas and resin and make a first class job of an old wreck, you *can* cover and strengthen a lot of areas which have begun to go, or soon would.

In this way, years can be added to the life of the boat. A boat of molded Fiberglas, or with a Fiberglas covered hull, will always command a higher price on the market or in trade.

Many small boats are carrying larger engines today than they were designed to handle. These engines drive at high speeds and in rough water. In so doing, they can open up a hull to the danger point. Small boats can be materially strengthened by the Fiberglas method, as this material has great tensile strength which it imparts to the hull. When a hull (including bottom, sides and transom) has been covered, you will get many of the advantages found in a molded hull.

In the spring, or "fitting-out" time, it will be only necessary to wash and launch the boat. No more laborious removal of old paint. No more sanding and caulking. No more "swelling up." If, after extended use, the boat looks a little shabby because of scratches and faded areas, it may be advisable to restore its beauty by painting.

It's fun to have a dry, waterproof hull, dry gear and dry feet—and a boat that's always ready to run.

That's the pleasant reward you get for taking the trouble to cover your boat the Fiberglas way.

Now let's see how to carry the job to the point of applying the covering.

First, you should be sure to buy good representative advertised materials. As with most anything else, cheap or cut-price materials, or materials about which extravagant claims are made, should be avoided. Next, you should carefully prepare the hull in the following manner.

How to prepare the hull.—Your boat, of course, should have been hauled and allowed to dry out thoroughly. Don't worry about shrinkage having opened it up, or because the seams are showing caulking. These are the natural results of drying.

Overturn small boats to make the bottom easier to get at. If possible, raise and tip larger hulls so as to expose more area. Choose a shaded or sheltered location, as exposure to direct sunlight sets up the resin too quickly.

Cleaning and Filling Seams. Rake out all loose putty or caulking. You don't have to dig deeply and remove every last vestige of seam filler or caulking. Simply remove any material that has loosened or is standing out beyond the surface. A small rattail file with the handle end bent to form a hook is an excellent tool. A putty knife is handy, too.

Fill all seams, cracks, screw holes, dings, etc., with a *non-oil base* putty such as Dura-tite, water-mixed wood putty, plastic wood or any similar material. This is important, because oil-base putty is not compatible with the resins used in the covering process. Don't just give this part of the job a lick and a promise. Be thorough! At this time, secure all loose fastenings. Also replace all badly damaged planking and other wood members.

Sanding. When the putty is dry and hard, the hull is ready for sanding. It pays to spend a little extra time on this operation, because any depressions will show up on the finished surface and may not be very pleasing to the eye.

If you decide to cover your boat late in the season after it has been in the water, haul it out and sand it immediately. The prompt removal of all paint will expose raw wood to the atmosphere and speed up the drying. But remember—the boat must be thoroughly dry before being covered.

All old paint and varnish must be removed, *right down to the bare wood!* Don't be afraid to take off some wood, even on the thinnest of plywood, or on planked hulls such as a canoe. The little wood you remove in the sanding operation will be replaced in thickness and strength many times over in the covering process.

If you're tempted to burn off old paint with a blow torch—*don't do it!* The heat drives the oil of the paint into the wood, and as previously stated, oil is not compatible with the resin. There is one exception described later. *Do not use a paint remover* for the same reason. It leaves a residue which doesn't help the process. Remove all paint by sanding—manually or mechanically. Wear it off!

If oil from the engine has soaked through the planking, you have to get that oil out sufficiently before you can cover the planking. Carbon tetrachloride must be used as a solvent to neutralize the oil and clean it from the area. One application will not necessarily do the job well enough. Go over the surface 3 or 4 times, if necessary. After this has been done, wash the surface with water and a good soap or detergent. Rinse thoroughly and allow to dry. Now sand it. The freshly exposed wood will be quite clean and ready to take the process.

You may find that the bottom is heavily soaked with oil. This is the time to use a blow torch, taking care not to burn or scorch the wood. Apply the heat to soften and vaporize the oil, so it comes to the surface. Then the carbon tetrachloride, soap and water technique may be used.

A solution of ¼ pound of lye to six quarts of water may be used to remove oil from planking also —rinse with clear water—allow to dry before covering.

A disc sander is recommended, with an 8″ disc having a very coarse grit, such as 4-16, which looks not unlike coffee grounds. Disc sanders may be rented from many hardware stores. Aluminum oxide grits are also very hard and make an excellent cutting surface.

Avoid Dead Smoothness. A coarse disc is recommended because it will help you speed the job along; because it won't "load up" readily, and therefore last longer, and because a rough disc produces a roughened surface which is the best base for the resin. Keep moving the sander back and forth over the surface. Do not dwell on one spot too long or you will sand too deeply.

Sanding is a dusty job. Try to do it in the open, or in some shop, barn or garage. Sanding *after* you have filled all the seams means that you do all the sanding, remove surplus putty at the seams and take off the paint in one lick.

With a coarse disc sander, it is possible to sand a 12′ boat bottom, sides and transom in 3½ to 4 hours, allowing even for a coffee break.

The hull is now ready to receive the materials.

Woods. The bond between the resin and the wood is important. The best adhesion will be established on soft, open grain woods which are dry and free from pitch. White pine and cedar are examples of woods which can be easily covered. Close grained hard woods such as cherry or birch are difficult to obtain a satisfactory bond.

Based on our field experience, we strongly advise not covering cherry or yellow pine. Cherry is a hard, very close grained wood; yellow pine, while soft, is usually heavy with pitch.

Since the bond is largely dependent on the penetration of the polyester resin into the wood body, any means of opening the pores of the wood is helpful. Coarse sandpaper will accomplish this job effectively. The use of a caustic solution is strongly recommended on oil borne woods or on old boats where the paint has soaked deeply into the grain.

THE COVERING MATERIALS.—By covering materials is meant the combination of Fiberglas fabric and resin (or plastic), a combination which produces a strong, tough covering for the boat.

The Fiberglas Cloth. The genuine Fiberglas fabric is made of strong, tough Fiberglas yarns. The fabric most commonly used and offered by most of the suppliers weighs about 10 ounces per square yard, and has a tensile strength of approximately 460 lbs. per inch of width. Lighter fabrics may be used on canoes and small, light boats such as prams and dinghies.

The weave is quite open in order to permit the fabric to conform to compound curves such as are found on boats having deep chines, without cutting the fabric. The open weave also permits "breathing"; consequently no air will be trapped under the fabric to cause blisters if reasonable care is used in the laying.

Important! When you buy materials, be *sure* the seller can assure you that the oil used on the yarn during the weaving operation has been removed by a special treatment. Untreated fabrics may have an oil residue, and as we know, oil is not compatible with the resin.

Do not worry about adding weight to your boat by using the heavier fabric. A Fiberglas covered hull does not pick up any measurable amount of water, whereas a floating wood hull absorbs a great deal of weight. The fabric comes in various widths, the most popular one being 44 inches. Rolls are as long as 125 yards. The 44-inch width satisfies many different sizes and kinds of boats. All kit suppliers cover this subject in their price lists.

How Many Plies of Fabric Should Be Used? Most small boats up to and including 16 feet may be covered with one layer of fabric. Larger boats, and boats of heavy, wide planking, power and speed should be covered by two or more plies of fabric to provide strength sufficient for the need.

Boats of 18 to 26 feet, clinker built or full planked, should have two plies of fabric, while boats of 32 to 45 feet in length should have three or four plies minimum.

Before deciding on the number of plies to use, read carefully the instructions furnished with the kit of materials you buy.

The Resin. The resin developed for this process is known as Polyester. It is made by a number of leading chemical houses in the country and is available through your kit supplier or his dealer. All Polyester resins are basically the same, although the kit or package varies somewhat from one supplier to another.

While Polyester resin is by far the most commonly used in this application, we have noticed increasing activity in the field with epoxy resin. Epoxy kits are largely being used for local repair on boats, automobiles and other applications which present special adhesion problems. At least one supplier is now offering an epoxy kit for the covering of entire hulls. We advise the use of Epoxy resins on hardwoods (such as oak or birch) or metals where it is difficult to get a satisfactory bond with the Polyester resin.

Epoxies are more expensive than Polyester and require a slightly different application technique.

Cuprinal. When cuprinal or other oil base preservatives have been used, the surface must be neutralized by a wash coat of acetone, mineral spirits (Savasol No. 5, a product of Standard Oil of New Jersey).

Now WE ARE READY TO COVER THE BOAT.—All resins are sold "unactivated"; that is, they must have a chemical added to start the action of curing and hardening. They also have a limited life "on the shelf" or in storage. In a temperature of about 70°, the shelf life is about 6 to 8 months. At higher temperatures it is less. Under refrigeration, the life of the resin in the can (unactivated) is over a year. Be sure you get fresh resin, just as you would insist on getting dated photographic film.

With the hull dry, the seams filled, all sanding done, and with the area dusted off, the job is ship-shape and clean—ready for covering.

First measure the boat and cut the first strip, allowing about 4 to 6 inches overage to avoid having to piece it out. Roll up this length on a paper tube. A mailing tube is easiest to handle, especially if you are working alone. Cut the additional strips you will need and gather them on another roll so that all the fabric you will need is convenient to handle. Lay the rolls aside in a clean place.

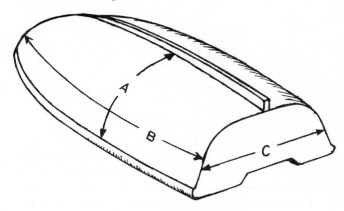

Fig. 98A. Measuring a boat for Fiberglas.

Now activate one quart of resin by adding the special chemical catalyst, following the directions furnished by your supplier. Avoid working with more than one quart of resin at a time.

Apply the first or prime coat directly to the bare wood with a brush or roller coater. If you use a roller, as many people prefer to do, run it in all directions, laying on a good full body of resin to satisfy the thirst of the wood. When using a brush, work the same—all directions of the compass.

After this first coat has been applied, let it stand about 15 to 20 minutes, if the temperature is, say, 70°—a little longer if the temperature is lower, and a shorter time if the room temperature is above 70°. Then apply a second coat. When this has become tacky, indicating that it is curing (about 15 to 20 minutes) you are ready to start applying the fabric.

(The nice thing about the whole Fiberglas boat covering process is that you can't make a serious mistake. The worst that can happen is that you activated a quart of resin too soon, waited too long to get it on the boat, or waited too long before laying the fabric. You'd lose the resin you had activated—that's all. No harm done. Just apply a fresh mix, the way you would apply a second coat of house paint.)

Pick up the fabric you have gathered on the tube and smooth the loose end at either end of the area to be covered. Unroll it a little at a time, and smooth it with your hand, pressing it into the resin. No tool is required.

Now you can apply resin on top of the fabric, waiting about 15 or 20 minutes for the undercoat to start curing. Usually two coats of resin (with or without added pigment) are applied to the fabric to obtain satisfactory appearance. In order to lose the pattern of the weave completely, however, 3 coats are usually applied.

Color. You have a choice of adding color to the resin or of painting the finished surface with one of the special paints developed for boat covering. A rather wide range of colors is available. When pigments are added to the resin, some fading must be expected.

About Expansion and Contraction. A boat will expand in the heat of the sun and shrink in the cool of the evening. It will expand in taking up water and shrink in drying out. These are tremendous forces to be reckoned with. Therefore, a large hull of heavy planking should not be covered with too little material, for it does not have sufficient strength.

The fact that there is some "give and take" to the Fiberglas fabric and the resin is helpful in combating the problem of expansion and contraction.

Now Your Boat Is Done! One of the nicest things about this Fiberglas-reinforced covering method is the fact that once you start applying the fabric and the resin, there's no long wait between coats. You're in the water soon. Furthermore, there's no long hull-scraping session . . . ever.

ELECTROLYSIS.—Sometime about the sixteenth century a scientist by the name of Galvanni discovered that an electric current was produced between two dissimilar metals immersed in a saline solution. Formerly, this was called galvanic action, today we term it electrolysis. The solution or electrolyte does not have to be salt water. Some acids will work as good, if not better. Formerly boats in our fresh water streams and lakes suffered little from electrolysis. Today industrial wastes are poured into our natural waters at an alarming rate, sometimes forming an electrolyte much stronger than sea water.

Electrolytic action takes place between any two distinctively different metals. The accompanying table will give the relative action between any two of them. Those in parenthesis are the best for boat work. Those farthest apart on the list will give the greatest action; i.e., magnesium and gold. Zinc and copper, or graphite, are the classic examples of the electric battery which you will find if you dismantle a flash light cell. Metals at the top of the list will *eat away*, those at the bottom of the list will have the least erosion.

All of our brasses and bronzes are mixtures of either zinc, tin or copper with other elements introduced in a small percentage to provide more strength. One of the first signs of bad electrolysis is de-zincification of the various brass and bronze alloys. Most of these will show a coppery red on their surfaces where the electrolysis is the worst. The red color is caused by the molecules of zinc following the electric current away from the bronze and actually leaving a mixture of pure copper.

GALVANIC SERIES OF METALS

CORRODED END (*anodic, or least noble*)
Magnesium
Zinc
Aluminum
Cadmium
Steel or Iron
Cast Iron
Chromium-iron (active)
Lead-tin solders
Lead
Tin
Nickel (active)
⎧ Brasses ⎫
⎪ Copper ⎪
⎨ Bronzes ⎬ *
⎪ Copper-nickel alloys ⎪
⎩ Nickel-copper alloys ⎭
Silver solder
Nickel (passive)
Chromium-iron (passive)
Silver
Graphite
Gold
Platinum
PROTECTED END (*cathodic, or most noble*)
*The metals and alloys bracketed are considered the best to use together in marine application.

Eventually, as the process progresses there is nothing left but a red powder which is the pure copper molecules. I have seen bronze strut bolts eroded down to less than a quarter of their original diameter. Sometimes zinc plates are secured to the metals that erode away. The zinc relieves the more noble metal of electrolytic action and is renewed when eaten away.

The action between zinc and the bronzes is not the only one which will give trouble. Stainless steel below the water will erode the bronzes away in short order. I know of one example of this in which everything except the propeller was of stainless. In two weeks in supposedly fresh water the propeller started to erode away on its thin tips. While some of this erosion was caused by cavitation, it was greatly aided by the de-zincification of the bronze. I know of another boat not yet overboard which has a stainless rudder, a galvanized iron rudder shoe and a bronze wheel and shaft. I shudder at the thoughts of the result.

Ofttimes stray electric currents set up between the boat's battery and the water outside the hull will be a prime offender. A micarta insulated coupling in the propeller shaft is the only cure for this. Watch your radio ground plate; this is often a vicious offender also.

TABLE — DECIMALS OF A FOOT

For Each Sixteenth of An Inch

0	1	2	3	4	5	6	7	8	9	10	11
	.0833	.1667	.250	.3333	.4167	.5000	.5833	.6667	.7500	.8333	.9167
.0052	.0885	.1719	.2552	.3385	.4219	.5052	.5885	.6719	.7552	.8385	.9219
.0104	.0937	.1771	.2604	.3437	.4271	.5104	.5937	.6771	.7604	.8437	.9271
.0156	.0990	.1823	.2656	.3490	.4323	.5156	.5990	.6823	.7656	.8490	.9323
.0208	.1042	.1875	.2708	.3542	.4375	.5208	.6042	.6875	.7708	.8542	.9375
.0260	.1094	.1927	.2760	.3594	.4427	.5260	.6094	.6927	.7760	.8594	.9427
.0312	.1146	.1979	.2812	.3646	.4479	.5339	.6172	.7005	.7839	.8672	.9505
.0365	.1198	.2031	.2865	.3698	.4531	.5365	.6198	.7031	.7865	.8698	.9531
.0417	.1250	.2083	.2917	.3750	.4583	.5417	.6250	.7083	.7917	.8750	.9583
.0469	.1302	.2135	.2969	.3802	.4635	.5469	.6302	.7135	.7969	.8802	.9635
.0521	.1354	.2188	.3021	.3854	.4688	.5521	.6354	.7188	.8021	.8854	.9688
.0573	.1406	.2240	.3073	.3906	.4740	.5573	.6406	.7240	.8073	.8906	.9740
.0625	.1458	.2292	.3125	.3958	.4792	.5625	.6458	.7292	.8125	.8958	.9792
.0677	.1510	.2344	.3177	.4010	.4844	.5677	.6510	.7344	.8177	.9010	.9844
.0729	.1562	.2396	.3229	.4062	.4896	.5729	.6562	.7396	.8229	.9062	.9896
.0781	.1615	.2448	.3281	.4115	.4948	.5781	.6615	.7448	.8281	.9115	.9949

CHAPTER XV

BUILDING THE BOAT

A REVIEW OF WHAT YOU SHOULD AND WHAT YOU SHOULD NOT DO BEFORE YOU START.

"Handsome is as handsome does" is a saying so old that its truth is no longer disputed. Many men have pictured their dream boats as something from which an ethereal light shone forth in glory. The desires of some have run to a boat resplendent in varnished mahogany and chrome-plated trim—something that would fly over the water with the speed of an airplane and possessing the comfort of a Pullman club car. The boats in this book were not designed with those thoughts in mind.

If on the other hand your yachting uniform consists of the dungarees that you wore in the engine room of the *Big Mo* when she steamed into Tokyo Bay; if you are willing to strike the bells of your ship's time on the bottom of your dish pan; if you are willing to curl up on a hard board berth; or at times, in the very bottom of your little boat, with nothing but the stars to light your ceiling as you sleep, then here is your boat.

Spit and polish are things to be admired in any craft and a certain amount of it is necessary to show the world your good ship's husbandry. However, the time spent in polishing could be just that much more time in which you could be sailing the little craft.

The boats on the following pages were designed to be built with the minimum of effort, therefore giving you the greatest amount of pleasure afloat. None of them is foolproof. A man who builds a racing craft must, at some time or other, expect to capsize. The man who will foolishly take a little craft out in the face of an impending storm can expect nothing less than disaster. Every summer the Coast Guard records show many disasters to pleasure boats. In almost every case the human element has been at fault. In cases of boatwreck, most disasters occur to poorly equipped or poorly built craft. Fire aboard pleasure boats is a terrible thing. I have seen enough of this to dread it. The only protection against it is good common sense and the rigid adherence to Coast Guard rules.

LAYING DOWN AND TAKING OFF

Most of the following information will be a resume of that contained in Chapter IV but it will not harm you a bit to read it again as it is the first step in the construction of any boat. Let us divide it into the two distinct phases of the entire operation.

LAYING DOWN

This embodies the drafting or layout of the lines of the boat. It is usually done on a large smooth floor. On some of the smaller boats it may be done on sheets of cheap plywood or if you are careful not to mar the actual plywood that will later form the planking of the boat, these may be used. The dimensions used are contained in the table of *offsets*. Some designers give their figures in feet, inches and eighths. For instance 7-3-6 would mean 7' 3-¾". Long ago I found that a professional builder who uses this procedure day after day has no trouble with it; to an amateur it is often confusing so all the figures for the designs in this book are those found in everyday use. Seven feet, three and three-quarters inches will be written just that way. Where the floor space will not permit, the lines may be contracted. The smaller boats may be laid out on large sheets of building paper and these rolled up when not in use.

The design fairing has been done as carefully as possible and the offsets are as correct as it was humanly possible to make them. The human animal is prone to err and no matter how carefully any project is checked there is still a chance of error. If you must be absolutely correct the only safe way is to lay the lines out full size and make them absolutely fair. If on the other hand you are willing to accept small errors, which generally fair themselves out in the long run, it will only be necessary to lay down the body plan.

Two methods of dimensioning the "V"-bottom boats have been used. Points of the frames are given on the *keel, chine* and *sheer* by the use of half widths and heights. A *half width* is always the distance from the centerline or midpoint of the boat. A *height* is always the distance *above* a given base line. The base line is not the same on all designs. Quite a lot of boats are more readily built inverted, or with their keels facing the sky. This will apply mostly to the plywood craft which are very easily turned over when the planking is completed. For these the base line is given as the *construction base line* (See Fig. A).

Where the boat is built in her normal position the offsets are given to the three same points namely *keel, chine* and *sheer* but the *base line* is given in its normal position, right where Noah placed it when he built the *Ark*.

OFFSETS FOR "V" BOTTOMS

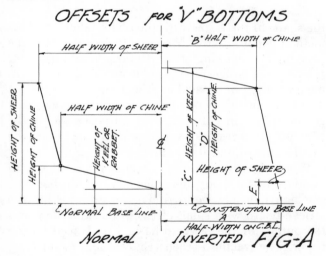

NORMAL   INVERTED   FIG-A

At one time in the history of shipbuilding there were very few "V" bottomed boats built. There *weren't* any, that I can find that were recorded before this country was founded. The earliest boats of this type were built on the Chesapeake Bay (this statement may be disputed) and were originally called *diamond bottom boats*. Round bottom boats were the mode and the method of dimensioning them has changed very little in recorded times. The dimensions for the frames of this type of boat, Fig. B, are given on a series of lines that are horizontal and parallel to the base lines called *water lines* and on

another series of lines which are vertical and which are parallel to the vertical centerline and these are called *buttocks*. In some boatyards they are called the *outs*. The combination of water lines and buttocks as viewed either from the bow or the stern form a

OFFSETS FOR ROUND BOTTOMS

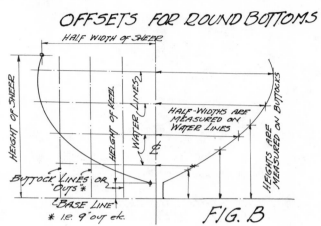

FIG. B

grid and it is over this grid that the *body plan* is drawn. The dimensions and drafting of the keel and sheer lines is done exactly as it was for the "V" bottom boats. The rounded frames are dimensioned by *half widths* on every water line that crosses them. These half widths are measured from the vertical centerline. Another series of dimensions are given along buttocks which they intersect and these are the *heights*.

Dimensions for the contour of the stems are given on a series of parallel and more or less equally spaced lines at the most convenient points of measurements for each individual boat. With all the round bottomed boats as well as any other curved lines which may be dimensioned, the batten should be run through all of the given spots. Even though the dimensions were taken from large-scale layouts it is still possible to misread a scale a bit and after running the line, and it does not appear fair, withdraw the nails and let the batten spring free at any spot that appears unfair. If this does not remedy the condition place it back in the original position and try another point. After the batten runs through, or as close to as many of the original spots as possible, you have it made and *that's it*.

In any case it will be necessary to lay down the *body plan*. Back in the days of all-wooden ships the body plan was laid down on a large wooden platform and the lines cut in to it with a scrieve knife. It was then taken to the frame yard and the wooden frames cut from and assembled over it. Later on the same was done for iron ships and it was placed near the furnace where the frames were heated to be bent. In this new process of the reversal of wooden ships and iron men the screive board retained its same name. There is no use in our changing it now. For

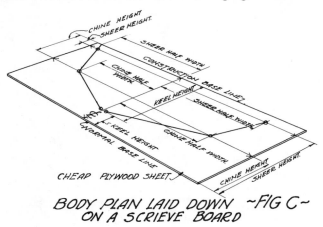

BODY PLAN LAID DOWN ~FIG C~
ON A SCRIEVE BOARD

our screive board we will require a sheet of cheap plywood 4' x 8' and ¼" thick. *Good one side* will be sufficient. Exactly in the center of each 8' edge we will cut a saw slot about ½" long. This permanently marks the vertical center of the *body plan* (See Fig. C). For "V" bottom boats it is best to measure the heights on each 4' edge and snap chalk lines the entire length of the sheet. If the measurements on each 4' end have been made properly you are sure that these lines are parallel to the base line. The half widths are laid off on these lines. Draw the body plan full so that the complete frame may be assembled over it. To avoid confusion use different colored pencils for the forward and aft bodies. For round bodied boats draw the grid of the water lines and buttocks on the scrieve board and lay out the frames on this.

TAKING OFF

Two of the boats in this book have their lines drawn to the *outside* of the planking. These are *Picaroon* and *Pelican*. On these the body plan must be laid down and the thickness of the planking taken off. For the "V" bottom boats this is relatively easy. By tacking a square strip the same thickness of the planking *inside* the body plan line and building the frames against these strips we have it made. For the round frame boats the take off is a "hoss of another color". Here a very thin batten is made the same width as the planking is thick or even more narrow

if possible. Little cubes of wood are glued to this at about 3" intervals. The total thickness of the batten at these cubes should be the exact thickness of the planking (1¾₁₆" for *Picaroon*) (See Fig. D). This batten is bent around the frame line on the body plan with the cubes outward, and their outer edges coinciding with the previously drawn frame line. By penciling inside the continuous strip of the batten we have

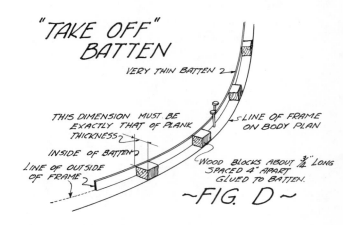

~FIG. D~

the shape of the frame with the plank taken off. This method is not exactly correct as it does not take the bevel of the planking across the frame into account. It would not be accepted by an inspector on a government contract or a naval architect on a racing yacht. The boats in this book are neither of these and it is good enough for all practical purposes. With the widely-spaced frames used in most of the boats, the small error will fair itself out.

Where it is necessary to transfer any shape to wood from the body plan, inexpensive draftsman's tracing paper may be used. The paper is held to the scrieve board with small pieces of masking tape and the outline of the piece to be laid off traced on the paper. The tracing is then removed and again fixed to the wood to be laid off with masking tape. Here it is pricked through with a sharp nail, awl or a tracing wheel. An elaboration on this method may be found in Chapter VI.

KEELS

The keel of any boat can be compared to the human backbone. It forms the main stem of the framing. To it the two ends of the boat, the stem and stern, are fastened and along its length the ribs that form the shape of the hull are attached. Some boats have very little or no keel at all. Others, especially those designed for sail, will have very husky keels that extend below the hull and form the fin which keeps the boat from crabbing sidewise across the water when the wind is somewhere on the beam. In some cases the keel is capped with a wide apron to receive the edges of the bottom planking. Anyone who has forced these wide timbers down on a keel with a heavy curve on its upper edge will appreciate the modern method of fitting cheeks to its sides. These cheeks being of smaller section are more easily bent than the apron. Whenever possible the cheeks should be through-bolted. When glued to the main keel with the new glues they become an integral part of the keel itself. *Pelican* has her cheeks sawed to shape and spiked to the main keel. They are made in short lengths and are fitted between the frames (intercostal). Various types of keels are shown in Fig. E.

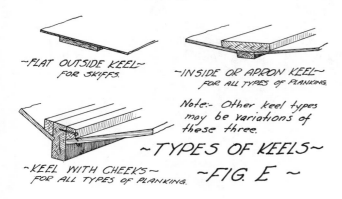

~FLAT OUTSIDE KEEL~
FOR SKIFFS.

~INSIDE OR APRON KEEL~
FOR ALL TYPES OF PLANKING.

Note:- Other keel types may be variations of these three.

~TYPES OF KEELS~

~KEEL WITH CHEEKS~
FOR ALL TYPES OF PLANKING.

~FIG. E ~

OUTSIDE BALLAST FOR KEELS.—Sail boats require some weight to counteract the press of their sails. To be the most effective it must be placed as low as possible. Metal, of course, is the heaviest material we can secure for this purpose. Next to this comes reinforced concrete with as much metal as it will safely hold imbedded within it. Let us consider each of these individually.

LEAD

This metal weighs 640 pounds for every cubic foot that we fit to the boat. Being dense and compact its center of gravity can be placed low on the keel where it will do the most work. As a general rule casting metal is beyond the realm of the amateur builder's capabilities. Lead can be secured in various forms of scrap—old lead pipe or sheet scrap melts easier;

lead or any large chunks of scrap are the hardest to melt. Old storage battery lead may be used if all of the element between the grids is thoroughly beaten from the plates. Lead also has the advantage that it can be cast in several heats if the surface of the previous pouring has been kept clean of dross and the surface is sprinkled with powdered resin or sal-ammoniac before the next heat is poured on top of it. It takes a great amount of heat to melt this material and a heavy iron pot will have to be secured for the melting. A heavy arc-welded melting pot may also be made for this purpose. The furnace to enclose the fire should be built of brick. Molds for lead may be made from wood, heavily whitewashed, or coated with water glass. They should be well braced to withstand the pressures of the molten lead. Plaster of paris may also be used for a mold where considerable shape is encountered. One last warning! *Be sure that the mold is dry.* Steam in molten lead can cause a terrific explosion. The writer owes his eyesight only to a miracle when this once happened to him.

CAST IRON.—This material is beyond the capabilities of the home workshop other than making the pattern and the core prints and boxes as shown in Fig. 91, Chapter XIV.

FABRICATED STEEL.—This type of keel is composed of steel plates welded together. The plates are made of either new or scrap material and are preferably arc-welded. If it is desired to make the keel of new material, plates of long, narrow proportions may be secured in various widths. These have a slightly-rounded edge which has no bearing on the end result. These plates are sold as *mill plates*. Be sure in stacking these up for welding that the proper spaces are left in the assembly for the entrance of the keel bolts. The usual method of cutting these plates is with an acetylene torch. Many builders have access to cutting torches and arc-welding machines and where these are handy the work should present no difficulty. Many of these keels have been manufactured from bridge shop or shipyard scrap. One requisite of the material is that it not be bent or kinked and will lie flat. As a general rule both cast iron and fabricated steel keels will range from 450 to 475 pounds per cubic foot.

CONCRETE.—Concrete in itself has very little strength compared to metal but properly reinforced with steel it becomes our most economical building material. For this reason it is imperative that every concrete keel have a sufficient number of steel reinforcing rods run the entire length. Another failing of concrete keels is that the edges chip off in grounding or when the entire weight of the boat comes on the concrete while on the railway. For this reason the concrete should have a wooden shoe of hardwood. Very hard oak, live oak, ironwood or greenheart should be used for this purpose.

The concrete in most cases should be cast with the backbone of the boat lying flat. One side may be closed with cheap plywood covered with waterproof building paper. Inexpensive 5-½″ roofers may also be used or the keel may be laid on a concrete walk or floor with building paper between. A dense aggregate should be used. One part of cement to one, or one-and-one-half, part of sharp, clean sand is proper and the mixture should be sufficiently wet to run freely to all corners of the keel. Where it is not desired to go to the trouble of mixing the aggregate, it can now be purchased in bags under various trade names. This has a higher percentage of sand than that specified but it will suffice. The type that contains gravel should be avoided.

The metallic filler should be clean. Rust will not be a detriment on iron if it is tight but all loose scale should be removed. Where the scrap is greasy it should be washed in caustic soda before use and thoroughly rinsed in clean water. If old storage battery plates are used be sure that all the non-metallic material is beaten from them and that the acid is thoroughly washed away. Beat all lead pipe scrap flat before inserting it in the concrete. Large-diameter scrap steel shafting laid next to the keel bolts is an excellent filler.

Pour ½″ layer of concrete first and then start adding the scrap. After the cavity is filled, tamp the surface to make sure that the mixture has flowed to every corner. Then slick off the upper surface with a trowel.

The concrete should be allowed to age as long as possible. For the final finish it should be wire brushed and given several coats of rubber base concrete paint before the anti-fouling is applied.

STEMS

Anyone who has laboriously shaped one of the old-style solid timber stems with its scarphs and through bolts will appreciate the new art of laminating these members. Two types of laminations are used and either type may be interchanged. This type of work is described in Chapter I, Fig. 6A and the various types of stems are shown in Fig. F. Either type of

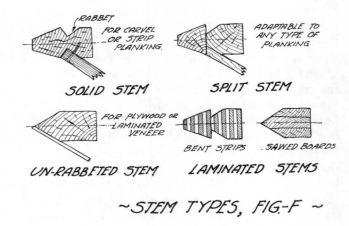

~STEM TYPES, FIG-F~

lamination may be used for any stem but the strip is easier to shape up than those made from laminated boards.

Most of the stems will have to be beveled on erection. This is accomplished by the use of a fairing batten as shown in Fig. G. Where it is necessary to rabbet the stem as in *Pelican* a batten of the same thickness as the planking is used and a series of notches cut into the stem at intervals as shown in Fig. G.

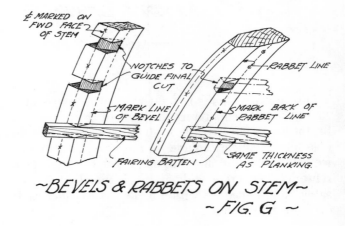

~BEVELS & RABBETS ON STEM~
~FIG. G~

TRANSOMS

These may take many shapes and divergent types of construction depending on the boat in which they are used. They should be made to their *developed* shape and not as they appear on the body plan. The heavier plank types are splined in their joints. A heavy saw cut is made along their adjoining edges and the groove for the spline cut from this. After the groove is finished a white pine spline is inserted and the pieces clamped up on resorcinal resin glue. If you are capable of making a good glue joint the splines may be dispensed with and locating dowels fitted to guide the pieces and hold them in line during the glueing process. Bar clamps will be necessary in the glueing process also. It is best to leave this type of transom in a rectangular form until entirely glued and then laid out and cut.

FRAMES

These are actually the ribs of the boat's body. In most cases they are built up from several members and either bolted or glued and nailed. Some of these frames are joined at the chine with gussets; others are overlapped. All frames should be built directly over their outlines on the body plan and checked after assembly to make sure that they conform to the correct outline. In some of the plywood boats, the bulkheads form the frames. In this case the bulkheads are assembled complete with their plywood before the hull is assembled. If by this time you are familiar with frames take one last look at Fig. 33, Chapter V, and another thing—*Don't forget the limber holes.*

INTERMEDIATE FRAMES

Some of the boats that are intended to use regular planking are fitted with intermediate frames between their main ones. As a general rule these are straight pieces of material and are set *normal* or at right angles to the run of the planking. If you decide to place a bulkhead where it will fall on any particular one of these intermediate frames it is well to bevel this one so that its face will lie square across the boat.

STRINGERS

These are longitudinal members connecting the frames. The principal ones are at the sheer and the chine and these receive the joints of the bottom and side planking and those of the side planking and the deck. In some of the boats the edge curvature will be too great to bend them. In this case they are laminated from thinner boards.

ERECTION

Two methods of erection are specified for the various type boats. The heavier types are erected in their upright or normal position. The lighter plywood types are erected inverted or upside down. Normally erected boats are set either on a keel horse as shown in Chapter V, Fig. 35, or on a series of keel posts as shown for *Kittiwake* in the following pages. In the case of the strip built boats they also are erected in the normal position due to the fact that the strips should be nailed from the keel out. Some of the smaller boats need no elaborate building jig; a pair of saw horses will suffice. The plywood boats are constructed on a building berth. (See Fig. 34, Chapter V).

In the case of the boats erected in the normal position the keel and complete backbone is fabricated first. It is then set up with all elements, level, plumb and true, and securely braced that way with temporary braces or spalls. Starting with the midship frame, this is set up as shown in Fig. H, and this member is

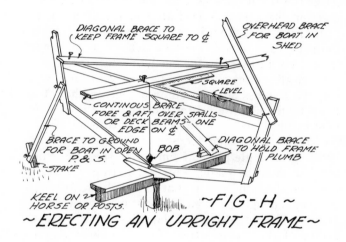

~FIG-H~
~ERECTING AN UPRIGHT FRAME~

also braced true in all directions. Each frame forward and aft of this is treated likewise. In *Kittiwake* spalls are placed across the frames so that in erection these will all form a level plane. With a wide board placed along them on the top of the spalls and one edge placed on their centerline, the entire series of frames can be accurately centered. Additional cross bracing will hold them plumb and square to the centerline.

With the plywood boats built on a berth it will only be necessary to plumb and center the frames if the spalls have been previously set square and level. The centerline and the width of the frames marked at each station are also a big erection help if this has been previously attended to. Where a level wooden floor is available a building berth will not be necessary. Temporary wooden blocks nailed to the floor in such positions as to receive the frame ends will suffice. The midship frames of these boats is also erected

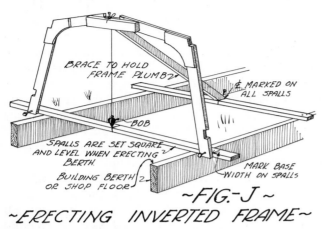

~FIG-J~
~ERECTING INVERTED FRAME~

first as shown in Fig. J. The rest of the frames are worked fore and aft of this frame in a similar manner. After the frames are set and checked in this type of erection the keel is placed atop of them and bolted in position. The stem is erected and securely bolted to the keel and its upper end (which is now the lower) is securely fastened to the berth or floor.

Once all frames of either type of erection are finally set, the notches for the chine are given their final bevel by the use of a fairing batten. The chine is then bent in and fastened to the stern and transom. Where the distance between the stern and transom is too great for a single piece of lumber to span the chine, a splice must be made. This is cut from a piece of material the same size as that to be spliced. It should be long enough to span the distance between the frames. The actual joint of the chine is made exactly center of the frame space. Try to make the splice where the run of the chine is the flattest. If necessary the butt block behind the splice should be slightly curved on the abutting side to prevent a flat spot. The splice should be screwed and glued.

The sheer stringer is treated in a like manner. In some cases the chine or sheer stringers will refuse to take the edge bend so that they may have to be laminated or sawed from a wider board. A very good example of this is shown in *Puffin* which follows in the next chapter.

Once the frame is rigidly set with the chine and sheer stringers in place, all other intermediate stringers, if any, are run in and securely fastened. The frames are then beveled with a fairing batten until the whole surface of the hull is fair to receive the planking. With the hulls that are designed for regular planking, now is the time to fit the intermediate frames. Some of these will have a slightly different

bevel between the head and heel. This is easily cut on the frame before it is finally fastened in place.

In beveling the keel chine and stem of the plywood-covered boats, a slightly different procedure will have to be used. We have seen in Chapter VII, Fig. 51, how plywood, or any sheet material for that matter, will only follow the surface of a cylinder or a cone. We must consider the bows of our plywood boats not as a single cone but as a series of cones. Starting at the chine end of the bottom midship frame we must divide the distance from here to where the chine meets the stem into a number of equal spaces. At a point about halfway between midship and the stem, we again divide the distance along the keel and stem to the chine into the same number of equal spaces as we did the chine. Now starting at the point where the stem and chine meet, we connect each pair of points with a straight edge and we notch down until the bevels meet the straight edge on both edges. We finally connect the notches to form one continuous bevel. The diagonal lines on which our straight edge laid are the radians of cones in which the plywood will bend. This is shown in Fig. K.

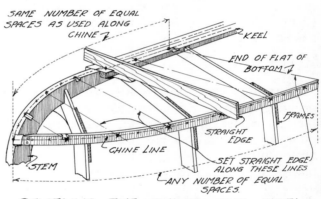

BEVELING THE CHINE AND KEEL
ON PLYWOOD HULLS ~ FIG-K ~

PLYWOOD PLANKING

After all of the framing has been properly beveled we are ready to apply the plywood. The bottom planking goes on first. When I first suggested this the Chesapeake boatbuilders let out a howl that could be heard in Norfolk. The time honored custom was to over-lap the bottom on the sides. All the dire predictions came to naught and now all plywood bottoms are fitted this way. The main reason for this is that the bottom sheets are hardest to get on and if the sides were planked it would be impossible to clamp the sheet to the chine where it needs it most. As the bow plank of the bottom is the hardest to get on, make a rough template of this and remove as much material as can be safely done to make the bending easier. Where the bevel of the chine stringer exceeds 45° start drilling ⅛″ holes on the corner of the chine and space these holes about 6″ centers until the stem is reached. Clamp the sheet home, working toward the bow, and after it is all set start marking it off. You will find that in the area where you have drilled the holes that it is fast becoming impossible to mark the chine. Go inside the boat and drive a six penny nail through the holes that you have previously drilled. The nails or their impressions will mark the line after the sheet has been taken off the frame, Fig. L.

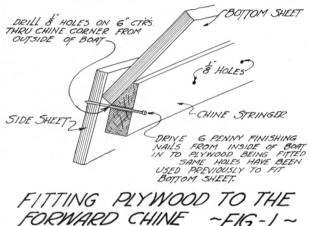

FITTING PLYWOOD TO THE FORWARD CHINE ~FIG.-L~

Just about where you started to drill the holes the chine bevel is starting to become so sharp that the plywood edge is losing its strength. Also if we continued to bevel we would have feather edges when we reached the stem. Discontinue the overlap and butt the sheet edges as shown in Fig. M. Allow

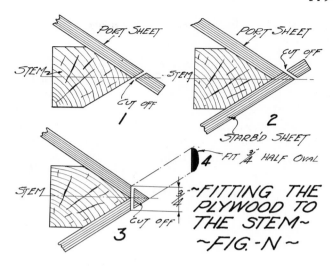

about an inch overlap of the sheets past the stem. When the sheet is fastened home, using the bevel of the stem as a guide saw it off, Fig. N. Do likewise for the starboard sheet using the face of the plywood as a guide. The final operation will be to take off the point and cap it with a piece of half oval metal.

Very little more can be said about plywood other than making the butts as in Fig. P. These are diamond-shaped pieces of plywood set between the stringers. The diamond shape allows more leeway of fit where there is a bit of twist at the joint. Where it is intended to tack the buttstrap it is the same thickness as the hull planking. This can only be used where the total thickness does not exceed ¾″. Other types of buttstraps are made from plywood glued and screw-fastened from the outside. Where considerable shape is encountered it is best to shape the surface of the buttstrap to fit the curvature.

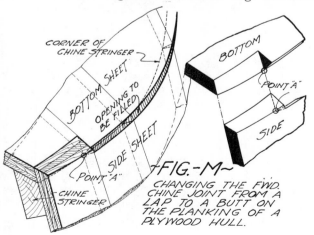

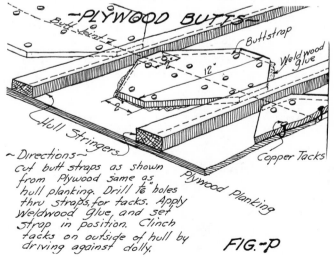

STRIP PLANKING AND LAMINATED VENEER

As these two subjects have been extensively covered in Chapter VII there will be no need of rehashing it here. Go back and review these methods thoroughly if you intend using either of them. There are some unconventional methods of ending the strips on the stem as shown in Fig. Q. If you intend to build a strip boat from plans in this book, the overlap method has been used for all boats except *Picaroon*. In all cases the port strip is sawed flush with the

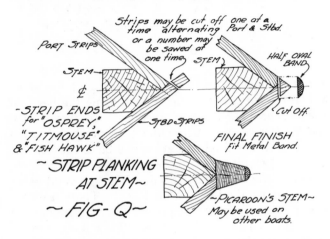

~ STRIP PLANKING AT STEM ~

~ FIG- Q ~

bevel and the starboard strip allowed to pass and is sawed off flush with the outside of the planking. It is well to allow the strips to pass until a number of them are ready to be sawed. This will give the stem the appearance of the corners of an old log cabin. Fairly soon you will find that the levels of the port and starboard strips are not matching. When this becomes the case, one or the other is notched down to allow its companion to pass. After the planking is completed the point is cut off and capped with a metal half oval as shown for the plywood stems, Fig. N. For the *Picaroon* the extra wood needed for the cutwater can be added to the stem and the ends of the strips sniped.

CARVEL PLANKING A LA MARYLAND

When it comes to comfort in a seaway nothing can equal a heavy boat. Plywood is an easy way to build a boat and it is the only way to get speed without ultra light and complicated construction. Personally I like a heavier boat. Plywood is like an alarm clock that ticks off the time at a furious rate; regular wood planking is like the old grandfather

clock that measures the same amount of time in the slow, measured swings of its heavy pendulum. Many types of "V" bottom boats have been built but none are as simple as the deadrise boats of the Chesapeake. These boats are built with a heavy keel all out of proportion and few, if any, cross frames. It is like framing a roof and carrying all the load on the ridge pole. If trusses were introduced in that roof the ridge pole becomes a very light piece of timber. I have seen several deadrise boats split their keels in a seaway because there were no frames tying their sides together. As a youngster I conceived the idea of introducing frames, thereby saving molds and lightening the keel. It was my old friend, the late Charles Hall, who christened this method *Construction a la Maryland*.

Actually what makes the construction native to Maryland is the cross-planked bottom. They tell me that they were doing this up in Connecticut even before the Indians came to Maryland, but that is neither here nor there. Actually I do believe that the *sharpie* was the grandmother of the *nancy boats* and the *skipjacks*. In planking these boats, start with the sides first. If you want to be real persnickety you can divide the side width into equal spaces at each frame and run in diminished planks. The easiest way is to use parallel planking. Butt two planks into one long, straight length and adjust it so that the distance to

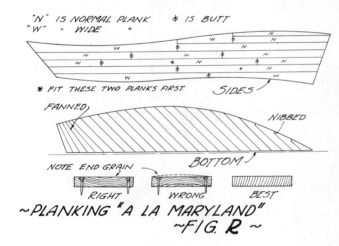

~PLANKING "A LA MARYLAND"
~FIG. R ~

the chine is nowhere greater than your widest board stock. This board is fastened on and the planking continued above it in parallel boards. Where a jib or short-pointed end would occur, the plank is butted and a wider plank fitted. (See Fig. R).

If the boat has been built in an inverted position the time has arrived to turn her over.

The smaller of the boats may be turned by two or three men without any trouble, but those having a beam of six feet or over become a problem. These take plenty of brains in planning the operation and much more brawn to complete it. Some sort of rig must be devised to turn the hull and the simplest is a gin pole and tackle. Even with the aid of this, it will take at least four husky men to complete the job.

Farmers when building a barn generally throw a party for all the neighbors when the sides are to be raised. These same tactics may be employed to turn the boat. A keg of beer or a wienie roast should help do the trick.

A gin pole of a length sufficient to allow the tackle to reach beyond the beam of the boat is needed, Figure S. This is set up near the midship frame and a rope sling is rove around the boat in such a manner that it will not slip. The tackle is hooked to this line and to the gin pole. The pole is now guyed securely so that its top will remain stationary. Be sure that everything is secure because a slip may destroy all the work that you have so far put into the boat.

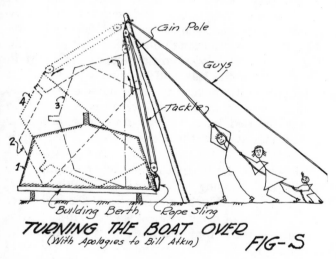

TURNING THE BOAT OVER
(With Apologies to Bill Atkin) FIG-S

With all the brawn at hand pulling on the tackle, the boat is hoisted from position 1 to position 2. In doing this it will be necessary for several men to lift on the low side of the sheer to help this point slide across the building berth. From position 2 the boat is hoisted further to position 3. Here the boat will reach its highest position on the tackle and the low sheer should be moved across the berth until the hull is ateeter. From here on it's lowered to position 4 and from there on it's plain duck soup. Lower away until the keel touches the building berth.

Several precautions should be taken in the turning operation. First be sure that the boat is securely shored from side to side, to prevent the hull from spreading apart in operations 1 to 3 and again to prevent the sides from crushing together from there on. Have plenty of old cushions or rolls of old carpet handy to prevent scarring the hull where it will come to rest during the various steps of the operations. Take it slow and watch every point. The building has taken a long time. The completion will take longer. *Don't hurry this part of the job.*

Once the boat is on her *feet* the frames again should be set up plumb so that levels and plumb bobs may be used to erect the joiner work and other operations requiring their use. A level line on the keel before she is turned over will help in the operation of setting her again. Once the boat is leveled in the fore-and-aft direction, she should be leveled transversely and then shored securely to keep her so.

OUTFITTING.—Now comes the tedious job of fitting all of the little odds and ends aboard the boat. The motor is installed along with its fuel tank and exhaust as previously described in Chapter VIII.

STEERING GEAR.—All of the sailboats shown on the plans in this book are steered with a tiller or stick inserted in the rudder head. Some of the smaller motorboats may be steered likewise. Somehow or other most motorboat men look with disfavor on the latter method and no matter how small the boat may be, the owner always dreams of sitting behind a wheel and handling his craft as though she were the *Queen Mary*. Such is the vanity of those who do their sailing with a monkey wrench in their hip pockets.

There are various forms of gear to connect the steering wheel with the rudder. The simplest of these and the one most in favor, due to its low cost, is that shown in Fig. T. The steering wheel is connected to a drum on which is wrapped enough cable to allow for the full swing of the rudder. At the point where the rudder is on centerline the cable is fastened permanently on the drum and enough turns are allowed each side of this point to permit the rudder to swing from *hard over* to *hard over*. To lead the cable aft to the quadrant or tiller, a series of sheaves is employed, as shown. Some means of taking up the slack as the rope or cable stretches must be devised. A turnbuckle is generally employed at this point, but I have found that even bronze turnbuckles have a bad habit of freezing in the threads due to infrequent use. When they reach this stage, they are the very devil to turn, especially when they are stuck away in some confined space beneath the floor. To cure this condition the tiller rope is spliced over two thimbles and a lacing of hard marlin cord is placed between them. This can be unrove and laced at any time necessary.

Rope for steering purposes is sold under the name of *tiller rope* and is generally a braided type such as is used for sash cord. Some of this has a flexible bronze center which increases the strength considerably and prevents stretching. All fabric ropes have a tendency to wear at the sheaves and the only recommendation is their low cost. For the best results extra flexible wire rope is the answer. Stainless steel heads the list.

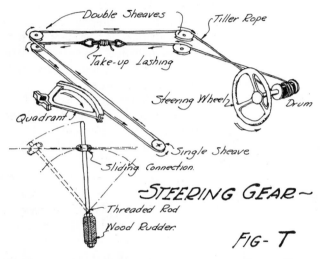

Where an outboard rudder is fitted the ordinary quadrant is out of the question. A metal or wooden tiller must be used in this case. As the tiller swings, the arc shortens or lengthens the tiller rope. To eliminate this nuisance a sliding connection as shown on Fig. T, must be used. Failing in this, the sheaves should be set so that the rope leads into the tiller at a position where it is halfway around its swing. By this method the least displacement of the rope is gained.

LEAKAGE.—Let us assume that your boat has been launched for the first time. Don't kid yourself; she is bound to leak. If she is of the planked type, her bottom seams must swell. If she is small the simplest thing to do is to let her sink until she has swelled sufficiently to be kept afloat without bailing. If the boat is large and has her motor installed, an old boatyard trick may be resorted to. When the boatyards get orders to launch a badly dried-out boat they concoct a gooey mixture of red lead paste mixed with melted tallow. The seams are puttied with this just before the boat is launched and as they swell the tallow is squeezed out. Ordinary window putty in this sort of work would harden, and its bulk in the

wide open seams between the planks would crush the wood as they swelled.

If, after the boat has been afloat some time, she is still making water, look for a bad leak. This sounds like a simple process but nine chances out of ten the leak is in a place that you can't get at. Screws that miss a frame and are withdrawn have a bad habit of leaving a hole which is never plugged. Stopwaters in keel timber joints are always forgotten some place in the construction, and failure to plug some part of bad construction is not a rare thing. Large leaks such as these are easy to discover by a rivulet of water inside the boat; their remedy is almost as easy.

Where these large leaks exist, the boat should be hauled at the earliest possible moment and the leaks corrected.

Sometimes these leaks can be stopped temporarily by putty from the inside of the boat, at other times no amount of work from the inside can stop them.

The watermen of the Chesapeake Bay possess a trick of stopping large leaks in a boat that is so old that it has grown whiskers. When a large leak develops, they snitch one of the old-fashioned ash sifters with a screen bottom and from the stable they secure a generous amount of dried horse manure. With the sifter on a long pole and filled to the brim with manure, it is worked down under the boat in the vicinity of the leak and vigorously shaken. The water going into the leak from the outside carries the manure in with it. In time the dried oats in the manure carried into the leak swell to twice their original size and jam the opening. Presto! the leak is stopped.

Horses are fast disappearing, and the material to stop leaks is passing with them, but other materials are just as good. The boat is taken into shallow water and a handful of dried oatmeal is placed in the vicinity of the leak from the outside. The oatmeal is clutched tightly to keep as much water as possible from it. The hand is placed over the leak and opened —oatmeal swells faster than digested oats and the leak stops quicker. A handful of sawdust from the power saw works almost as well.

The large leaks are not the ones that are the most troublesome or the hardest to track down. It is the slow drip-drip leak running continuously all week long that causes a half hour's pumping on the week end. The remedy is to first find the leak. The boat is sponged dry and the leak located by plugging the limbers with putty and watching to see in which frame space the water accumulates. Once the leak is localized, it is tracked down by the water trickle.

Often this is small and the planking must be wiped dry to find it. A bit of aluminum powder sprinkled on the surface of the remaining water will show the direction of the waterflow when everything else fails.

The trend in boating has changed since the first edition of this book was written. People all over the country are now boat conscious and it is not uncommon to see a boat in a back yard a hundred miles from the nearest water. The boat fan today will put his boat on a trailer behind the family car and drive two or three hundred miles to his favorite cruising grounds.

Home workshop tools have opened up a whole new field for the "do-it-yourself" man and the expression has come into common usage. With these new tools, boat work has become so simple that it is no longer necessary to make the design ultra-easy to build. Kit boats are on the market which can be assembled so easily that their builders look around for other worlds to conquer. Styles in boats, like women's clothes, change from year to year. The modern factory-built boat is as much a thing of beauty as the modern car and it is these criteria that set the taste in the back yard boat shop. The foregoing chapters are, for the most part, as good as the day they were written but popular demand has changed the selection of boats to be built.

Most every boy today learns to read blueprints in high school and he demands complete plans with plenty of detail. To this end, working plans have been included in the book. These are the plans that the architect would furnish to the builder and they give all information necessary to build the boat. Due to the format size they are necessarily small but all are readable. Where necessary, the use of a reading glass brings out details that are otherwise not clear.

In most cases the lines plan has been included in the set. These have been as carefully faired as it was humanly possible to do. There is still chance of error due to the fact that the original drawing was made at one-eighth or one-twelfth the actual size of the boat, and, to be absolutely sure, the lines should be laid down full size as this multiplies the error the scale amount in the layout. Often the layout may be made on the very plywood sheets you order to plank the boat. If you are willing to trust the designer (and many boats have been built this way), it will only be necessary to lay down the body plan and the stem outline. This may be done on cheap plywood with the advantage that it can be stood against a wall, out of the way, when not in use. Laying out the lines gives one big advantage, all bevels for frames and stem may be lifted directly from the layout.

If an apparent error does seem to exist, check your own layout first before sitting down and writing a nasty letter to the publisher or to me. One classical example of this is in *Sandpiper* which was first published in one of the popular "how-to-do-it" magazines. I received over fifty letters complaining that the transom dimensions were given an inch too long, and some of these letters were rather sharp. It just so happened that the dimension measured along the slope of the transom was an inch greater than it was shown in the body plan. All of this was done in spite of a note on the drawing that read "Transom figures are developed". Designers are busy men and they do not put notes on drawings for practice in improving their lettering. Most errors will amount to an even inch or an even foot. Look for this first. Sure! the designers make boo-boos, who doesn't?

Do not try to improve on the design unless you are qualified to do so. One case in particular was that of an aircraft designer (who should have known better). Using material on hand, which was far heavier than that specified, he cried bitterly when the performance of the boat went below that expected. Pay no attention to the words of your uncle or sister-in-law but build the boat as specified.

Just a few words to clear up another sore point. "What speed will the boat make?" This can best be answered by a host of other questions: "How much power do you have?", "What wheel are you using?", "What is the R.P.M. of the motor?", "How heavy is the boat?", "How smooth is the bottom?". All of these factors are needed to answer the first question intelligently. It is a popular delusion that the converted *jeep* motors will develop sixty horsepower. I will eat every one of them that will develop over forty-five. The same applies, in proportion, to all converted auto engines.

Outboard motors as a general rule will exceed their A.P.B.A. rating. This is due to the keen racing competition which caused improvements in them that added to their power after the formula was developed. The war also added to their performance by financing extensive research for their use in the armed forces. While my very first boat motor was one of the early *Evinrudes*, later years taught me to distrust all outboards. But no one can be an ostrich and keep his head in the sand forever. Today they have the same reliability as the high-speed inboards. They have untold advantages for the small boat. In the first place they give valuable room to the interior of the boat that an inboard would occupy. Couple this with the fact that you need no water or exhaust piping, no shaft, tank, strut or log and you have a monetary gain which is, in itself, an item. If you are not mechanically inclined the overhaul of an inboard is an expensive proposition. Add to this the fact that a large percentage of the mechanics doing this work today would be better employed at a cobbler's bench repairing shoes. When anything goes haywire with your outboard you place it in the trunk of your car and take it to a factory-trained mechanic who does not stay in business very long if he does sloppy work.

You can insure your outboard at reasonable rates and get a high trade-in value when you want another. You can get electric starting, remote control and oversize fuel tanks; you can even use two of these mills for more reliability or carry a small spare one for an emergency. What more is desired, except perhaps, more economy?

One of the biggest detriments to the start of building a boat is the prospective builder's apprehension about his ability. At first all problems appear as mountains which shrink into mole hills after they are conquered. If you have enough intellect to build a boat in the first place this same attribute will give you the know-how later. Where there is a will, so help me, there are at least three ways: the right way, the wrong way and the way you do it. The other nine hundred and ninety-seven don't count. Select the boat you want to build, order your material, sharpen your tools and have fun.

Mrs. Oscar Thomas (Marian) added a postscript when she typed this manuscript. I can do no more than include it for she is the wife of a backyard boat builder, and these gals have an angle too, so here it is:

(P.S.—Sam, don't you think that after he selects his boat and sharpens his tools, he should consult his wife before he orders the material so that she can get the household money out of the sugar bowl to pay the delivery man when the material arrives??)

BUILDING THE PLYWOOD BOATS

As all plywood boats are similar in construction and differ only in their sizes, the construction of any one will entail the same procedure. They may be constructed upside down or on a keel horse. The advantages of working down on the plywood will well repay any amount of effort expended in turning them over later. In any event, the framing is erected and well braced at the start of the job. The straight stringers are run in and fastened to the frames. Forward of the midship frame, the bottom stringers are not screwed to the frames but are bound in their notches by a piece of wire passed over the stringer and around the frame. As the natural shape of the plywood will take a curve on the bottom frames forward, this wire is later cut and withdrawn. A wedge the same width as the stringer is inserted between the frame and stringer and the stringer is then forced out against the plywood after the keel and chine joints are finally screwed up. An extra screw is then driven through the plywood, stringer and wedge into the frame.

After all intermediate stringers are erected and fastened securely the chine stringer is fitted. Due to the excessive curvature on the forward end of the chine, in some boats, it is well to saw this piece to shape rather than to subject the framing to the strain of edge bending this member. For this reason, wider boards have been specified and a layout is given on some of the lines plans so that this may be done. The shape of these members, due to the method of development used, is not entirely correct but they are close enough that a little springing up or down will make them fit. It is far easier to do this than to try to spring the curvature into them.

After the frame has been securely fastened it is ready for beveling. As a general rule in the power boats, the frames on the bottom will need no bevel aft of midship. Forward, where the plywood starts to arc away from them, there will be no point in doing this. All of the frames on the topside above the chine will require bevel, but in some places this will be small enough to be neglected.

The chine bevel forward of midship is likely to cause the greatest trouble. As we have read before, the plywood will have a tendency to arc away from the frames. This may appear to be double curvature, but in reality it is only the frame cutting across the surface of a large cone whose straight radial lines run to a point somewhere off the boat which would be the apex of this cone whose radians lie along the line of the chine and the stem-to-keel curvature. The closest we can approach these radians is to divide the distance along the chine, from the midship frame to the point where it meets the forward edge of the stem, into a given number of equal spaces about 1′ apart. The distance along the keel, between the next frame forward of midship and the stem point of the chine, is also divided into the same number of equal spaces. A straight edge laid between corresponding points will simulate the radians and if the structure is beveled to this line, we are as close as we can come to a fit. After the plywood is bent on for the trial fit, some alterations to the bevel may be necessary. For this reason it is best not to fully cut it.

Starting at the stem the bottom planking is applied first. If this sheet is templated and roughly cut to within 3″ of its finished shape the job will be much easier. The sheet is clamped along the keel and chine, at as many places as you have clamps. Along the stem you will find places where the bevel will kick it off no matter how hard you try to make a clamp hold.

The only answer to this problem is to use temporary screws with large washers under their heads. Another expedient is to use double-headed nails which may be readily withdrawn or ordinary nails with plywood squares under their heads.

When the sheet is finally set down tight, the marks for the final cut may be put on. Follow the outer edges with a pencil and go inside and mark the outlines of all frames and stringers on both of their edges. These are for outdrilling the screw holes later.

By this time you have probably discovered that at the extreme end of the chine it is impossible to mark the line due to the flat bevel. Due also to this condition, we must change the overlap of the bottom and topside sheets to a butt seam. The best place to locate this point is where the bevel of the bottom sheets start to exceed 45°. From this point forward to the stem, drill a series of ⅛″ holes about 6″ apart and clear through the chine stringer. Drill these holes on the very point of the bevel so that they will divide the angle about equal. After the sheet has been secured, go inside the boat and drive six-penny finishing nails through the chine into the plywood. When the sheet is removed, the nails, or their impressions, give a series of spots through which to draw the line of the cut. This same series of holes is later used to mark the topside sheet when it is fitted. Allow about 1″ past the stem for the final cut of the sheet after it is fastened down and then with the opposite side of the stem as a guide, saw it off flush with that side at the same bevel. On the other side of the boat do the same, using the outer surface of the first sheet in the same manner. The remaining pointed edge is later cut down to the width of the stem band.

After the first bottom sheet has been fitted, the rest of the bottom and topsides will be easy sailing. There is little more to say about the planking except

that if fiberglas (in whole or in part) is *not* to be used, the seams should be well buttered with sealing compound. Butt blocks of ¾″ plywood, glued and screwed from the outside, are an improvement on the diamond buttstraps formerly used. Where there is curvature in the plywood sheet these blocks should be saw-kerfed every 3″ to allow them to follow the curvature.

When fiberglas is to be used anything resembling paint or oil should be kept as far away from the hull as possible as it prevents a good bond between the resin and the wood. For this reason do not use wax crayons for marking, or any preservative on the wood until the fiberglasing is completed. Even though it is not contemplated to fiberglas the entire hull, a 6″ strip of this material along all seams and over all joints will do more for watertightness than all the fancy joints or seam compositions ever invented. All plywood should be thoroughly primed with a primer recommended by the plywood manufacturers after all work is done.

After the boat is turned on her keel (assuming that she has been built inverted) comes the time to fit her deck. Prepare a board the full beam of the boat and cut the camber out of this to form a female mold. In this the camber forms a hollow as it would on the underside of a deck beam. In fact one of the deck beams cut a bit wider than the boat would answer the same purpose. Use this to bevel the sides of the boat to the camber. Use it also to mark off all the beam knees or gussets and install the deck beams wherever necessary.

When the deck has been framed the plywood decking may be laid. Where excessive curvature occurs on the camber, the plywood may be seamed along any of the stringers if it cannot be pulled down to the sheer stringer. Along the edge of the sheer, round the plywood to a radius equal to its thickness. Deck-covering materials have a tendency to crack as years go by and this always starts where it has been pulled over a sharp corner. Delay the covering of the deck until all coamings have been fitted. If any of the coamings are of plywood, do not turn the canvas up inside of them. Fiberglas again appears to be the best deck-covering material.

After all cabin coamings are in place and beams fitted we are ready for its top covering. Two layers of ⅛″ x 3″ mahogany make the best covering where excessive double curvature occurs. Any other wood of the same thickness may be used if the top is to be canvassed. Starting in a diagonal line, from one corner to the other, fit the first strip. A *Bostitch* stapling machine is handy for this work. In lieu of this, tack the strip down with ½″ brads or small *Hold-fast* nails. One edge of the next strip is carefully planed to an exact fit with the first strip laid. The work then progresses by fitting one edge and leaving the other straight until the whole first layer of the cabin top is finished, nailing at each beam and stringer as you go. The next layer is fitted to the opposite diagonal, fastening the strips in the same manner, but laying up their under surfaces in *Elmer's Glue*. On this upper layer it is best to temporarily fit four or five strips at a time. Mark their sequence and remove them to spread the glue. Set them back (as they were removed) in the glue and nail them tight. On *Puffin*, where the forward edges meet the deck, carefully bevel them and fit a backing strip to the deck before applying them. After the glue has hardened, carefully set all the brads and sand the entire surface smooth.

From here on in, it's a straight job of filling, staining and varnishing until the entire job shines like a futuramic *Caddy*. Where plywood cabin tops are applied, treat them accordingly.

After the first couple of coats of cabin varnish have been applied it's time to fit the windows. While they are more expensive than plate glass, *Plexiglas* or *Lucite* have the advantage of being capable of being sawed, thus saving the expensive cutting of regular glass to shape. These plastic sheets can also be bent to a radius and thus lend themselves better to curved surfaces. Being quite easy to drill, the setting of these materials is further simplified. Frames for this type of window are made from No. 12 or 14 Ga. aluminum sheet sawed to shape on a jig saw with metal cutting blades. These frames are made about 1-¼″ larger than the window opening and the plastic sheets are cut to the outside of the frame. No. 8 aluminum or chrome-plated machine screws are spaced on about 3″ centers around the frame and extend through the glass and cabin sides with the nuts on the inside. The holes in the plastic should be drilled about 3/16″ in diameter to allow for expansion and contraction of the material.

Kuhls Bedlast or some similar material should be placed between the glass and the wood to form a watertight seal. The excess material is removed from the glass and surrounding wood with a rag moistened in turpentine. Flat oval aluminum strips form the dress-up trim. A much better appearance results if these strips are machine-screwed from the inside of the boat. In this case, the holes in the oval are tapped and the points of aluminum screws are filed off flush with the outside of the strip. Aluminum automotive drip moldings will find good use around the cabin top edges to prevent messy spots from drainage. Almost all of these special moldings can be secured from companies that handle auto-trailer supplies. The new *Reynolds* "Do-It-Yourself" aluminum shapes and sheets can now be purchased at the larger hardware and building-supply stores. This material may be worked with ordinary hand tools and will find hundreds of uses aboard the boat. It is good policy to guard all aluminum surfaces with a good weatherproof metal lacquer.

THE BILLS OF MATERIAL

In all material bills included along with the plans of this book, the stock has been estimated within reasonable limits as any boatbuilder would estimate it. The system used gives a generous allowance for waste, miscuts and bad wood. All material has been ordered nominal size. Dressing will deduct from 3/16″ to 3/8″. Large timbers and others which are not stock have been laid down in the layouts as losing ¼″ in the dressing process. For instance, the keel timbers of *Picaroon* are assumed to measure 2-¾″ thick, those of *Pelican* to be 5¾″. In all cases where the lines of the boat or notches in framing depend on exact timber sizes, it is very good practice to measure the exact thickness of the wood involved before making a cut or laying down a line.

In listing the hardware it is evident that screws and nails cannot be counted down to the last individual piece. A professional boatyard would keep these items as running stock and order screws by the dozen-gross and nails by the keg. This cannot be done in the backyard boatshop as there would often be more nails left over than used. For this reason most of these items which are easily purchased will be on the shy side of that needed so that the builder can purchase more of these as the work progresses.

Manufactured boat fittings are more or less standardized. Two manufacturers in this country cater to the yachting trade and turn out a complete line of excellent fittings for small boats. *The Wilcox Crittenden Co.* of Middletown, Conn., and the *Perkins Marine Lamp and Hardware Corp.* of Brooklyn, N.Y., have complete lines of fittings and these are so universally used that you can secure them in any large marine hardware store in this country. For this reason the fittings have been specified from the *W-C* or *Perko* catalog and their figure numbers are used. Most marine hardware companies will list the *W-C* line in their catalogs under the same identical figure number.

Bolts, screws, nails, rope and other items not manufactured by *W-C* and *Perko* are also listed in the catalogs of marine hardware dealers. Each may have a slightly different make-up in his catalog. Most dealers will have in their files copies of the catalogs of other marine dealers. The *W. Tiebout Company* in New York City has, in the writer's lifetime, been one of the large companies which cater to a boatbuilder's needs. They carry everything from boat spikes to lampwicking, and to help identification of all items not strictly in the class of fittings, the figure numbers have been taken from the *Tiebout* catalog. If you do not buy from *Tiebout* your own dealer can identify your needs by the *Tiebout* figure numbers.

Now as to material for cabin interiors. This writer often has labored hours in designing an interior which he considered as near perfect as possible. On inspecting the boat later he found an entirely different layout. The hours spent in figuring the material to construct the original interior was so much time wasted. It took him a long time to realize that every *Jack Tar,* his wife, his mother-in-law and all his kissing cousins have their own particular ideas of cabin layout. It must be a grand feeling to lie in a bunk with your knees up under your chin and, contemplating every convenience that one would find on the *Queen Mary* exclaim, "Gee, this is sure one grand cabin layout. That guy Rabl don't know his oats at all." For this reason no material for interior layouts has been given.

I have often been asked to specify paint. Sometimes the builder will apply this over a damp surface or use an improper thinner. After the paint blisters and cracks the man who recommended it is a heel of the first order. No Sireeee! You can choose your own paint and be happy with it.

CHAPTER XVI

BOAT PLANS

UNCLE GABE'S FLATTIE SKIFF

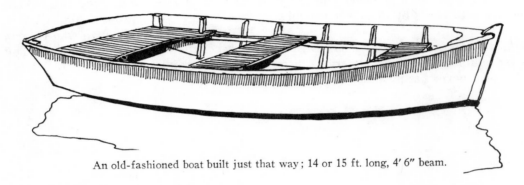

An old-fashioned boat built just that way; 14 or 15 ft. long, 4′ 6″ beam.

On several occasions in the preceding chapters I have mentioned old Uncle Gabriel Moses, the negro skiff builder who lived over on Bodkin's Creek. Uncle Gabe built the sweetest rowing skiffs that I have ever come in contact with. When they were fitted with a small sail they performed equally well. Back in the days when old Gabe lived we could still get cypress boat sides sixteen and eighteen inches wide. Today these widths can only be obtained in redwood from our West Coast. Toward the end, old Gabe started making his sides from two boards and without a doubt this was one of the things that contributed to his broken heart and hastened his death. We will assume that wide boards are no longer available and describe the construction using two boards to a side.

Secure boards of such a width that a total of sixteen inches may be used for the sides. Two ten-inch boards and two sixes or four eights will do the trick. The length depends on how long you want to make your skiff. While Uncle Gabe built a twelve -foot skiff occasionally, the fourteens and sixteens were his most frequent orders. When the boards are in your shop lay the two intended for one side together. Don't worry if the edges are an eighth-inch or so out of perfect straight line. Reverse one of the boards and

see if they will then match within an eighth-inch. If the gap is more than an eighth get your plane to work and match them.

Now divide the lengths of the boards into three equal spaces, Plan I. This will be 5′4″ for the sixteen-foot boards of 4′8″ for the fourteens. Starting four inches from the end of the board that is to be the bow, mark off a point and three inches from the stern end, another. Measure up on the stern line three inches and mark this spot. Measure up on the first third length from the bow a distance of two inches and put a mark here. Now with a thin batten connect the stem mark, the two-inch mark at the first third, the bottom of the board at the second third length and the spot at the stern. Draw a line along the batten. This will give the bottom of the sides the shape of a very elongated S. With a ripsaw cut away the excess lumber on the bottom of the plank and then put the two planks together again. From them mark the boards for the opposite side of the boat and cut them so that both sides are identical.

From two oak boards mark off the chines using the shape of the bottom of the sides as a template. Put these back to back and bevel their tops as shown on Plan I. Uncle Gabe always beveled his chines for

128

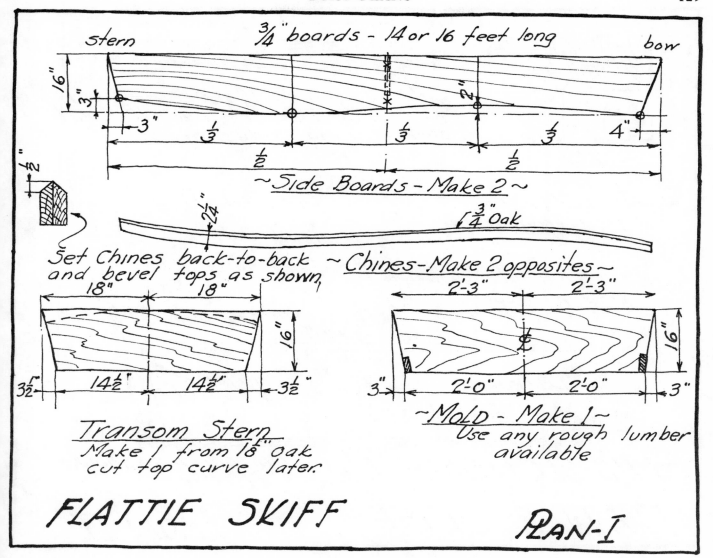

stern · ¾" boards - 14 or 16 feet long · bow

16" · 3" · 3" · ⅓ · ⅓ · 2" · ⅓ · 4"

½ · ½

~Side Boards - Make 2~

½" · 2¼ · ¾" Oak

Set Chines back-to-back and bevel tops as shown. · ~Chines-Make 2 opposites~

18" · 18" · 16" · 2'-3" · 2'-3" · 16"

3½" · 14½" · 14½" · 3½" · 3" · 2'-0" · 2'-0" · 3"

Transom Stern
Make 1 from 18" oak
cut top curve later.

~Mold - Make 1~
Use any rough lumber
available

FLATTIE SKIFF · Plan-I

this prevented water from lying on their tops. Some builders consider this an unnecessary refinement, but old Gabe's skiffs were the best.

From one or two pieces of 1⅛" oak, cut the transom stern boards as shown. If two pieces are used, the best practice is to dowel and spline them together. The bevel on their edges and the crown of the tops is cut later.

From any rough or cull lumber available make the mold as shown on Plan I and be sure to cut the notches for the chine to pass through. Make these notches large enough so that they will not cause you trouble later.

The stem is cut from a piece of 3" x 7" oak as Uncle Gabe used to make them and the rabbet was given a two-inch curvature in the 22" of length. The

forward edge was curved to suit this. If this sort of curved stem is to be used, the forward ends of the side planks will also have to be curved to fit the stem rabbet. If a straight stem is fitted (and there have been thousands of skiffs built this way), the stem may be cut from a piece of 3" x 6" or even 3" x 5".

When all the component parts are finished, the side boards are screw-fastened to the stem. If you use nails to fasten your boat, this point at least should be screwed because it will take the pull of the side-board bend until the bottom is planked. After one board is screwed to the rabbet, it is turned over and the other side board fastened in. Some sort of prop will have to be placed under the end of this plank if you want to screw it in flat. Otherwise the boards are set vertical and the last one is clamped in position

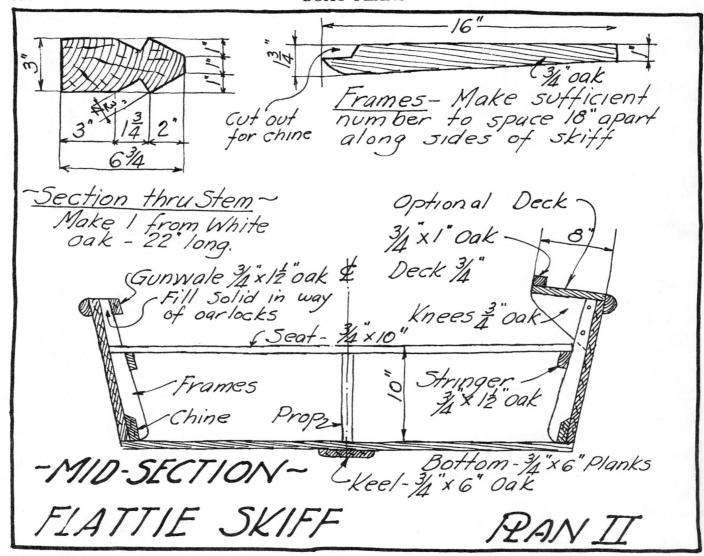

3"

1"

3" 3/4" 2"

6 3/4

Cut out for chine

3"
3/4"

16"

3/4" oak

1"

Frames— Make sufficient number to space 18" apart along sides of skiff

~Section thru Stem~
Make 1 from White Oak - 22" long.

Optional Deck
3/4" x 1" Oak
Deck 3/4"

8"

Gunwale 3/4" x 1½" oak ₵
Fill Solid in way of oarlocks

Knees 3/4" oak

Seat - 3/4" x 10"

Frames

Chine   Prop

10"

Stringer
3/4" x 1½" oak

~MID-SECTION~

Keel - 3/4" x 6" Oak

Bottom - 3/4" x 6" Planks

FLATTIE SKIFF   PLAN II

while the screws are placed. If the sides are in two pieces fit only the bottom strakes at this time, allowing the upper ones to wait until later.

The boards and stem are now set up on saw horses and the mold is fastened into the point as shown Temporary nails are driven through the side boards to keep them in position. A couple of turns of rope are taken around the side boards about a foot from their aft ends. This rope is drawn tight until the side boards meet the width of the transom stern. The bevel for the stern is taken and cut to suit. If there is not enough brawn present to draw the boards into the transom, a stick is inserted between the ropes and a tourniquet is made by twisting on the stick. Be sure, before the transom is finally screwed in place, that enough material projects below the side planks

to allow for the bevel where the bottom planking will overlap. Long screws should be used to fasten the side boards to the transom. Some builders fit a batten along the transom sides so that the side board screws will not have to be driven in the end grain of the transom boards. Uncle Gabe used such hard white oak that this was never necessary on his skiffs.

Once the side boards are bent and fastened to the transom, the boat is checked for alignment. Some side boards will bend more than others, throwing the mold off center. A string run from the center of the stem to the center of the transom should pass over the center of the mold. If this is out of line, a temporary brace may be nailed to the port side of the mold and the starboard side of the transom, or vice versa, to spring the boards into their proper position. This is

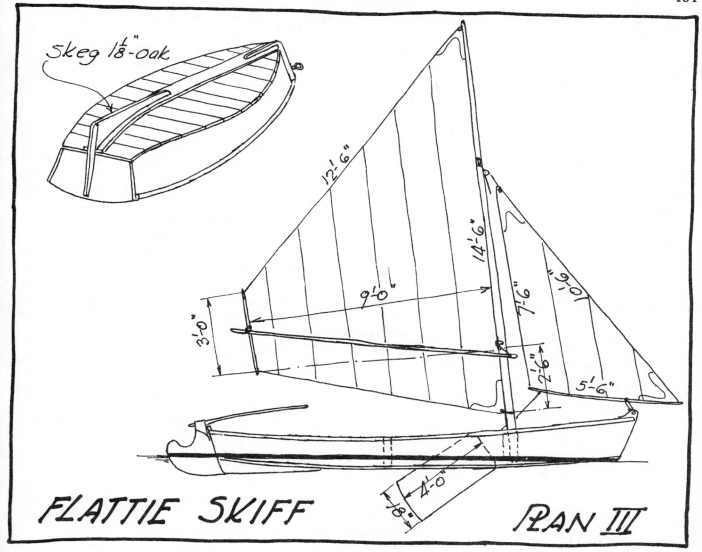

skeg 1⅛"-oak

FLATTIE SKIFF   PLAN III

allowed to remain until the bottom is planked.

The chines are now fitted by either being nailed or screwed to the side boards from the inside. They are cut to a neat fit at their ends to meet the stem and transom. Some builders set them a little above the line of the bottom planks to save a bit of beveling.

The boat is now turned bottom up and a straight-edge laid across the bottom of the side planks and chines. The sides are beveled until the straightedge will lie flush across them on both sides of the boat. Some builders are fussy about this fit and finally lay the straightedge flat after rubbing it with black bowling alley crayon. The flat side of the straightedge is rubbed against the chines, leaving black marks where the high points occur.

Six-inch boards are recommended to plank the bot-

tom and if the boat is a fourteen-footer, 125 lineal feet of this material will be required. If the length is sixteen feet, 150 lineal feet will be needed. Starting from the mold the boat is planked forward and aft. A board is laid across the bottom and marked off. It is then removed for cutting, put back and fastened with nails or screws. Nails are preferred by most of the builders including Uncle Gabe. Some method to make the chine seam tight must be used. Uncle Gabe always bought the worn-out woolen trousers that his ragpicker nephew secured in his trade. He would tear these in strips about an inch wide and, after soaking them in white lead, place them between the chines and bottom planks. Wool has the property of not rotting as quickly as cotton and holding the lead better. In modern work a strand of lampwicking soaked in black *Staytite* or *Miracle Adhesive* type *M-T* may be used. A saw is laid between the planks to space them apart as they are fitted. Never fit the bottom planks tight if they are of cypress, pine or redwood. Even a six-inch plank will buckle under this condition and an eight-inch plank has been known to leave the chine.

When the bottom is completely planked, the boat is turned right side up again and the frames fitted. These are made from oak about ¾" thick as shown on plan II. Enough of these to space 18" apart along the sides are needed. They are set normal to the side planks and allowed to extend their full length above the lower side boards. After they are all fitted, the upper side boards are bent in and fastened to them. If the seam between the two boards does not want to come tight, a bar clamp or a little work with a plane will fix them.

When the sides are complete, the seat and gunwale stringers of ¾" x 1½" oak as fitted as shown on plan II. Some builders let these into the frames so that they stand vertical. It is of little importance how they actually set. If side decks, or washboards as they are called on the Chesapeake Bay, are to be fitted the gunwale strips are omitted. The side deck is made from 12" planks butted as necessary to preserve the width of 8".

The boat is now turned over and the keel strip of ¾" x 6" oak fitted as shown on plan III. The skeg, sternpost and grounding strip are also fitted. The keel strip is fastened from inside the boat with screws.

If a sailing rig is to be fitted, two lines of bottom fastenings will have to be made in way of the trunk. The screws are driven from the planking into the keel and staggered from side to side. Some builders prefer to fit the keel strip inside the boat. Uncle Gabe contended that this was wrong because it prevented bilge water from draining from side to side and that the strip on the outside reduced wear on the bottom when the boat was dragged up on a beach. Perhaps he was right.

If a sailing rig is fitted, by all means fit the washboards as they will prevent a lot of water from running inside the boat. The centerboard trunk is made twelve inches deep above the inside bottom. A total width of about fifteen inches will be necessary for the trunk sides. The trunk is located about four and a half feet aft of the stem head in the sixteen-footers and about four feet in the fourteens.

The mast is seventeen feet long and about three inches in diameter at its butt. Uncle Gabe used to get a straight pine sapling, peel the bark off and season a full year before using. The spreader is two inches in diameter at its center, tapering to an inch at each end. The jib club and the mainsail spreader are about one inch in diameter. No standing rigging is fitted to the mast. The jib is set flying and the mainsail is laced to the mast. The whole rig is removed when not in use. The only block necessary is a small one for the jib halyard.

I have received numerous letters from the first edition whose writers complained that their sailmakers had never seen a sail cut like that shown. Their sailmakers are not as yet dry behind the ears, or have never been on the Chesapeake Bay. In the days when I was a kid, many skiff sails were cut thus. If you prefer a more modern sail have it clothed like that of the *Teal*.

BOAT PLANS

MIDGE

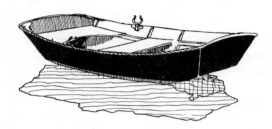

A plywood dink that everybody needs; 7' 0" long, 4' 0" beam.

Many of the boats in this book are big enough to sport a tender of the type described here, and if they are anchored offshore this sort of boat is almost indispensable. It is of the simplest design possible, yet it is very seaworthy and will carry three full-grown persons if called upon to do so. The little tub will tow on any length of rope and is light enough to be taken aboard by one man. It will row with the greatest of ease and can turn on the proverbial dime, and its roped sheer will keep it from marring the high finish of any yacht's topsides.

The construction is the acme of simplicity. Only four frames are required, the seat acting as a brace amidship and the two ends frame the rest of the boat. Two simple molds are made as shown on plan II. The bow and the stern are made from any stock boards available. While mahogany will make a natty looking job for the ends, any sort of board can be used if the boat is to be painted. As the molds are useless after the boat is planked they may be made of scrap lumber. The molds and ends are set upside down on the floor at the positions shown and securely braced.

The chine strips are bent in and fastened to the ends. As there is quite a bit of bend to the chines, it is recommended that they be soaked overboard for a week or steamed before the bending is attempted. If it is found that they persist in twisting at an angle that does not line up with the side planks they should

be worked on until they do by screwing a clamp on them, and giving an opposite twist.

The side planks are gotten out by setting the edge of the plywood sheet at the transom where it

Author and friend in the original *Midge*.

touches the floor, bending it around the sides of the boat and clamping it to the bow plate. The shape along the chine is then marked off and the sheet removed. The side sheet is then cut out roughly along the chine line. The operation is then repeated for the

133

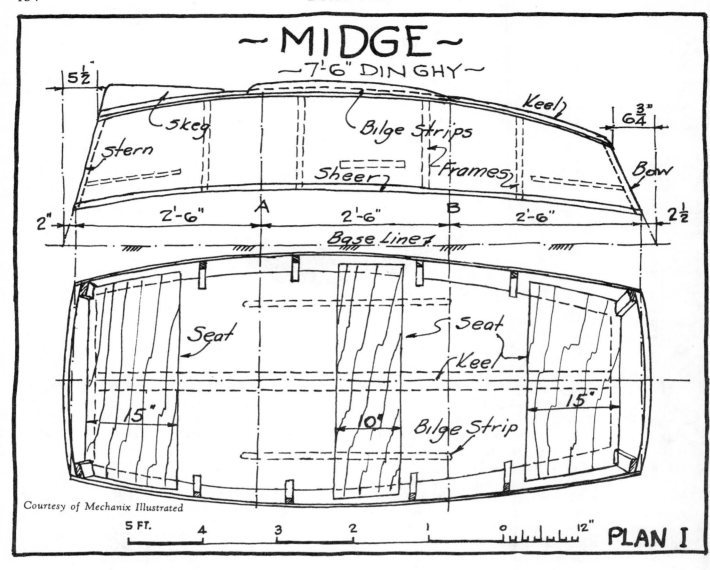

~MIDGE~
~7'-6" DINGHY~

Courtesy of Mechanix Illustrated

PLAN I

other side. The sides are next put back on the frame and the line of the chine accurately marked off. The sheets are then marked off for the ends, and a thin strip of wood bent along the edge nearest the floor to mark the sheer line shown on the drawings. Holes for the screws are also drilled at this time and the sheets removed for accurate cutting. Saw out the sheer line, replace the planks on the frame and fasten.

The chine, side planking and ends are then beveled so the bottom will lie flat across them. Be sure that the screws through the side planks to the chine (about two inches apart) are placed high enough in the chine so that the beveling process will not cut into their heads. When you are sure that the bottom sheet

of plywood will lie flat all around the boat and that no high spots exist, the sheet is laid on the bottom and marked off. It is cut to shape with a small allowance for planing later, put back and drilled for screws on 2" centers. After removing for burr cleanage, it is fastened in place with flannel and marine glue, or white lead and varnish in the seams. The screws are then driven home. The ends are planed off to match the bow and stern and the keel strip is then bent around the bottom along its center. This strip is fastened to the stern and bow only, the fastenings through the bottom being driven after the boat is turned over.

The boat is now cut loose from the floor, turned

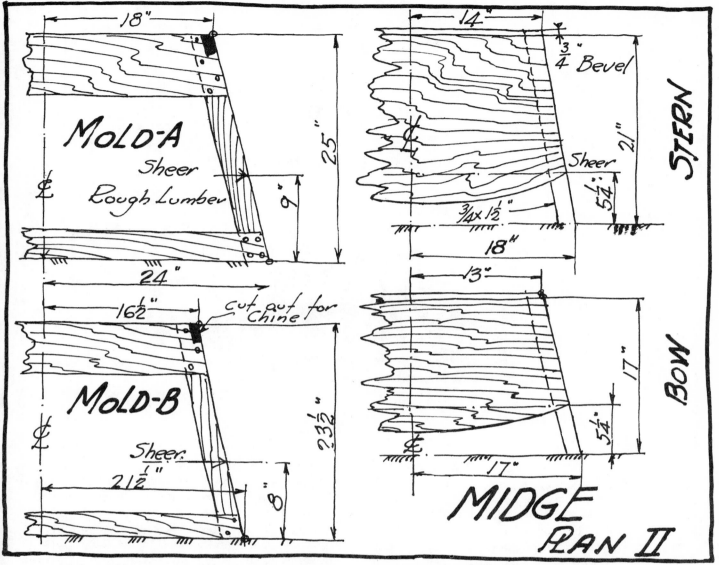

over and the molds removed after the sheer strip is in place. The frames are next installed and screwed from the outside. The whole inside of the boat is given a coat of aluminum priming paint. Seats are fitted next, and the inside given its final painting before they are fastened in permanently. The outside is then painted, preferably to match the color of the parent boat. The rope around the edge is attached by drilling holes through the sheer strip every three inches and lacing the rope to the strip with Italian yacht marline of medium thickness or heavy fish line. The rope should be well stretched as it is put on. The ends of the rope should be served to prevent unraveling. Oarlocks and towing ring complete the boat.

BILL OF MATERIAL

1 Sheet Plywood 48"x96"x¼"—Sides

1 Sheet Plywood 48"x144"x⅜"—Bottom
  (4'0" waste makes end seats)
2 Pcs. ⅝"1¼"x8 ft. Oak—Chines
2 Pcs. ⅝"x¾"x8 ft. Oak—Sheer Strips
1 Pc. ⅞"x1¾"x8 ft. Oak—Keel
1 Pc. ⅞"x15"x8 ft. Oak or Mahogany—Ends
1 Pc. ⅞"x1¾"x16 ft. Spruce—Seat Strips
1 Pc. ⅝"x10"x16 ft. Spruce—Seat amidship
3 Gross ¾" No. 6 Flat Head Wood Screws (Brass)
1 Gross 1½" No. 8 Flat Head Wood Screws (Brass)
20 Ft. ¾" diameter Cotton or Manila Rope
1 Ball Italian Yacht Marline (Medium)
1 Pint Liquid Marine Glue (Jefferies)
1 Quart Paint—For Outside
1 Quart Paint—For Inside
1 Pair Oarlocks (Wilcox Crittenden—Fig. 440)
1 ¼"x2" Towing Ring (Wilcox Crittenden—Fig. 213)

BOAT PLANS

TEAL: A 15-FOOT PLYWOOD SKIFF

An original *Teal* undergoing static test.

When Uncle Gabe launched his last skiff on Bodkins Creek, plywood was a thing to experiment with but not to trust. The wide cypress boat-side lumber that he used was becoming a thing of the past even before Gabe passed on. The outboard motor was increasing in power to the point where Gabe's skiffs no longer performed satisfactorily ahead of them. A new era had started. A new kind of skiff was required. Starting where Gabe left off, I experimented with various bottom shapes. A boat that will perform well under power is hard to row; one that is easy to row does not perform well under power. So there you have it. *Teal,* therefore, had to be a compromise.

The first step in constructing *Teal* is to saw out the two sides from a sheet of ⅜" plywood, 4' wide and 16' long. If you desire an ultra-light boat the sides may be ¼". Mark off the ordinates shown on the plans from one straight side of the sheet and measure the required distance in on each. Do not saw the stem end as yet. After one side is sawed, use it to mark the other.

Now, get out the stem as shown and work it to the required bevel. From any scrap lumber you may

have, make the mold, and from 1-⅛" oak fabricate the transom. Using the bottom curvature of one of the sheets as a pattern, mark off the chine stringers and saw them to shape.

Now, take a piece of heavy cardboard or thin wood and tack it on the bevel of the stem. Mark the forward edge of the stem on this pattern. When this pattern is removed you will find it slightly different than the line you used to mark off the stem curvature. Apply the pattern to the proper position on your side pieces and saw them to this shape.

With plenty of sealing compound between the joints, screw-fasten the plywood sides to the stem with 1-¼" No. 10 flat-head wood screws. The aft ends of these boards will have a considerable spread so be sure you have enough room before you attempt this operation.

Putting the mold between the sheets at its proper location, fasten it temporarily with nails through the sheets. The boat should be upside down during this operation. With a rope wrapped around the aft ends pull them together until they are almost the width of the transom. Now, measure from the starboard edge of the aft end of the sheet to the port side of the mold. The distance on the opposite diagonal should be the same. Theoretically, both sheets of plywood should bend the same, but in practice they very seldom do, and often temporary braces are required on the sheer to make them *even up*.

The transom is now screwed in using applications of wood preservative and seam compound in the joint. If the draw rope is used as a tourniquet the sheets may be drawn fairly tight against the transom but do not carry this too far.

The chine strips are now bent in and screwed about every 4″ to the side sheets. Use liberal applications of wood preservative between the surfaces. In setting the chines, let them project about 3/16″ above the plywood. After the chines are in, some builders have used spreaders at the quarter lengths on the bottom for'd and aft of the mold to give a more rounded shape to the chine.

With a straight-edge across the bottom, bevel the sides and chines until they are in line. Lay on the bottom sheet, tack it, and mark it off. After it is cut to shape, butter the edges with sealing compound and lay a strand of lampwick packing from end to end of both sides and across the transom. Screw on the bottom sheet with 1″ No. 10 flat-head screws on 3″ centers and plane off the excess flush with the sides.

Note that no longitudinal framing, with the exception of the chines, is inside of the boat. The reason for this becomes evident the first time you have to wash out the boat for repainting. There is not a single edge behind which dirt can lodge when washing out the interior. The keel and stringers are put outside on the bottom and screwed from the inside. The side frames are made and fastened in at the positions shown. The sheer stringer is bent around the outside and the seat stringers bent inside after the mold is removed. The seat locations may be changed to suit your own fancy. The type of oarlocks shown have been found best for this type of boat. Be sure to fit the reinforcing pieces as shown, glueing up the 3/4″ plywood from two pieces of 3/8″ scrap. Shape the skeg and screw it on with bolts and lag-screws, being sure to use washers inside the boat. A slat floor may be installed inside the boat if desired.

If the boat is to be used with an outboard motor, cut the center portion of the transom down to a depth of 15″ and fit an oak knee to reinforce it.

A sailing rig is shown and may be fitted if desired One sheet of 3/4″ plywood 4′ 0″ x 8′ 0″ will be required to make the centerboard, trunk, rudder and mast thwart. The mast is 17′ 6″ high. The diameter at the step is 2 3/4″ and at the head is 1 1/2. It may be made from one piece of spruce timber or from a laminate of smaller pieces glued with *Elmer's Glue*. The sprit is made from a piece of 2″ x 2″ and is 12′ 0″ long. The diameter of the center is 1 3/4″ and at the ends is 1 1/4″. The sail is laced to the mast and rolled upon it when not in use. Large brass screweyes should be placed on the mast to take the head and tack lashings as well as the sprit lashing. Similar screweyes are placed in the ends of the sprit to take up the lashings at those points. As the sail is portable, no stays are fitted and are not needed unless you find your timber to be too limber when in use. It is best to have this type of mast a bit limber as it gives to the wind in sudden gusts.

BILL OF MATERIAL — TEAL

Lumber

2	pcs.	Plywood	4'-0" x 16'-0" x 3/8"	
1	pc.	Plywood	4'-0" x 8'-0" x 3/4"	for sail only
4	pcs.	Oak	1" x 2" x 16'-0"	Sheer & Clamps
4	pcs.	Oak	1" x 2" x 8'-0"	Frames
2	pcs.	Oak	1" x 2" x 12'-0"	Protection Strips
2	pcs.	Oak	1" x 2" x 12'-0"	Seat Stringers
1	pc.	Oak	1" x 4" x 14'-0" or 1" x 8" x 14'-0"	Keel
2	pcs.	White Pine	1" x 10" x 12'-0"	Seats
1	pc.	Oak	1 1/8" x 10" x 14'-0"	Transom & Knees
1	pc.	Oak	2" x 8" x 6'-0"	Stem & Knee
1	pc.	Oak	2" x 2" x 6'-0"	Seat Supports
1	pc.	Spruce	3" x 3" x 18'-0"	Mast
1	pc.	Spruce	2" x 2" x 12'-0"	Spreet

Hardware

2	Gross	1" - #10 Fl. Hd. Galv. Wood Screws	
1	Gross	1 1/2" - #10 Fl. Hd. Galv. Wood Screws	
2		Oarlocks	W.C. Fig. 440
1	Set	Rudder Fittings	W.C. Fig. 4601
1	Qt.	Elmers Glue	

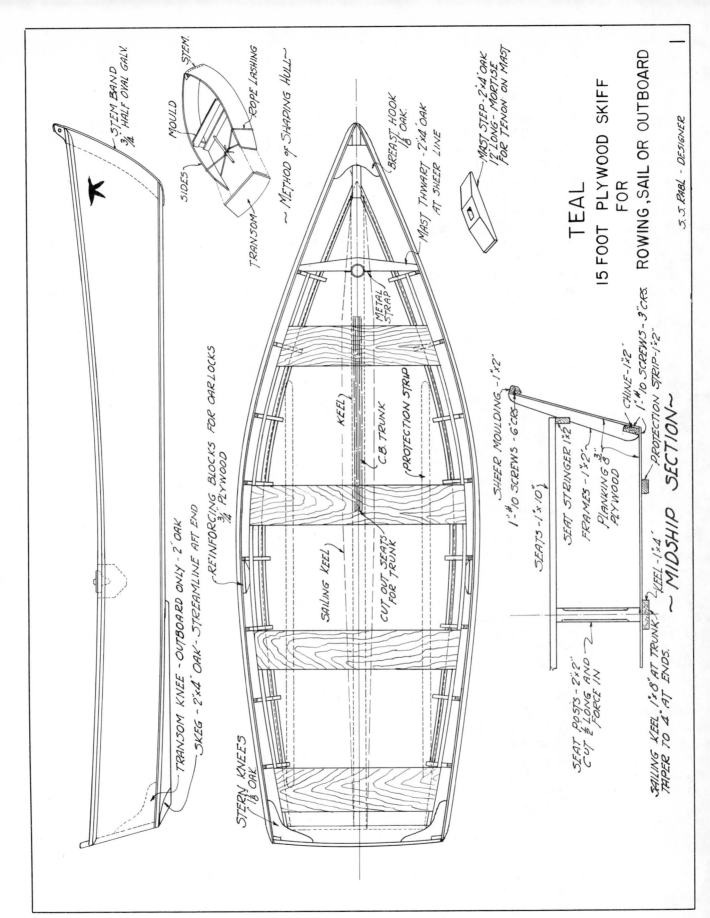

STEM BAND ¾ HALF OVAL GALV.

STEM.

MOULD

SIDES

ROPE LASHING

~ Method of Shaping Hull ~

TRANSOM

BREAST HOOK ⅞ OAK.

MAST THWART - 2"x4" OAK AT SHEER LINE

MAST STEP - 2"x4" OAK 12" LONG - MORTISE FOR TENON ON MAST

METAL STRAP

KEEL

C.B. TRUNK

PROTECTION STRIP

SAILING KEEL

CUT OUT SEATS FOR TRUNK

TRANSOM KNEE - OUTBOARD ONLY - 2" OAK

SKEG - 2"x4" OAK - STREAMLINE AFT END

REINFORCING BLOCKS FOR OARLOCKS ¾ PLYWOOD

STERN KNEES ⅞ OAK

TEAL

15 FOOT PLYWOOD SKIFF
FOR
ROWING, SAIL OR OUTBOARD

S. S. RABL - DESIGNER

SHEER MOULDING - 1"x2"
1" #10 SCREWS - 6" CRS.

SEATS - 1"x10"

SEAT STRINGER 1"x2"

FRAMES - 1"x2"

PLANKING ⅜ PLYWOOD

CHINE - 1"x2"
1" #10 SCREWS - 3" CRS.

PROTECTION STRIP - 1"x2"

SEAT POSTS - 2"x2"
CUT ½" LONG AND FORCE IN

KEEL - 1"x4"

SAILING KEEL 1"x8" AT TRUNK TAPER TO 4" AT ENDS.

~ MIDSHIP SECTION ~

138

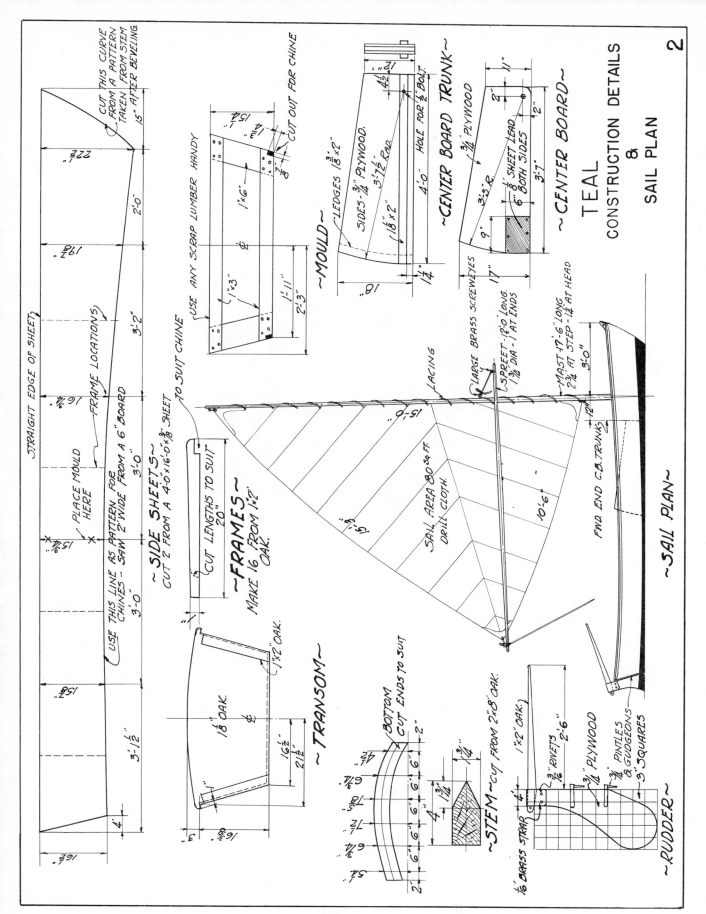

CUT THIS CURVE FROM A PATTERN TAKEN FROM STEM. 15" AFTER BEVELING.

CUT OUT FOR CHINE

~SIDE SHEETS~
CUT 2 FROM A 4'-0"x16'-0"x⅜" SHEET

USE THIS LINE AS PATTERN FOR CHINES - SAW 2" WIDE FROM A 6" BOARD

STRAIGHT EDGE OF SHEET

FRAME LOCATIONS

PLACE MOULD HERE

TO SUIT CHINE

USE ANY SCRAP LUMBER HANDY

~MOULD~

LEDGES 1⅛"x2"

SIDES - ¾" PLYWOOD.

~CENTER BOARD TRUNK~

¾" PLYWOOD

HOLE FOR ½" BOLT

~CENTER BOARD~

⅛" SHEET LEAD BOTH SIDES

LARGE BRASS SCREWEYES

~FRAMES~
MAKE 16 FROM 1½" OAK.
CUT LENGTHS TO SUIT

SPREET-12'-0" LONG. 1⅜" DIA-1" AT ENDS

MAST-17'-6" LONG 2¾" AT STEP-1¾" AT HEAD

SAIL AREA 80 SQ.FT.
DRILL CLOTH.

LACING

FWD END C.B. TRUNK

~SAIL PLAN~

~TRANSOM~
1½" OAK.

18 OAK.

~STEM~ CUT FROM 2"x8" OAK.
BOTTOM CUT ENDS TO SUIT

1"x2" OAK.

¾" PLYWOOD

BRASS STRAP

RIVETS

PINTLES & GUDGEONS

3" SQUARES

~RUDDER~

TEAL
CONSTRUCTION DETAILS
&
SAIL PLAN

2

139

BOAT PLANS

SANDPIPER

A modernization of the author's famous *Porpoise* design; 15′ 0″ long, 4′ 6″ beam.

One of the most popular outboard boats that I have ever designed was *Porpoise* which was published in *Mechanix Illustrated* in 1948. So many of these were built that I have lost track of the number. Designed as a rough-water fishing boat for motors of 5 H.P. and under, it had widespread appeal. It can be framed from almost any wood that will hold fastenings, and uses up the plywood ordered for it to such a degree that waste is almost entirely eliminated. No special wood sizes are required except for the keel which can be dressed down at any lumber mill from a standard 2″ x 6″. The stem is a laminate bent from ¼″ or ⅜″ strips, 3″ wide, or from three thicknesses of 1″ stock laid flat, nailed and glued. The original hull was built from standard sizes of North Carolina pine treated with *Cuprinol* before assembly and today is in almost perfect condition.

Many improvements were made on the original design by various builders over the years. The original required a small piece of plywood at the stem head to attain the designed overall length. The new

length is a bit shorter to eliminate this. The original floor was made from wide boards fastened directly to the frames. A removable slat floor makes cleaning and painting far easier. Originally the stern seat was one wide expanse of plywood. Longitudinal seats at this point make for handier control of the motor. Some builders have raised the sides with a 4″, or 6″ board which made a decided improvement for real rough-water work. The original depth was designed as a maximum of what could be gotten from a standard 4′ sheet. *Sandpiper* today is the same boat with all the foregoing improvements incorporated.

The first step in the construction is to assemble the frames. Draw their shapes on the floor and nail and glue the pieces over the outlines. Note how the chine gussets are cut from one piece of 8″ x 24″ plywood. The center cut angle is the same for both sides of the boat. The gussets are glued to the frame timbers with *Elmer's Glue* and held there with 1¼″ patent nails. The center connection is made in the same manner. Note also, in making the frames, how the gussets at Frame 1 form the support for the stern seat and how Frame 7 is constructed entirely of plywood in its lower portion. In making both the frames and the transom note how all the pieces are cut from the 4' x 8' sheet of ½" plywood. In making the transom, fit the ½" plywood covering with temporary screws so that it may be easily removed for access to the interior of the boat later. Also decide on the question of the depth of the boat before cutting the notch for the sheer. If the sheer is to be raised, the normal sheer line is the center of a ½" x 1½" seam batten. If the additional depth is not desired, the sheer line is the top of a 1" x 2" sheer stringer which will actually measure $1^{3}\!/_{16}$" x 1⅝". If the depth is to be increased the top of the sheer stringer is moved 4" above its normal position and the notch moved up accordingly. If for any reason you should desire to increase the depth more than 4" it may be accomplished by using a hogged sheer which may be cut from a 6" board. If the sheer is to be increased, order a board 2" wider and use the wasted width for the seam batten.

The stem is glued up from thin strips of wood, 3" wide. Cut a series of wedge-shaped blocks from scrap 2 x 4's and nail these to the floor about 18" apart. These blocks are set to the line of the inside of the stem. It is best to lay out the stem shape on a piece of brown wrapping paper and lay this on the floor as a pattern for setting the blocks. Place another series of blocks about 1" away from the outline of the forward edge to act as wedging pieces when assembling the strips. Coat both sides of the strips except the first and last with *Elmer's Glue* and bend them in. Small nails driven on the exact center of the strips will aid a lot in holding the strips until they are all in place and the wedges finally driven up. If you have an abundance of *C* clamps, the wedge blocks may be eliminated except at the ends. The stem may also be made from three flat laminations of 1" material similar to the method used in *Titmouse* and *Osprey*.

The boat is built inverted. Frame 4 is set up square to the centerline and plumb, as shown in Plan No. 3, Page 145. All other frames are set according to this. The keel may be prebeveled from the figures given or worked off later on the job. It is bolted to the stem and this assembly is then erected and fastened to the frames and transom. The sheer stringer and the chine are now bent in and securely fastened. The chine stringer is beveled off to receive the planking. The actual chine line at the stem is the exact center of the chine stringer. On the corner of the chine

stringer forward of Frame 6, drill a series of ⅛" holes about 6" apart, all the way through the stringer to the inside of the boat. Use 2" No. 10 flat-head screws in all framing.

Forward of Frame 5 the bottom plywood will start to take a curvature. The bottom stringer is wedged out to accommodate this at Frame 6. Do not screw the stringer to Frame 6. Wire it down temporarily and after the boat is turned over, remove the wire and wedge it securely against the bottom plywood. Fasten it to the frame with a long screw from the outside.

Now take the 16' plywood sheets and lay off the cut lines as shown on the plans. Saw them to these lines. Each sheet makes a bottom and a side and half the deck. Temporarily tack a piece of 1" x 2" along the flat of the keel and fit the first bottom sheet to this. Clamp it down well and mark it off along the chine. Remove the plywood from the transom and crawl inside the boat. Forward of Frame 6 drive six penny finishing nails through the holes in the chine, into the plywood, to mark the cut where it was impossible to mark with a pencil. Mark the location of the bottom stringer and all frames on the inside of the sheet. Remove the sheet and cut it out, making all cuts square to the surface. Drill all holes for the stringer and frame connections on 6" centers from the inside of the sheet, between the previously marked outlines. Give all the abutting surfaces of the framing and the sheet a coat of *Cuprinol, Wood Life* or *Woodtox*. Do not do this on any wood before glueing. Butter the keel, chine, and stem joints with sealing compound and put the sheet back, drill into the frames and stringers and fasten them home. 1" No. 10 screws are used in the plywood and should be 3" apart along the edges. After all fastenings are in place bevel off the chine edge of the sheet aft of Frame 6.

The side sheets are placed in a similar manner. Shape the skeg and fasten it to the keel between the edges of the bottom sheets, buttering the joint with sealing compound before it is finally bolted in place. The transom plywood is finally fastened tight and the frames cut loose from the floor. The boat is now turned right side up for final finishing. The interior arrangement may be as shown on the plans or may be as elaborate as you care to make it. Remember, in fitting a motor to this boat, that she was designed for 5 H.P.; 10 H.P. is the limit of power that she will take and still remain safe, and this statement is from actual experience.

BILL OF MATERIAL — SANDPIPER

Lumber

8	pcs.	Y. Pine	1" x 3" x 10'-0"	Frames
2	pcs.	Y. Pine	1" x 3" x 16'-0"	Chines
2	pcs.	Y. Pine	1" x 2" x 16'-0"	Sheer Str.
2	pcs.	Y. Pine	1" x 2" x 16'-0"	Sheer Guards
1	pc.	Y. Pine	2" x 6" x 12'-0" Dress to 1 1/4"	Keel
1	pc.	Y. Pine	2" x 6" x 8'-0"	Skeg
2	pcs.	Y. Pine	1" x 2" x 12'-0"	Seat Str.
1	pc.	Oak	2" x 12" x 4'-0"	Stern Knees
1	pc.	Oak	1 1/4" x 10" x 18"	Motor Pad
1	pc.	W. Pine	1" x 10" x 10'-0"	Seats
14	pcs.	W. Pine	1" x 3" x 10'-0"	Floor
2	pcs.	Oak	1/2" x 2" x 12'-0"	Protection Strip
8	pcs.	Oak	3/8" x 3" x 8'-0"	
		or		Stem
3	pcs.	Oak	1" x 8" x 8'-0"	
2	Sheets	Harborite	4' x 16' x 3/8"	
1	Sheet	Harborite	4' x 8' x 1/2"	

Hardware

2	Gross	1" -#10 Fl. Hd. Wood Screws Galv.		
1	Gross	1 1/2" -#10 Fl. Hd. Wood Screws Galv.		
2	lbs.	4 penny head nails	Galv.	
4		3/8" x 3 1/2" Galv. Carriage Bolts	Tiebout	3614
1		3/8" x 2" Galv. Carriage Bolts	Tiebout	3614
3		3/8" x 3' Galv. Lag Screws	Tiebout	3598
45	Lin. ft.	3/4" Half oval Alum.	W. C. Fig.	5456
1	Pair	Bow Chocks - 4" -Sealume	W. C. Fig.	414
1	Pair	Oarlocks Galv.	W. C. Fig.	4476
1		Bow Handle	W. C. Fig.	813
2		Stern Handles	W. C. Fig.	814
1		Cleat - 4 1/2"	W. C. Fig.	810
2	Qts.	Elmers Glue		
		Equipment to Comply to U.S.C.G. Rules		

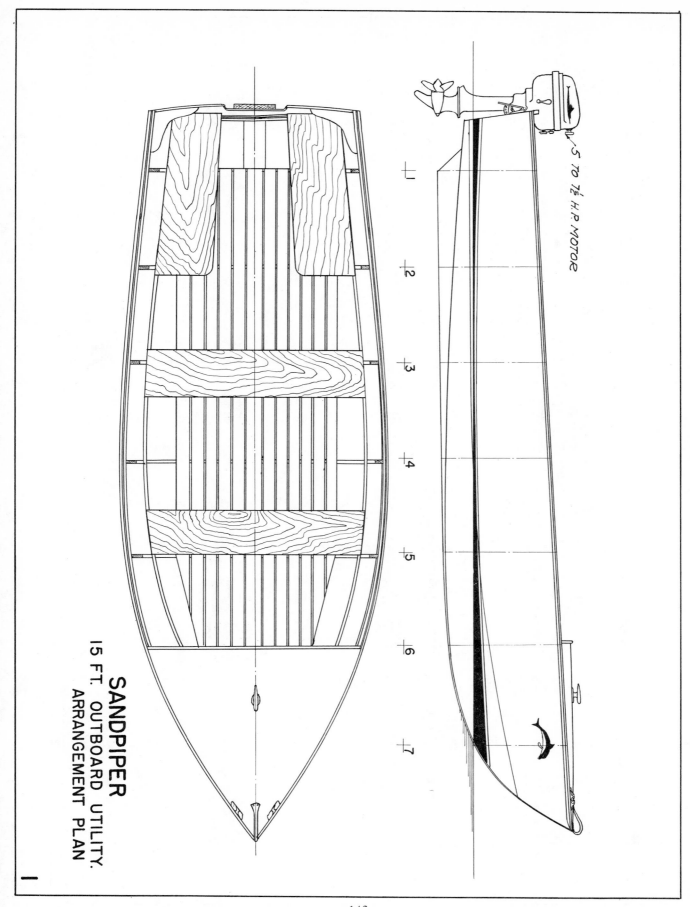

5 TO 7½ H.P. MOTOR

SANDPIPER
15 FT. OUTBOARD UTILITY.
ARRANGEMENT PLAN

143

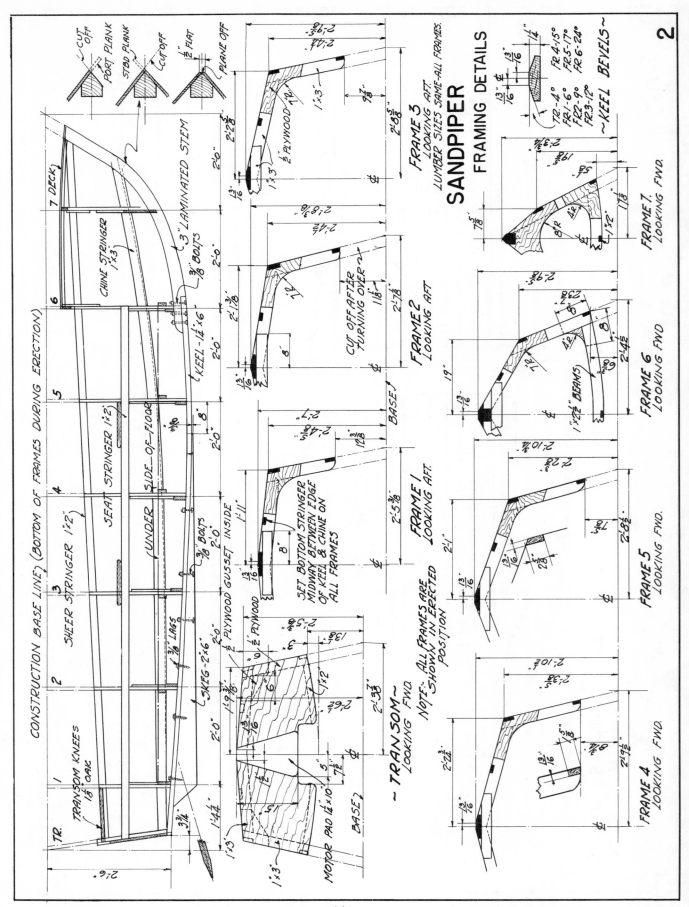

CONSTRUCTION BASE LINE (BOTTOM OF FRAMES DURING ERECTION)

SANDPIPER
FRAMING DETAILS

~ KEEL BEVELS ~

FR.2-4° FR.4-15°
FR.2-9° FR.5-17°
FR.3-12° FR.6-24°

FRAME 3
LOOKING AFT.
LUMBER SIZES SAME-ALL FRAMES.

FRAME 7.
LOOKING FWD.

FRAME 2
LOOKING AFT.

FRAME 6
LOOKING FWD

FRAME 1
LOOKING AFT.

FRAME 5
LOOKING FWD.

~ TRANSOM ~
LOOKING FWD.

NOTE:- ALL FRAMES ARE
SHOWN IN ERECTED
POSITION

FRAME 4
LOOKING FWD.

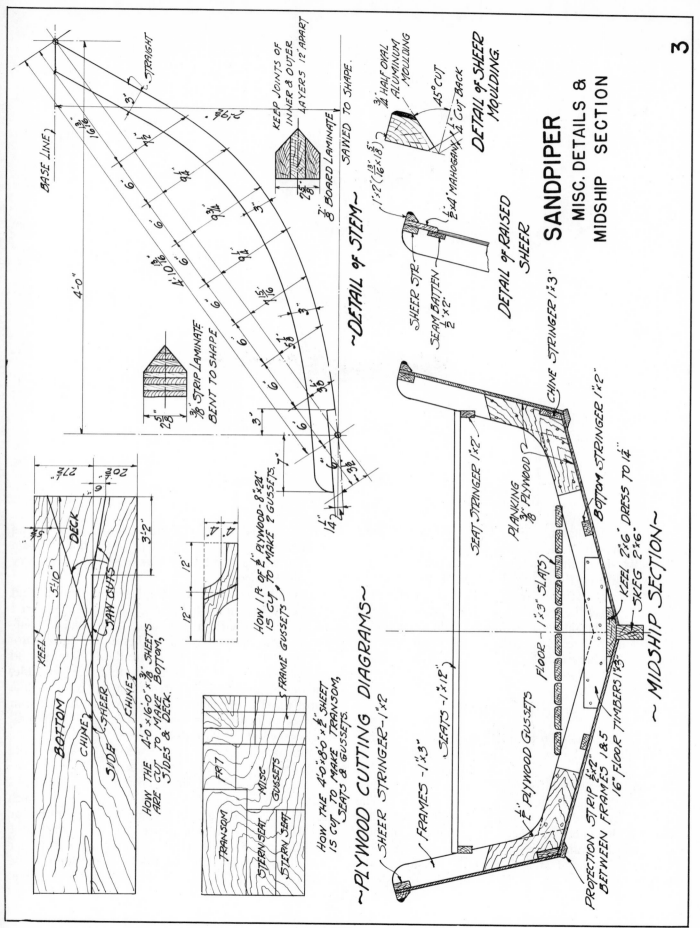

~ DETAIL OF STEM ~

KEEP JOINTS OF INNER & OUTER LAYERS 12" APART

⅜" BOARD LAMINATE SAWED TO SHAPE.

BASE LINE

STRAIGHT

3"

4'-0"

⅜" STRIP LAMINATE BENT TO SHAPE.

2⅝"

HOW 1 Pc. OF ½" PLYWOOD-8"×24" IS CUT TO MAKE 2 GUSSETS.

3" PLYWOOD CUTTING DIAGRAMS ~

SANDPIPER
MISC. DETAILS &
MIDSHIP SECTION

¾" HALF OVAL ALUMINUM MOULDING

45° CUT

2×4" MAHOGANY

1"×2" (13/16"×1⅝")

~ DETAIL OF SHEER MOULDING ~

SHEER STR.

SEAM BATTEN ½"×2"

DETAIL OF RAISED SHEER

CHINE STRINGER 1"×3"

SEAT STRINGER 1"×2"

PLANKING ⅜" PLYWOOD

BOTTOM STRINGER 1"×2"

KEEL 2"×6" DRESS TO 1½"

SKEG 2"×6"

FLOOR - 1"×3" SLATS

SEATS - 1"×12"

½" PLYWOOD GUSSETS

FRAMES - 1"×3"

PROJECTION STRIP ¾"×2"

16" FLOOR TIMBERS 1"×3"

BETWEEN FRAMES 1 & 5

~ MIDSHIP SECTION ~

BOTTOM

KEEL

CHINE

SIDE

SHEER

CHINE

DECK

SAW CUTS

HOW THE 4'-0"×16'-0"× ⅜" SHEETS ARE CUT TO MAKE BOTTOM, SIDES & DECK.

FR 7

MISC. GUSSETS

TRANSOM

STERN SEAT

STERN SEAT

HOW THE 4'-0"×8'-0"× ½" SHEET IS CUT TO MAKE TRANSOM, SEATS & GUSSETS.

SHEER STRINGER - 1"×2"

S. FRAME GUSSETS

3

BOAT PLANS

OSPREY

An outboard runabout in the modern trend; 15′ 0″ long, 6′ 0″ beam.

If you are looking for a boat that will reward your efforts in building her, *Osprey* is that boat. Actually she is little more than an oversized water ski with a beautifully flared hull built above it. She will take any outboard from 10 H.P. to 35 H.P. and get up and go like a scared cat. The bottom is of flat boards and the sides are stripped. While she will take a bit longer to construct than a plywood boat the work is less laborious and the end result more beautiful.

SPECIFICATIONS

FLAT BOTTOM.—To be made of ¾″ or 1³⁄₁₆″ material glued and doweled. The center strake is 8″ wide, the others 6″. The whole bottom is glued before cutting. The intermediate battens are spaced between the frames and are of 1⅛″ x 2″ oak. The dowels are made from 20-penny galvanized nails cut to 3″ long and are spaced on 16″ centers to come between the frames and the battens. Battens and frames are screw-fastened from the outside of the bottom with 1½″ No. 12 flat-head, galvanized wood

screws, spaced about 3″ centers. Stagger the screws in the battens. Lay out the shape of the bottom from the half widths and add *outside of this* the necessary amount for bevel.

If the bottom is to be fiberglased, the dowels and glue may be eliminated and the thickness reduced to ⅝″. If the bottom is doweled and glued the outline may be cut with a *Skilsaw* before the battens are fastened. The total depth of both dowel holes should be at least 3¼″. If the necessary tools are available, the dowels may be eliminated and a ¼″ x ¾″ spline substituted in the joints. If desired, the flat bottom may be made of ¾″ plywood with a ¾″ square oak strip glued along its outer edges.

FRAMES.—These are cut from 1⅛″ oak and the side frames measure 2″ wide at the sheer and 3″ at the bottom. Their inner bottom edges are 6½″ away from the edge of the bottom. The bottom frames are of 1⅛″ x 2″ oak. In laying out the patterns for the frames use tracing paper and mark the outer lines. By moving the tracing outboard the proper amount at top and bottom, the inner outline may be readily traced from the same line as the outside.

Joints with the straight bottom wooden frame are made with glue and 2″ No. 12 galvanized screws or ¼″ bolts. If the lines have been laid down full size the bevels of the frames may be picked up from these, otherwise the frames must be beveled off to the sweep of a longitudinal fairing batten.

TRANSOM.—Glued and doweled from 1⅛″ x 12″ oak or mahogany. Outside edges and motor doubling are of 1⅛″ oak, screwed and glued to inner face with 2″ No. 12 screws. Bevel the bottom edge to meet the flat and a 1⅛″ x 2″ batten is secured to the bottom boards to take the bottom of the transom.

STEM.—Glued up from three thicknesses of ⅞″ or 1³⁄₁₆″ oak to dimensions shown. Glue and secure to flat bottom with six 2″ No. 12 wood screws. Bevel forward edge to a sharp point at the centerline either from the laid-down lines or with a fairing batten.

SHEER STRINGER.—To be of oak ¾″ to ⅞″ thick as received from mill. Minimum width on bottom to be 2″. As there will be considerable edge bend forward, this portion is sawed from a 12″ board to the dimensions shown on the lines and the construction plans. The next curved portion aft is sawed from a 6″ board. Joints are made either by edge-screwed scarphs 12″ long or by butts with backing pieces 18″ long beneath them. The stringers are fastened to the frames with one No. 12 wood screw at each.

STRIP PLANKING.—To be ripped ⅝″ thick and as wide as received from mill, ¾″ or ⅞″. To be edge-nailed every 6″ with 4 penny galvanized wire nails cross-toed.

DECKING.—To be of ⅜″ marine plywood canvased. If a better finished job is desired use ¼″ plywood overlaid with ¼″ x 3″ mahogany strips and ¼″ edging all glued to the plywood. The appearance may be further enhanced by the insertion of ⅛″ x ¼″ white holly or ash strips in all joints and seams. If the latter procedure is followed, use no stain whatsoever on the mahogany, instead filling the pores with a clear wood filler followed with spar varnish. If desired, the hull may be finished as an open boat. In this case the sheer stringer is capped with ½″ mahogany.

ERECTION.—The flat bottom is laid on an open work table about 24″ above the floor. It is secured to this with double-headed nails for easy removal later. The frames are erected and plumbed and then securely braced to any convenient point. 1″ x 2″ cross spawls should be fitted to temporarily hold the sheer half width to its given dimension. If decking is to be fitted, the deck beams will serve this purpose. After

the sheer stringer is fitted the planking is started from the flat bottom working toward the sheer. Connection of the frames, stem and transom, are with four-penny galvanized head nails toed blind through every other strip. Resorcinal resin glue should be used throughout the boat.

BILL OF MATERIAL — OSPREY

Lumber

Qty		Material	Dimensions	Use
1	pc.	Oak or Mahogany	1 1/4 x 12″ x 12′-0″	Transom
2	pcs.	Oak	1 1/8″x 12″ x 12′-0″	Frames
6	pcs.	Oak	1 1/4 x 2 x 10′-0″	Frs. & Battens
2	pcs.	Oak	3/4″x 12″ x 10′-0″	Sheer Stringer
1	pc.	Oak	3/4″x 6″ x 10′-0″	Sheer Stringer
1	pc.	Oak	3/4″x 2″ x 10′-0″	Sheer Stringer
2	pcs.	Oak	3/4″x 12″ x 12′-0″	Stem & Knee
3	pcs.	Oak	3/4″x 8″ x 12′-0″	Beams
1	pc.	Optional	3/4″ x 8″ x 14′-0″	Flat Bottom
2	pcs.	Optional	3/4″ x 6″ x 14′-0″	Flat Bottom
5	pcs.	Optional	3/4″ x 6″ x 12′-0″	Flat Bottom
100 Bd. Ft.		Mahogany	5/8″ Random widths & Lengths	Stripping
4	Sheets	Fir	4′-0″ x 8′-0″ x 3/8″	Plywood - Decks, Etc.
1	Gallon	Elmers Glue		

Hardware

Qty		Description	
1	Gross	2″-#10 Fl. Hd. Wood Screws Galv.	
1	Gross	1″-# 7 Fl. Hd. Wood Screws Brass	
10	lb.	6 penny finishing Nails	Galv.

Fittings

Qty		Description		
35	Lin. ft.	Moulding Strip	Size 2	W. C. Fig. 5455
2		Lifting Handles		W. C. Fig. 6200
1		Bow Handle		W. C. Fig. 9971
1	Set	Windshield Brackets		W. C. Fig. 816A
1	Set	Bow Chocks		W. C. Fig. 812
5	Swivel	Blocks & Straps		W. C. Fig. 5781
6		Tiller Rope Guides		W. C. Fig. 576
1		Steering Wheel		W. C. Fig. 536

Lights & Equipment as required by U. S. C. G.

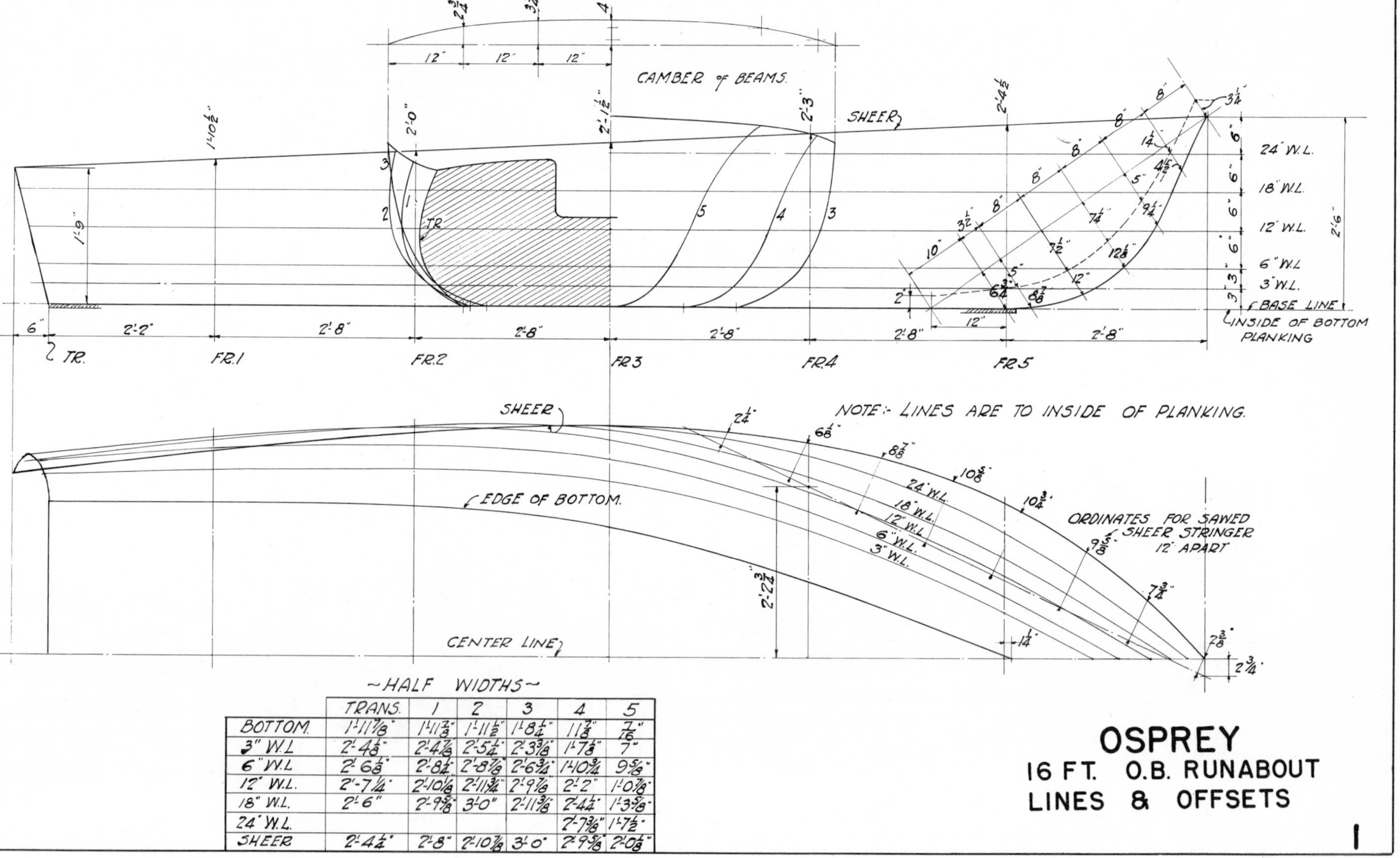
CAMBER of BEAMS.
SHEER
24" W.L.
18" W.L.
12" W.L.
6" W.L.
3" W.L.
BASE LINE
INSIDE OF BOTTOM PLANKING
TR.
FR.1
FR.2
FR.3
FR.4
FR.5
NOTE:- LINES ARE TO INSIDE OF PLANKING.
EDGE OF BOTTOM.
ORDINATES FOR SAWED SHEER STRINGER 12" APART
CENTER LINE

~HALF WIDTHS~

	TRANS.	1	2	3	4	5
BOTTOM.	1'-11 7/8"	1'-11 7/8"	1'-11 1/2"	1'-8 1/4"	11 7/8"	7/16"
3" W.L	2'-4 1/8"	2'-4 7/8	2'-5 1/4"	2'-3 3/8"	1'-7 1/8"	7"
6" W.L	2'-6 1/8"	2'-8 1/4"	2'-8 7/8"	2'-6 3/4"	1'-10 3/4	9 5/8"
12" W.L.	2'-7 1/4"	2'-10 1/8	2'-11 3/4"	2'-9 7/8"	2'-2"	1'-0 7/8"
18" W.L.	2'-6"	2'-9 5/8"	3'-0"	2'-11 3/8"	2'-4 1/4"	1'-3 5/8"
24" W.L.					2'-7 3/8"	1'-7 1/2"
SHEER	2'-4 1/4"	2'-8"	2'-10 7/8	3'-0"	2'-9 5/8"	2'-0 1/8"

OSPREY
16 FT. O.B. RUNABOUT
LINES & OFFSETS

1

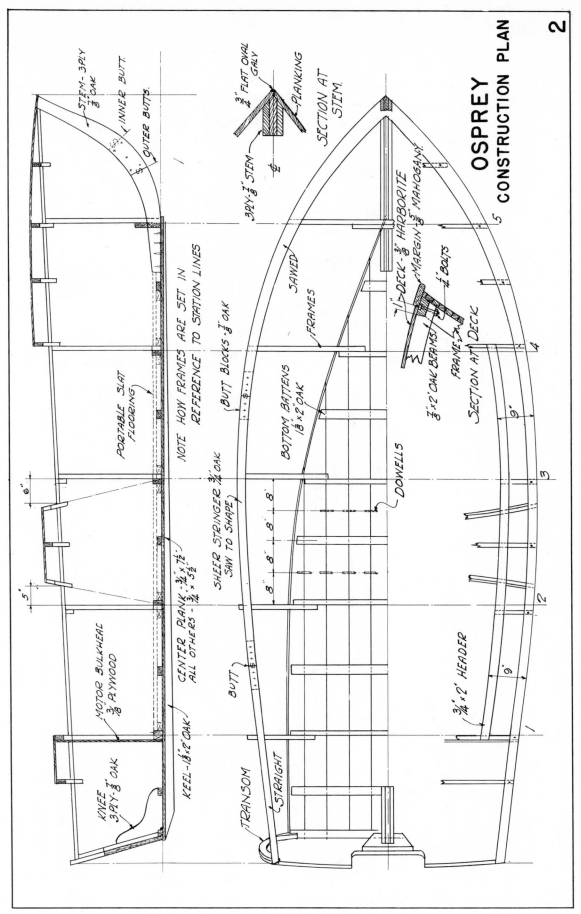

OSPREY CONSTRUCTION PLAN

SECTION AT STEM.

SECTION AT DECK.

STEM-3PLY ⅞ OAK

INNER BUTT.

OUTER BUTTS.

¾" FLAT OVAL GALV.

PLANKING

3PLY-⅞ STEM

1"→DECK-⅜ HARBORITE

MARGIN ⅝ MAHOGANY

¼ BOLTS

⅞×2" OAK BEAMS

FRAME

SAWED

FRAMES

PORTABLE SLAT FLOORING

NOTE HOW FRAMES ARE SET IN REFERENCE TO STATION LINES

BUTT BLOCKS-⅞ OAK

SHEER STRINGER ¾ OAK SAW TO SHAPE)

BOTTOM BATTENS 1⅝×2" OAK

DOWELLS

MOTOR BULKHEAD ⅜ PLYWOOD

CENTER PLANK-¾×7½" ALL OTHERS-¾×5½

KEEL-1⅝×2" OAK

KNEE 3PLY-⅞" OAK

TRANSOM

BUTT

STRAIGHT

¾×2" HEADER

6"

5'

8"   8"   8"

8"   8"

9'

9"

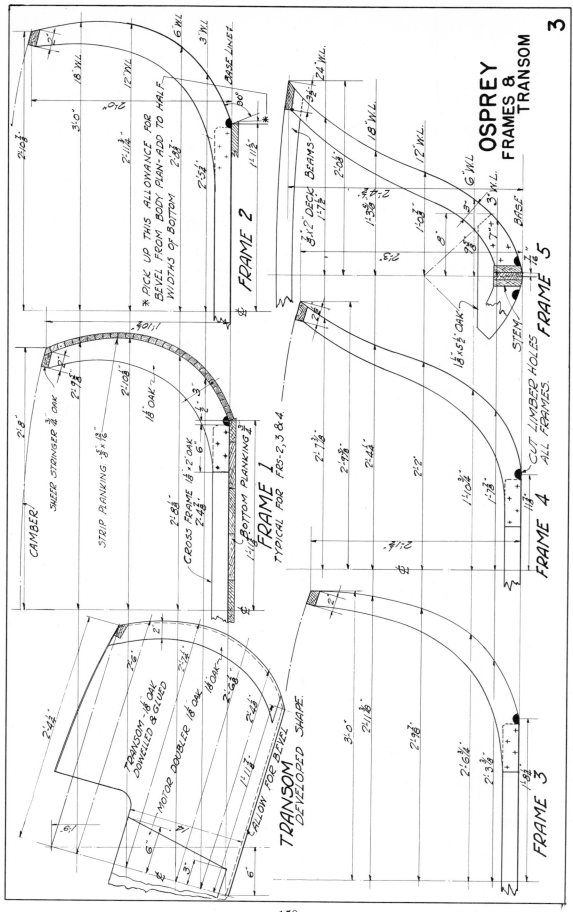

OSPREY
FRAMES &
TRANSOM

FRAME 5

FRAME 4

CUT LIMBER HOLES
ALL FRAMES.

FRAME 3

STEM

1⅝"×5½" OAK

3"×2" DECK BEAMS

24" W.L.

18" W.L.

12" W.L.

6" W.L.

3" W.L.

BASE

FRAME 2

6" WL
3" WL
BASE LINE

* PICK UP THIS ALLOWANCE FOR
BEVEL FROM BODY PLAN-ADD TO HALF
WIDTHS OF BOTTOM.

18" WL
12" WL

90°

FRAME 1
TYPICAL FOR FRS-2,3 & 4.

CAMBER

SHEER STRINGER ¾" OAK

STRIP PLANKING · ⅝"×4¾"

⅛" OAK

CROSS FRAME 1⅝"×2" OAK

BOTTOM PLANKING ¾"

TRANSOM
DEVELOPED SHAPE.

TRANSOM - 1⅝" OAK
DOWELLED & GLUED

MOTOR DOUBLER 1⅝" OAK

1⅝" OAK

ALLOW FOR BEVEL

3

150

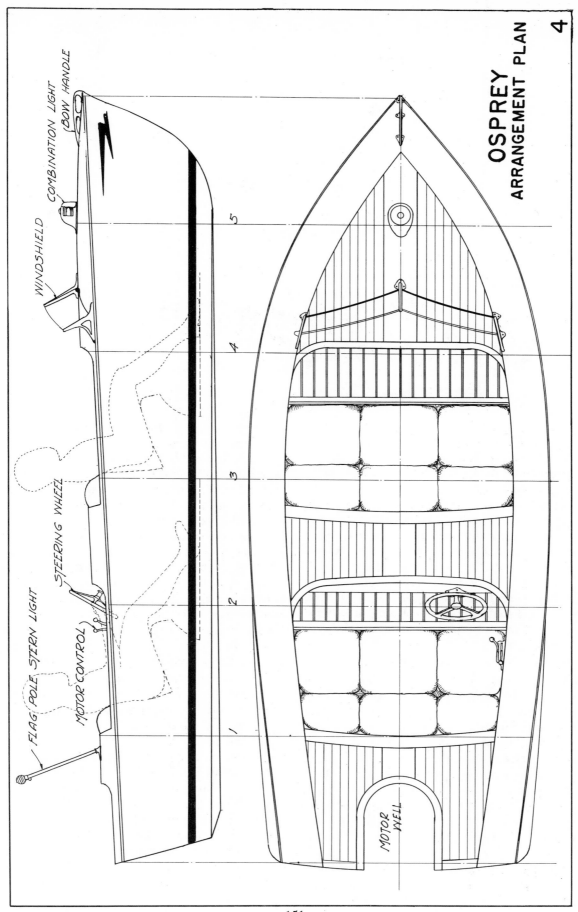

OSPREY
ARRANGEMENT PLAN

4

FLAG POLE STERN LIGHT

MOTOR CONTROL

STEERING WHEEL

WINDSHIELD

COMBINATION LIGHT
(BOW HANDLE)

MOTOR WELL

151

BOAT PLANS

TITMOUSE

A sailing cruiser which will fit a trailer; 15′ 0″ long, 6′ 0″ beam.

This *Titmouse* is quite a bit different from the one in the first edition, and while it will take a bit more time to build her she will be no more difficult. She was designed along the lines of many readers' letters for an improvement on *Titmouse* that would be a sassy-looking boat which could be trailered to any location and used for short cruises in sheltered waters.

Many years ago, more than I care to remember, our English cousins developed a particular type of boat which they called a canoe yacht. They were so popular that the best designers gave them their attention. They were designed to transverse the shoal English coastal broads and go exploring up the numerous rivers which were blocked in many places by bridges. In the height of their development they possessed two features that are good today.

Most of them had their cabin tops hinged at the forward end so that they could be raised to provide sitting room aft. A *Vee*-shaped curtain closed the opening when the top was raised. This gave a livable little cabin, very necessary in the inclement English weather. A primus stove and primitive W.C., plus a good pair of oars, were the capital items of the outfit. The hinged mast which most of them carried may or may not be a necessity to pass under bridges today but it most certainly works a lot easier than stepping or unstepping a mast every time the boat is put on a trailer.

The first step in making the boat is to assemble the bottom. The center plank is of 1″ oak, 8″ wide;

the others are of the same material you choose for the hull stripping and are 8″ and 6″ wide. The best way to make this assembly is on a wooden floor covered with old newspapers to prevent the glue from sticking. The center plank, with the trunk slot already cut and the centerline marked on both sides, is nailed to the floor with double-headed nails in about four places. The inboard edges of the two next adjacent planks are glue-coated and drawn against the center plank with bar clamps or wedged against it with wedges and temporary blocks nailed to the floor. After the glue has set this process is repeated for the other two outer planks. Lay off but do not cut the edge curvature as yet. Mark the position of all battens and frames on the flat bottom, and glue and screw the battens to the planking. Cut all battens 1/2″ clear of the edge curvature. After all glue has set, remove the assembly from the floor and turn it over. Back mark the frame stations on this side also and lay off the curved edge with the proper allowance for the bevel. A *Skilsaw* will easily travel around the amount of curvature you have to cut. Keep about 1/16″ away from the line and finish it with a plane.

The stem and transom are next constructed with nailed and glued joints. The flat bottom of the transom should be beveled beforehand; the sloping bottom and sides may be roughly beveled to save a lot of work later. The stem pieces are cut out and glued up from dimensions given on the lines. After the glue has set, the centerline is scribed on the forward

152

face and the bevel lines marked on both sides. The stem edge is then beveled off from the side marks to the centerline. This bevel is not exact and there is a small allowance to be cut off later.

The frames are next made as per the details. Do not cut Frame 3 entirely away from the trunk as yet. Cut up from the bottom allowing about 1" of wood to be cut out later when the trunk is fitted. Note how the plywood knees are cut from the ¾" sheet. Before cutting the knees from the sheet, lay off the centerboard, trunk and rudder. The knees are made from the plywood that remains. The beams are made whole and cut later.

Make the transom knee and assemble the transom to the flat bottom. Glue and bolt the stem to its proper position on the forward end.

The boat is built right-side-up on a straight keel horse. Lagscrew the flat bottom to the keel horse and block up the ends to the proper curve. A piece of galvanized-wire clothes line stretched from the stem head to the center of the transom will aid in forming the curve on the bottom. The weight of one man standing amidship will bend all the curvature necessary if the end blocks are set first. One-eighth inch or so difference in the curvature at any one point is of no importance. Holes for the hold-down lags are plugged later.

After the bottom is securely fastened, and leveled across its width, the frames are erected. Starting with Frame 2, all frames are set plumb. Frame 2 is plumbed and it is then screw-fastened from the under side. As this will be a frequent operation set the top of the keel horse at least 2' above the floor for working room beneath the boat. Brace Frame 2 securely so that it will not move. Run one edge of a straight 1" by 3" batten from the center of the stem head across the marked centerline of the beam on Frame 2 to the centerline of the transom top. This will form a brace to keep the other frames upright and center them at the same time. Check the bottom bevel of all of these frames, then square and plumb each.

After all frames have been set plumb and square, bend in and fasten the sheer stringer. Where this member meets the stem head, be sure that its outer surface fairs with the centerline of the stem on its forward edge, then fit the breast hook and quarter knees.

Take a square strip of the planking material and with this as a guide, bevel off the edge of the flat bottom by making this strip fit neat at every frame. After this has been done work the material off between the frames in a good fair curve. After this

edge has been faired start applying the strips. Allow the forward edges of the strips to run past the stem for several inches, alternately sawing off one side and then the other to let the opposite strip pass. Where one strip is high, notch it down much in the same manner as the logs of an old log cabin were worked at the corners. As the planking progresses the stem will look like a porcupine's back but all this is sawed off later. When all the ends on both sides are sawed off flush with the run of the planking the bow of the boat will end in a sharp point.

When the strips reach the sheer and start to run above it, discontinue the use of finishing nails and use headed nails which will be withdrawn later. When the glue has hardened along the sheer the strips are roughly cut down, withdrawing the nails as you go. After all nails are set or withdrawn, the planking and stringer are plane-beveled to match the camber. Fit the extra beams and the doubling pieces under the mooring bitt and in way of the tabernacle posts.

Now we are ready for the deck. The first operation is to get out the margin plank. Clamp a wide board along the sheer and mark its outer edge from the outside of the planking. With three of these boards butted where necessary, run the entire length of the boat. Do not as yet cut their inner edges. When all pieces have been fitted fasten them on temporarily and measure in 3" and mark them at frequent intervals. Set a strip of planking along these marks and scribe the inner edge. Remove the boards and saw to the line. It is imperative that the inner line be absolutely fair so that the decking strips will make a good joint with it. Fasten the margins down securely with glue to the sheer stringer and beams. When these are securely fastened lay the center planks of the deck.

The deck is now laid in strips the same as the planking. Working in from the margin, continue in until a distance of 9" is reached. Due to the strip widths this may vary ½" or so. This is of no import, so use your own judgment as to how wide you want your deck. Forward of the cabin front continue the stripping until the forward deck is completed. Do the same for the aft deck.

If you really want a snazzy deck, use mahogany for the margin and center and white pine for the strips and finish it natural. On the other hand I know of one youngster who made his deck this way and was justly proud of it, only to see it badly dented by a terrific hailstorm not three hours after the boat was launched. This kind of deck takes careful carpentry. The deck, if not finished natural, may be painted or canvassed. Putty and gunk in this case will hide a lot of sins.

Sand the hull and decks at the same time especially if you have to rent a heavy sander. Dust all the surfaces thoroughly and apply a priming coat or filler. Where openings exist between the strips use *Kuhl's Brushlast* and work across the seams to get it down deep. After all paint or filler is thoroughly dry, sand again and where any hollows appear in the way of any seams, fill with *Trowelast* worked in with a putty knife. As this material has a slight shrinkage you may have to go over and touch up some places to bring them out flush. After a final sanding the finishing coats may be applied.

The centerboard trunk is fitted after the hull is removed from the keel horse. Be sure that the forward ledge is a tight fit under the deck beam. The beam at Frame 3 will be removed to do this. Set the trunk down in glue and screw it up from the outside. The bottom edges of the plywood and the ledges finish flush with the outside of the bottom planking. The sills of the trunk are glued and screwed from the inside of the trunk. Try all parts to the boat for fit before final assembly, even when fitting the forward beam.

Between all beams on the inner edges of the deck, in the way of cockpit and cabin, fit a 1″ x 2″ header, sawed to shape, then glue and screw this to the decking. Be sure that the inner edge of these pieces lies vertical, then cut out the beams at Frames 1, 2 and 3 to match the line of the deck. Fit the inner coaming and allow it to project 1″ above the top of the deck planking. Nose off the top and bottom inner edges of this coaming to take away its sharp edges. After it is fitted and screwed in place, erect a temporary mold to take the bend of the outer or cabin coaming. Take a rough spiling for the main coamings and cut them roughly to shape. Bend them into position and scribe the final fit. Fit the forward end of the cabin. The top of this has no camber as this forms the hinge line.

You must decide at this time whether or not you want a bulkhead at the after end of the cabin. A bulkhead has an advantage in that all duffle can be placed in the cabin and locked away from petty larceny when you leave the boat unattended while cruising, and it stiffens the cabin coaming where it needs it most. On the other hand, it takes valuable floor room that will be used for sleeping. A compromise may be made and if the bulkhead is cut from one piece of ¼″ plywood it will be fairly stiff even though only 4″ is allowed inside the coaming.

The cabin top is now framed with the outer edge of the beam sill projecting ³⁄₁₆″ to ¼″ outside of the main coaming. If scrap 1″ x 2″ material is fastened to the inside of the coaming the difference in thickness between the coaming and the beam sill when bent around them will give this amount. The 1″ x 2″ beams are notched down into the beam sill ½″, as shown, and #8 wood screws are driven both ways on each side. The coaming should be free of all strains and have its natural set before the hinged top is fitted.

If any temporary bracing is removed from the coaming after the top is fitted, the spring may bind the cabin top. Be sure also that the total distance from the front to the back of the roof does not exceed 4′-0″ so that it may be covered with one sheet of plywood. After the top is completed and hinged to your satisfaction, reinforce the inside corners with sheet brass angles and fit the ³⁄₈″ facing strips. The top is then covered with plywood and fabric. Delay cutting the port holes as long as possible so that the coaming will take its natural set. Be careful in cutting these so that no undue strain is put on the coaming to split it. The lights themselves are best made of *Plexiglas* or *Lucite* with rims sawed from 14 Ga. aluminum sheet.

The mast is made of 1″ x 3″ white pine stock, the lower part from two 12′ lengths and the upper lengths to suit. Build the mast in a jig nailed to the floor and stretch lines to make sure the supports are straight. Spacers are inserted between the 1″ x 3′s to make a total of 3¼″ (4 thicknesses of ¹³⁄₁₆″). These are made 8″ long and should be 16″ where the main members are butted. They are spaced on 4′-0″ centers. Above the shrouds the mast is tapered to a total section of 2″ x 2″ at the top. Before the frame of the mast is removed from the jig, one side of the plywood is glued and nailed every 6″ with 4-penny galvanized nails. Do not think you can get away without a jig even though the members are perfectly straight; you will end up with an unholy mess. This advice is prompted by my own experience. After both sides of plywood are applied, the corners are rounded off and the nails set and filled. The back of the mast is a straight line from top to bottom. The top of the mast is mortised for the halyard sheave and a piece of ³⁄₈″ x ¹³⁄₁₆″ wood strip is nailed and glued in the center of the aft side for the length of the sail track. Either a full-length mast may be fitted in the conventional manner or the hinged mast installed for trailer operation. On the hinged mast an extra spacer made of oak should be inserted in way of the hinge bolt. A blitz rod at the top, with connections to the forestay and the water, is good protection. The boom is standard *Tee* construction.

If the boat is to be used as a day sailer without a cabin, carry the decks in 20″ from the sides and fit the inner coamings flush with the top of the deck. Also fit a small breakwater ahead of the mast.

The final operation is to plane off the sharp end of the stem to ½″ and fit a ½″ half-round brass band from the sheer to about 6″ aft of the beginning of the flat bottom. The sheer is trimmed out with a piece of ¾″ flat oval galvanized or aluminum band. Mortise the chain plates in and under this.

The floor is installed in 1″ x 3″ slats with their tops at the 6″ waterline. This is made in portable sections divided as you see fit. For short cruises the beds are made up right on the floor using inflatable air beach mats as the mattresses. These may be deflated and stowed during the day. A portable galley, such as that fitted to the *Picaroon*, completes the outfit. A tent covering the cockpit may turn an otherwise miserable, rainy day into one of pleasure.

BILL OF MATERIAL — TITMOUSE

Lumber

3 pcs.	Oak	1″ x 8″ x 12′-0″	Bottom
2 pcs.	Oak	1″ x 6″ x 10′-0″	Bottom
2 pcs.	Oak	1″ x 2″ x 12′-0″	Bottom Battens
1 pc.	Oak	2″ x 6″ x 6′-0″	Skeg
2 pcs.	Mahogany	1″ x 8″ x 10′-0″	Transom
1 pc.	Oak	1″ x 6″ x 10′-0″	Transom
1 pc.	Oak	1″ x 3″ x 3′-0″	Transom
4 pcs.	Oak	1″ x 2″ x 3′-0″	Transom
1 pc.	Oak	1″ x12″ x 12′-0″	Frames
1 pc.	Oak	1″ x 10″x 12′-0″	Frames
1 pc.	Oak	1″ x 8″ x 12′-0″	Frames
2 pcs.	Oak	1″ x 3″ x 8′-0″	Frames
3 pcs.	Oak	1″ x 8″ x 8′-0″	Stem
1 pc.	Oak	1″ x 3″ x 8′-0″	C.B. Trunk
1 pc.	Oak	2″ x 6″ x 3′-0″	C.B. Trunk
1 pc.	Oak	2″ x 2″ x 3′-0″	C.B. Trunk
4 pcs.	Oak	1″ x 6″ x 12′-0″	Beams-Coamings, Etc.
2 pcs.	Oak	1″ x 2″ x 16′-0″	Sheer Strs.
2 pcs.	Oak	1″ x 10″ x 8′-0″	Misc.
2 pcs.	Oak	1 3/8″ x 6″ x 6′-0″	Beams
2 pcs.	Oak	1 3/8″ x 4″ x 6′-0″	Tabernacle
7 pcs.	Spruce	1″ x 3″ x 12′-0″	Mast & Boom
2 pcs.	Mahogany	1″ x 12″ x 10′-0″	Cabin Trunk
175 Bd. ft.	Mahogany	5/8″ Finished Thickness, For Stripping trim, etc. Random Length & Widths.	

2	Sheets	Plywood	4′-0″ x 8′-0″ x 1/4″	Mast & Cabin
1	Sheet	Plywood	4′-0″ x 8′-0″ x 3/4″	Trunk Rudder, Etc.

Hardware

10 lbs.	6 penny Galv. Finishing Nails	
5 lbs.	4 penny Galv. Head Nails	
2 Gross	1 1/2″ - #10 Fl. Hd. Wood Screws (Galv.)	
1 Gross	1 1/4″ - #8 Fl. Hd. Wood Screws (Galv.)	
3 Qts.	Elmers Glue	
2	Rudder Pintles Size 0	Perko Fig. 1071
2	Rudder Gudgeons Size0	Perko Fig. 1072
1	Cleat 6 1/2″	Perko Fig. 572

Fittings

2	Bow Chocks	Size 1	Perko Fig. 160
1	Deck Pipe	Size 0	Perko Fig. 741
1	Bitt	Size 1	Perko Fig. 597
1	Bow Plate		Perko Fig. 181
1	Bow Ring	Size 2	Perko Fig. 238
2	Deck Blocks	Size 0	Perko Fig. 87
1	Masthead Sheave	Size 4	Perko Fig. 154
1	Cheek Block	Size 1	Perko Fig. 95
1	Centerboard Block	Size 1	Perko Fig. 827
1	Outhaul Block		Perko Fig. 885
20 feet	5/8″ Sail Track		W.C. Fig. 120
2	Chain Plates		W.C. Fig. 630
2	Finishing Plates		W.C. Fig. 6301
2	Mast Tangs	Size 2	W.C. Fig. 9892
1	Bail	Size 0	W.C. Fig. 6390
1	Gooseneck		W.C. Fig. 6484
3	Release Hooks	(Shrouds & Forestay)	W.C. Fig. 978
2	Halyard Shackles		W.C. Fig. 2870
1	Jib Halyard Block		W.C. Fig. 954
4	Sheet Blocks		W.C. Fig. 952
2	Fairleads	Size 2	W.C. Fig. 5811
32 ft.	Moulding Strip	Size 3	W.C. Fig. 5455
8 ft.	Moulding Strip	Size 1	W.C. Fig. 5456
100 ft.	1/4″ Rope	Manila	
30 ft.	5/16″ Rope	Manila	
65 ft.	1/8″ Rope	Flexible Steel Wire	
6	Thimbles for 1/4″ Wire rope		
6	Thimbles for 1/8″ Wire rope		
2	Thimbles for 5/16″Wire rope		
3	Turnbuckles	1/4″ Size	W.C. Fig. 3162
1	Set Sails including Bag, slides and snaps.		

The following letter was received from Mr. John T. Durnin of Wayne, Pa., which speaks for itself:

Dear Mr. Rabl,

Enclosed is a picture of your *Titmouse*. I've sailed it all summer and it certainly is a fine little boat. As you can see, I finished it without a cabin and with decks only 8" wide. This gave me a cockpit over 9 ft. long. The seats on each side are 8 ft. long by 16" wide.

I kept the boat near Wildwood, N.J., where I received many favorable comments. Even fishermen liked it, because it was so roomy.

The planking was western cedar, the frame was white oak and the decking ⅜" plywood. The mast was made according to your plans and turned out very well. The only real trouble I had was getting the correct bevel on the stem. The top part was O.K. but the bottom was a mess.

The sails I had made by Thurston out of 3.6 oz. Dacron. A 3.6 h.p. outboard hung on a transom bracket worked out pretty good but a 5 h.p. would be better.

I've sailed alone in some pretty rough water and with winds of 18 to over 20 m.p.h. and this little boat stood up to it very well. At times though, it was pretty wet going. For normal use, I found this to be a perfect small "family boat." My wife, two children and myself could comfortably spend the whole day either sailing, fishing, crabbing or just poking around.

The entire boat—motor, hardware, etc., cost me about $475.00 to build.

I'm ready now to build something a little bigger, probably *Picaroon*. With the strip planking, it should be easier to build.

Sincerely,
John T. Durnin

October 9, 1957

Mr. John T. Durnin's *Titmouse.*

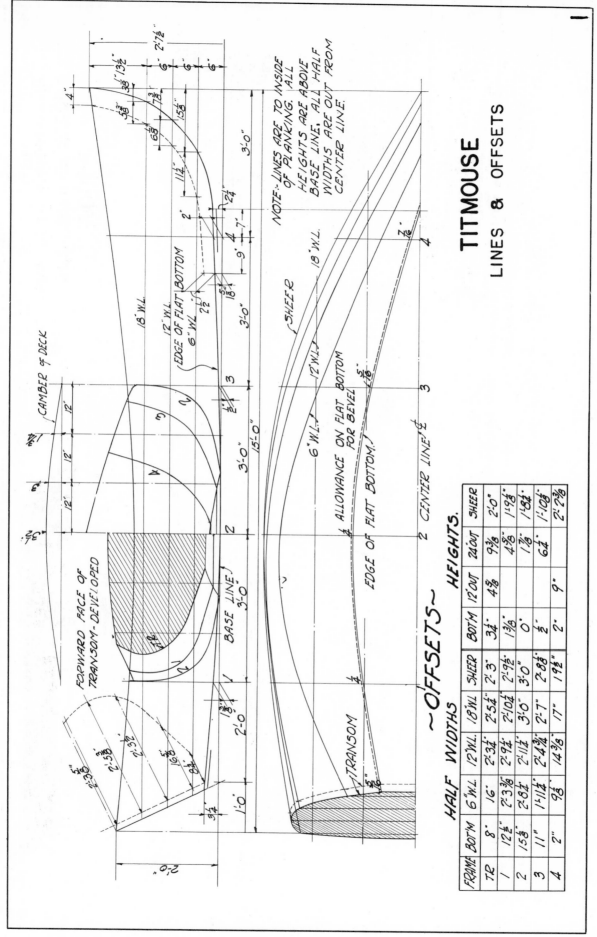

TITMOUSE
LINES & OFFSETS

NOTE:-LINES ARE TO INSIDE OF PLANKING. ALL HEIGHTS ARE ABOVE BASE LINE. ALL HALF WIDTHS ARE OUT FROM CENTER LINE.

CAMBER OF DECK

FORWARD FACE OF TRANSOM - DEVELOPED

EDGE OF FLAT BOTTOM

ALLOWANCE ON FLAT BOTTOM FOR BEVEL

EDGE OF FLAT BOTTOM

SHEER

TRANSOM

18" W.L.

12" W.L.

6" W.L.

BASE LINE

CENTER LINE

~OFFSETS~

HALF WIDTHS

FRAME	BOT'M	6"W.L.	12"W.L.	18"W.L.	SHEER
TR	8"	1'6"	2'3¼"	2'5¼"	2'3"
1	12½"	2'3⅜"	2'9¼"	2'10¼"	2'9½"
2	15⅝"	2'8¼"	2'11¼"	3'0"	3'0"
3	11"	1'11¼"	2'4¾"	2'7"	2'8⅝"
4	2"	9⅝"	14⅜"	17"	19½"

HEIGHTS

FRAME	BOT'M	12 OUT	24 OUT	SHEER
TR	3¼"	4⅞"	9⅜"	2'0"
1	1⅜"	4⅜"	4⅜"	1'9⅝"
2	0"		1⅞"	1'8¼"
3	½"		6¼"	1'10⅝"
4	2"	9"		2'2⅞"

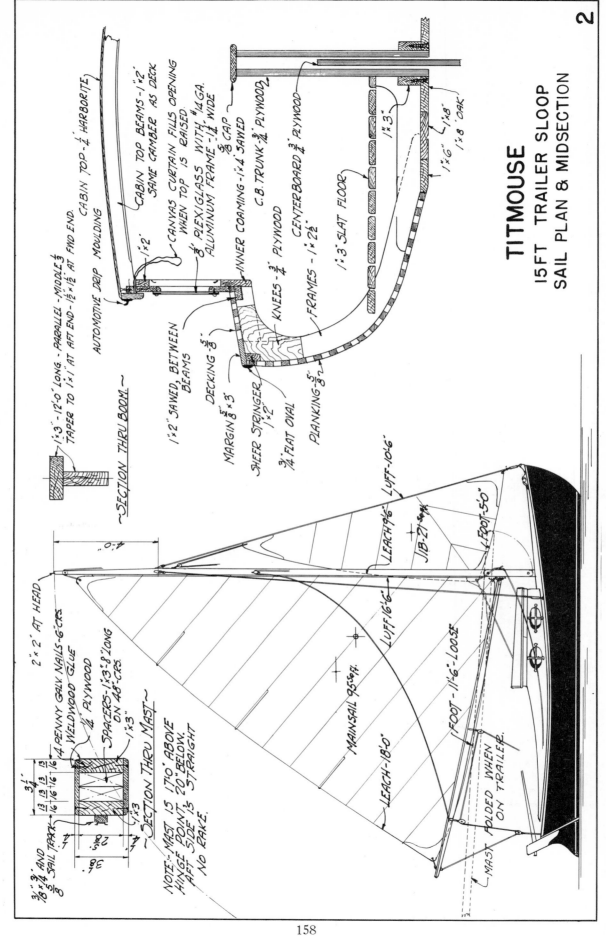

TITMOUSE
15FT TRAILER SLOOP
SAIL PLAN & MIDSECTION

2

CABIN TOP BEAMS - 1"×2"
SAME CAMBER AS DECK

CANVAS CURTAIN FILLS OPENING
WHEN TOP IS RAISED.

⅜" PLEXIGLASS WITH #14 GA.
ALUMINUM FRAME - 1¼" WIDE

⅝" CAP
INNER COAMING - 1"×4" SAWED

C.B. TRUNK - ¾" PLYWOOD

KNEES - ¾" PLYWOOD

CENTERBOARD ¾" PLYWOOD

FRAMES - 1"×2½"

1"×3" SLAT FLOOR

1"×3" - 12'-0" LONG - PARALLEL - MIDDLE ⅓
TAPER TO 1"×1" AT AFT END - 1½"×1½" AT FWD END.

CABIN TOP - ¼" HARBORITE

AUTOMOTIVE DRIP MOULDING

~SECTION THRU BOOM~

1"×2"

1"×2" SAWED BETWEEN
BEAMS

DECKING ⅜"

MARGIN ⅝"×3"

SHEER STRINGER
1"×2"

¾" FLAT OVAL

PLANKING ⅝"

1"×3"
1"×6" 1"×8"
1"×8" OAK

2"×2" AT HEAD

~SECTION THRU MAST~

4 PENNY GALV. NAILS - 6" CRS.
WELDWOOD GLUE

¼" PLYWOOD

SPACERS - 1"×3" - 8" LONG
ON 48" CRS.

1"×3"

¾"×¾" AND
⅝" SAIL TRACK

3¼"
⅓ ⅓ ⅓
16 16 16 16

¾"
2½"
38"

NOTE:- MAST IS 17'-0" ABOVE
HINGE POINT, 20" BELOW.
AFT SIDE IS STRAIGHT
NO RAKE.

MAST FOLDED WHEN
ON TRAILER.

4'-0"

LUFF 10'-6"

LEACH 9'-6"

JIB 21 sq.ft.

FOOT 5'-0"

LUFF 16'-6"

MAINSAIL 95 sq.ft.

FOOT 11'-6" LOOSE

LEACH 18'-0"

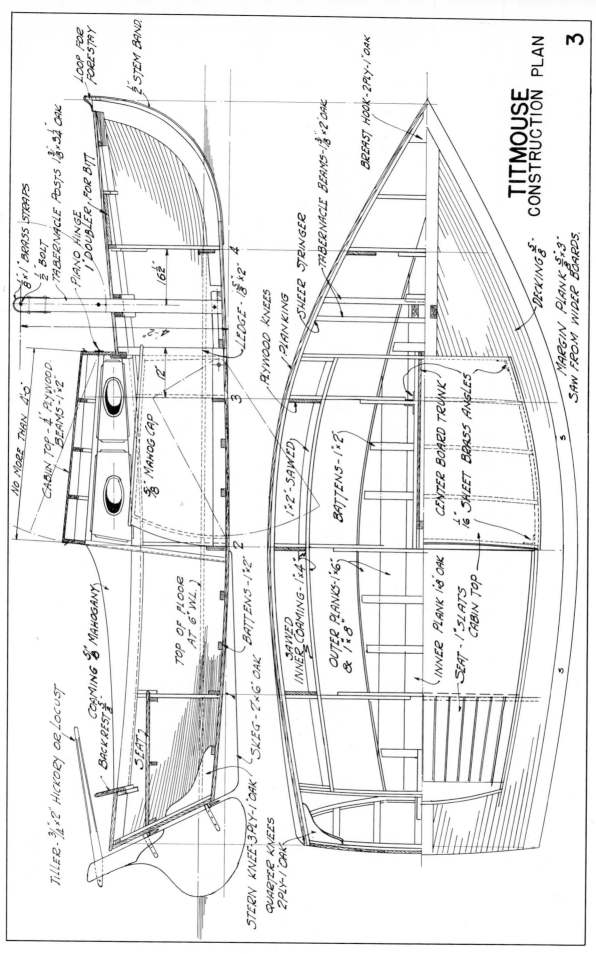

TITMOUSE
CONSTRUCTION PLAN

3

BREAST HOOK - 2 PLY - 1" OAK

DECKING 5/8"

MARGIN PLANK 5/8" x 3"
SAW FROM WIDER BOARDS.

TABERNACLE BEAMS - 1 3/8" x 2" OAK

SHEER STRINGER

PLYWOOD KNEES

PLANKING

1" x 2" - SAWED

BATTENS - 1" x 2"

SAWED
INNER COAMING - 1" x 4"

OUTER PLANKS - 1" x 6"
& 1" x 8"

CENTER BOARD TRUNK

1/16" SHEET BRASS ANGLES

INNER PLANK 1 x 8 OAK

SEAT - 1" SLATS
CABIN TOP

5

5

LOOP FOR
FORESTAY

1/2" STEM BAND.

TABERNACLE POSTS 1 3/8" x 5 1/4" OAK

1" DOUBLER FOR BIT

PIANO HINGE

1/8" x 1" BRASS STRAPS

1/2" BOLT

16 1/2"

LEDGE - 1 5/8" x 2"   4

CABIN TOP - 1/4" PLYWOOD.
BEAMS - 1" x 2"

NO MORE THAN 4'-0"

4 - 2"

5/8" MAHOG CAP

3

2"

12"

TOP OF FLOOR
AT 6" W.L.

BATTENS - 1" x 2"   2

COAMING 5/8" MAHOGANY)

BACKREST 5/8"

SEAT

TILLER - 3/4" x 2" HICKORY OR LOCUST

SKEG - 2" x 6" OAK

STERN KNEE 3 PLY - 1" OAK

QUARTER KNEES
2 PLY - 1" OAK

159

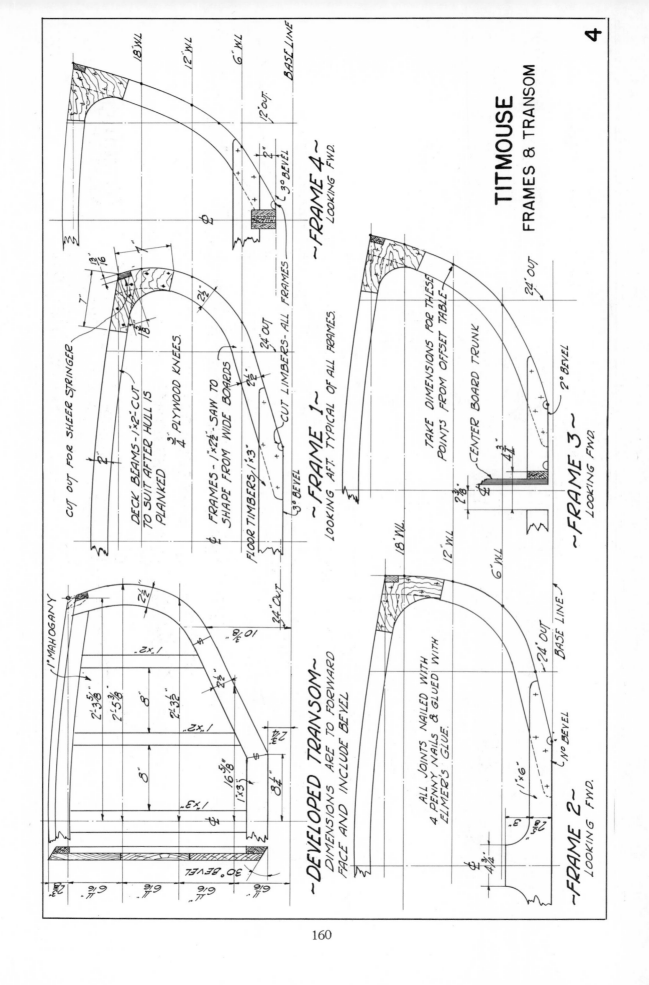

TITMOUSE
FRAMES & TRANSOM

~FRAME 4~
LOOKING FWD.

~FRAME 1~
LOOKING AFT. TYPICAL OF ALL FRAMES.

~FRAME 3~
LOOKING FWD.

~DEVELOPED TRANSOM~
DIMENSIONS ARE TO FORWARD
FACE AND INCLUDE BEVEL

~FRAME 2~
LOOKING FWD.

CUT OUT FOR SHEER STRINGER

DECK BEAMS - 1½"2" CUT
TO SUIT AFTER HULL IS
PLANKED

¾ PLYWOOD KNEES.

℄ FRAMES - 1"x2½" - SAW TO
SHAPE FROM WIDE BOARDS

FLOOR TIMBERS, 1"x3"

CUT LIMBERS - ALL FRAMES

TAKE DIMENSIONS FOR THESE
POINTS FROM OFFSET TABLE

CENTER BOARD TRUNK

ALL JOINTS NAILED WITH
4 PENNY NAILS & GLUED WITH
ELMER'S GLUE.

1" MAHOGANY

160

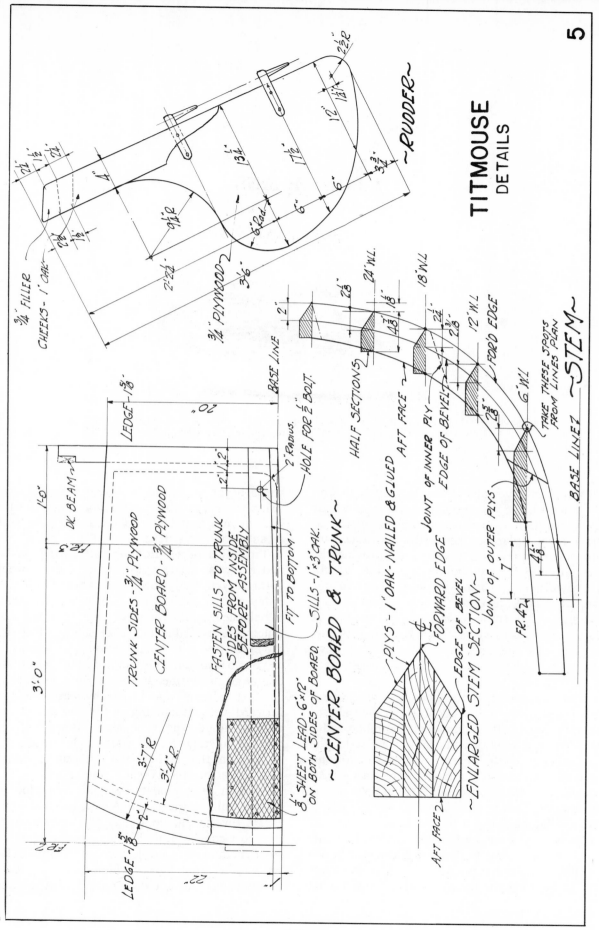

~RUDDER~

¾" FILLER
CHEEKS - 1" OAK

¾" PLYWOOD

TITMOUSE
DETAILS

TRUNK SIDES - ⅜" PLYWOOD
CENTER BOARD - ½" PLYWOOD

DK. BEAM

LEDGE - 1⅝"

FASTEN SILLS TO TRUNK
SIDES FROM INSIDE
BEFORE ASSEMBLY

FIT TO BOTTOM
SILLS - 1"×3" OAK.

2" RADIUS.
HOLE FOR ½" BOLT.

BASE LINE

HALF SECTIONS

24" W.L.

18" W.L.

12" W.L.

6" W.L.

FORD EDGE

JOINT OF INNER PLY
EDGE OF BEVEL

JOINT OF OUTER PLYS

AFT FACE

TAKE THESE SPOTS
FROM LINES PLAN

BASE LINE ~STEM~

PLYS - 1" OAK - NAILED & GLUED

FORWARD EDGE

EDGE OF BEVEL

~ENLARGED STEM SECTION~

AFT FACE

⅛" SHEET LEAD - 6"×12"
ON BOTH SIDES OF BOARD.

~CENTER BOARD & TRUNK~

LEDGE - 1⅝"

BOAT PLANS

FISH HAWK

A sport fisherman with unusual features. Designed by the author for his own use. Inboard powered; 18′ 0″ long, 7′ 0″ beam, 20″ draft, power from 25 to 100 h.p.

Fish Hawk is a versatile boat. Lightly built and heavily powered, she will satisfy the cravings of our younger generation. Constructed of good substantial timbers and inch planking she will have enough inertia to move slowly in a seaway and provide the comfort required by old duffers who, like myself, have become tired of being bounced about in our modern, ultra-light creations. The maximum amount of floor space that could be incorporated in a boat of this size was necessary for crabbing and fishing, and it should be flat and level, especially so when the first mate is not as steady on her feet as she used to be.

My first conception of the boat was one with a beautiful flare forward. This conception died aborning when inverted bell sections took too much width off the berth, and cramped the foot room under the hatch. As finally drafted, *Fish Hawk*'s forward lines might have come directly out of Chapman's *Architecturus Navalis Mercatoria* published in 1769. Boats of that time were not wrong in light of modern thinking. When planing the full bow is out of water. At slow speeds it will not knife down in a sea as our modern boats are wont to do. Our Navy still builds a lot of its service craft this way, so utility won over beauty. In building the model, a lot of longitudinal strips broke at Frame 6. There were only two answers to prevent this: either fine down the forward lines or fit a cant frame. To keep the bow as it was, a cant frame was fitted.

Two other necessities were also fitted—a *Johnnie* and a forward hatch. As one gets older, when *you gotta go* you really must, and where is there a man today who is so heartless as to expect the first mate to balance herself over a galvanized pail when marine toilets are available in pastel shades. Fitted under the berth, and with the curtains down, it is as private as your bathroom. The forward hatch was first fitted on one of my former boats, the *Pamar*. It is a great comfort to know that in rough weather one can go forward, without hanging on to hand rails, by simply ducking under the windshield. It's a still greater comfort to stand almost waist high in a hatch when hauling in the anchor line without expecting the next wave to pitch you into the drink.

Modern requirements demand a steering seat as comfortable as those in the cars we drive. On *Fish Hawk* this was made a copy of *Pamar*'s which was the most comfortable. Fishing requirements call for some method of steering from the cockpit. This also was copied from *Pamar* which had a vertical tiller. Fishing solo, this could be moved with the knees or hips, and with both hands busy on the rod the boat could be maneuvered to bring her in position to take an ornery striper over the side.

After weighing the good and bad of all types of motor installations, a small inboard such as the *Universal Atomic Four* was chosen. In spite of the claims for outboards or Vee-drives, even a larger motor than shown gave the most workable cockpit space. The motor box serves as a table or a seat as occasion may demand. For a man in retirement, using his boat almost every day, the fuel and oil economy of the inboard presents a big argument for its use. The *Atomic Four* should give *Fish Hawk* from eight to ten honest miles per hour without undue strain.

Fish Hawk was not designed to be built overnight. She will not plank as fast as a plywood job, but she may be built solo and, again for a retired man, this means a lot as most of his work will be done when young helpers are at their daily tasks. There is no piece of wood in the whole of the construction which is over a foot wide and which may not be cut on the smallest of home workshop bandsaws. No one item of work on the hull is arduous, so that even some of those men who have suffered a coronary will find it within their capabilities. All of the wood is standard lumber yard stock and, perhaps with the exception of the oak, may be purchased in your own locality. If oak is not available there are acceptable substitutes for it. In these days of wood preservatives which really work, even some of the woods that were formerly frowned upon for boat work will be acceptable. After all, how long can a man who retires at sixty expect to use a boat?

For the framing I have selected North Carolina Pine. This should be what the lumber dealers call "trim quality". It is a wood almost as strong as oak, takes glue readily and will last longer than a lot of oak we buy today. The decks and transom are of *Harborite* with all raw edges shielded by glue joints. These edges are the weak points of all plywood and too great care cannot be exercised here.

The frames are sawed from boards as shown on the plans and assembled over the body plan. The joints are laid up with a resorcinal resin glue such as *Elmer's* or *Weldwood*. They are then screw-fastened, eliminating the necessity of a flock of clamps, which, if purchased for one boat, will cost more than ten times all the screws you will use. The flat face of the frame is laid downward and the joint pieces attached to the upper side. The deck gussets of plywood are glued and nailed to the frames and beams. Note that the beams on Frames 1 to 4 inclu-

sive are made of 1″ x 6″ boards and that only those necessary to frame the deck are shaped. Later when the deck is laid these pieces are cut away. They are not wasted as they can be re-sawed to frame the many little parts within the hull. Cut the notches for all longitudinals for a tight fit; this is important for assembly reasons.

The stem, forward sheer members and transom are next fabricated and then the keel is made. The keel apron should be beveled where it projects beyond the keel proper, to an angle of 6°.

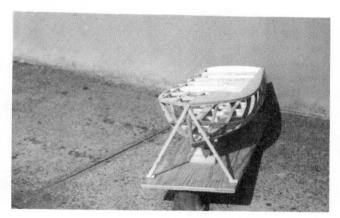

Bow view of *Fish Hawk's* model.

Do not cut the stem bevel all of the way down. Leave some of this to be done on erection and then only bevel enough for the day's operation. In this way the wood preservative on the surface of the wood is removed, exposing a clean surface to the glue. If the boat is erected under cover, the wood preservative coating can be eliminated until the boat is finally planked. If the boat is to be erected outside, do the preserving before erection. If you anticipate a long erection job, a coat or two of priming paint over the preservative will do no harm. Be sure to keep all wood preservative from glued surfaces or cut it away on erection. A *Stanley Surform* file or plane will come in handy, or a wood rasp will do yeoman service in beveling the members.

When erecting the model it was surprising how simple the process became. Bolt the stem to the keel with glue in the joint and set these level on blocks or sawhorses high enough to conveniently work below the boat. Plumb the stem and brace it rigid. Set the transom on the aft end of the keel to its proper rake, level it and brace it in this position. Erect Frame 3, square it across the keel, plumb it and then brace it in position. Bolt frames 5 and 6 in position; the sheer members will brace them later. Erect the forward sheer members fitting frames 5 and 6 in their proper notches. Brace Frame 5 level. If the forward sheer members are correct they will hold this frame plumb. Frame 6 will center itself. Fasten the 1" x 2" sheer stringers to the forward members and erect frames 4, 2 and 1. As you go aft, the sheer stringer will hold these frames in position. Glue and screw all joints. A set of *Stanley Screw Mates* in your electric drill will facilitate this work. One and a half inch, No. 10 flat-head galvanized screws are used throughout the work. You will also note that $^{13}\!/_{16}$" has been used for all wood thickness as this is standard. It might be well to check your lumber to confirm this before cutting any notches. One and five-eighths has been used as the width for all 1" x 2" stock. Three-eighths inch less than the nominal size has been used for all other widths.

After the frame has been erected it is well to give it a final check. The cant frames, bilge stringer and hatch opening are then framed and the plywood deck is laid. The deck may be fastened with *Hold Fast* nails or 1", No. 8 flat-head screws as you prefer. Be sure to set the center joint, either in bedding compound or glue, as the sheets are laid. For that matter, a coat of bedding compound or glue on all deck faying surfaces can do no harm.

Now is the time to lay the flooring. The first three flooring planks past the motor foundation should be glued in their joints and screwed and glued to the frames for these strips will form sister keelsons and contribute a big amount of rigidity to the frame. Lay the floor with the grooves inboard, ripping them off on the innermost planks so as to form a better edge for the removable floor sections on the centerline. Personally I would continue to lay the floor clear out to the sides. All of the flooring past the center strips may be nailed with galvanized nails driven blind. On my own boat I want the floor tight against the sides to prevent even Liliputian crabs from scampering down in the bilges where they can hide with impunity and stink to high heaven when they die there.

Once the floor is laid the frame will be rigid enough to remove the exterior bracing. If she is to be strip-planked the cross beams in way of the cockpit can be removed. If other planking is to be fitted leave them in. All of the work that can be done on the interior before planking will be a lot easier in handling and making fits as you can do this from the ground instead of going up and over the side every time it is necesary. It may also be advantageous to remove one of the bilge stringers temporarily for this work. A number of ways of planking the hull are possible and what you can do on the interior depends on this. We will deal with each method separately.

STRIP PLANKING.—Strip planking would be my own personal choice for this hull. The cover should consist of square strips cut from mahogany finished ¾" and ripped 1" wide. If you rip the boards yourself, cut only what is necessary for the day's work to avoid distortion. On the model it was found to be far easier to plank the flat deadrise with boards rather than to strip it. These flats should be assembled on the shop floor where wedge blocks could be used rather than having to resort to bar clamps. After the boards are glued, the intermediate battens which will measure approximately $^{13}\!/_{16}$" x 1¼" would be screwed to the planking. These would be ripped from standard 1" x 3" stock which comes about 2⅝" wide. The final cut of the outside edge is delayed until last. The port and starboard units would then be assembled to the keel and apron with screws and glue before erection. It might not be amiss to mention again that the face of the apron, where it projects from the keel, should be beveled 6°. There is little further to say about the strip planking that has not been covered already in this book except that, until the vertical portion of the stem is reached, it will be far easier to butt the port and starboard strips on the centerline as shown on the plans rather than try to cross them. If you do not make a good joint at this point there is always the last resort to fiberglas putty or a gunk made from resorcinal resin glue and sawdust. Quite unlike a lot of the other strip-built boats, where the strips will reach the sheer at the ends of the boat first, you will find that on this one they will touch first amidships. On my own boat I would be tempted to make them follow the sheer, after the bilge was turned, by fitting stealers forward and aft.

DOUBLE DIAGONAL PLANKING.—For this method, and all others following, additional stringers will be necessary in the frame. These are split 1" x 3" material finishing 1¼" wide. Two are fitted between the keel and bilge stringer and two between the bilge stringer and the sheer. In each case the distance along the frame edges is divided equally for their centers. It will be advantageous to turn the frame over and it will be stiff enough to do this. Do not remove the cross beams in way of the cockpit on frames 1 to 4 inclusive. Set the frame up on temporary blocking and level it for working position.

The planking proper consists of two layers of $^3\!/_{16}$" x 4" mahogany strips applied diagonally. Leave one edge straight and fit the abutting edge of the next strip to it. On both layers use ¾" *Hold Fast* nails. Gluecoat all faying surfaces before the final nailing. After the first layer is applied sloping aft from the keel, mark the positions of all frames and stringers as a guide to nailing the second layer to be laid in the opposite direction. Where the outer planks will not lie flat on the inner ones, a $\frac{1}{2}''$ copper tack clinched against a dolly on the outside will do the trick. After the planking is complete it is given one coat of fiberglas fabric and resin.

DIAGONAL VENEER.—This method of planking is very much like the one just described except that three layers of $\frac{3}{32}''$ mahogany veneer are applied with glue between them. Staples are used in lieu of nails and a single coat of Fiberglas is applied over the shell.

VENEER AND FIBERGLAS.—In this method only a single layer of $\frac{1}{16}''$ mahogany veneer is applied. It should be glued and stapled to the frame. Over this a coating of fiberglas to a total thickness of $\frac{3}{16}''$ is applied. Instructions for doing this are found elsewhere in this book.

FINISHING THE HULL.—*Fish Hawk* may be built as plain or as fancy as your pocketbook dictates. The *Harborite* deck may be painted or veneered with $\frac{1}{4}''$ x 3'' mahogany strips glued on. In this case it would be folly to use the material specified so substitute a good uncoated marine plywood in its place. If you lean toward a mahogany transom it also can be veneered with $\frac{3}{8}''$ material. For the transom I would use *Harborite* as there will still be the exposed inner side. If veneer is intended it should be applied before planking. The berth and seat, as well as the motor box, should be built of $\frac{3}{8}''$ *Harborite*.

The windshield and standing top are separate units. The windshield is built permanently to the boat but the top may be removed and left ashore if and when desired. The metal used in its construction is *Reynold's Do-it-Yourself* stock. Foam rubber for the berths can be bought cheaply from auto graveyards and with a little ingenuity and some plastic upholstering material, transformed into workable cushions for the seat and berths.

As to a motor, anything from 25 H.P. on up will work. Regardless of the motor chosen, the center of the shaft should pass through the center of the hole in Frame 2. The maximum size wheel on the 15° angle shown is 12''. For a longer wheel the strut and rudder may be altered. Before ending this epistle, be sure you comply with all U.S. Coast Guard requirements and when the boat is finished use her as any sane person should.

In the event that an outboard motor is contemplated, *Fish Hawk* will take the most powerful. Speed, of course, is dependent on how lightly she is planked. She was not designed for extremely high speeds but the straight run of her buttocks aft are no detriment in this respect. A breaker strip, parallel to centerline located on the 24'' buttock and running from the transom forward to frame 2, will be a big aid in planing. For outboard motors, Frame 1 should be made a watertight bulkhead and the transom braced similar to that of *Puffin*.

Where extreme lightness is desired, all of the present 1'' members may be reduced to $\frac{5}{8}''$ in thickness and constructed of spruce. The stem and keel should remain as is. The decks may be reduced to $\frac{1}{4}''$ in thickness. Three layers of mahogany veneer with one layer of fiberglas will provide the lightest hull. For more powerful inboard engines, stringers beside the motor beds at the present floor level will be necessary. For outboards the keel thickness of 2'' is carried all the way back to the transom, where its end should be streamlined for better performance.

FISH HAWK UNDER CONSTRUCTION.—Before this edition got into print, I decided to build *Fish Hawk* for myself. She is now completely framed and went together fair. The only trouble encountered was with the laminated sheer stringer at the bow. The force required to twist this to the camber was so great that it threatened to disrupt the whole frame. The stringer was finally set level and shimmed up an eighth of an inch above its given position. Transversely, its top is level. The extra eighth inch of height was dressed down to the normal sheer position to suit the curve of the camber. This gives about an inch of landing for the plywood deck on its outboard edge. North Carolina pine, which had no less than eight annular rings per inch, was selected for the frames. This was a tall order for the lumber yard but it finally was obtained by selecting from a large amount of wood. It was decided to strip-plank the frames and Philippine mahogany, ripped in to $\frac{3}{4}''$ x 1'' strips, is on hand for this work.

The extra-light standing top was abandoned and a top, fashioned from $\frac{3}{4}''$ mahogany in the good old-fashioned mood, was fitted. One of the first things that was done, after the framing had been regulated and faired, was to lay the cockpit flooring. This gave a working platform on which to do all of the deck work in a way that no amount of temporary boards laid on the frames could do. All of the frames were fabricated in the basement workshop and erected completely assembled. The erection took place on a keel horse set 27'' above the ground to allow plenty of room to work beneath the hull.

In the original design, the 1″ x 3″ bilge stringer was fitted to hold the frames in line during the planking operation. When the decision to lay the cockpit floor early in the construction was made, it also became apparent that this alone would hold the alignment of the frames in a way that no other means could equal. The notches in the frames were eliminated, as they could be fitted later if the stringer was necessary. The theory that the floor would hold the alignment was correct and the stringer was eliminated permanently. Another example of the advantage of leaving off the planking became apparent when the framing for the berth was fitted. Some means of supporting the outboard edge of the plywood berth top was necessary. With the planking off, it was an easy matter to fit a ribband in notches in the frames at the berth level to accomplish this end. Fairing battens bent around the bow showed that the cant frames were an actual necessity.

MIRACLE ADHESIVE.—One of the greatest assets to the construction was the adhesive used. Early in the planning stages I began to look for an adhesive that did not have the disadvantage of working at 70° as do all of the resorcinal resin glues. It had been planned to work late in the Fall and even in Winter when the weather allowed. For work at these low temperatures, the resorcinals were out. The ideal glue was discovered in Miracle Adhesive N.P. 428. This is made by the makers of "Black Magic," The Miracle Adhesives Corporation, 250 Pettit Avenue, Belimore, N.Y. This adhesive will set up at freezing temperatures, has a bond strength greater than any wood and is not fussy to mix. The proportions of the epoxy resin and the catalyst are 50–50 but this is not critical; 40–60 or 60–40 will make little difference except in hardness or flexibility. It has been used to bond all the framing and laminations and will be used to bond the strip planking when this is fitted.

One big lesson learned in the construction is not to plank the hull until all of the interior work, including the motor, is complete. It is so much easier to do a lot of the work standing on the ground and to climb into the hull through the frames, not to mention the fact that all dirt may be swept off the floor onto the ground. The garboards were fitted temporarily and removed and laid away in the shop until the time when they will be needed for planking. The itch to see the strips go on becomes, at times, almost overpowering but the sensible thing to do is to resist it.

Nuclear power for the hull is not as yet available, so the next best thing to it, is to be fitted. This is the Universal Atomic four as originally specified. This little mill is far more economical than an outboard, and when, in a few years, I retire from my present bread-and-butter job, economy will be a big factor. This motor is one of the few manufactured today that is not an automotive conversion. All parts of this motor are marine engineered and its reverse gear is built in, not simply bolted on. All of the outboard

Miracle Adhesive in use in building *Fish Hawk*. Tin spouts were soldered to the lids of the cans for easier pouring of the viscous liquids in small quantities. A pinch-ended beer can was used to lay a small bead of glue on the edge of a board. A strip of the planking with guides on each side was used to spread the bead of glue evenly over the edge of the board.

fittings were fabricated rather than cast, as described in Fig. 90, Chap. XIV. Another innovation in connection with the power plant will be in the gas tank. This will be made of ⅜″ Harborite, lined with Fiberglas impregnated with the Miracle Adhesive N.P. 428 which is impervious to gasoline.

And so-o-o, another boat takes shape on the shipways of Sam Rabl's own back yard.

BILL OF MATERIAL — FISH HAWK

Lumber

INDIVIDUAL FRAMES

Frame 1

1 pc.	1″ x 12″ x 4′-6″	N. C. Pine
1 pc.	1″ x 8″ x 10′-0″	N. C. Pine
1 pc.	1″ x 6″ x 8′-0″	N. C. Pine
1 pc.	1″ x 2″ x 6′-0″	N. C. Pine

Frame 2

1 pc.	1″ x 10″ x 6′-0″	N. C. Pine
1 pc.	1″ x 8″ x 10′-0″	N. C. Pine
1 pc.	1″ x 6″ x 8′-0″	N. C. Pine
1 pc.	1″ x 2″ x 6′-0″	N. C. Pine

Frame 3

1 pc.	1″ x 10″ x 6′-0″	N. C. Pine
1 pc.	1″ x 8″ x 10′-0″	N. C. Pine

1 pc.	1" x 6" x 8'-0"	N. C. Pine		
1 pc.	1" x 2" x 6'-0"	N. C. Pine		

Frame 4

2 pcs.	1" x 8" x 8'-0"	N. C. Pine
1 pc.	1" x 6" x 8'-0"	N. C. Pine
1 pc.	1" x 2" x 6'-0"	N. C. Pine

Frame 5

2 pcs.	1" x 8" x 8'-0"	N. C. Pine
1 pc.	1" x 6" x 8'-0"	N. C. Pine
1 pc.	1" x 2" x 6'-0"	N. C. Pine

Frame 6

2 pcs.	1" x 10" x 6'-0"	N. C. Pine
1 pc.	1" x 6" x 6'-0"	N. C. Pine
1 pc.	1" x 2" x 4'-0"	N. C. Pine

Cant Frame

| 2 pcs. | 1" x 10" x 5'-0" | N. C. Pine |

Transom

1 Sheet Harborite 3/4" x 4'-0" x 8'-0"   also makes gussets and hatch rings

| 3 pcs. | 1" x 8" x 6'-0" | N. C. Pine |
| 1 pc. | 1" x 2" x 6'-0" | N. C. Pine |

Sheer Stringers

| 4 pcs. | 1" x 8" x 10'-0" | N. C. Pine |
| 2 pcs. | 1" x 2" x 12'-0" | N. C. Pine |

Stem

| 3 pcs. | 1" x 8" x 8'-0" | N. C. Pine |

Bilge Stringer

| 2 pcs. | 1" x 2" x 14'-0" | N. C. Pine (Select) |
| 1 pc. | 1" x 2" x 10'-0" | N. C. Pine |

Deck Stringers

5 pcs.	1" x 2" x 8'-0"	N. C. Pine
2 pcs.	1" x 2" x 6'-0"	N. C. Pine
1 pc.	1" x 3" x 6'-0"	N. C. Pine

Keel

1 pc.	1" x 6" x 16'-0"	Oak
1 pc.	2" x 3" x 12'-0"	Rock Elm
1 pc.	1" x 3" x 6'-0"	Rock Elm

Deck

2 Sheets Harborite 3/8" x 4'-0" x 8'-0"

Flooring

100 Sq. ft. (laid)   1" x 2 1/2" T. & G. Flooring
Vert. Grain Douglas Fir

Planking, Windshield and all Trim

350 bd. ft.   3/4" Mahogany
random lengths & widths

Berth, Seats and Motor Box

1 Sheet Harborite 3/8" x 4'-0" x 8'-0"

1 Sheet Harborite 1/2" x 4'-0" x 8'-0"

Hardware

15	lb.	6 penny Galv. finishing nails	
3	Gross	1 1/2" - # 8 Fl. Hd. Galv. Wood Screws	
3	Gross	1 1/2" - #10 Fl. Hd. Galv. Wood Screws	
2	Gross	1" - # 7 Fl. Hd. Galv. Wood Screws	
1	Gross	1 1/2" - #10 Fl. Hd. Brass Wood Screws	
6	Bolts Brass	3/8" x 2 1/2" Rd. Hd. Hex nut	Stern Brg.
2	Bolts Brass	3/8" x 3 1/2" Rd. Hd. Hex nut	Strut.
8		Brass Washers for above.	
3		Carriage Bolts 1/2" Dia. x 4 1/2" Long	
5		Carriage Bolts 1/2" Dia. x 3 1/2" Long	
13		Carriage Bolts 3/8" Dia. x 3" Long	

Fittings

1	Comb. Light	Size 1	Perko Fig. 598
1	Stern Light		Perko Fig. 422
1	Dash Light		Perko Fig. 184
1	Ignition Plate		Perko Fig. 518
3	Switches		Perko Fig. 718
2	Drain Plugs		Perko Fig. 124
1	Steerer		Perko Fig. 570
1	Rudder	Size 1	Perko Fig. 818
1	Rudder Port	1" Size	Perko Fig. 1089
1	Rudder Collar	1" Size	Perko Fig. 815
1	Rudder Quadrant	10" Size	Perko Fig. 651
1	Shaft Log	#3 Size	Perko Fig. 671
1	Strut	1" Shaft - 7" Drop	Perko Fig. 1019
2	Cleats	6 1/2"	Perko Fig. 572
1	Pair Bow Chocks	Size 2	Perko Fig. 160
2	Stern Chocks	Size 11	Perko Fig. 161
1	Deck Pipe	Size 1	Perko Fig. 741
1	Cheek Block	Size 1	Perko Fig. 95
1	Cheek Block	Size 11	Perko Fig. 96
2	Tiller Rope Pullies		Perko Fig. 592
8 ft.	Fender Mould (Stem)		Perko Fig. 199
45 ft.	5/8" Fender Mould (Sheer)		Perko Fig. 193
20 ft.	Drip Moulding (Top)		Perko Fig. 192
30 ea.	"Lift the Dot" Fasteners		Perko Fig. 114, 116, & 118

Fish Hawk in frame in Sam Rabl's own back yard.

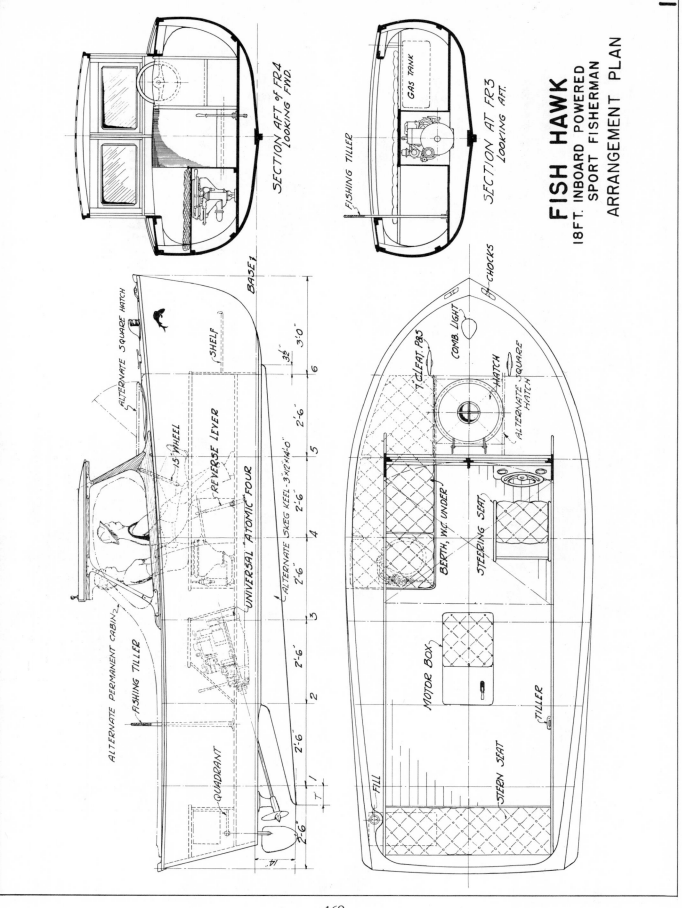

SECTION AFT of FR4
Looking Fwd.

SECTION AT FR3
Looking Aft.

FISH HAWK
18 FT. INBOARD POWERED
SPORT FISHERMAN
ARRANGEMENT PLAN

GAS TANK

FISHING TILLER

ALTERNATE SQUARE HATCH

SHELF

3'-0"

3²"

ALTERNATE PERMANENT CABIN

ALTERNATE SKEG KEEL-3"x12"x4'-0"

UNIVERSAL "ATOMIC FOUR"

15" WHEEL

REVERSE LEVER

FISHING TILLER

QUADRANT

BASE 1

2'-6"   2'-6"   2'-6"   2'-6"   2'-6"   2'-6"   2'-6"
7"   2'-6"   14"

8 - CHOCKS

7" CLEAT P&S

COMB. LIGHT

HATCH

ALTERNATE SQUARE HATCH

BERTH, W.C. UNDER

STEERING SEAT

MOTOR BOX

TILLER

STERN SEAT

FILL

169

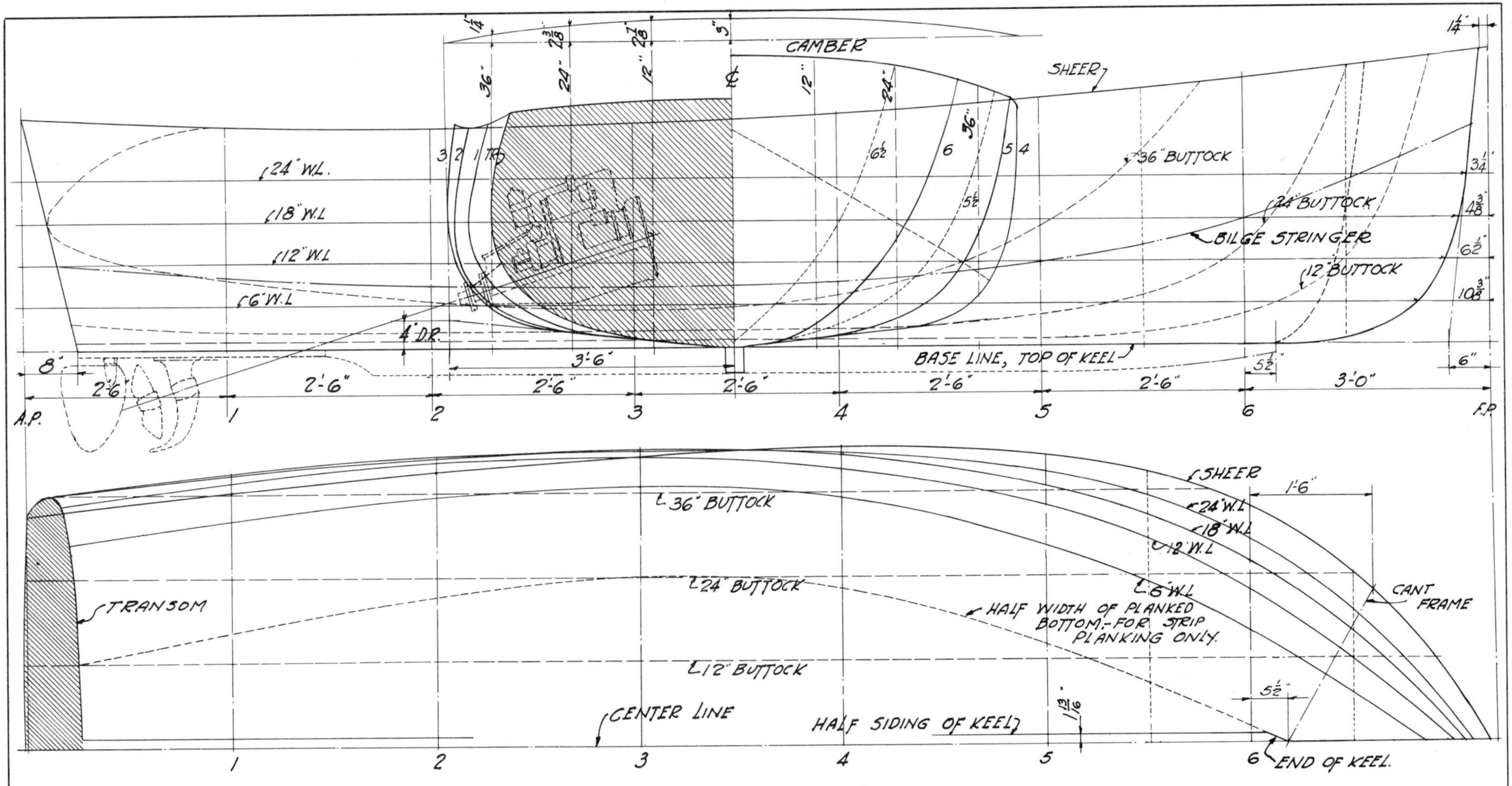

~OFFSETS~

	HALF WIDTHS					HEIGHTS.				
FRAME	6" W.L	12" W.L	18" W.L	24" W.L	SHEER	12" BUT.	24" BUT	36" BUT.	BLG. STR	SHEER.
TRNSM	2'-4 3/4	2'-10 3/8	3'-0"	2'-11 5/8	2'-9"	1 1/4"	3 3/4	1'-6"	1'-0"	2'-9"
1	2'-8 1/8	3'-2"	3'-3 3/8	3'-2 3/8	3'-0 1/4"	1 1/4	2 5/8	9 1/8	10 1/4"	2'-7 3/4
2	2'-11 7/8	3'-4 5/8	3'-5 3/8	3'-4 3/4	3'-3 1/8	1 1/4	2 1/8	6 1/8	8 7/8	2'-7 3/8
3	3'-0 5/8	3'-5 1/4	3'-6 3/8	3'-6 1/8	3'-5 1/8	1 1/4	2 3/8	5 5/8	8 5/8	2'-8"
4	2'-10 7/8	3'-3 1/4	3'-4 7/8	3'-5 5/8	3'-6 1/2"	1 1/4	2 3/8	7 1/8	9 1/8	2'-9 1/2"
5	2'-4 1/8	2'-10"	3'-1 1/8"	3'-3"	3'-5 1/4	1 1/4	4"	1'-4"	11 7/8	2'-11 1/8
6	1'-3 3/4"	1'-9 3/4	2'-1 3/4	2'-4 7/8"	2'-9 5/8	3 3/8	1'-3 3/8		1'-5 7/8	3'-1 7/8
F.P.									2'-7"	3'-6"

NOTE:- OFFSETS ARE TO INSIDE OF PLANKING.- + OR - 1/8". TRANSOM FIGURES ARE NOT DEVELOPED.

FR 5 1/2	1'-11"	2'-5 1/8	2'-8 1/2	2'-11 1/4	3'-2 5/8	THESE FIGURES FOR FAIRING ONLY.	3'-0 1/2
FR 6 1/2	6 7/8	11 5/8	1'-3 5/8	1'-6 3/4	2'-0 1/8		3'-3 1/2
CANT FR	11 1/8	1'-3 3/8	1'-6 1/2"	1'-8 7/8	2'-1"		3'-3 1/8

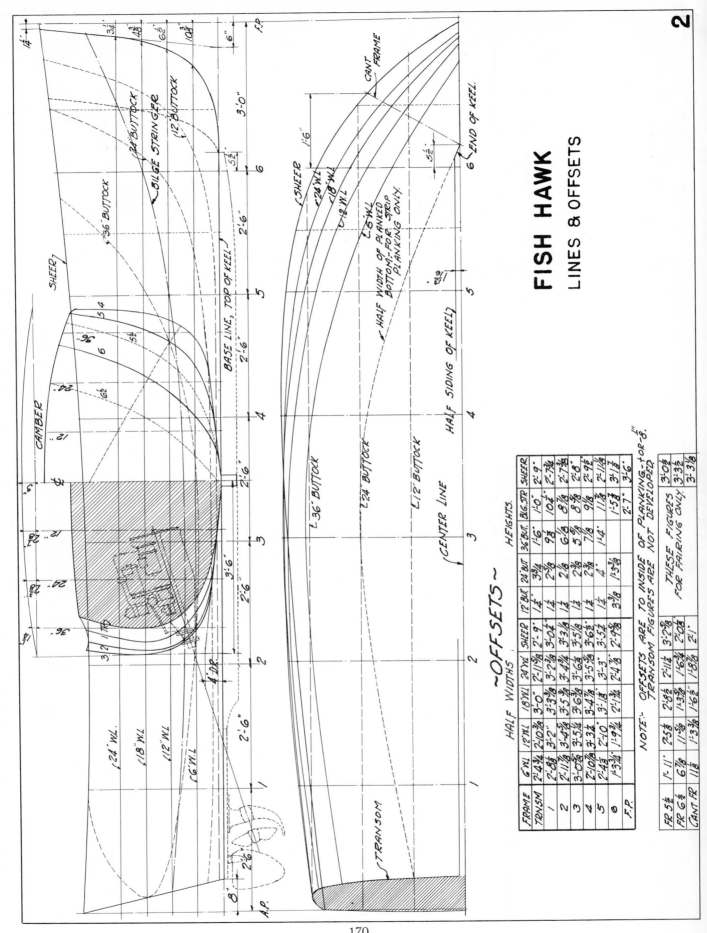

FISH HAWK

LINES & OFFSETS

2

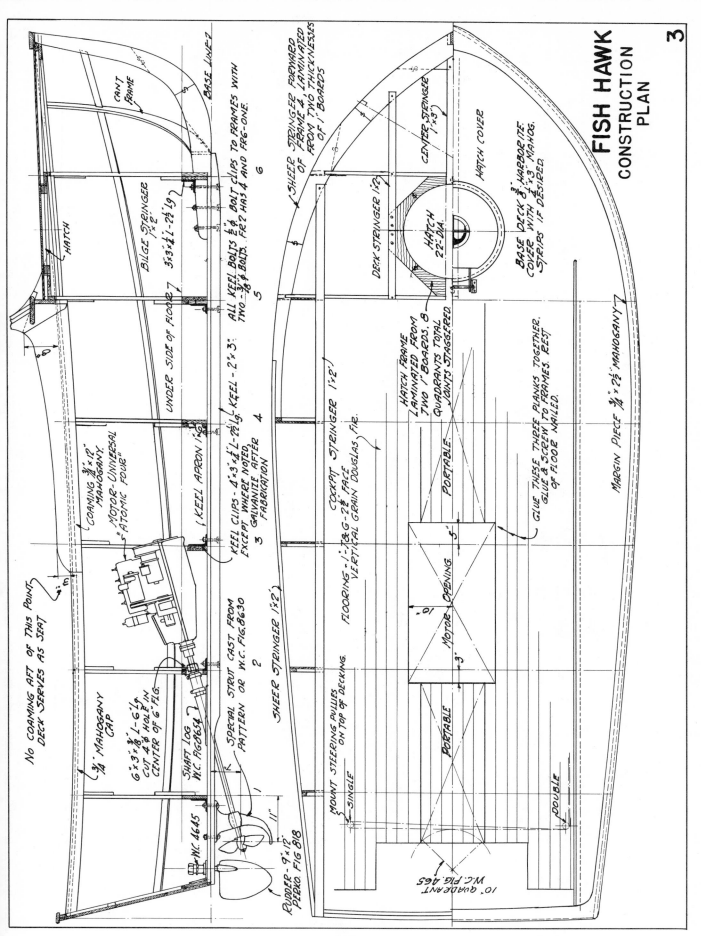

FISH HAWK
CONSTRUCTION PLAN

3

No COAMING AFT OF THIS POINT,
DECK SERVES AS SEAT

HATCH

CANT FRAME

BASE LINE

BILGE STRINGER 1"×2"

COAMING 3/4"×12" MAHOGANY.

MOTOR-UNIVERSAL "ATOMIC FOUR"

3/4" MAHOGANY CAP

6"×3"×3" L-6'Lg.
CUT 4"∅ HOLE IN
CENTER OF 6 FLG.

SHAFT LOG
W.C. FIG 8654

W.C. 4645

SPECIAL STRUT CAST FROM
PATTERN OR W.C. FIG. 8630

UNDER SIDE OF FLOOR 7

ALL KEEL BOLTS 5/8 ∅ BOLT CLIPS TO FRAMES WITH
TWO - 3/8 ∅ BOLTS. FR.2 HAS.4 AND FR.6-ONE.

KEEL CLIPS - 4"×3"×1" L-2½"Lg.
EXCEPT WHERE NOTED,
GALVANIZE AFTER
FABRICATION

KEEL - 2"×3"

KEEL APRON 1"

SHEER STRINGER 1"×2"

RUDDER - 9"×12"
PERKO FIG 818

COCKPIT STRINGER 1"×2"

FLOORING - 1"-T&G-2½" FACE
VERTICAL GRAIN DOUGLAS FIR.

MOUNT STEERING PULLIES
ON TOP OF DECKING.

SINGLE

10" QUADRANT
W.C. FIG. 465

SHEER STRINGER FORWARD
OF FRAME 4, LAMINATED
FROM TWO THICKNESSES
OF 1" BOARDS

CENTER STRINGER
1"×3"

DECK STRINGER 1"×2"

HATCH COVER

HATCH
22" DIA.

BASE DECK 3/8" HARBORITE
COVER WITH 1"×3" MAHOG.
STRIPS IF DESIRED

HATCH FRAME
LAMINATED FROM
TWO 1" BOARDS. 8
QUADRANTS TOTAL
JOINTS STAGGERED

PORTABLE

5"

MOTOR OPENING

10"

3"

PORTABLE

DOUBLE

GLUE THESE THREE PLANKS TOGETHER.
GLUE & SCREW TO FRAMES. REST
OF FLOOR NAILED.

MARGIN PIECE 3/4" × 2½" MAHOGANY

171

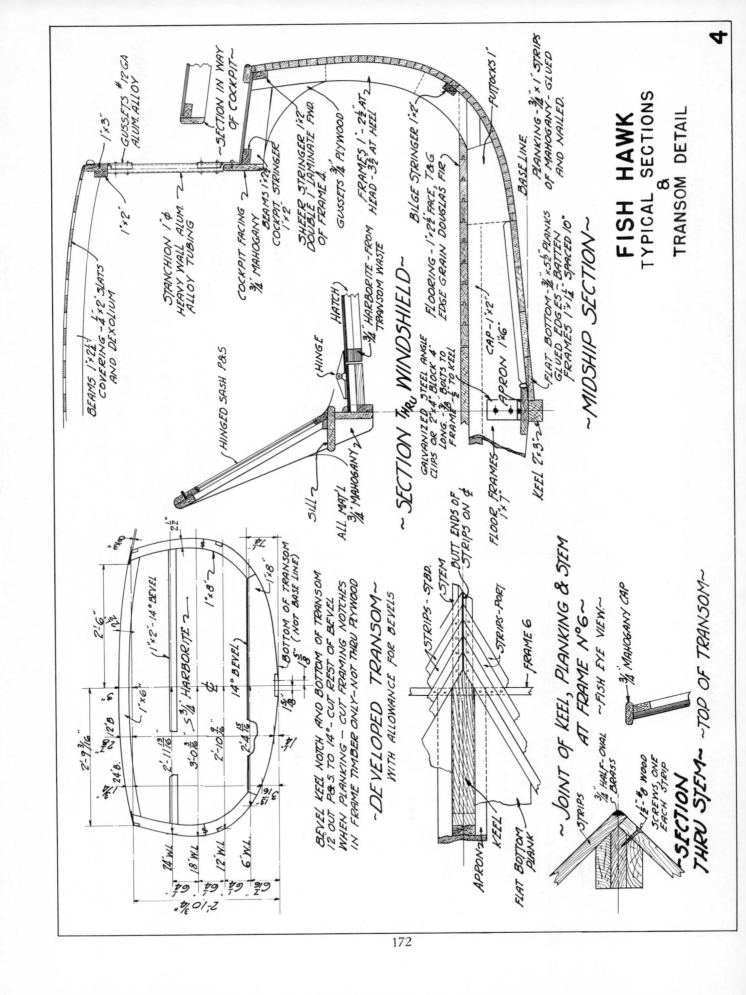

FISH HAWK
TYPICAL SECTIONS
&
TRANSOM DETAIL

4

172

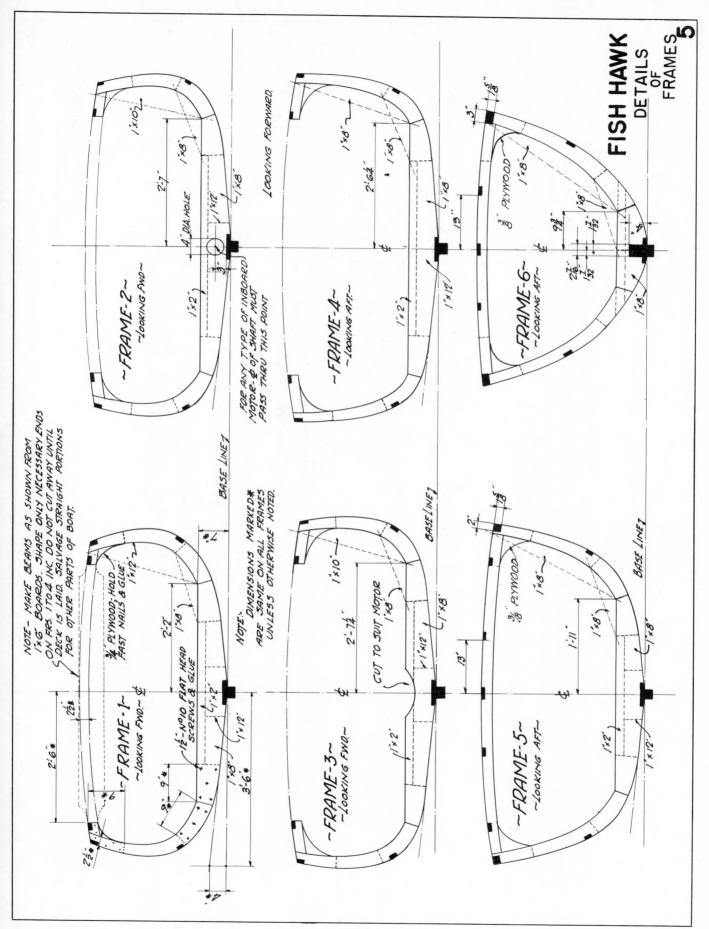

FISH HAWK
DETAILS
OF
FRAMES **5**

~FRAME·2~
~LOOKING FWD~

~FRAME·4~
~LOOKING AFT~

~FRAME·6~
~LOOKING AFT~

~FRAME·1~
~LOOKING FWD~

~FRAME·3~
~LOOKING FWD~

~FRAME·5~
~LOOKING AFT~

LOOKING FORWARD

FOR ANY TYPE OF INBOARD
MOTOR-℄ OF SHAFT MUST
PASS THRU THIS POINT

BASE LINE

NOTE- MAKE BEAMS AS SHOWN FROM
1"×6" BOARDS. SHAPE ONLY NECESSARY ENDS
ON FRS. 1 TO 4 INC. DO NOT CUT AWAY UNTIL
DECK IS LAID. SALVAGE STRAIGHT PORTIONS
FOR OTHER PARTS OF BOAT.

NOTE:- DIMENSIONS MARKED *
ARE SAME ON ALL FRAMES
UNLESS OTHERWISE NOTED.

BASE LINE

BASE LINE

BASE LINE

¾" PLYWOOD; HOLD
FAST NAILS & GLUE

1½-N°10 FLAT HEAD
SCREWS & GLUE

CUT TO SUIT MOTOR

⅜" PLYWOOD

⅜" PLYWOOD

173

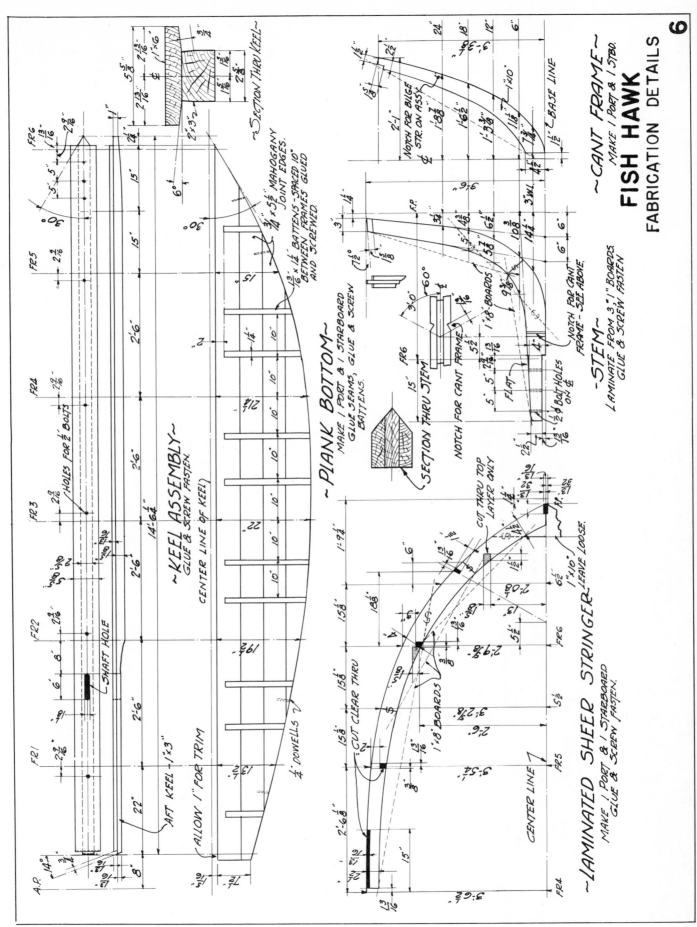

FISH HAWK
FABRICATION DETAILS

6

BOAT PLANS

PUFFIN

An outboard cruiser designed for trailer operation; 18′ 0″ long, 7′ 6″ beam.

Puffin was designed for the man who wants a small cruiser that can be carried on a trailer and taken to the faraway cruising grounds behind the family car. The construction is in no way complex and what has been said about the construction of the other plywood boats in this book applies as well to this one.

The boat is constructed upside down and the bottom sheets applied first. Note that the frames are built to the inside of the stringers rather than to the plywood. This eliminates a lot of notching and gives a bottom which is easily cleaned inside as there are no frames for the dirt to lodge against at the stringers.

The keel is a piece of 2″ x 6″ and is straight from the transom to Frame 5. The stem is laminated from three 1″ boards and glued and screwed. All of the frames carry the plywood from side to side to form lateral support for the floor and act as gussets also. Frame 1 is a watertight bulkhead to separate the motor compartment from the rest of the boat and render it safe should a wave rise above the motor opening. Build the motor bracing between this frame and the transom as shown.

The cabin top is constructed of glued mahogany strips finished natural. If this looks like too much work for you, a conventional cabin may be fitted to the lines shown.

Puffin will perform with a minimum of 15 H.P. and should carry a maximum of 30 H.P.

BILL OF MATERIAL — PUFFIN

Lumber

12	pcs.	Optional Oak or Spruce	1" x 3" x 8'-0"	Frames
1	pc.	Oak	2" x 6" x 16'-0"	Keel
1	pc.	Oak	2" x 4" x 12'-0"	Floors
8	pcs.	Oak or Spruce	1" x 2" x 16'-0"	Stringers
3	pcs.	Oak or Spruce	1" x 3" x 16'-0"	Stringers
2	pcs.	Oak or Spruce	1" x 12" x 10'-0"	Sheer Stringer
2	pcs.	Oak or Spruce	1" x 2" x 10'-0"	Sheer Stringer
20	Strips	Oak	1/4" x 3" x 10'-0"	Stem
2	pcs.	Spruce	1" x 6" x 6'-0"	Cabin Sills
6	pcs.	Spruce	1" x 6" x 6'-0"	Cabin Beams
45	Sq. ft.	Mahogany	1/8" x 3"	Cabin Top
75	Lin. ft.	Spruce	1/3" x 2"	Interior
3	Sheets	Harborite	3/4" x 4'-0" x 8'-0"	Transom, Floor, Etc.
2	Sheets	Harborite	1/4" x 4'-0" x20'-0"	Side Shell
2	Sheets	Harborite	3/8" x 4'-0" x12'-0"	Bottom Shell
2	Sheets	Harborite	3/8" x 4'-0" x 8'-0"	Bottom Shell
4	Sheets	Harborite	3/8" x 4'-0" x 8'-0"	Bulkheads & Trim
2	pcs.	Mahogany	5/8" x 14" x 14'-0"	Cabin Sides
3	pcs.	Mahogany	1" x 3" x 8'-0"	Trim
1	pc.	Mahogany	1" x 6" x 10'-0"	Trim

Hardware

4	Gross	1" -#10 Fl. Hd. Wood Screws Galv.		
2	Gross	1 1/4" -#10 Fl. Hd. Wood Screws Galv.		
2	Gross	1 1/2" -#10 Fl. Hd. Wood Screws Galv.		
8		Galv. Carriage Bolts 1/2" x 6"		
4	Qts.	Elmers Glue		
16	Lin. ft.	1/8" x 1 1/2" Galv. Iron Flat Bar	Keel	
1		Combination Light	Perko Fig.	1247
1		Stern Light	Perko Fig.	1148
2		Clam Shell Vents	Perko Fig.	323
1		Steering Wheel	Perko Fig.	570
1	pr.	Bow Chocks Size 1	Perko Fig.	160
1		Bitt Size 1	Perko Fig.	597
5		Tiller Rope Pulleys	Perko Fig.	592
108	Ft.	Fender Moulding 3/4"	Perko Fig.	193
1		Continous Hinge 1 1/2" x 60"	Perko Fig.	211
1		Aluminum Angle 1 1/2" x 1 1/2" x 1/8" x 3'-0"		
2		Aluminum Sheets #14 Ga. 12" x 48"	Windows	
2		Plexiglass Sheets 1/8" Thick 12" x 48"	Windows	
2		Aluminum Sheets #14 Ga. 8" x 14"	Windows	
2		Plexiglass Sheets 1/8" Thick 8" x 14"	Windows	

1/4" Plate Glass to Fit Windshield

Equipment as required by U. S. Coast Guard

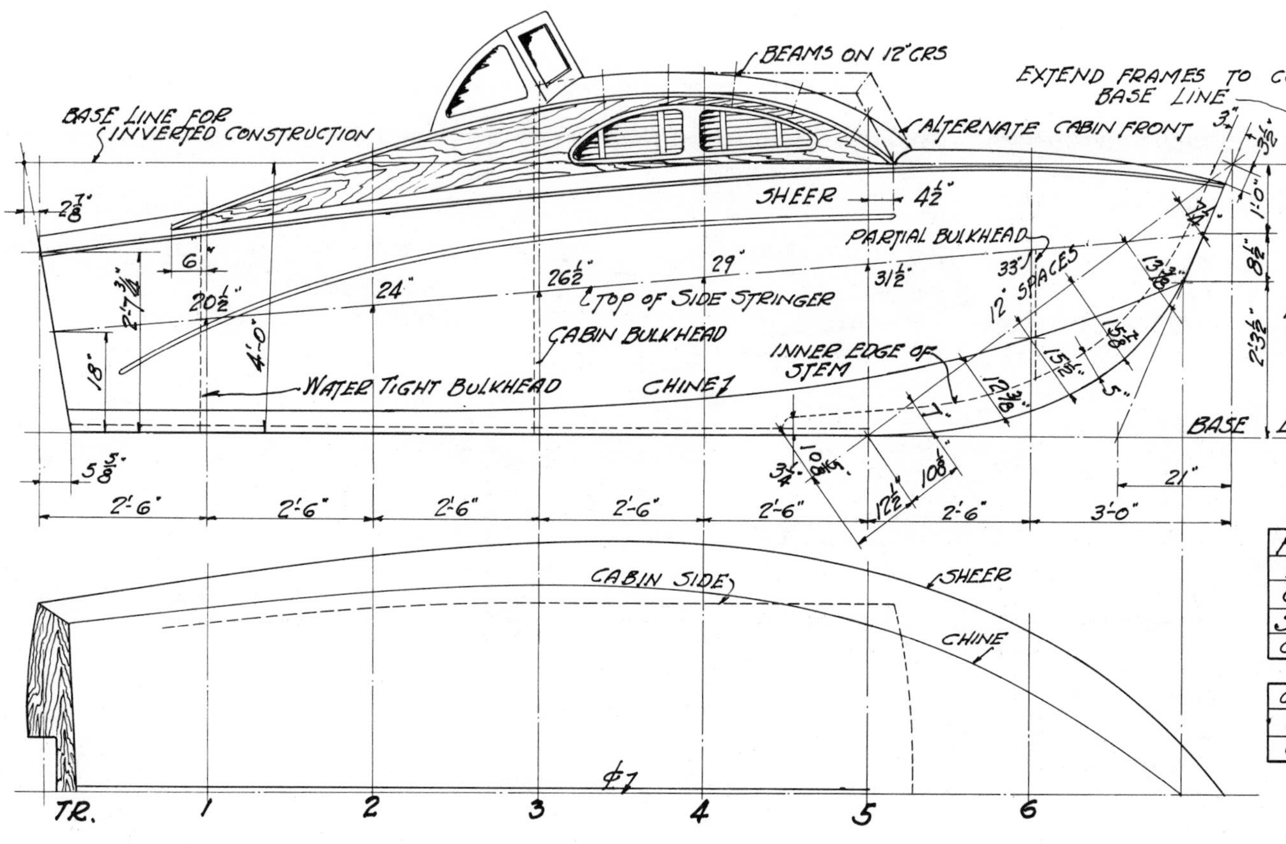

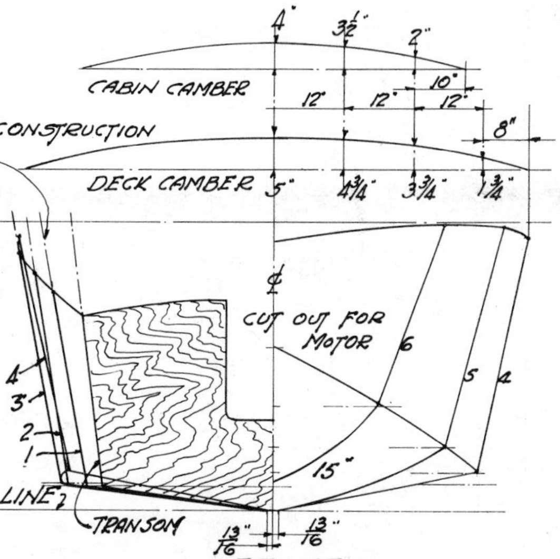

~OFFSETS~

HEIGHTS

FRAME	TR.	1	2	3	4	5	6
KEEL	0"	0"	0"	0"	0"	0"	4¾"
CHINE	4⅜"	4¼"	4¼"	4½"	6⅜"	10⅜	1'-5½"
SHEER	2'-8⅜"	2'-11½"	3'-3¼"	3'-6½"	3'-9¼"	3'-10⅞	3'-11¼"
CABIN		3'-3"	4'-1¾	4'-9½"	5'-0¼"	4'-3½"	

HALF WIDTHS

CHINE	2'-5¾"	2'-8½"	2'-11⅜"	3'-0¾	2'-11½"	2'-5¾"	1'-6"
SHEER	2'-9"	3'-2"	3'-5¾"	3'-8¼"	3'-8"	3'-3¼"	2'-4⅝
CABIN		2'-6"	2'-8¾	2'-10"	2'-10"	2'-10"	

OFFSETS ARE TO INSIDE OF PLYWOOD.
TRANSOM FIGURES ARE TRUE SHAPE.

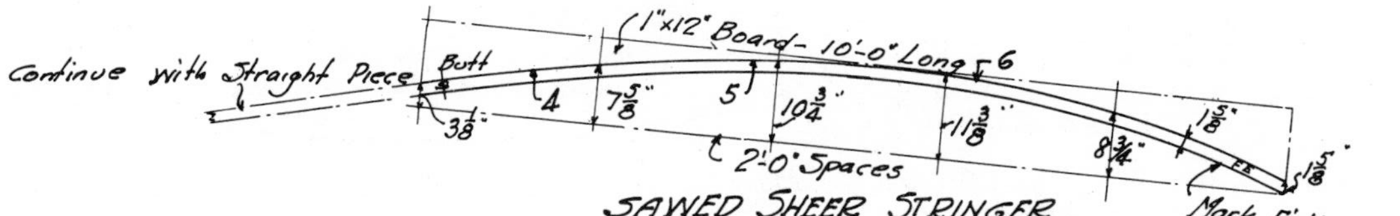

SAWED SHEER STRINGER FROM STEM HEAD AFT PAST #4

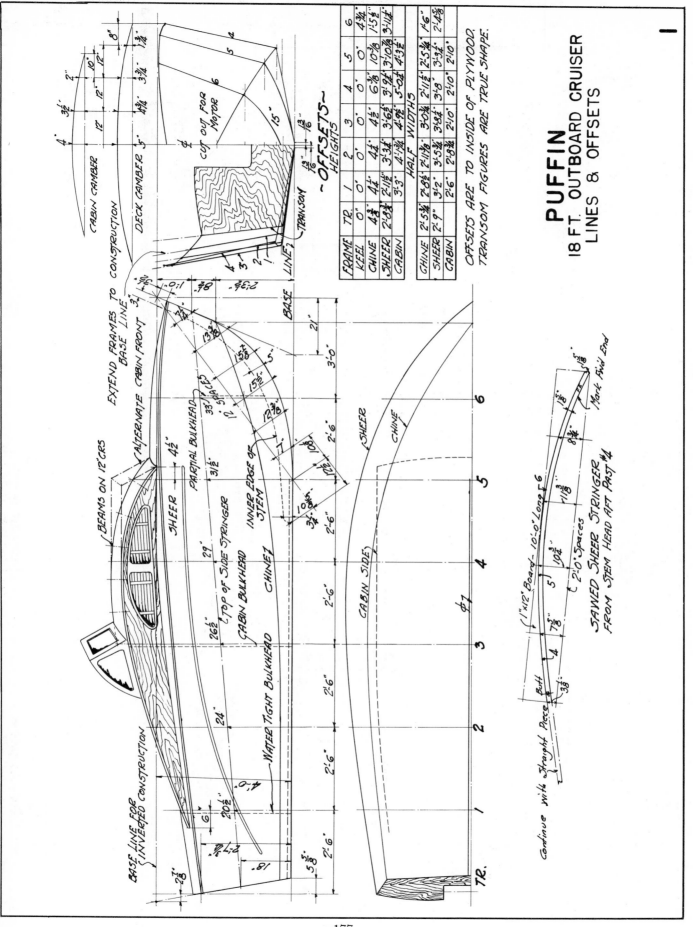

PUFFIN

18 FT. OUTBOARD CRUISER
LINES & OFFSETS

1

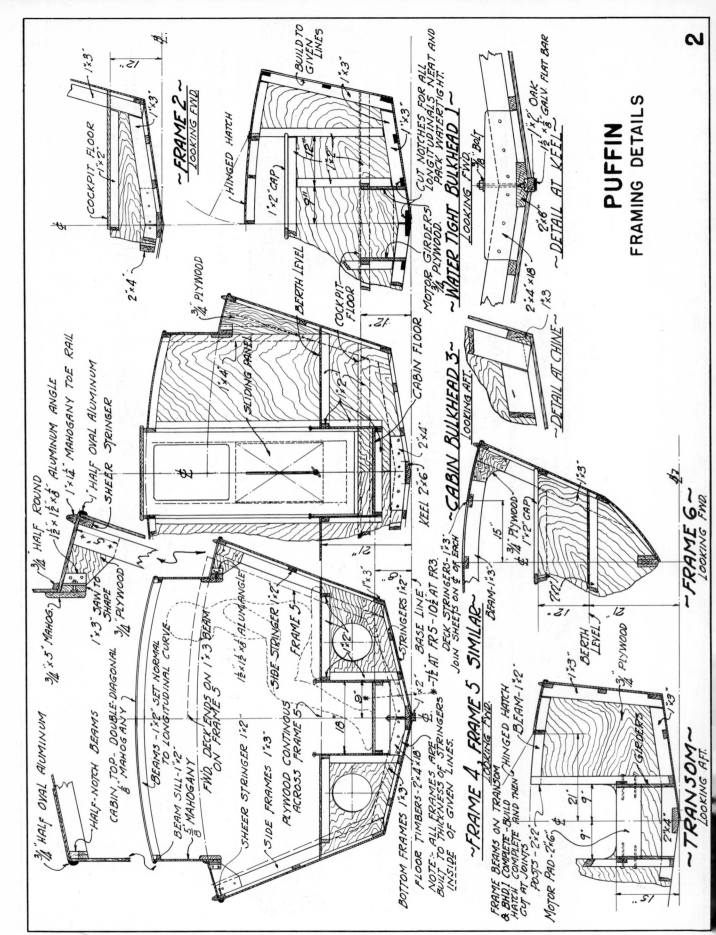

~FRAME 2~
Looking Fwd.

1"x3"
21"
1"x3"
COCKPIT FLOOR 1"x2"
BUILD TO GIVEN LINES
2"x4"
HINGED HATCH
1"x3"
12"
1"x2"
9"
1"x2" GAP
BERTH LEVEL
3/4" PLYWOOD
CUT NOTCHES FOR ALL LONGITUDINALS NEAT AND PACK WATERTIGHT.
MOTOR GIRDERS 3/4" PLYWOOD.
COCKPIT FLOOR

~WATER TIGHT BULKHEAD 1~
Looking Fwd.

~DETAIL AT KEEL~
7/8" BOLT
1"x2" OAK
1 1/2"x 1/8" GALV. FLAT BAR
2"x6"
2"x4"x18"
1"x3"

PUFFIN
FRAMING DETAILS

2

~DETAIL AT CHINE~

3/4" HALF OVAL ALUMINUM
3/4"x 5" MAHOG.
1/2"x 1 1/2"x 1/8" ALUMINUM ANGLE
1"x 1 1/4" MAHOGANY TOE RAIL
SHEER STRINGER
HALF-NOTCH BEAMS
3/4" HALF ROUND
CABIN TOP - DOUBLE DIAGONAL 1/8" MAHOGANY
3/4" PLYWOOD
1"x3" SAW TO SHAPE
5"
1/2" HALF OVAL ALUMINUM
BEAM SILL-1"x2"
5/8" MAHOGANY
BEAMS - 1"x2" SET NORMAL TO LONGITUDINAL CURVE
SLIDING PANEL
1"x4"
1"x2"
£
FWD. DECK ENDS ON 1"x3" BEAM ON FRAME 5
SHEER STRINGER 1"x2"
SIDE STRINGER 1 1/2"x2"
SIDE FRAMES 1"x3"
PLYWOOD CONTINOUS ACROSS FRAME 5
1 1/2"x 1 1/2"x 1/8" ALUM. ANGLE
FRAME 5
1"x2"
CABIN FLOOR
2"x4"
KEEL 2"x6"
12"
£
£.21.
BERTH LEVEL
COCKPIT FLOOR
3/4" PLYWOOD
1"x3"

~FRAME 4, FRAME 5 SIMILAR~
Looking Fwd.

BOTTOM FRAMES 1"x3"
FLOOR TIMBERS - 2"x4"x18"
NOTE:- ALL FRAMES ARE BUILT TO THICKNESS OF STRINGERS INSIDE OF GIVEN LINES.
1"x2"
STRINGERS 1"x2"
- 7 1/2" BASE LINE J
* - 7 1/2" AT FR.5 - 10 1/2" AT FR.3.
DECK STRINGERS - 1"x3".
JOIN SHEETS ON £ OR FR.3.
9"
9"
18"
1"x3"
9"
8"
1"x3"

~CABIN BULKHEAD 3~
Looking Aft.

FRAME BEAMS ON TRANSOM & BHD.1 COMPLETE - BUILD HATCH COMPLETE AND THEN CUT AT JOINTS
POSTS - 2"x2"
MOTOR PAD - 2"x6"
BEAM-1"x3"
BEAM-1"x2"
CHINGED HATCH
1"x3"
15"
3/4" PLYWOOD
£ 1"x2" GAP
£
2"x2"
BERTH LEVEL
3/4" PLYWOOD
1"x3"
21"
12"
21"

~FRAME 6~
Looking Fwd.

~TRANSOM~
Looking Aft.

9"
9"
9"
21"
51"
GIRDERS
2"x4"
3/4" PLYWOOD
1"x3"
1"x3"
BERTH LEVEL
£

178

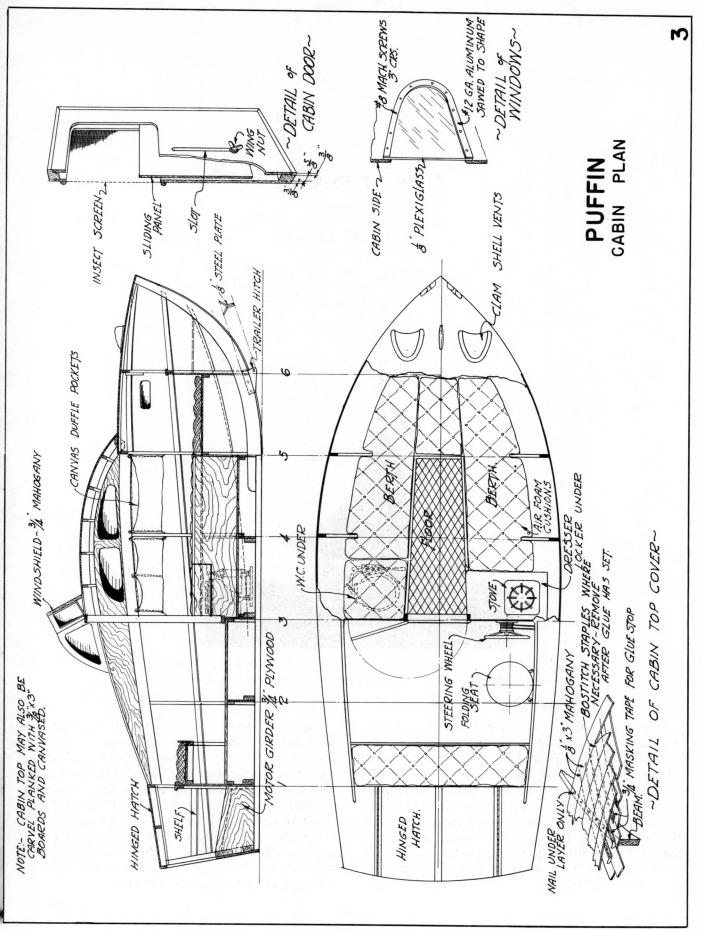

NOTE:- CABIN TOP MAY ALSO BE
CARVEL PLANKED WITH 3⁄8"x3"
BOARDS AND CANVASED.

WINDSHIELD~3⁄4" MAHOGANY

CANVAS DUFFLE POCKETS

HINGED HATCH

SHELF

MOTOR GIRDER 3⁄4" PLYWOOD

INSECT SCREEN

SLIDING PANEL

SLOT

1⁄8" STEEL PLATE

TRAILER HITCH

~DETAIL of CABIN DOOR~

WING NUT

5⁄8" 3⁄8"

3⁄8"

#8 MACH. SCREWS
3 CRS.

#12 GA. ALUMINUM
SAWED TO SHAPE

~DETAIL of
WINDOWS~

CABIN SIDE

1⁄8" PLEXIGLASS

CLAM SHELL VENTS

PUFFIN
CABIN PLAN

W.C. UNDER

BERTH

FLOOR

BERTH

AIR FOAM CUSHIONS

DRESSER
LOCKER UNDER

STOVE

STEERING WHEEL

FOLDING SEAT

BOSTITCH STAPLES WHERE
NECESSARY~ REMOVE
AFTER GLUE HAS SET.

1⁄8"x3" MAHOGANY

3⁄4" MASKING TAPE FOR GLUE STOP

BEAM.

NAIL UNDER
LAYER ONLY

~DETAIL OF CABIN TOP COVER~

HINGED HATCH.

6

5

4

3

2

1

179

3

BOAT PLANS

PICAROON I and II

An improved version of a world-famous tabloid cruiser; 18' 0" long, 7' 6" beam, 3' 6" draft, inboard auxiliary power. *Picaroon II* is a round-bottom copy of *Picaroon*.

Picaroon is that same little boat that Brice Johnson built for me in Cambridge over thirty years ago, the same boat in which Hank Hemingway had his great adventure in the Gulf of Mexico, sailing from Mobile to Neuvitas in Cuba. The same tabloid cruiser of which Westy Farmer wrote: "A delight to the eyes of every sailorman," and to which the late Charles Hall attached the title of the "Perennial Picaroon". She is the same little ship that was destined to become world-famous and to have been built on every continent of this globe.

Modern methods of construction have afforded some improvement in her construction but have detracted not a whit from her seaworthy lines. Plywood has produced a better hull, there is no reason why she cannot still be built much in the same manner as *Kittiwake* with main frames of 1⅛" x 3¾", and intermediates of 1⅛" x 2¼" on 12" centers. The chine, sheer and bottom stringers would be 1⅛" x 2¾" and the planking of 1" dressed material which will measure ¹³⁄₁₆". For this reason the lines are drawn to the outside of the planking.

All pieces of the backbone are detailed so that no lay down is necessary. The keel, stem and all parts are assembled and set right-side-up on a keel horse. The frames are erected and braced and the stringers run in. By this time the reader has become familiar with the methods used in constructing other boats in this book so a detailed step-by-step instruction would be senseless.

The frames are a combination of oak and plywood and form bulkheads and partial bulkheads as they are assembled in the boat. Properly fabricated, it is possible to assemble them in such a manner as to eliminate over 75% of the interior work. Even the motor beds are detailed for pre-fabrication so that they may be assembled along with the frames. If you have a little knowledge of lofting it is also possible to pick up from the body plan the shape of such flat surfaces as the berth tops and cockpit flooring and fit these items before the planking is applied. Make extensive use of *Elmer's Glue* and patent nails in all the assemblies.

The motor fitted is a *Universal Blue Jacket Twin*. This motor develops 12 H.P. at full speed and is thoroughly reliable. While it has more power than is needed it will not be overstrained to maintain cruising speed. It also has electric starting which is a must in most single-handed work. Electric starting gives the added advantage of power for lighting and an automatic bilge pump.

The cabin arrangement is primitive. The head is an ordinary galvanized pail with a homemade *Johnnie* seat to cover it and make its use more comfortable. The galley is self-contained and built around a *G.I. Coleman* stove and which may be stowed anywhere that loading conditions may permit. Inflatable beach mattresses will work well on the berths, and for clothes stowage there is nothing better than the traditional sea bag which still exists in our atomic Navy much in the same form that it did on *Old Ironsides*.

The sailing rig is much the same as I used with complete success on my last little auxiliary, the *Meg*. The loose-footed sail permits brailing against the mast without lowering, keeps clean in this way, and removes the temptation to soil it with hands slimy from fish or bait if it were stowed on the boom. One thing that I would personally carry would be a combination sail with slides on one edge and jib snaps on the other, and which would serve the double purpose of either storm jib or storm trysail as occasion would demand.

Both the mast and boom are hollow spars built up from lumber and plywood and should present no difficulties.

The outside ballast may be a weldment or a casting, either of which will cost about the same unless you have a friend who is familiar with acetylene cutting and arc welding. The original *Pic* carried all of her ballast inside and this boat will do the same if you wish to eliminate the weighted keel. Still another alternative is to cast the keel in concrete, filling in as much lead or iron scrap as the aggregate will permit. In this case it will be well to cap the entire keel bottom with two pieces of 1″ x 3″ flat iron bar and weld the lower ends of the keel bolts to this as well as tack-welding the two bars together. This iron alone will weigh about 40 pounds per running foot and will be down where it will do the most good. A good coating of *Rustoleum* paint on all of the iron work will eliminate a lot of corrosion.

BUILDING PICAROON WITH PLANKING

Picaroon was originally built as a cross-planked *a la Maryland* job. She was thus when Hank Hemingway sailed her across the Gulf, and she can still be built this way if you so desire. The backbone timbers are almost identical. The only change is to add ⅜″ to the top of the keel and the horn timber to make up the difference between the ½″ plywood bottom and the ⅞″ (or 1³⁄₁₆″) board planking which you will use.

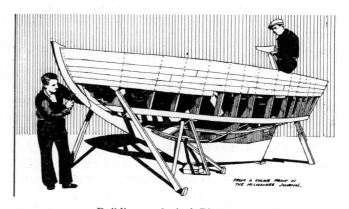

Building a planked *Picaroon*.

The original main frames were 1⅛″ x 3¾″ set on the same stations shown on the line plan. As the lines are drawn to the outside of the planking they remain the same but a different amount is *taken off* to allow for the thicker planking. The chine corners of the frames are gusseted with an oak board 1⅛″ x 8″ and their joint at the keel is made with a 2″ x 4″, 2′ long.

The transom is made up of 1⅛″ oak boards with 1⅛″ x 2¼″ edging. Between the main frames on the sides, intermediate frames of 1⅛″ x 2¼″ stock are inserted on 12″ centers much in the same manner as they are on *Kittiwake*. Note that the frames just aft of the stem take a slight curve. The bottom is diagonally planked with 1″ x 6″ boards. The bottom stringer is 1⅛″ x 2¼″. The topside planks are 1″ x 6″ run parallel.

Fair Dinkum. A *Picaroon* built by Mr. Dean T. Stephens of Alameda, California. She carries a Genoa and a "Captain's Handkerchief", plus his wife and four kiddies.

The deck may be laid in 1″ boards the same as with *Kittiwake* and canvased as it originally was. The original rudder was made from a single oak plank 1¾″ thick and 22″ wide, tapered to ½″ on its aft edge. It still may be made of this same material in narrower boards joined with long iron dowels. The interior bulkheads and joiner work were originally of ½″ T & G beaded staving. They can still be made thus.

The original mast was solid of 3″ x 4″ Sitka Spruce worked pear-shaped and had a set of 12″ spreaders at the top of the forestay. The very first rig that the little hull carried was gaft-headed with a 20′ spar. It can still be made thus if a long solid spar of light wood is not obtainable.

Picaroon II is a round bottom stripped hull built on the same keel as *Picaroon*. She has approximately the same displacement as the *Pic* but has prettier lines than the original.

All details are the same as the *Pic* with the exception of the frames, which like the straight ones, are fabricated from sawed lumber and plywood. The hull is strip planked with 1″ lumber finished to 13/16″ x 1″ and glued with *Elmer's Glue* and nailed as described in the article on strip planking.

A board 8″ wide is fitted against the keel. After its inboard edge is fitted it is tapered down to nothing at its forward and aft ends in a long sweeping curve. The strips are carried up from the edge of this garboard plank to the sheer with their 1″ faces against the frames. The deck is best laid in strips like the hull over a base of ¼″ plywood. Sails, rigging, interior arrangement and motor installation are exactly the same as for *Picaroon*.

~ OFFSETS ~

TRANSOM DEVELOPMENT PICAROON II Sheet 3

Note, Fwd face of plywood and Aft face of Frame, - Same.	AFT FACE OF PLYWOOD	FWD FACE OF PLYWOOD	FWD FACE OF FRAME.
Dist. out from ℄ 42″ W.L	26¾″	27¾″	30⅛″
″ ″ ″ 51″ W.L.	32″	32¼″	32⅝″
″ ″ ″ 60″ W.L	30¾″	30 15/16″	31¼″
″ Below 51″ W.L 1⅜″ Out	19⅝″	20¾″	22 5/16″
″ ″ ″ 9″ ″	16¾″	17 13/16″	19⅜″
″ ″ ″ 18″ ″	13 5/16″	14 5/16″	15⅞″
″ ″ ″ 27″ ″	8 13/16″	9⅝″	11 3/16″
Sheer above 51″ W.L - ℄	14½″		
″ ″ ″ 9″ out	14 5/16″		
″ ″ ″ 18″ ″	13 15/16″		
″ ″ ″ 27″ ″	13 5/16″		

NOTE - 42″ & 60″ ON W.L's ARE FOR DESIGNATION ONLY - NOT TRUE ELEVATION - 13/16″ PLANKING HAS BEEN TAKEN OFF.

BILL OF MATERIAL — PICAROONS List I

Lumber

Note: The following material is common to all hulls regardless of type.

1	pc.	Oak	3″ x 12″ x 12′-0″	Main Keel
1	pc.	Oak	3″ x 8″ x 4′-0″	Lower Horn
1	pc.	Oak	3″ x 12″ x 4′-6″	Upper Horn
1	pc.	Oak	3″ x 4″ x 1′-6″	Stern Knee
1	pc.	Oak	3″ x 3″ x 2′-0″	Stern Post
8	pcs.	Oak	1/2″ x 3″ x 8′-0″	Stem
2	pcs.	Oak	2″ x 2″ x 16′-0″	Keel Cheeks
3	pcs.	Oak	1 1/4″ x 2 1/2″ x 16′-0″	Sheer Stringers

4	pcs.	Oak	1 1/4" x 2 1/2" x 12'-0"	Deck Stringers
2	pcs.	Oak	1 1/2" x 1 1/2" x 14'-0"	Deck Stringers
5	pcs.	Oak	1 1/4" x 8" x 8'-0"	Deck Beams
5	pcs.	Oak	1" x 6" x 6'-0"	Cabin Beams
3	pcs.	Oak	1" x 2" x 16'-0"	Sheer Mould
2	pcs.	Mahogany	3/4" x 12" x 14'-0"	Cabin Sides
2	pcs.	Mahogany	1" x 12" x 8'-0"	Joiner Work
2	pcs.	Mahogany	1 1/4" x 8" x 8'-0"	Joiner Work
4	Sheets	Plywood	4'-0" x 8'-0" x 3/8"	Decks & Joinery
2	Sheets	Plywood	4'-0" x 8'-0" x 3/4"	Floors & Rudder
3	Sheets	Plywood	4'-0" x 8'-0" x 1/4"	Masts & Cabin Top

Hardware

2	Gross	1" #10 Fl. Hd. Galv. Wood Screws	
2	Gross	1 1/2" #10 Fl. Hd. Galv. Wood Screws	
14	Lin ft.	1/2" Dia. Galv. Iron Rod	Drifts
2	Doz.	1/2" Clinch rings	W. C. Fig. 836
8	Lin ft.	3/8" Dia. Galv. Iron Rod	Blind Drifts
12	Lin ft.	3/4" Dia. Galv. Iron Rod	Keel Bolts
3		1/2" Carriage Bolts 8" Long (Galv.)	
4		3/8" Carriage Bolts 6" Long (Galv.)	
6		1/2" Lag Screws 8" Long (Galv.)	
4		3/8" Lag Screws 4" Long (Galv.)	
6		Wire Rope Thimbles 1/4" Rope	W. C. Fig. 323
8		1/4" Screw Pin Anchor Shackles	W. C. Fig. 290
2		Shoulder Eye Bolts 1/2" x 3 1/4"	W. C. Fig. 2181
3		Rigging Turnbuckles 3/8" Dia.	W. C. Fig. 3162
3	*	Wire Rope Sockets 3/16" Size	W. C. Fig. 949
3	*	Wire Rope Sockets 3/16" Size	W. C. Fig. 950

* Electroline may be substituted

2		Deck Blocks	Size 1	W. C. Fig. 3800
2	lgths.	5/8" Sail Track		W. C. Fig. 120
1		Mast Head Sheave		W. C. Fig. 8460
6		Fairleads		W. C. Fig. 995
1		Boom Traveller	No. 1	W. C. Fig. 6390
1		Goose Neck		W. C. Fig. 6484
2		Halyard Shackles		W. C. Fig. 2870
1		Open Shell Block	Size 1	W. C. Fig. 9520
2		Open Shell Blocks	Size 1	W. C. Fig. 952
1		Jib Halyard Block	Size 1	W. C. Fig. 954
1		Cheek Block	Size 1	W. C. Fig. 382
1		Outhaul Block No. 1	Size 2	W. C. Fig. 5800
1		Outhaul Slide	Size 1	W. C. Fig. 9800
4		Cleats	6" Size	W. C. Fig. 400

1		Cleat	4" Size	W. C. Fig. 400
1		Stuffing Box	Size to suit	W. C. Fig. 865
1		Stern Bearing	Size to suit	W. C. Fig. 864
2		Outside Ports	4" Dia.	W. C. Fig. 525
2		Rudder Pintles	3/4"	W. C. Fig. 460
1		Mooring Bitt	Size 0	W. C. Fig. 4190
2	Qts.	Elmers Glue		

BILL OF MATERIAL — PICAROON   List II

Lumber

Note: The following material is in addition to List I for a V bottom plywood planked hull.

3	pcs.	Oak	1 1/4" x 3" x 12'-0"	Chines
2	pcs.	Oak	1 1/4" x 2 1/2" x 16'-0"	Bottom Strs.
3	pcs.	Oak	1 1/4" x 2 1 2" x 12'-0"	Side Strs.
3	Sheets	Plywood	4'-0" x 8'-0" x 3/8"	Frames
1	Sheet	Plywood	4'-0" x 8'-0" x 3/4"	Frames & Trnsm.
3	pcs.	Oak	1 1/4" x 3" x 12'-0"	Frames
3	pcs.	Oak	1 1/4" x 2 1/2" x 14'-0"	Frames
1	pc.	Oak	1 1/4" x 4" x 6'-0"	Frames
4	pcs.	Pine	1" x 2" x 12'-0"	Frames
2	pcs.	Harborite	4'-0" x 20'-0" x 3/8"	Topsides
2	pcs.	Harborite	4'-0" x 16'-0" x 1/2"	Bottom

Hardware

4	Gross	1" No. 10 Fl. Hd. Wood Screws	
3	Gross	1 1/4" No. 10 Fl. Hd. Wood Screws	
3	Qts.	Elmers Glue	

BILL OF MATERIAL — PICAROON II   List III

Note: The following material is in addition to List I for a round bottom stripped hull.

5	Sheets	Plywood	4'-0" x 8'-0" x 3/8"	Frames & Dk.
1	Sheet	Plywood	4'-0" x 8'-0" x 3/4"	Flooring
3	pcs.	Oak	1 1/4" x 6" x 10'-0"	Beams
4	pcs.	Oak	1 1/4" x 12" x 12'-0"	Frames
2	pcs.	Oak	1 1/4" x 8" x 12'-0"	Frames
1	pc.	Oak	2" x 4" x 12'-0"	Floors
6	pcs.	Pine	1" x 2" x 8'-0"	Floors
2	pcs.	Cedar or Mahogany	1" x 8" x 12'-0"	Garboards
250	Sq. ft.	Cedar Or Mahogany	Random Widths & Lengths	Planking
10	lbs.	6 penny nails (Galv.)		
3	Gross	1 1/2" - #8 Fl. Hd. Wood Screws		
1	Gal.	Elmers Glue.		

BILL OF MATERIAL — PLANKED PICAROON   List IV

The following material is in addition to
List I for a hull planked with standard
board lumber.

3	pcs.	Oak	1 1/4" x 3" x 12'-0"	Chines
2	pcs.	Oak	1 1/4" x 2 1/2" x 16'-0"	Bottom Strs.
60	lin. ft.	Oak	1 1/4" x 2 1/2"	Int. Frames
80	lin. ft.	Oak	1 1/4" x 4"	Main Frames
1	pc.	Oak	2" x 4" x 12'-0"	Floor Frames
1	pc.	Oak	1 1/4" x 8" x 12'-0"	Frame Knees
2	pcs.	Oak	1 1/4" x 12" x 10'-0"	Transom
1	pc.	Oak	1 1/4" x 2 1/2" x 12'-0"	Transom
460	lin. ft.	Cedar	1" x 6" random length	Planking

For Planked Decks And Cabin Top

Deduct from List I

4	Sheets	Plywood	4'-0" x 8'-0" x 3/8"	Decks & Joinery
1	Sheet	Plywood	4'-0" x 8'-0" x 3/4"	(one retained for rudder)
2	Sheets	Plywood	4'-0" x 8'-0" x 1/4"	(one retained for mast)

Add in addition to List IV

4	pcs.	Douglas Fir	1" x 12" x 12'-0"	Side Decks
100	lin. ft.	Douglas Fir	1" x 1 1/2"	Forward Deck
80	Sq. ft.	Douglas Fir	T. & G. Flooring-2 1/2" Face	Flooring
120	Sq. ft.	White Pine	T. & G. and Beaded Staving	Joinery & Cabin Top
5	pcs.	White Pine	1" x 12" x 8'-0"	Berths

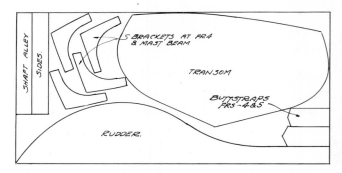

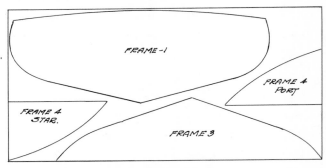

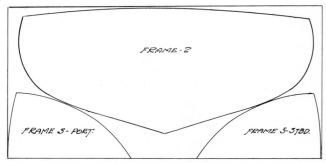

Cutting diagrams for *Picaroon.* Frames, transom and rudder
cut from three sheets of plywood.

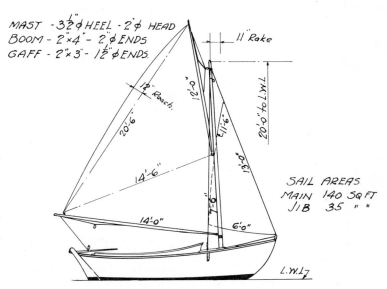

MAST -3½"⌀ HEEL -2"⌀ HEAD
BOOM - 2"×4" - 2"⌀ ENDS
GAFF - 2"×3" - 1½"⌀ ENDS.

SAIL AREAS
MAIN 140 SQ FT
JIB   35 " "

Original rig of *Picaroon* as a day sailer—1926.

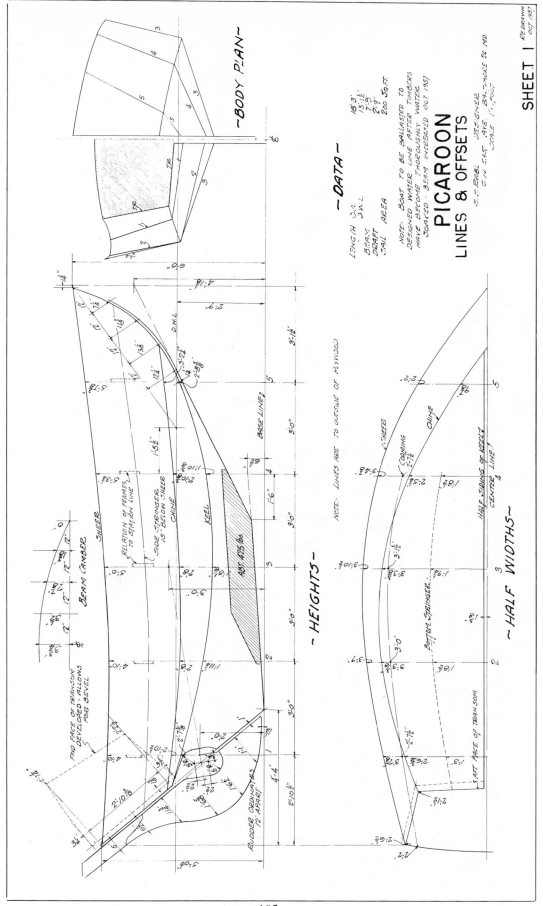

~BODY PLAN~

~DATA~

LENGTH O.A.   18'3"
J.W.L.   13'1½"
BEAM   7'9"
DRAFT   2'9"
SAIL AREA   200 SQ.FT.

NOTE: BOAT TO BE BALLASTED TO
DESIGNED WATER LINE AFTER TIMBERS
HAVE BECOME THOROUGHLY WATER
SOAKED - BEAM INCREASED OCT 1957

PICAROON
LINES & OFFSETS

S. S. RABL, DESIGNER
G.N. EAST AVE., BALTIMORE 24 MD.
SCALE 1½"=1 FOOT

SHEET I

REDRAWN
OCT. 1957

NOTE: LINES ARE TO OUTSIDE OF PLYWOOD

~ HEIGHTS ~

~ HALF WIDTHS ~

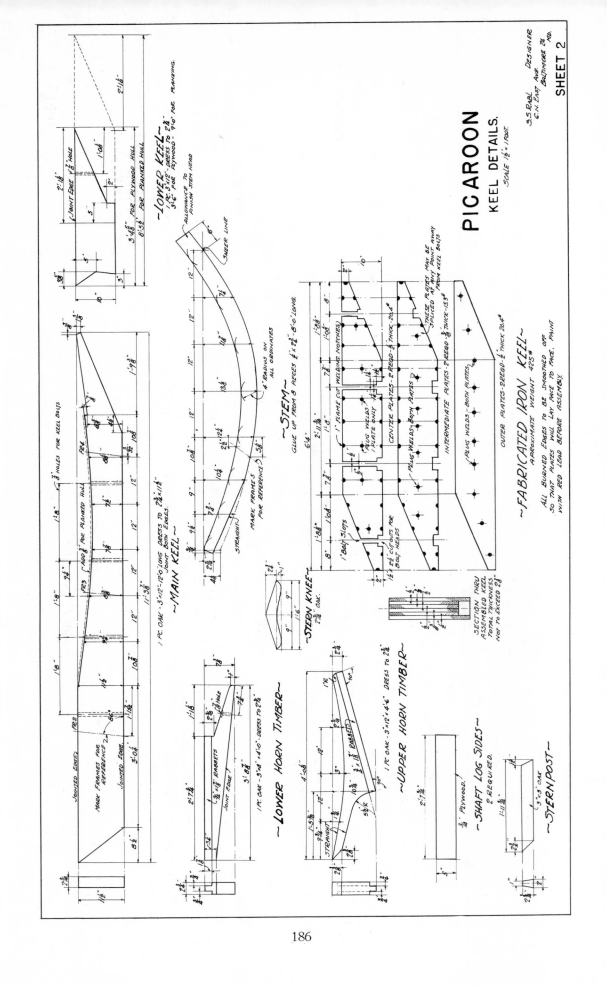

PICAROON

KEEL DETAILS.

SCALE 1½" = 1 FOOT.

S.S. RABL   DESIGNER
6.N. EAST AVE.
BALTIMORE 24
MD.

SHEET 2

186

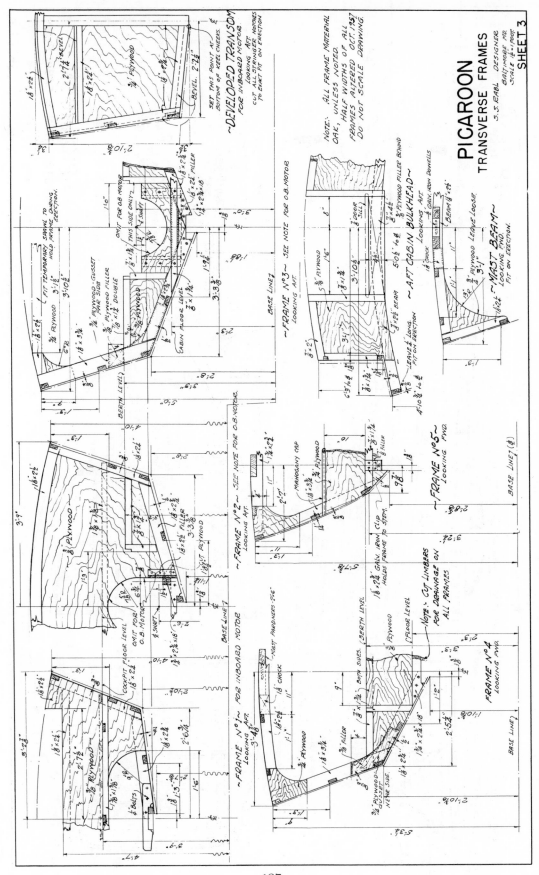

~DEVELOPED TRANSOM~
FOR INBOARD MOTOR
Looking Aft.
CUT ALL STRINGER NOTCHES
TO EXACT FIT ON ERECTION.

SET THIS POINT AT
BOTTOM OF KEEL CHEEKS.

NOTE:- ALL FRAME MATERIAL
OAK, UNLESS NOTED.
HALF WIDTHS OF ALL
FRAMES ALTERED OCT. 1957.
DO NOT SCALE DRAWING.

PICAROON
TRANSVERSE FRAMES
S.S. RABL DESIGNER
BALTIMORE MD.
SCALE 1½"=1 FOOT
SHEET 3

~FRAME No.3~ SEE NOTE FOR O.B. MOTOR
Looking Aft.

~AFT CABIN BULKHEAD~
Looking Aft.

~MAST BEAM~
Looking Fwd.
FIT ON ERECTION.

~FRAME No.2~ SEE NOTE FOR O.B. MOTOR
Looking Aft.

~FRAME No.5~
Looking Fwd.

~FRAME No.1~ FOR INBOARD MOTOR
Looking Aft.

~FRAME No.4~
Looking Fwd.

NOTE:- CUT LIMBERS
FOR DRAINAGE ON
ALL FRAMES.

187

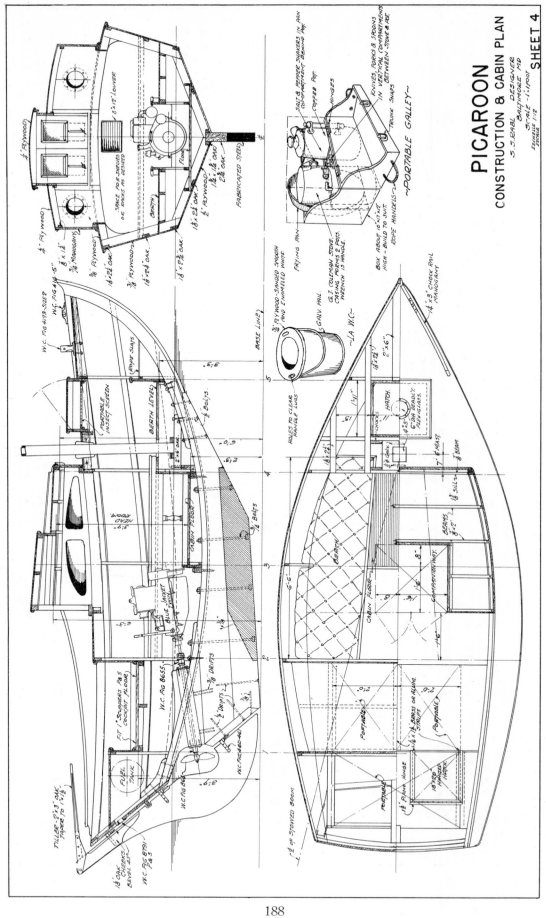

PICAROON
CONSTRUCTION & CABIN PLAN
S.S. CRAIL DESIGNER
BALTIMORE MD
SCALE 1":1 FOOT
ECHELLE 1:12

SHEET 4

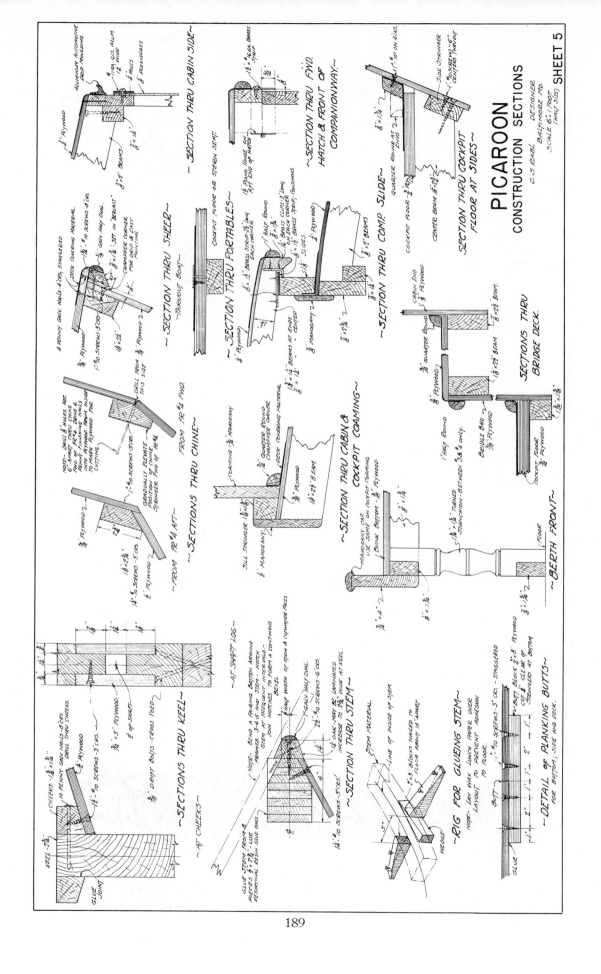

PICAROON
CONSTRUCTION SECTIONS

S. S. RABL   DESIGNER
BALTIMORE MD.
SCALE 6" : 1 FOOT
(HALF SIZE)   **SHEET 5**

~SECTION THRU CABIN SIDE~

~SECTION THRU FWD. HATCH & FRONT OF COMPANIONWAY~

~SECTION THRU SHEER~
~THRUOUT BOAT~

~SECTION THRU PORTABLES~

~SECTION THRU COMP. SLIDE~

~SECTION THRU COCKPIT FLOOR AT SIDES~

~SECTIONS THRU CHINE~
~FROM FR #4 FWD.~
~FROM FR #4 AFT~

~SECTION THRU CABIN & COCKPIT COAMING~

~SECTIONS THRU BRIDGE DECK.~

~BERTH FRONT~

~SECTIONS THRU KEEL~
~AT CHEEKS~

~AT SHAFT LOG~

~SECTION THRU STEM~

~RIG FOR GLUEING STEM~

~DETAIL OF PLANKING BUTTS~
FOR BOTTOM, SIDE AND DECK.

189

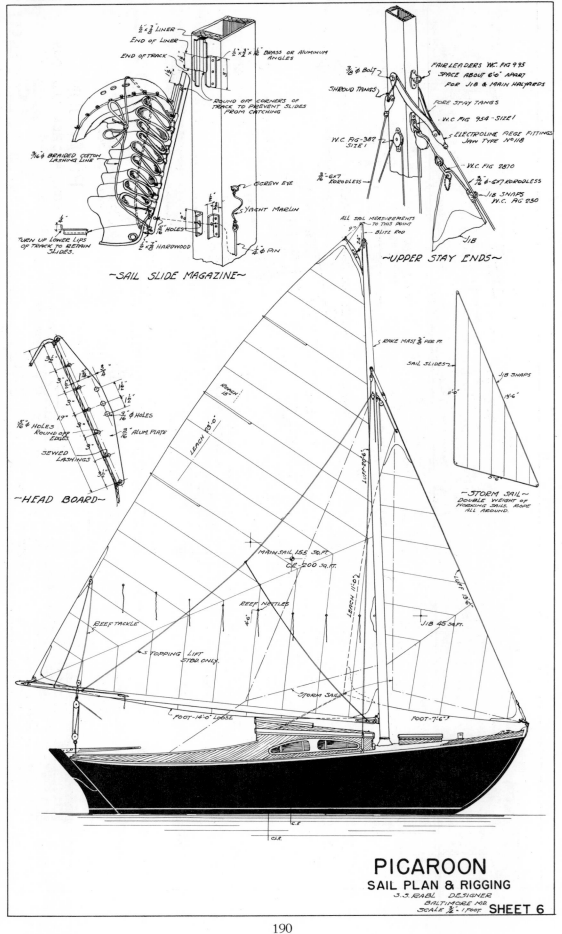

~SAIL SLIDE MAGAZINE~

~UPPER STAY ENDS~

~HEAD BOARD~

~STORM SAIL~
DOUBLE WEIGHT OF
WORKING SAILS. ROPE
ALL AROUND.

PICAROON
SAIL PLAN & RIGGING
S.S. RABL   DESIGNER
BALTIMORE MD.
SCALE ½"= 1FOOT.   **SHEET 6**

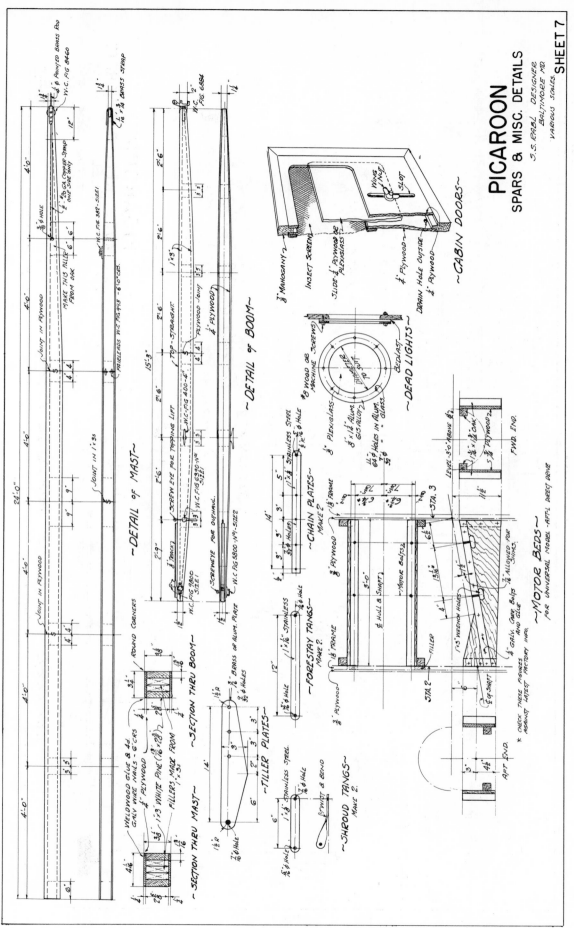

~DETAIL OF MAST~

~DETAIL OF BOOM~

~SECTION THRU MAST~

~SECTION THRU BOOM~

~TILLER PLATES~

~SHROUD TANGS~
MAKE 2.

~FORESTAY TANGS~
MAKE 2.

~CHAIN PLATES~
MAKE 2.

~DEAD LIGHTS~

~CABIN DOORS~

~MOTOR BEDS~
FOR UNIVERSAL MODEL ~AFF'L DIRECT DRIVE

* CHECK THESE FIGURES
AGAINST LATEST FACTORY INF'R.

PICAROON
SPARS & MISC. DETAILS
S. S. ERBL DESIGNER
BALTIMORE MD
VARIOUS SCALES. **SHEET 7**

191

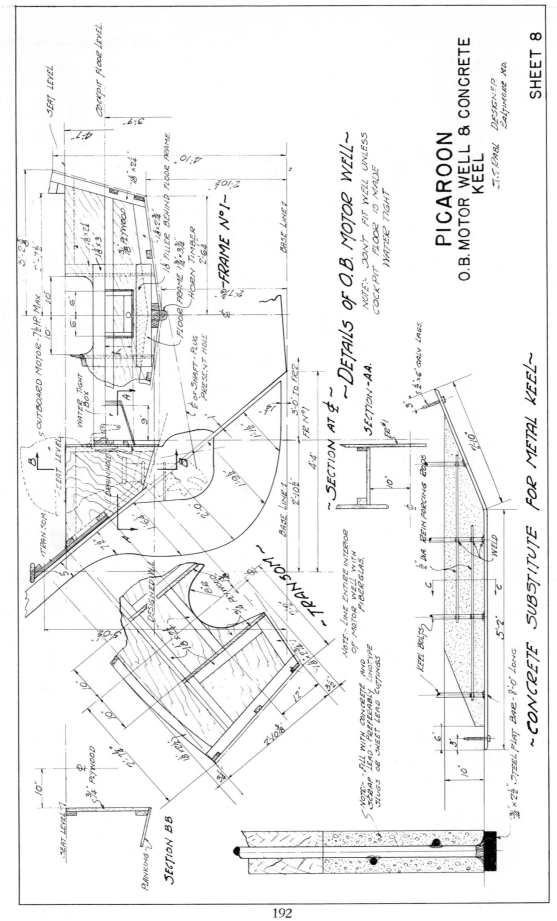

PICAROON

O.B. MOTOR WELL & CONCRETE KEEL

SHEET 8

~ DETAILS OF O.B. MOTOR WELL ~

~ CONCRETE SUBSTITUTE FOR METAL KEEL ~

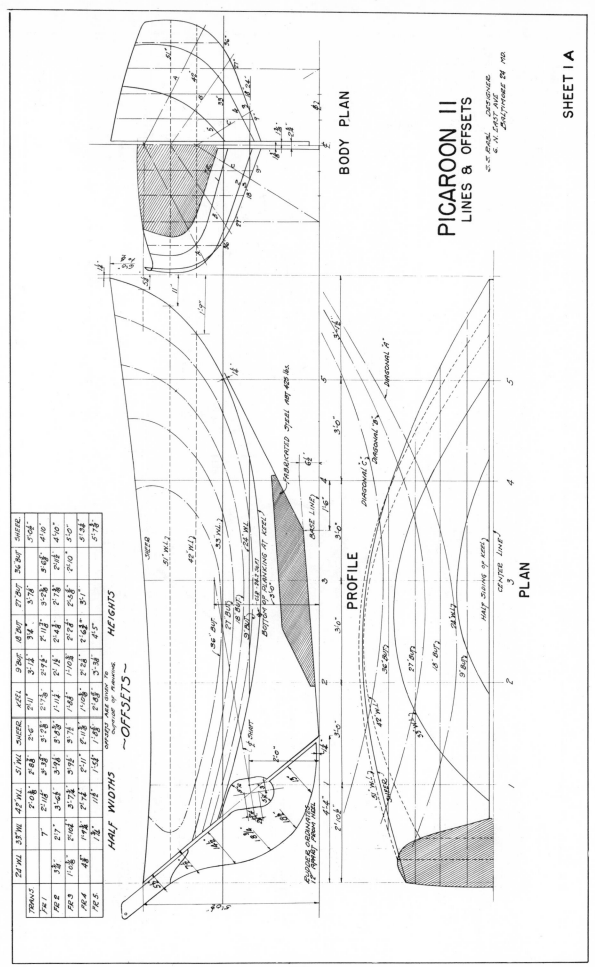

	24" W.L.	33" W.L.	42" W.L.	51" W.L.	SHEER.	KEEL	9" BUT.	18" BUT	27" BUT	36" BUT	SHEER.
TRANS.			2'-0 3/8"	2'-8 7/8"	2'-6"	2'-11"	3'-1 1/4"	3'-4"	3'-7 1/8"		5'-0 1/2"
FR 1		7"	2'-11 1/8"	3'-3 5/8"	3'-2 7/8"	2'-7 3/8"	2'-9 1/2"	2'-11 7/8"	3'-2 3/8"	3'-6 5/8"	4'-10"
FR 2	3 3/4"	2'-7"	3'-6 1/2"	3'-9 1/8"	3'-8 3/8"	1'-11 1/4"	2'-1 1/2"	2'-4 3/8"	2'-7 3/8"	2'-11 1/2"	4'-10"
FR 3	1'-0 3/8"	2'-10 1/4"	3'-7 3/4"	3'-9 1/2"	3'-7 1/2"	1'-8 8/8"	1'-10 3/4"	2'-2 8/8"	2'-5 5/8"	2'-10"	5'-0"
FR 4	4 5/8"	1'-9 3/4"	2'-7 1/4"	2'-11"	2'-11 3/8"	1'-10 3/8"	2'-2 1/8"	2'-6 3/4"	3'-1"		5'-3 1/4"
FR 5.		1 3/4"	11 1/2"	1'-5 1/4"	1'-8 5/8"	2'-8 5/8"	3'-3 1/8"	4'-5"			5'-7 3/8"

HALF WIDTHS — OFFSETS ARE GIVEN TO OUTSIDE OF PLANKING. — HEIGHTS

~OFFSETS~

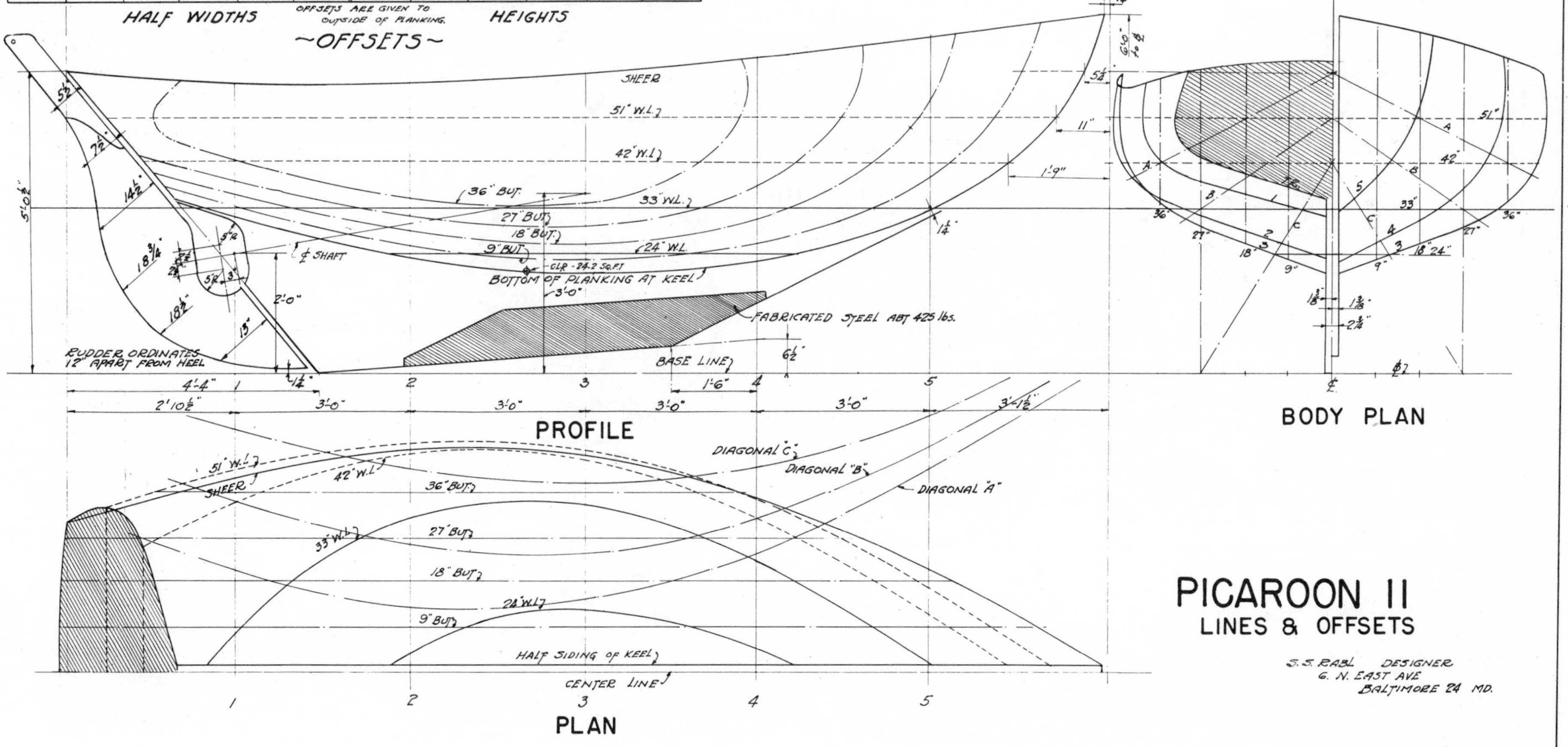

SHEER
51" W.L.
42" W.L.
36" BUT.
33" W.L.
27" BUT.
18" BUT.
9" BUT.
24" W.L.
℄ SHAFT
CLR - 24.2 SQ.FT
BOTTOM OF PLANKING AT KEEL
FABRICATED STEEL ABT 425 lbs.
BASE LINE
RUDDER ORDINATES 12" APART FROM HEEL
5'-0 1/2"
4'-4"
2'-10 1/2"
3'-0"
3'-0"
3'-0"
3'-0"
3'-1 1/2"
1'-6"
6 1/2"
2'-0"
PROFILE
DIAGONAL "C"
DIAGONAL "B"
DIAGONAL "A"
SHEER
HALF SIDING OF KEEL
CENTER LINE
PLAN
BODY PLAN

PICAROON II
LINES & OFFSETS

S. S. RABL DESIGNER
6. N. EAST AVE
BALTIMORE 24 MD.

SHEET 1 A

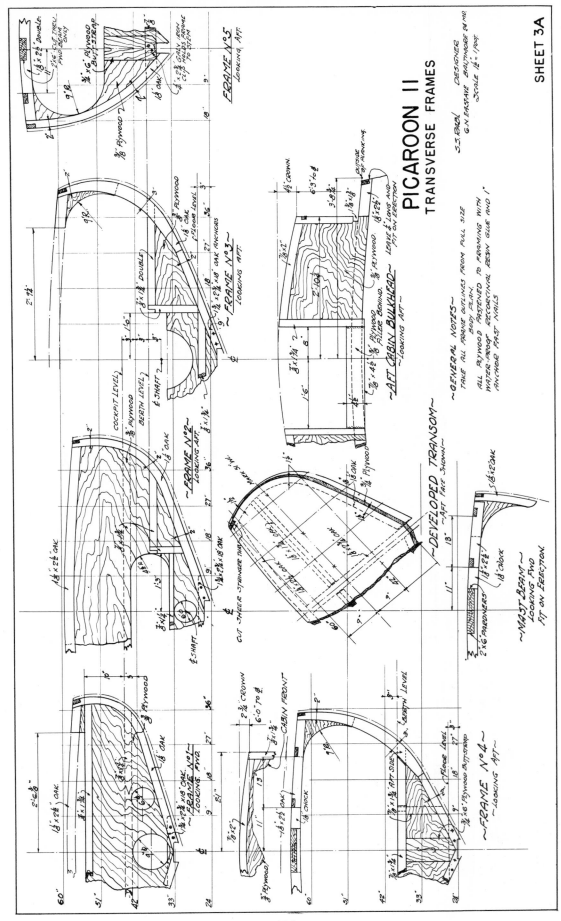

PICAROON II
TRANSVERSE FRAMES

S.S. RAABL   DESIGNER
G.N. EASTAVE BALTIMORE 24 MD.
SCALE 1½" = 1'0"

~GENERAL NOTES~
TAKE ALL FRAME OUTLINES FROM FULL SIZE
BODY PLAN.
ALL PLYWOOD FASTENED TO FRAMING WITH
WATER-PROOF RESORCINAL RESIN GLUE AND 1"
ANCHOR FAST NAILS

SHEET 3A

BOAT PLANS

KITTIWAKE

An inexpensive boat for the water gypsy. No spit and polish, but with good, sensible accommodations; 24′ 0″ long, 8′ 9″ beam, 2′ 0″ draft.

There has always been the man who does not take his yachting seriously. To him a boat is just a boat. He has no dreams of grandeur, cares not a whit for spit or polish and has no desire to show his jet tail-pipes to the rest of his brethren. His yachting uniform probably consists of the pair of faded dungarees that he wore in the engine room of the *Big Mo* when she entered Tokyo Bay and he strikes out the watch bells on the bottom of a dishpan. He is a water gypsy and there must be a lot of his ilk for Jack Hanna's *Dorothy*, Charles Hall's *Gannet* and my own *Oriole* have ever been popular boats. For this man, and with these three boats as a criterion, *Kittiwake* was created.

Kittiwake is just a good old-fashioned boat designed without any fancy construction features and whose materials can be purchased in almost any lumber yard. Boats like her have been built long before power tools were ever dreamed of, and while it would be folly to deny the benefits of power tools, she can still be constructed with the ordinary hand tools. Two good, sharp saws, a rip- and a cross-cut, a sharp hatchet, several planes, several chisels, a

brace and a set of bits, a draw-knife and a coarse rasp, plus all the clamps you can beg, borrow, or steal, should be sufficient. These, or even power tools, will not work while you sit idle. The ability to use them is of prime importance.

Kittiwake may be built of almost any lumber available in your own locality and, with a few exceptions, may be nail-fastened throughout. Thousands of similar boats have been built of native pine in the little tidewater boatyards of Maryland far from any electric power line. One form of bottom, copied from *Oriole*, may be planked as easily as a flattie skiff and no spilings have to be taken for any single piece of lumber in the whole of the hull.

The other form, which is true Chesapeake Bay deadrise construction, will be a bit more tedious to construct and takes a bit better carpentry, but is in no way difficult. It will produce a slightly better sea boat and takes away the blunt appearance of the bow.

Almost any power will give satisfactory performance, anything from 20 H.P. to 60 H.P. will suffice. *Kittiwake* was not designed as an express cruiser, so bear this in mind in selecting the motor. The power plant may be an auto conversion, it may be a rebuilt marine engine or a new one as suits your pocketbook, remembering always that the increased speed in this type of boat never justifies the additional horse-power.

The interior arrangement may be simple and primitive with a galvanized pail for the head and an auto camp stove and ice box for the galley, or it may be resplendent in stainless steel and mahogany trim. Far be it from me to dictate which.

There will be no fairing of the lines as detail drawings have been furnished so that you may lay out directly on the wood. There will be no tedious boring of the shaft hole with the necessity of long bitts or an attack of ulcers from worry as to where the far end of the hole is coming out.

All of the keel material is of 3″ stock. This will finish 2¾″ or perhaps ⅛″ less but be sure that all the thicknesses are the same. The best material for this is, of course, white oak, but pine or any other type of hard wood will be usable. If the bottom of the keel is capped with a 1″ x 3″ strip of hardwood, Western Fir will answer.

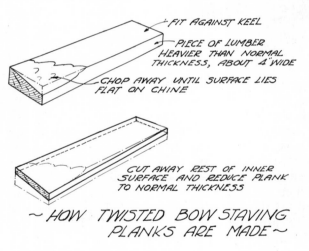

~ HOW TWISTED BOW STAVING
PLANKS ARE MADE ~

The main keel is straight 3″ x 4″ stock. If it can be secured in one length, all well and good, otherwise scarph it as shown. The skeg timber is laid off as per the drawing. If a band saw is not available, notch down to within 1″ of the finished line with a sawcut about every 8″ and split most of the wood away. Finish the cut with a sharp hatchet or adz. A *Skilsaw* will be handy in cutting the rabbet but longer and more difficult rabbets than this have been cut by hand. The horn timber is worked in a similar manner. Assemble the various members with ⅜″ lag screws or through bolts. If you have a stock and dies, the

bolts may be made to suit from a length of ⅜″ diameter galvanized rod with nuts on both ends. The sides of the shaft log are best assembled with *Elmer's Glue* but if this is not available, forget it. Butter all joints with a good sealing compound. In spite of all the fancy products on the market there is none better than common asphaltum roofing cement. The keel cheeks, of 2″ x 2″ stock, are next fixed to both sides of the keel. Splice the cheeks anywhere that their run is straight. Discontinue them forward of Frame 5 if the sharp bow is to be fitted. The stem knee and inner stem are made as per details and assembled on the backbone. The outer stem is not to be erected as yet for it will be easier to cut off the plank ends if this is not done.

The frame shapes are laid down on a smooth floor to both sides of the centerline and the actual frame assembled over these lines. Use ¼″ galvanized bolts in the frame joints. Ordinarily the frames are made from 1-⅛″ oak stock. Standard pine, or fir, 2 x 4's and 2 x 6's may be dressed down to 1¼″ in the mill where you purchase them. If you are not fussy about the weight of the boat they may be used as is. The cross spalls which will be removed later may be of any available rough lumber. Mark their centerline and keep them all at the level shown. The transom may be planked when its frame is made, or later. If planked later the ends of the stringers will be covered.

As a general rule there will be no enclosure large enough to build the boat under cover. Select a level piece of ground and drive a series of heavy stakes in a line to support the keel. Stretch a level string to represent the base line and another to represent the slope of the keel bottom. Cut off the tops of the stakes to match the line of the keel bottom and brace them tight. Erect the backbone and firmly brace it plumb. Erect Frame 3 in its proper position. Level, square and plumb it, holding it in its proper position with temporary braces so that it will not move. Erect the other frames in a similar manner and tie the whole structure together with temporary ribbands around the frames and across the cross spalls.

The sheer stringer and chine pieces are next bent in and fastened. These are made from 2 x 3's dressed down to a 1¼″ thickness. They will have to be spliced, so do this where the run is comparatively straight using butt pieces of the same material. It is best to screw-fasten these members to the main frames with 2½″ # 12 screws. On the sharp bow model be sure that the chine line, where it meets the stem, is at the center width of the stringer at this point to allow for the planking fits.

The intermediate frames run from sheer to chine in a straight line. They are made from 1-⅛" x 2-¾" oak or common 2 x 3's dressed down to 1¼". To space them, divide the distance between frames on both sheer and chine into four equal parts and set the intermediates on these points. All of these frames are set square to the line of the stringers and planking so therefore are set with only enough bevel to fit the sheer and the chine.

The bottom stringers are next run in and fastened. It is very good practice to leave one of these loose. Lay it aside after fitting, as the space where it comes out is very good access to the interior of the boat during construction.

The side planking is applied to the frames in straight parallel strakes 6" wide. Run the line of the first plank straight from stem to transom in such a way that at no point is the distance any greater than 12" above the bottom of the chine stringer. The plank should lie on the frames *natural* without any spring in its width.

Two 14' planks, overlapped and clamped so that their edges form one straight line, may be adjusted on the hull to obtain the run of this first plank. Continue planking up until the sheer is reached. Here you will have to start using the 8" planks either to drop out or to add a strake. Where the 6" width, if continued, would fall below the stringer, the plank is cut and an 8" width butted to it. This 8" width is again continued and when it starts to run off, another 6" and an 8" or two 6" planks are continued. In no case should the end of a plank be less than 2" wide. This process will save the ripping of planks where the nibbed system would require it.

The planks next to the chine are done in a similar manner. All topside planking should be outgaged for caulking. Be sure to space the butts in adjacent planks well apart.

Delay planking the bottom as long as possible. Make it the very last operation. In this way you save the laborious job of cleaning out the boat after the interior joiner work is completed.

On the simplified bottom, 6" planks are laid at 45° to the keel and sloping aft. Allow the width of a hack saw blade, but no more, between them so that they will swell tight afterward without caulking. These planks have no outgage. Lay their inner and outer edges on flannel or wool strips about 1" wide. Soak this flannel or wool well in seam-sealing compound or roofing cement. As the cloth will be on the the under side of the buttered surface, tack it at intervals with small copper tacks. If the bottom plank-

ing is delayed until all interior work is finished, and you no longer need the level and plumb lines, the boat may be leaned away from one side and the exposed bottom planked very much easier.

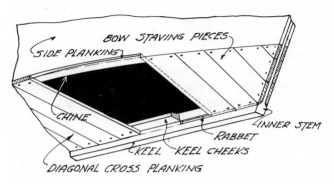

~ SHARP BOW PLANKING ~
WORM'S EYE VIEW.

If the sharp bow is to be fitted, it will be found that the twist of the cross planking forward would be so excessive as to prohibit its use. There are two ways of planking the bow. The first method is to build in a series of closely-spaced frames at about 12" intervals forward of Frame 4 between the keel and the chine and these carvel-planked with longitudinal strakes. These strakes will have to be outgaged and caulked in the regular manner. The method in general use in the little tidewater boatyards of the Chesapeake Bay, where this type of boat originated, is to cross-plank with narrow planks into which the twist is worked from wood of greater thickness. As a general rule these planks are worked from 2" x 4", or 2" x 6" stock. While this is generally done with an adz, a sharp hatchet will also do a yeoman job. The square edge of the stock is held against the keel and the chine edge chopped away until a good fit is procured. Lines are then laid off on the edges to the twist and thickness required and then the excess wood is chopped away and the plank planed smooth. In some cases I have seen only the fitting edges and the outside of the plank worked off. The inside of the boat in this case takes the appearance of a series of steps until the uniform thickness planks are reached. As all this rough work is inside the boat and in an obscure place, what matters? All of these staving planks, as they are called, should be outgaged and caulked the same as carvel planking.

The question of plywood is bound to arise. Use it if you desire. The thickness should be ½" throughout. Considerable difficulty may be encountered in the sharp bow but it can still be done. If plywood is to be used, eliminate the intermediate frames on the sides and substitute in their places a longitudinal stringer 1¼″ x 2-¾″ halfway between the sheer and the chine.

After the side planking is completed, make the beam mold and trim down the entire sheer until it matches the camber of the mold. Make what deck beams are necessary and install them, either forward of the intermediate frames if they are forward, or aft of them if they are aft. Bevel off their extremities to fit the intermediate frames and secure them with a ¼″ galvanized bolt. Run in the 1″ x 2″ coaming stringer and fit the 2″ x 4″ spacer beams between this and the sheer stringer. Frame out the forward hatch and fit its coamings. After all deck framing is completed the plank sheers are fitted. Lay these in with lengths of 12″ boards and butt them where they no longer fill the width. Forward and aft, where the decking will be fitted to them, cut and fit the 1″ x 3″ backing pieces between the beams which will receive the ends of the decking. Bed all joints down well in white or red lead paste. This precaution is a good guard against rot and may save a lot of grief later.

The straight decking is standard tongue-and-groove flooring material. Vertical grain Douglas fir is best for this but use the best you can procure. Bed the joints of this down in white lead paste or *Bedlast*. There are some rubber sealing compounds on the market today which will come and go with the wood and keep the deck permanently tight. If the job of laying the deck is done well and bedded it need never be canvased.

Now fit the inner coamings. These will need to be sawed to shape as there is too much edge curvature to spring them. Save a pattern of this shape to cut the main coamings later. Bed these inner coamings well at their joints with the coaming stringer and the deck.

Build in the motor foundation to suit the motor you have selected. The floor timbers of Frames 1, 2, and 3 are wide enough to take the beds of almost any engine you select. At the width of the beds, lagscrew a pair of 2 x 4's over these frames and bolt the main foundation timbers to these, thus distributing the thrust over three main frames.

When the motor is installed you will have enough clearance in the shaft tunnel to move the shaft about 3″ higher on its forward end if necessary. At the inner end of the tunnel, install either a patent shaft log or a 6″ x 6″ block of oak bored to take a flexible stuffing box. A plain stern bearing at the aft end will complete this installation. The rudder stock is brought inboard

through a standard stuffing box. It was for this reason no stern knee was fitted. The value of a knee at this point is doubtful anyway.

It will be a lot easier to fit the exhaust piping and shaft as well as the steering gear if the cockpit floor is delayed. The cockpit floor beams are 1-⅛″ x 2-¾″, or thereabouts, set on all main and intermediate frames. It will be well to support every beam with a post down to the keel or bottom stringers. The flooring itself will be standard tongue-and-groove stock the same as the decking. It may be very easily made watertight and self-bailing.

Two cabin profiles have been given. You can make your own choice. The interiors may be built of plywood or the good old fashioned 1″ T & G staving. They may be arranged as you see fit. If you have ever ridden in a light all-plywood boat, this one will be a revelation. She will be easy in a sea-way if not driven too hard and the best comparison that you can make with a plywood boat is the difference between a light sports car and a good old-fashioned heavy *Packard* in their actions on the road.

The cabin construction is simple. The ends are erected first and three rather heavy battens are run close to the outboard edges and on centerline between these. The beams are left longer than desired and temporarily fastened to the battens. This gives a straight-line cabin top. By plumbing up from the inner coaming, the end cuts of the beams are obtained. At the same time keep a record of the measurement down to the deck at each beam to shape the top of the cabin coaming. The beams are now removed and cut to their proper lengths, numbering them for installation later. The cabin and cockpit coaming is now bent in and fastened to the ends and to the inner coaming. Be sure that the lower edge is well bedded against the deck or caulk this joint later. In the way of the cabin, the coaming will be two boards high. The joint of these boards may be either splined or doweled, with glue in both cases. The joint may also be made with vertical battens spaced astride the port light locations and covered with a thin longitudinal batten on the inside. The top is planked with regular T & G flooring material and canvased. Vee-edged staving or wainscote material will make a better appearance if it can be obtained. The cabin and cockpit flooring is T & G of the same material used for flooring in building construction. If the cockpit is to be watertight and self-bailing it should be canvased. In way of the cabin floor leave 10″ or 12″ of the floor removable for access to the bilges. If the cabin floor is run out to the sides a lot more available storage space will be secured under the berths.

The standing top is constructed as shown on the plans. Note that the sides in way of the windshield have a rake-in or tumble home. This takes away its otherwise boxy appearance and brings its width to a reasonable figure at the aft end where it meets the stanchion, and yet keeps parallel construction. The front sash is hinged; the sides are fixed. The cabin arrangement is more or less standard for this type of boat. By all means fit the forward hatch. It has many advantages. First of all, it is an emergency escape in case of fire at the motor or galley. It gives good ventilation to the cabin and a good place to stand in when handling anchor lines in heavy weather. In addition to all of these, it gives additional headroom over the W.C. and comes in handy at this location when mastheading your dungarees.

The motor shown on the plans is a *Universal Utility Four* which develops 25 H.P. at 2600 R.P.M. This is a good, husky engine designed especially for Marine use and is all the power that will ever be needed in this type of boat. Be sure that it is installed in accordance with U.S. Coast Guard regulations and that the required vents are installed as shown.

If the boat is not intended for extensive cruising, the half cabin may be fitted as shown. This will contain two berths with a W.C. under the hatch. It gives a good shelter in inclement weather and a good place to snooze when the fish stop biting. With this arrangement *Kittiwake* will make a wonderful boat for following the schools of stripers or snappers wherever they go. Being rather heavy she will be comfortable and, of all the boats in this book, she would be one choice for my own personal use.

BILL OF MATERIAL — KITTIWAKE

Lumber

1 pc.	Oak	3" x 4" x 16'-0"	Main Keel
1 pc.	Oak	3" x 4" x 10'-0"	Main Keel
1 pc.	Oak	3" x 12" x 12'-0"	Skeg
1 pc.	Oak	3" x 12" x 8'-0"	Horn & Stem Knee
1 pc.	Oak	3" x 4" x 10'-0"	Stems
5 pcs.	Oak	1 1/4" x 6" x 8'-0"	Frames
1 pc.	Oak	2" x 6" x 12'-0"	Floors
6 pcs.	Oak	1 1/4" x 4" x 8'-0"	Side Frames
120 Lin. ft.	Oak	1 1/4" x 3"	Int. Frames
60 Lin. ft.	Oak	1 1/4" x 3"	Floor Beams
5 pcs.	Pine	1" x 12" x 12'-0"	Planksheers
10 pcs.	Oak	1 1/4" x 3" x 16'-0"	Chines & Sheer
2 pcs.	Oak	1" x 2" x 16'-0"	Coaming Stringer
4 pcs.	Pine or Mahog.	1" x 6" x 12'-0"	Inner Coaming
2 pcs.	Pine or Mahog.	1" x 12" x 16'-0"	Cabin Sides
2 pcs.	Pine or Mahog.	1" x 6" x 12'-0"	Cabin Sides
5 pcs.	Oak	2" x 3" x 16'-0"	Bottom Stringers
2 pcs.	Oak	2" x 4" x 12'-0"	Motor Stringers
8 pcs.	Oak	1 1/4" x 6" x 6'-0"	Deck & Cabin Bms.
175 bd. ft.	Cedar or Pine	1" x 6" Random lengths	Bot. Plkg.
200 bd. ft.	Cedar or Pine	1" x 8" Random lengths	Side Plkg.
160 Sq. ft.	Laid	2 1/3" face	T. & G. Flooring
130 Sq. ft.		3"	T. & G. Vee Edge Staving
2 pcs.	Oak	2" x 2" x 8'-0"	Stanchions
4 pcs.	Pine	1" x 2" x 8'-0"	Windshield & Top
4 pcs.	Pine	1" x 3" x 8'-0"	Windshield & Top
1 pc.	Pine	1" x 4" x 12'-0"	Windshield & Top
6 pcs.	Pine	1" x 6" x 8'-0"	Windshield & Top
1 pc.	Pine	1" x 8" x 8'-0"	Windshield & Top
2 pcs.	Plywood	4'-0" x 8'-0" x 1/4"	Windshield & Top

Hardware

70		1/4" x 3 1/3"	Carriage Bolts -Galv.	
65		1/4" x 3"	Carriage Bolts -Galv.	
80		1/4" x 2 1/2"	Carriage Bolts -Galv.	
1 Gross		2 1/2" -#12 Fl. Hd. Galv. Wood Screws		
2 Gross		2" -#12 Fl. Hd. Galv. Wood Screws		
3 Gross		1 1/2" -#10 Fl. Hd. Galv. Wood Screws		
15 lbs.		2 1/4"	Boat nails	Tiebout Fig. 3639
10 lbs.		2 3/4" Boat nails		Tiebout Fig. 3639
5 lbs.		3 1/2" Boat nails		Tiebout Fig. 3639
16 ft.		1/2" Dia. Galv. Rod		Drifts
20		1/2" Clinch Rings Galv.		Tiebout Fig. 836
12		1/2" Sq. Nuts & Washers		Tiebout Fig. 3623
1	Comb. Light			Perko Fig. 1140
1	Stern Light			Perko Fig. 422
2	Transom Vents			Perko Fig. 1069
1 Pair	Motor Vents			Perko Fig. 762
1	Inlet. Connection			Perko Fig. 64
1	Scoop Strainer			Perko Fig. 66
6	Portlights	6" Dia.		Perko Fig. 317
2	Portlights	4" Dia.		Perko Fig. 317
1	Drum Steerer	16"		Perko Fig. 661
1	Cruiser Rudder	Size 6		Perko Fig. 816
1	Quadrant	12"		Perko Fig. 651
1	Shaft Log			Perko Fig. 671
1 Set	Bulwark Chocks			Perko Fig. 751
1	Bitt	Size No. 1		Perko Fig. 608
1	Deck Pipe	Size No. 1		Perko Fig. 741
1	Rudder Port	1" Size		Perko Fig. 1089
1	Stern Bearing			W. C. Fig. 864
1	Rudder Skeg			Tiebout Fig. 4642
60 Lin ft.		3/4" Galv. Half Oval		

Mr. Erik Duffy's *Kittiwake*. (Top left) Main frames erected on keel. (Top right) Sheer and chine stringers bent in. (Bottom left) The first side planks going on. (Bottom right) Side planking completed above chine.

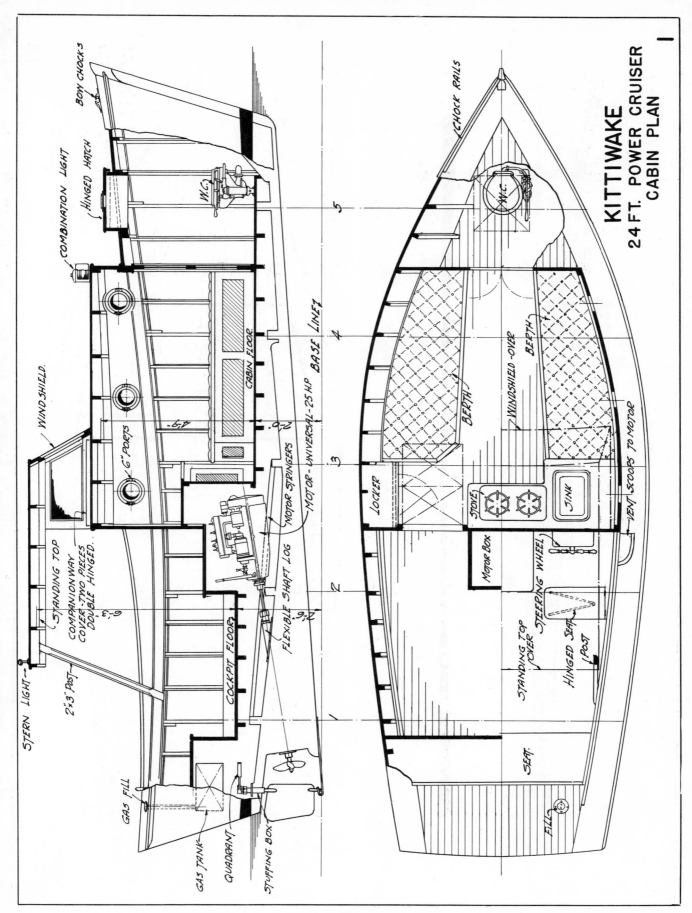

KITTIWAKE
24 FT. POWER CRUISER
CABIN PLAN

CHOCK RAILS

W.C.

BERTH

WINDSHIELD - OVER

BERTH

LOCKER

STOVE

SINK

VENT SCOOPS TO MOTOR

MOTOR BOX

STEERING WHEEL

STANDING TOP OVER

HINGED SEAT

POST

SEAT

FILL

COMBINATION LIGHT

BOW CHOCKS

HINGED HATCH

W.C.

WIND SHIELD.

6" PORTS

CABIN FLOOR

4'-6"

2'-6"

BASE LINE

MOTOR - UNIVERSAL - 25 H.P.

MOTOR STRINGERS

FLEXIBLE SHAFT LOG

2'-6"

COCKPIT FLOOR.

STANDING TOP

COMPANION WAY COVER - TWO PIECES DOUBLE HINGED.

3'-3"

STERN LIGHT.

2"x3" POST.

GAS FILL

GAS TANK

QUADRANT

STUFFING BOX

5

4

3

2

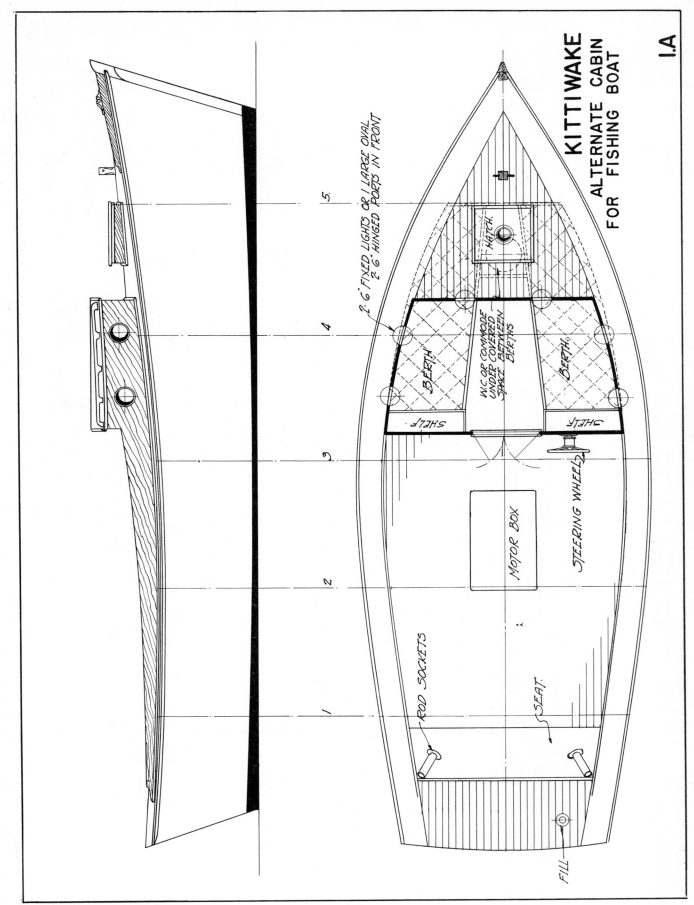

KITTIWAKE

ALTERNATE CABIN
FOR FISHING BOAT

I.A

2 6' FIXED LIGHTS OR 1 LARGE OVAL
2 6' HINGED PORTS IN FRONT

HATCH.

BERTH

W.C OR COMMODE
UNDER COVERED
SPACE BETWEEN
BERTHS

BERTH

SHELF

SHELF

STEERING WHEEL

MOTOR BOX

ROD SOCKETS

SEAT.

FILL

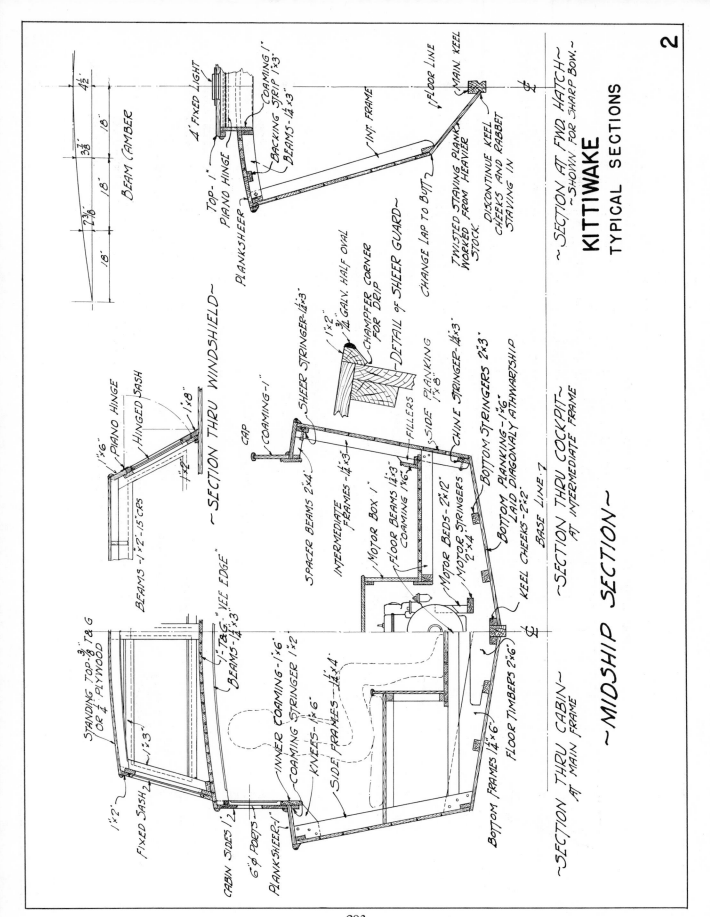

BEAM CAMBER

18" 2⅜ 18" 18" 18"

4½ 3⅞ 18"

~SECTION THRU WINDSHIELD~

4' FIXED LIGHT

COAMING 1"
BACKING STRIP 1"x3"
BEAMS - 1¼"x3"

Top - 1"

PLANKSHEER

PIANO HINGE

INT. FRAME

FLOOR LINE

MAIN KEEL

TWISTED STAYING PLANK
WORKED FROM HEAVIER
STOCK.

DISCONTINUE KEEL
CHEEKS AND RABBET
STAYING IN

CHANGE LAP TO BUTT

~SECTION AT FWD HATCH~
~SHOWN FOR SHARP BOW.~

KITTIWAKE
TYPICAL SECTIONS

PIANO HINGE
HINGED SASH

1"x6"

1"x8"

1"x2"

BEAMS - 1"x2" - 15 CRS

¾ T&G ½" VEE EDGE

SHEER STRINGER - 1¼"x3"

CAP

COAMING - 1"

1"x2"

¾ GALV. HALF OVAL

CHAMPFER CORNER
FOR DRIP

~DETAIL OF SHEER GUARD~

SIDE PLANKING
1"x 8"

FILLERS

CHINE STRINGER - 1¼"x3"

SPACER BEAMS 2"x4"

INTERMEDIATE
FRAMES - 1¼"x3"

MOTOR BOX 1"

FLOOR BEAMS 1¼"x3"

COAMING 1"x6"

MOTOR BEDS - 2"x12"

MOTOR STRINGERS
2"x4"

BOTTOM STRINGERS 2"x3"

BOTTOM PLANKING - 1"x6"
LAID DIAGONALY ATHWARTSHIP

KEEL CHEEKS - 2"x2"

BASE LINE 7

~SECTION THRU COCKPIT~
AT INTERMEDIATE FRAME

STANDING TOP - ⅜" T&G
OR ¼" PLYWOOD

1"x6"
PIANO HINGE

1"x2"

FIXED SASH 2"

CABIN SIDES 1½"

6" Ø PORTS

PLANKSHEER - 1"

INNER COAMING - 1"x6"

COAMING STRINGER 1"x2"

KNEES - 1"x6"

SIDE FRAMES - 1¼"x4"

BOTTOM FRAMES 1¼"x 6"

FLOOR TIMBERS 2"x6"

~SECTION THRU CABIN~
AT MAIN FRAME

~MIDSHIP SECTION~

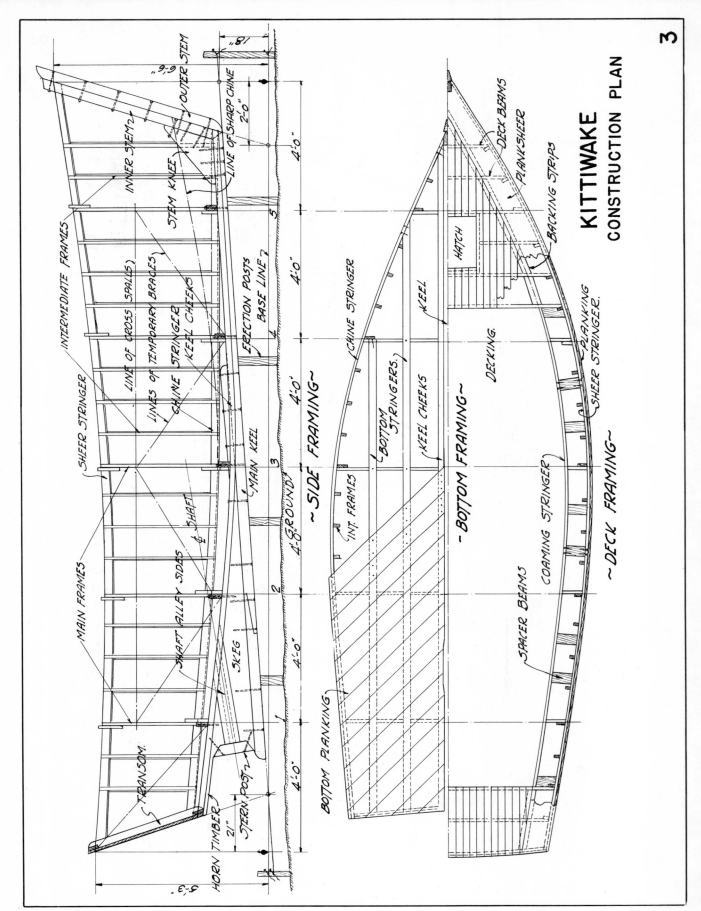

KITTIWAKE
CONSTRUCTION PLAN

3

~SIDE FRAMING~

OUTER STEM
INNER STEM
STEM KNEE
LINE OF SHARP CHINE
INTERMEDIATE FRAMES
SHEER STRINGER
LINES OF CROSS SPALLS
LINES OF TEMPORARY BRACES
CHINE STRINGER
KEEL CHEEKS
ERECTION POSTS
BASE LINE
MAIN KEEL
MAIN FRAMES
SHAFT VALLEY SIDES
℄ SHAFT
SKEG
TRANSOM
STERN POST
HORN TIMBER

~BOTTOM FRAMING~

BOTTOM PLANKING
CHINE STRINGER
BOTTOM STRINGERS
KEEL
KEEL CHEEKS
INT. FRAMES

~DECK FRAMING~

DECK BEAMS
PLANKSHEER
BACKING STRIPS
HATCH
DECKING
PLANKING
SHEER STRINGER
COAMING STRINGER
SPACER BEAMS

2'-0"
4'-0"
9'-6"
21"
9'-3"
"8'"
4'-6"(ROUND)

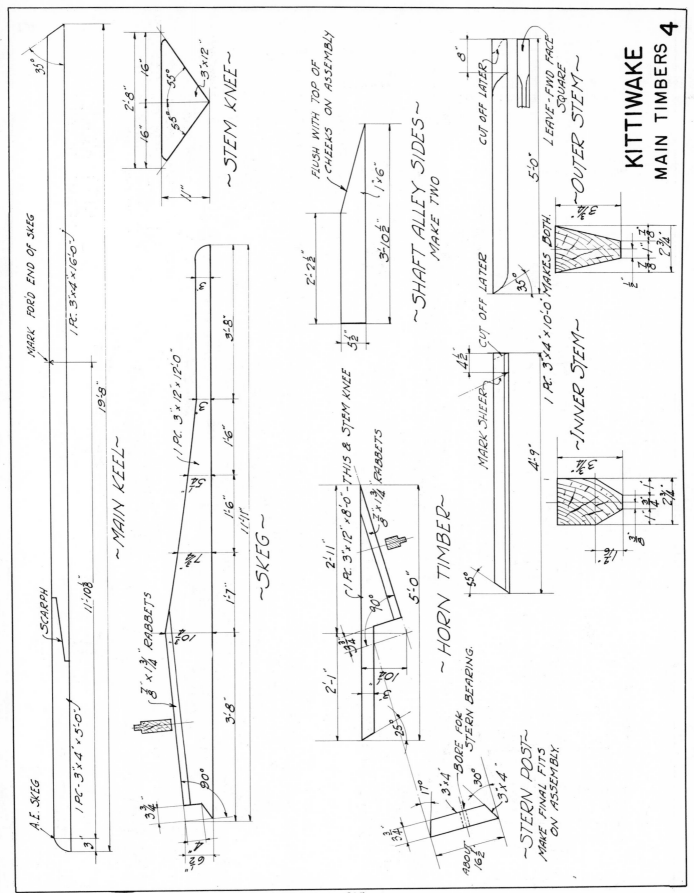

KITTIWAKE
MAIN TIMBERS 4

~STEM KNEE~

~MAIN KEEL~

~SKEG~

~SHAFT ALLEY SIDES~
MAKE TWO

~OUTER STEM~

~INNER STEM~

~HORN TIMBER~

~STERN POST~
MAKE FINAL FITS
ON ASSEMBLY.

FLUSH WITH TOP OF
CHEEKS ON ASSEMBLY

CUT OFF LATER

LEAVE-FWD FACE
SQUARE

CUT OFF LATER

MARK SHEER

BORE FOR
STERN BEARING.

A.E. SKEG

SCARPH

MARK FOR'D END OF SKEG

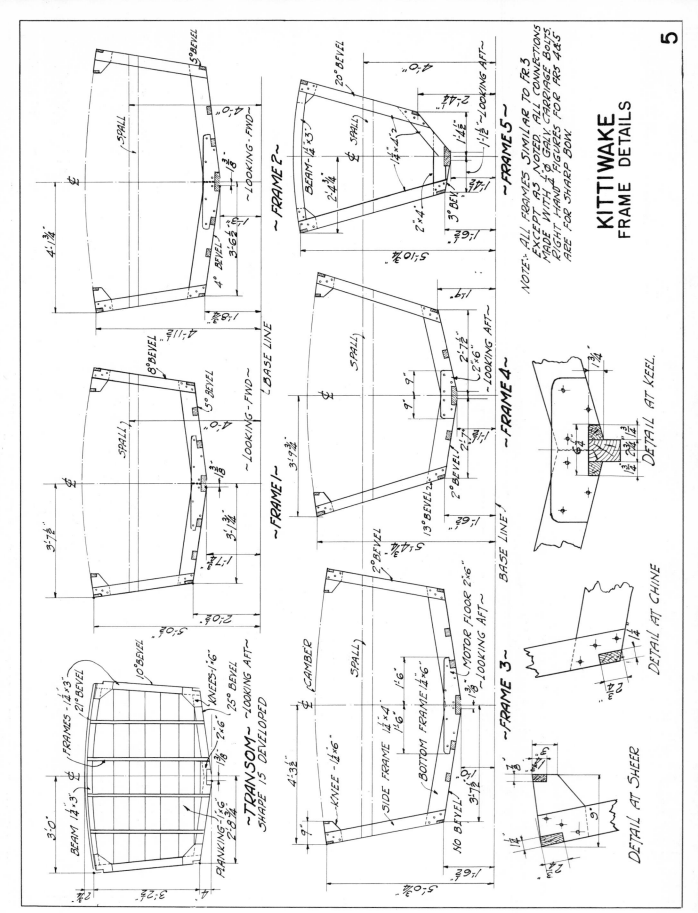

KITTIWAKE
FRAME DETAILS

~FRAME 2~

~FRAME 5~

NOTE:- ALL FRAMES SIMILAR TO FR.3
EXCEPT AS NOTED. ALL CONNECTIONS
MADE WITH ¼⌀ GALV. CARRIAGE BOLTS.
RIGHT HAND FIGURES FOR FRS 4&5
ARE FOR SHARP BOW.

~FRAME 1~

~FRAME 4~

DETAIL AT KEEL.

~TRANSOM~
SHAPE IS DEVELOPED
~LOOKING AFT~

~FRAME 3~

DETAIL AT CHINE

DETAIL AT SHEER

206

5

BOAT PLANS

PELICAN

A 24-ft. auxiliary cruiser, A companion boat to *Kittiwake* for the wind sailors; 24′ 6″ long, 9′ 0″ beam, 3′ 6″ draft, 260 sq. ft. sail area, 12 to 25 h.p., inboard auxiliary power.

The ink was hardly dry on the plans of *Kittiwake* before the windship sailors began to clamor for something similar. Opinions were shuttled back and forth until out of a conglomeration of conflicting ideas, a definite pattern began to form. First and foremost was that the little ship be an enlargement of *Picaroon*, and that the lines be retained in the larger size and only altered in consistence with the enlarged proportions. This was to carry out the spirit of a recent remark on the *Pic*'s having lines like a washtub and the seaworthiness of the *Queen Mary*.

While it is true that almost any old tub with a motor installed becomes a motor boat, it is decidedly not the case in a boat which must sail. It was also decided that she would be a loaf-along cruiser and capable of going coastwise. For every thousand of the water gypsies who use their boats on week ends, there is only one who takes his boat on an extended ocean voyage. For that reason a real seagoing self-bailing cockpit was not fitted at the sacrifice of livable room aft.

As a general rule the average backyard builder is chock full of ambition and empty of cash. For that reason labor-saving short cuts in the use of modern materials were discarded and the final outcome was a good old-fashioned boat like your granddaddy used to build before the days of power tools and all the new gunks and plastics of this present age. The only concessions to modernism were the rudder and spars. Anyone who has doweled a large wooden rudder or laboriously worked down a solid spar will know exactly what I mean.

The question of trunk cabin or raised deck was the hardest to settle. Personally I do not like a raised deck. Practically, I cannot urge against the additional room inside the boat nor against the fact it is far easier for the amateur to build and a much stronger job than the trunk. The question of an enclosed toilet or a commode called for a decision. The toilet enclosure took valuable room from the cabin that could be well used for other purposes. Berth end bulkheads render the commode semi-private. A curtain between these bulkheads would make it more so. In the end, common decency, if not self defense, would clear the cabin of other occupants while the toilet is in use.

Now don't throw up your hands in horror. The boat is nail fastened! Good old-fashioned boat nails that will hold in oak until the cows come home are a lot less expensive than screws and a lot less labor to apply. *Picaroon* lived thirty years with these in her vitals and they outwore her timbers. The ends of the topside planking and its butts should be screw-fastened. All the framing wherever possible is bolted. Nothing will hold any better than a bolt which will pull up the faying surfaces of the timbers airtight and contribute rigidity to a joint, so much so that knees are almost unnecessary. In some cases square boat spikes are used. Drill a hole for these the same diameter as the side of the square and don't forget to insert the chisel edge of the spike across the grain.

Pelican has husky timbers. You will generally not find these in a big city lumber yard, but if you do you will pay for them through your nose. Visit some of the country lumber yards and find out where there is a backwoods sawmill working. In all probability you will have this material cut from selected standing timber. It will come to you green but will be easier to work in this state. Be sure to coat the timbers immediately with raw linseed oil or pine tar oil and turpentine on reception. If there is a lumber mill or boatyard near you that has a bandsaw, take your timbers there to have them cut after you have laid them out. If the foregoing is not the case, work them down by hand just like your granddaddy did.

The question is now forming in the minds of many readers: "How about plywood planking?" The answer is "Nix!" Only plywood of comparative weight to the material specified will work. The boat

was designed to get away from this. There are many struggling young naval architects who will gladly redesign the boat for you if you insist. The bottom planking is 1-⅛", the side planking is ⅞". This may come to you 1/16" less, which is of no importance. Your large timbers *are* important and if the finished sizes are not what is specified, make allowance for this when you lay down the frames. The raised deck is laid in straight tongue-and-grooved material without any fancy margin pieces. Vee-edged wainscote material is best for this. The Vee should be laid down to form the cabin ceiling. Beaded material is also O.K. or, in a pinch, a good grade of flooring will answer. I will submit to ⅝" plywood here if you care to use it. Regardless of material used it should be fabric-covered. *Dexolium* would be my choice for covering as it is non-slip and everlasting but canvas has been used for deck covering on ships that were built long before my friend Carlos Von Dexter, or I for that matter, were even thought of. I would not use the gunk that he supplies to lay this material in. I have found good old *Kuhl's* canvas cement to work better when climatic conditions are unfavorable.

Now as to the motor. I know that Harold Goodwin would want to use his *Packard straight eight*. Someone else will want to use his *Ford Vee*. Look at *Pelican's* stern. There are no jet tailpipes or after-burners there. From 12 H.P. to 25 H.P. will be ample. My choice would be the husky *Universal Blue Jacket Twin*. I might install this same company's *Atomic* or *Utility Four* for greater speed. In my experience they make the best marine motors in this country.

There will be no necessity to lay down the lines full size. They have been pre-faired and all the important timbers have been detailed. Lay down only the frame lines full size. Take off the plank thickness and build the frames to the resultant line. The transom has been laid down to its true development shape and its forward face is the aft side of the stern post. Frames may be beveled after erection or the bevel picked up from a model if you have made one. So far, so good; let's start building her.

The main keel timber is made first. If you have to work it by hand, saw a series of cuts down to the line and split away as much of the wood as possible. Be careful in this operation and observe the run in the grain. A split in the wrong direction may mean disaster. The final finishing is done with an adz or sharp hatchet. If you do not have an adz do not buy one especially for this work. Adz work cannot be learned in a day. In using a hatchet make a series of close cuts at right angles to the line and chip the wood away between the shallow cuts. Sharpness of the hatchet is important; grind the cutting edge much keener than is usual. Even though your timbers have been sawed there is still considerable work to fairing down their ends. A broad chisel and a draw knife will come in handy at this point. Cut in the rabbet lines on both sides of all the timbers with a scrieve knife or a series of chisel marks; this will be important later.

Assemble the timbers over an extreme outline to check their accuracy. Where joints are not exactly wood-to-wood all along, they may be made so by running a saw cut between them. When everything is proper, temporarily nail the timbers together and bore the holes for the fastenings and keel bolts. Note that the extreme aft bolt must be recessed. Take the timbers apart and butter all the joints with roofing cement and then set up all fastenings except the upper nuts of the keel bolts. The keel bolts are tightened after the concrete has cured.

Wire the reinforcing rods to the keel bolts and their ends to the turned-up ends of the lower one. Lay the assembled backbone flat. Close the lower side of the keel aperture and pour the aggregate, adding as much scrap as it will safely hold. Tamp the concrete down well and trowel off its upper surface. Allow about three days for the concrete to harden properly before disturbing it.

Set up the assembled backbone in its proper position with all elements checked for plumbness and level. Brace everything securely so that it will not move, Now stand off and admire your work; a keel has been laid and a little ship is born.

Draw the body plan to its full entirety both sides of the centerline, using a red pencil for the forward frames and a blue one for the after ones. Do this on a flat floor or platform where having your drill go entirely through the frame timbers will not matter. The drilled hole should be the same size as the bolts for a tight fit. Rip a square strip off both the bottom and side planking and tack inside of the frame lines. These take off the plank thickness, so build your frames directly against these. Lay the bottom frames and the raised deck frames against the floor. Lay the side frames, the floor timbers and the deck beams on top of these. Mark off the positions of all cut-outs for the keel and all stringers and cut them to suit. Note that the inner face of the main sheer stringer is always vertical. Nail all timbers together temporarily so that they will not move in drilling. Take the timbers apart and give all abutting surfaces a coat of wood preservative before assembly. Bolt the

timbers together and lay the assembled frame back on the body plan for a check of its accuracy. If everything is correct, install the temporary braces and start another frame.

After all frames are finished, erect them on the backbone in their proper order and brace them securely so that they will not move during the remainder of the erection.

Run in the sheer stringer first. As in all probability this cannot be secured in one piece, it must be spliced. The splice is best made over a backing piece. Make the splice where the run of the stringer is flat aft. Even here the backing piece will have to be slightly curved on its outer side to prevent a flat spot. The heads of the carriage bolts used in the stringers are about ³⁄₁₆″ thick. The stringers must be counter-bored for these. Note also that the forward ends of the stringers will not end on the rabbet line but a plank-thickness behind it. Here they should be screw-fastened. Leave off the bottom stringers for the present for better access to the boat's interior.

The intermediate side frames and the deck beams are now erected. The intermediate side frames forward of #5 will take a slight curvature to meet the stem. This is determined with a fairing batten.

The planking is now applied to the sides and raised sheer of the boat. Some of our more affluent brethren will want to use mahogany for the raised sides and finish it natural. All well and good as this is what I would do, but the boat will sail just as well without it. As boat nails are to be used, ⅛″ holes should be bored for all of them. Be sure also to drive the point across the grain of the framing. Set the heads down flush with a large nail set and putty them after painting. What was said about planking *Kittiwake* need not be repeated here. You will also find that some of the short planking on the bottom aft of the stem may have to be staved.

The raised deck and the small one aft are laid as one would lay ordinary flooring with six-penny galvanized nails. As there is no point in toe-nailing, except to pull up an obstinate strip, the boards may be through-nailed. The beams in way of the dog house are cut away only after all of the decking has been completed. After the wood has been laid, all raised edges of the boards should be taken off with a disc sander.

Lay the fabric across the boat so that all seams lap aft. Turn the outboard edges down 1-¼″ and allow sufficient canvas or *Dexolium* to turn up the same amount around all openings. Space ½″ copper or galvanized tacks about ¾″ apart on all seams and edges. Before applying the priming coat of paint to canvas wet it down thoroughly. By doing this the paint will not penetrate the cotton fibers and they remain pliant a lot longer.

Install the motor and all of the interior before planking the bottom. This will keep the bilges clean. Note that on this boat the keel cheeks are sawed to shape and not bent as in some of the others. These cheeks run intercostal between frames and may be pre-beveled before fitting, thus eliminating the tedious job of beveling to fit the planking down under the boat in a cramped space. Note also how a slight rabbet is cut in the keel so that the bottom planks meet square to the wood. This is the ideal way to do this job but no great harm will incur if you elect to bevel the keel ends of the bottom planking.

The spars are built up of spruce and plywood pieces nailed and glued with *Weldwood*. The rigging is simple and if you cannot make a good wire rope splice use poured sockets or *Electroline Fiege* fittings.

The boat will require enough inside ballast to bring her down to her designed water line. Do not be in too big a hurry to fit this as the timbers will absorb several hundred pounds of water after she has been launched a month. The inside ballast should be of concrete and scrap, cast in a form so that it will straddle the keel and the cheeks. Its weight should not rest on the bottom planking. The little ship should prove able and smart. She will follow much in the order of a waterfront ditty about a pelican that I have heard for more years than I care to remember.

BILL OF MATERIAL — PELICAN

Lumber

1	pc.	Oak	6" x 12" x 16'-0"	Main keel
1	pc.	Oak	6" x 12" x 6'-6"	Lower Stem
1	pc.	Oak	4" x 8" x 5'-0"	Upper Stem
1	pc.	Oak	4" x 8" x 3'-6"	Stem Knee
1	pc.	Oak	6" x 8" x 10'-0"	Stern Post
1	pc.	Oak	6" x 8" x 3'-0"	Stern Knee
1	pc.	Oak	4" x 6" x 3'-6"	Shaft Alley
1	pc.	Oak	6" x 12" x 3'-6"	Horn Timber
1	pc.	Oak	6" x 8" x 5'-0"	Fore Foot
1	pc.	Oak	2" x 6" x 6'-6"	Shaft Alley
1	pc.	Live Oak or Greenhart	2" x 6" x 10'-6"	Ballast Shoe
4	pcs.	Oak	2" x 4" x 12'-0"	Keel Cheeks
6	pcs.	Oak	1 1/4" x 6" x 8'-0"	Bottom Frames

160	Lin. ft.	Oak	1 1/4" x 3"	Side Frames
50	Lin. ft.	Oak	1 1/2" x 3 (Long lengths)	Chines
50	Lin. ft.	Oak	1 1/2" x 3 (Long lengths)	Sheer
100	Lin. ft.	Oak	1 1/2" x 3 (Long lengths)	Bottom Strs.
30	Lin. ft.	Oak	1 1/4" x 6	Frame Caps Aft.
2	pcs.	Oak	2" x 12" x 12'-0"	Transom
1	pc.	Oak	2" x 6" x 6'-0"	Transom
250	Bd. ft.	Cedar, Cypress or Mahogany	1 1/4" x 6"	Bottom Planking
200	Bd. ft.	Cedar, Cypress or Mahogany	1" x 6"	Topside Planking
50	Bd. ft.	Wood	1" x 8"	Topside Planking
300	Bd. ft.	Pine or Fir	1" x 2 1/2" face "V"Edge	Staving Decks, Etc.
100	Bd. ft.	Pine or Fir	1" x 2 1/2" T. & G.	Flooring Decks Etc.
1	Sheet	Fir	4'-0" x 8'-0" x 1"	Plywood Rudder
10	pcs.	Spruce	1" x 3" x 12'-0"	Masts
1	pc.	Spruce	3" x 4" x 8'-0"	Masts
2	pcs.	Fir	4'-0" x 8'-0" x 1/4"	Plywood Mast
1	pc.	Spruce	2" x 4" x 12'-0"	Main Boom
1	pc.	Spruce	2" x 4" x 8'-0"	Miz. Boom
1	pc.	Spruce	2" x 3" x 10'-0"	Main Gaff
1	pc.	Oak	3" x 3" x 6'-0"	Mooring Bitt
7	pcs.	Oak	1 1/4" x 8" x 10'-0"	Dk. Beams
5	pcs.	Oak	1 1/4" x 6" x 8'-0"	Dk. Beams & Rudder
1	pc.	Oak	1 1/4" x 3" x 8'-0"	Cabin Sail
6	pcs.	Mahogany	1" x 2" x 8'-0"	Dog House
6	pcs.	Mahogany	1" x 3" x 8'-0"	Dog House
4	pcs.	Mahogany	1" x 6" x 8'-0"	Dog House
1	pc.	Mahogany	1" x 8" x 8'-0"	Dog House
1	pc.	Oak	1 1/4" x 6" x 16'-0"	Dog House Beams
1	pc.	Oak	1 1/4" x 8" x 12'-0"	Dog House Beams

Hardware

220	1/4" x 2 1/2"	Galv. Carriage Bolts	Frames		Tiebout Fig. 3614
100	1/4" x 3"	Galv. Carriage Bolts	Frames		Tiebout Fig. 3614
40	3/8" x 3 1/2"	Galv. Carriage Bolts	Frames		Tiebout Fig. 3614
12	3/8" x 5"	Galv. Carriage Bolts	Shaft Alley		Tiebout Fig. 3614
6	1/2" x 6"	Galv. Lag Screws			Tiebout Fig. 3598
25	Lin ft.	1/2" Dia. Galv. Iron Rod	Bolts & Drifts		
12	Lin. ft.	1" Dia. Black Iron Rod	Keel Bolts		
60	Lin ft.	1/2" Sq. Reinforcing Bar	Keel		
100	1/4" x 4"	Galv. Boat Spikes			Tiebout Fig. 3654
2	pcs.	6" x 12" - 1/4"	Brass Plate	Rudder Head	
50			1/2" -Sq. Nuts -Galv.		Tiebout Fig. 3623
50			1/2" Washers -Galv.		
30			1/2" Clinch Rings -Galv.		Tiebout Fig. 836
15	lbs.	2 1/4" Boat Nails			Tiebout Fig. 3639

3	Gross	1 1/2" - #10 Fl. Hd. Wood Screws Galv.
1	Gross	2" - #12 Fl. Hd. Wood Screws Galv.

Fittings

8		Screw Pin Anchor Shackles 3/16"		W. C. Fig. 290
1		Bronze Shoulder Eyebolt (Pintle)		W. C. Fig. 2180
10		Rope Thimbles 1/4" (For Manila)		W. C. Fig. 323
1		Rope Thimble 3/8" (For Manila)		W. C. Fig. 323
18		Rope Thimbles 3/16" (For Wire)		W. C. Fig. 323
9		Turnbuckles 5/16"		W. C. Fig. 310
5		Fast Eye Blocks Size 7		W. C. Fig. 368
2		Fast Eye Blocks Size 7 1/2		W. C. Fig. 370
2		Fast Eye Blocks Size 8		W. C. Fig. 369
2		Cheek Blocks Size #1		W. C. Fig. 382
1		Cheek Block Size #11		W. C. Fig. 383
1		Deck Pipe 1 1/2" Size		W. C. Fig. 672
5	Lgths	Sail Track 5/8		W. C. Fig. 120
2		Eyebands 2" I. D.		W. C. Fig. 6350
8		Fairleads		W. C. Fig. 995
8		Chain Plates 10 1/2"		W. C. Fig. 630
4		Mast Tangs Size 2		W. C. Fig. 9892
2		Boom Travelers Size 1		W. C. Fig. 6390
1		Gooseneck		W. C. Fig. 6483

2		Goosenecks		W. C. Fig. 6484
2		Halyard Shackles		W. C. Fig. 2870
1		Clew Outhaul Size 0		W. C. Fig. 9800
1		Clew Outhaul Size 1		W. C. Fig. 9800
2		Outhaul Cheek Blocks Size 1		W. C. Fig. 5800
1		Jib Halyard Block Size 1		W. C. Fig. 954
1		1" Rudder Gudgeon Brass		W. C. Fig. 462
2		1" Rudder Pintles Brass		W. C. Fig. 460

Cordage

320	Lin ft.	1/4" Manila Rope	Halyards
40	Lin ft.	5/16" Manila Rope	Miz Sheet
50	Lin ft.	3/8" Manila Rope	Main Sheet
200	Lin ft.	3/16" Flexible Steel Wire Rope for Standing Rigging	
2	Hanks	1/8" Braided cotton	Flag Halyards, etc.
2	Balls	Yacht Marlin	Serving
1		Complete set of sails with all slides, snaps and a stowage bag included. Slides on masts and spars	

Adhesives

3	Qts.	Elmers Glue
4	Qts.	Kuhls Canvass Cement
1	Gallon	Roofing Cement (Asbestos Fiber)

PELICAN
24 FT AUXILIARY CRUISER
SAIL PLAN & PROFILE

50 SQ. FT.

16'-0"

6'-6"

14'-0"

14'-6"

9'-6"

155 SQ. FT.

265 SQ. FT.

110 SQ. FT.

11'-0"

23'-0"

11'-6"

17'-0"

60. SQ. FT

17'-0"

7'-3"

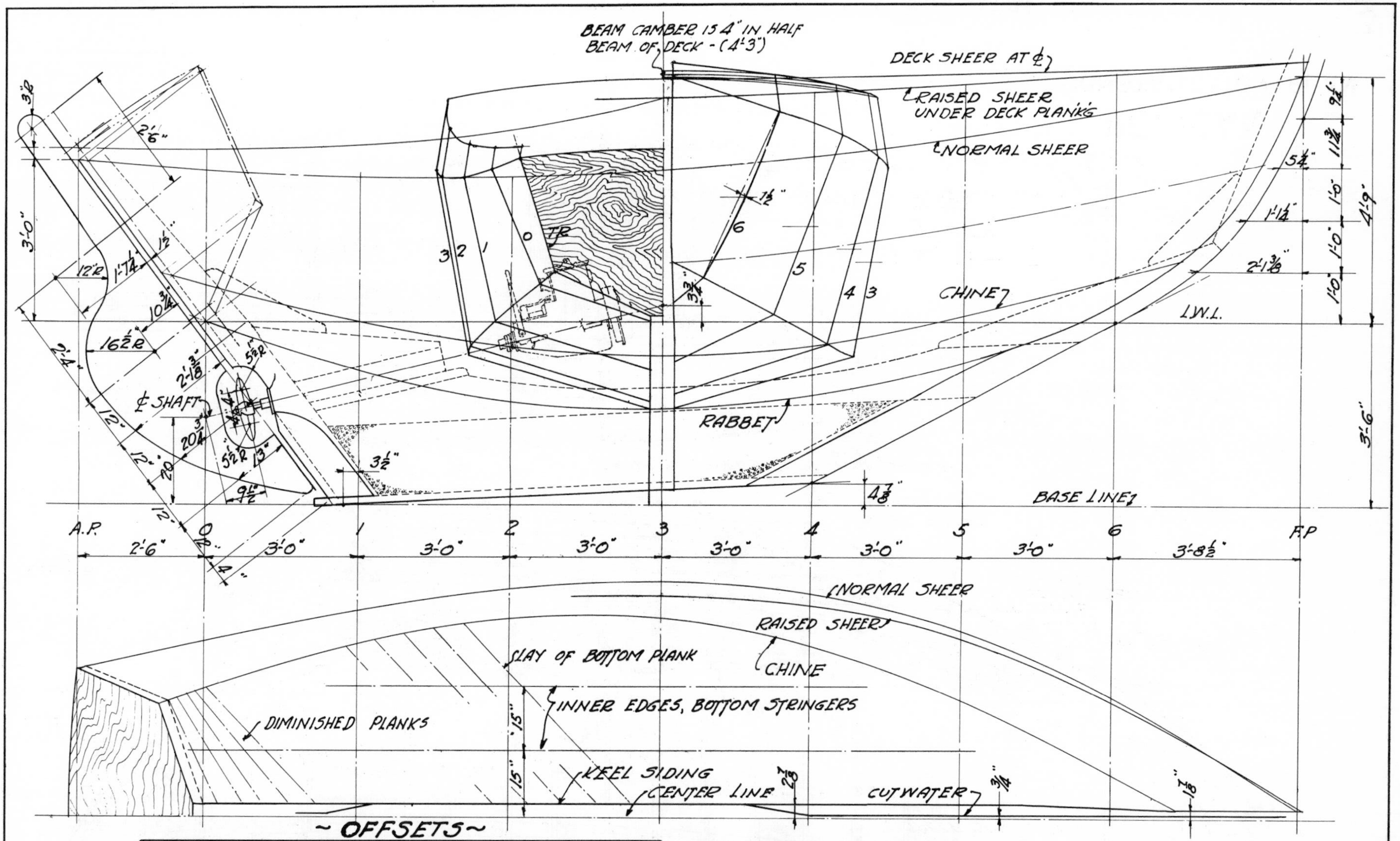

~ OFFSETS ~

	FRAME	TR	1	2	3	4	5	6
HEIGHTS	RABBET	3'-6"	2'-6⅝	1'-11⅝"	1'-10"	2'-1¼	2'-8⅞"	3'-10⅝
	CHINE	4'-4¾	3'-6"	3'-0¼"	2'-10¼	3'-0⅝	3'-7⅝	4'-4¼"
	N. SHEER	6'-6⅞"	6'-3⅜	6'-3½"	6'-5"	6'-8⅜"	7'-0¾	7'-6¾
	R. "	6'-10"	6'-10¾	7'-2¼"	7'-9⅝"	7'-10⅞"	8'-0¾"	8'-3¼"
HALF WIDTHS.	CHINE	2'-2"	3'-3¾	3'-9⅞"	3'-10"	3'-3⅝"	2'-3¼"	10⅛"
	N. SHEER	2'-10"	3'-11½"	4'-4⅝"	4'-6⅜	4'-3½"	3'-7⅛"	2'-4"
	R. SHEER	2'-9⅝"	3'-10⅛"	4'-2¾	4'-3⅛"	4'-0⅞	3'-5¼"	2'-2⅞"

NOTE, OFFSETS ARE GIVEN TO OUTSIDE OF PLANKING. DEDUCT PLANK THICKNESS TO OBTAIN SHAPE OF FRAMES. TRANSOM FIGURES ARE TO AFT FACE - NOT DEVELOPED.

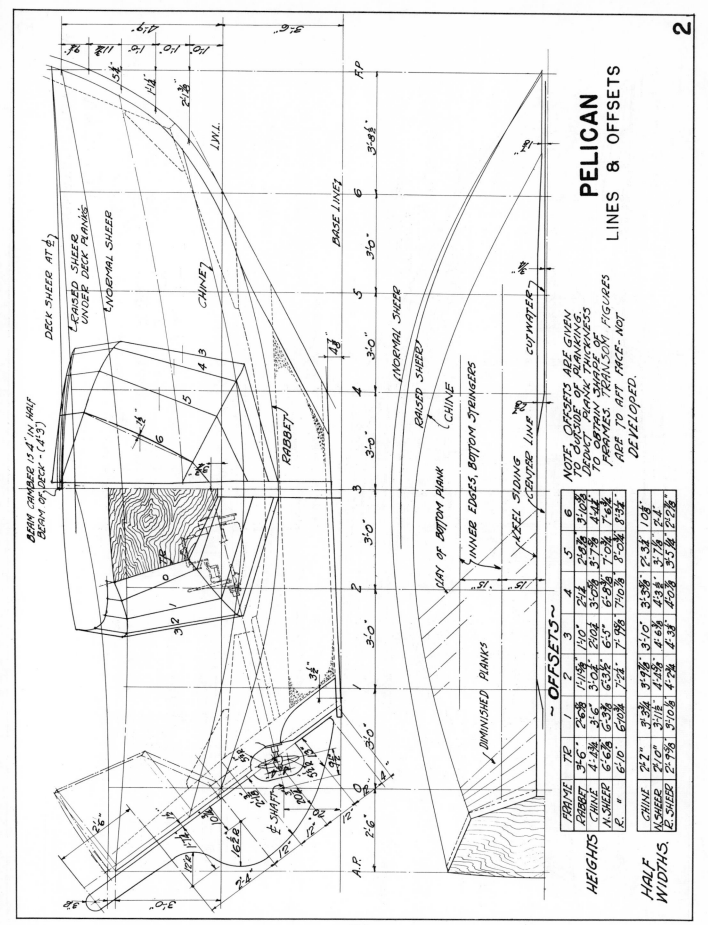

PELICAN
LINES & OFFSETS

2

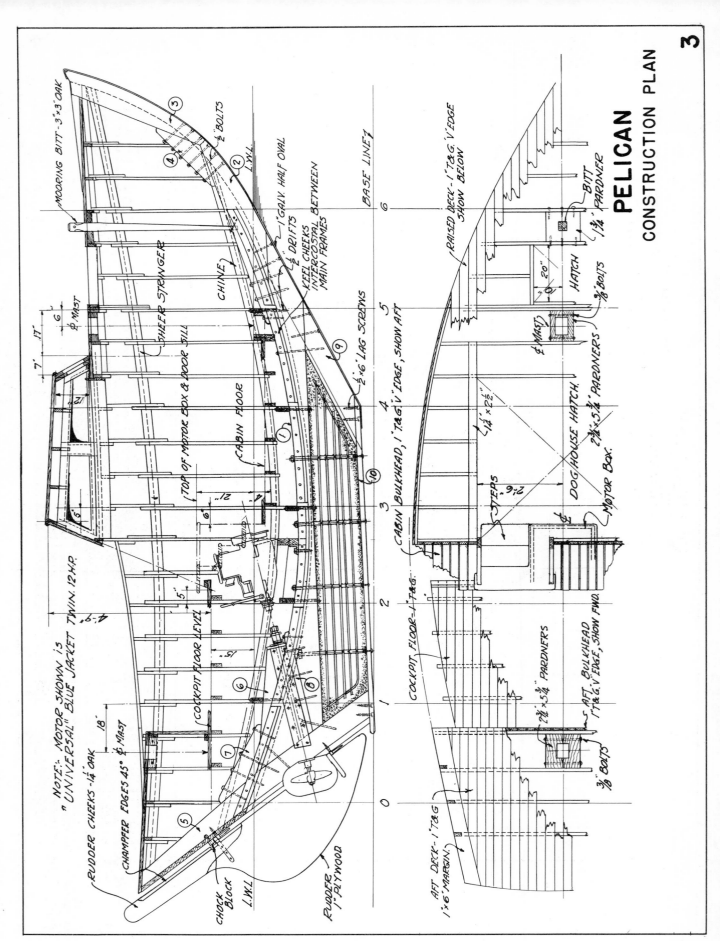

PELICAN
CONSTRUCTION PLAN

3

214

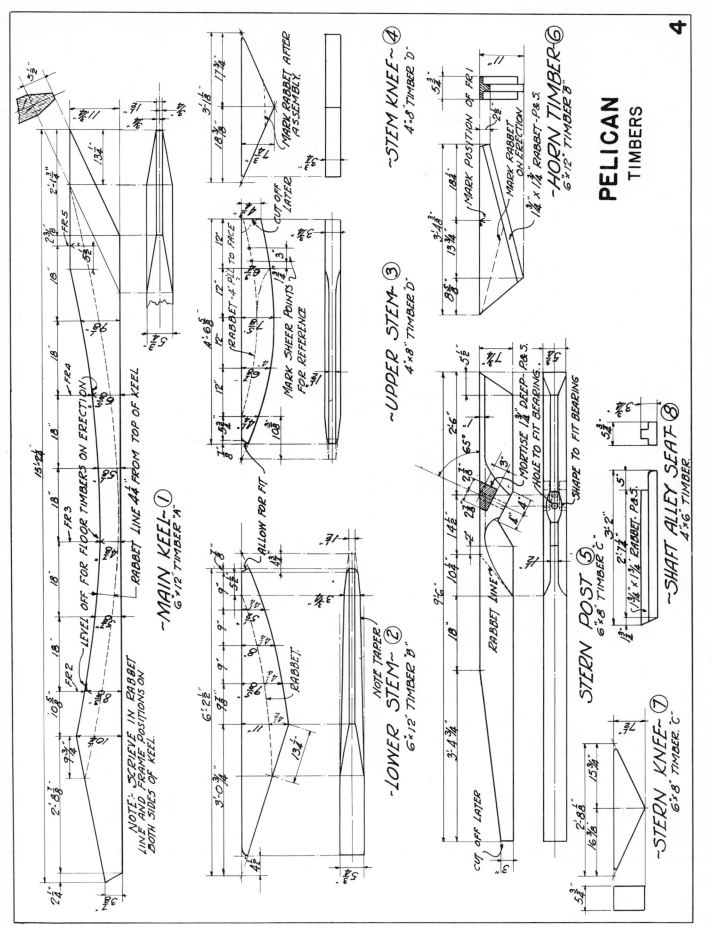

PELICAN TIMBERS

~MAIN KEEL~ ①
6"x12" TIMBER "A"

~LOWER STEM~ ②
6"x12" TIMBER "B"

~UPPER STEM~ ③
4"x8" TIMBER "D"

~STEM KNEE~ ④
4"x8" TIMBER "D"

~STERN POST~ ⑤
6"x8" TIMBER "C"

~HORN TIMBER~ ⑥
6"x12" TIMBER "B"

~STERN KNEE~ ⑦
6"x8" TIMBER "C"

~SHAFT ALLEY SEAT~ ⑧
4"x6" TIMBER.

NOTE:- SCRIEVE IN RABBET LINE AND FRAME POSITIONS ON BOTH SIDES OF KEEL.

4

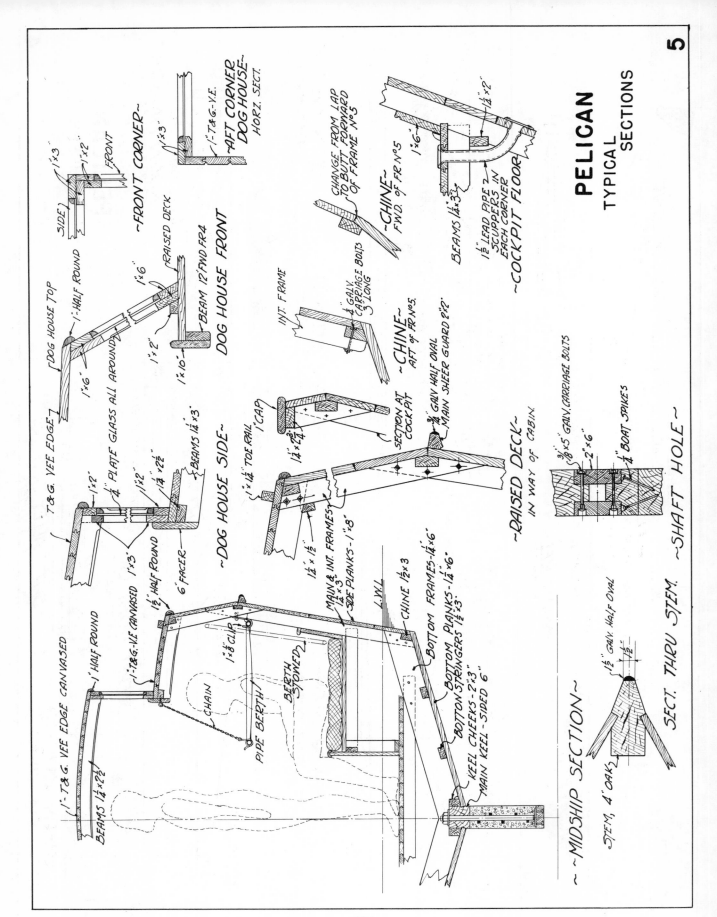

PELICAN
TYPICAL SECTIONS

~FRONT CORNER~

~AFT CORNER
DOG HOUSE~
HORZ. SECT.

1"-T&G.-V.E.

1"×3"

1"×2"

FRONT

SIDE

1"-T&G. VEE EDGE

DOG HOUSE TOP

1" HALF ROUND

1"×6"

RAISED DECK

BEAM 12" FWD. FR.4

DOG HOUSE FRONT

1"×6"

1"×2"

1"×10"

CHANGE FROM LAP
TO BUTT FORWARD
OF FRAME No.5

~CHINE~
FWD. OF FR. No.5

1"×6"

1¼"×2"

1½" LEAD PIPE 2
SCUPPERS IN
EACH CORNER

BEAMS 1¼"×3"

~COCKPIT FLOOR~

INT. FRAME

¼" GALV.
CARRIAGE BOLTS
3" LONG

~CHINE~
AFT OF FR. No.5

SECTION AT
COCKPIT

¾" GALV. HALF OVAL
MAIN SHEER GUARD 2"×2"

~DOG HOUSE SIDE~

T&G. VEE EDGE

1"×2"

¼" PLATE GLASS ALL AROUND

1½" HALF ROUND

1½"×2"

1¼"×2½"

BEAMS 1¼"×3"

1"×3"

6" FACER

1" 1¼" TOE RAIL

1" CAP

1¼"×2½"

1¼"×2½"

~RAISED DECK~
IN WAY OF CABIN.

⅜"×5" GALV. CARRIAGE BOLTS

2"×6"

¼"×4" BOAT SPIKES

~SHAFT HOLE~

~MIDSHIP SECTION~

1"-T&G. VEE EDGE CANVASED

1" HALF ROUND

1"-T&G.-V.E. CANVASED 1"×3"

1½" HALF ROUND

BEAMS 1¼"×2½"

1¼"×2½"

1¼"×3"

CHAIN

PIPE BERTH

BERTH
STOWED

1"×8 C.I.P.

MAIN & INT. FRAMES
1¼"×3"

SIDE PLANKS - 1"×8"

1¼"×1½"

L.W.L.

CHINE 1½×3

BOTTOM FRAMES-1¼"×6"

BOTTOM PLANKS 1½"×6"

BOTTOM STRINGERS 1½"×3"

KEEL CHEEKS - 2"×3"

MAIN KEEL - SIDED 6"

STEM, 4" OAK

1½" GALV. HALF OVAL

½"

SECT. THRU STEM.

5

PELICAN
DETAILS OF FRAMES

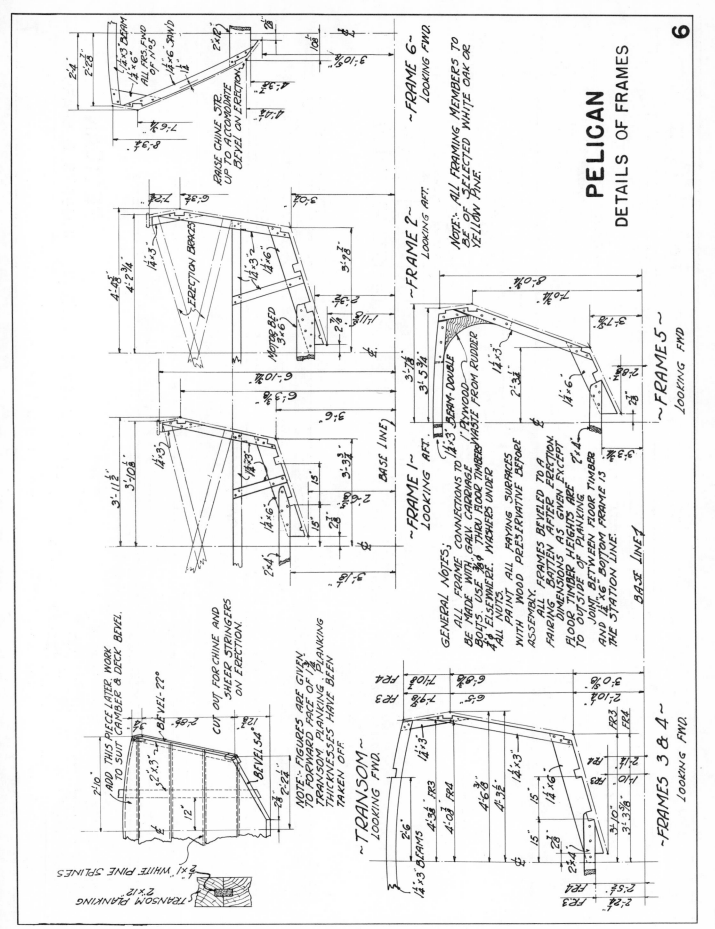

~FRAME 6~
LOOKING FWD.

~FRAME 2~
LOOKING AFT.

NOTE: ALL FRAMING MEMBERS TO BE OF SELECTED WHITE OAK OR YELLOW PINE.

~FRAME 1~
LOOKING AFT.

~FRAME 5~
LOOKING FWD.

GENERAL NOTES:

ALL FRAME CONNECTIONS TO BE MADE WITH GALV. CARRIAGE BOLTS. USE ⅜∅ THRU FLOOR TIMBERS & ⅝∅ ELSEWHERE. WASHERS UNDER ALL NUTS.

PAINT ALL FAYING SURFACES WITH WOOD PRESERVATIVE BEFORE ASSEMBLY.

ALL FRAMES BEVELED TO A FAIRING BATTEN AFTER ERECTION.

DIMENSIONS AS GIVEN EXCEPT FLOOR TIMBER HEIGHTS ARE TO OUTSIDE OF PLANKING.

JOINT BETWEEN FLOOR TIMBER AND 1¼"x6" BOTTOM FRAME IS THE STATION LINE.

BASE LINE

~TRANSOM~
LOOKING FWD.

~FRAMES 3 & 4~
LOOKING FWD.

ADD THIS PIECE LATER. WORK TO SUIT CAMBER & DECK BEVEL.

BEVEL 72°

CUT OUT FOR CHINE AND SHEER STRINGERS ON ERECTION.

BEVEL 54°

NOTE: FIGURES ARE GIVEN TO FORWARD FACE OF 1¼ TRANSOM PLANKING. PLANKING THICKNESSES HAVE BEEN TAKEN OFF.

TRANSOM PLANKING 2"x12"

½"x1" WHITE PINE SPLINES

RAISE CHINE STR. UP TO ACCOMODATE BEVEL ON ERECTION.

ERECTION BRACES

MOTOR BED 3"x6"

BASE LINE

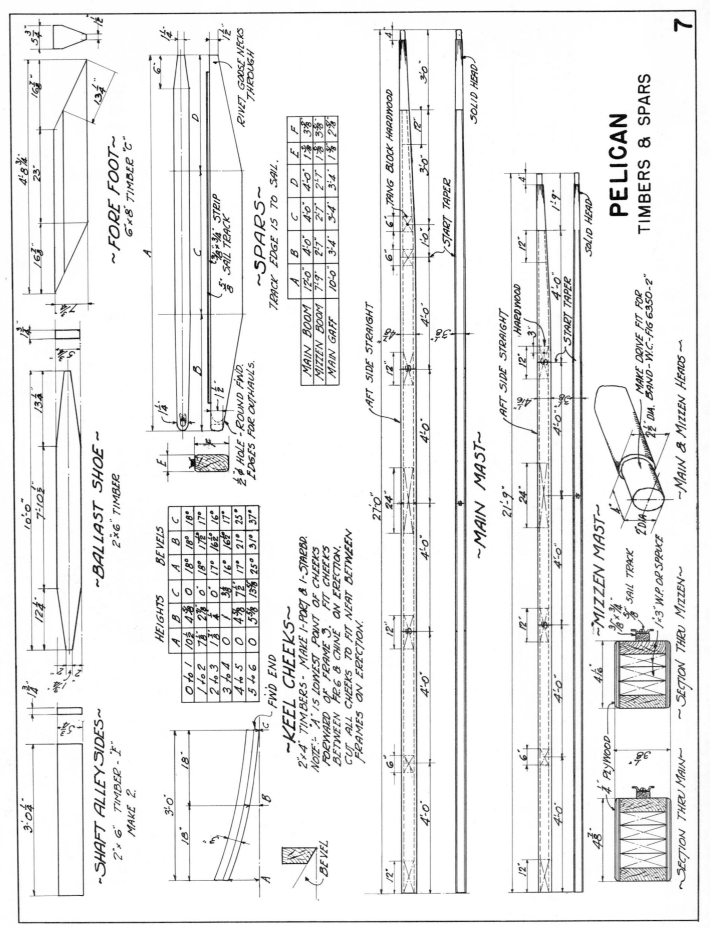

PELICAN
TIMBERS & SPARS

~SPARS~
TRACK EDGE IS TO SAIL.

	A	B	C	D	E	F
MAIN BOOM	12'-0"	4'-0"	4'-0"	4'-0"	1½	3⅜
MIZZEN BOOM	7'-9"	2'-7"	2'-7"	2'-7"	1⅞	3⅜
MAIN GAFF	10'-0"	3'-4"	3'-4"	3'-4"	1⅞	2⅞

~FORE FOOT~
6"x 8" TIMBER 'C'

~BALLAST SHOE~
2"x 6" TIMBER

~SHAFT ALLEY SIDES~
2"x 6" TIMBER - 'I' -
MAKE 2.

BEVELS

HEIGHTS		A	B	C		A	B	C
0 to 1		10¼	4⅝	0		18°	18°	18°
1 to 2		7⅜	2⅞	0		18°	17½	17°
2 to 3		1⅜	⅞	0		17°	16½	16°
3 to 4		0	1	3⅜		16°	16⅝	17°
4 to 5		0	4⅜	7½		17°	21°	25°
5 to 6		0	5⅜	13⅝		25°	31°	37°

~KEEL CHEEKS~
2"x 4" TIMBERS - MAKE 1-PORT & 1-STBD.
NOTE :- 'A' IS LOWEST POINT OF CHEEKS
FORWARD OF FRAME 3. FIT CHEEKS
BETWEEN FR. 6 & CHINE ON ERECTION.
CUT ALL CHEEKS TO FIT NEAT BETWEEN
FRAMES ON ERECTION.

~MAIN MAST~

~MIZZEN MAST~

~MAIN & MIZZEN HEADS~

~SECTION THRU MIZZEN~

~SECTION THRU MAIN~

RIVET GOOSE NECKS THROUGH

7

YOUR BOAT AND THE U. S. COAST GUARD

One of the first things that you do as your boat is nearing completion is to have her registered with the Coast Guard headquarters in your district and get her registry number. This only applies if she has an inboard motor or is over sixteen feet and carries an outboard motor and is operated on navigable waters under the jurisdiction of the Coast Guard. Your nearest Coast Guard office will furnish the necessary forms to fill out and will then give you the registry certificate and the boat's number.

A bill of sale for the hull materials and the motor is now required to receive a certificate.

If building on a lake or stream not under Coast Guard jurisdiction, you should register your boat with the proper State Department having authority. A letter to your Secretary of State at your state capital will bring you the necessary information.

All through her life the boat will be under the watchful eyes of the Coast Guard or the proper state authority. A word about the Coast Guard Service may be helpful.

First of all do not consider these chaps as policemen. Each and every ruling that has been formulated by this service is for your own particular protection. In times of trouble the Coast Guard boys are out there in a storm to tow you in or perform other rescue work if necessary. Many of the men of this service have given their lives that some foolish motorboat sailor might live to regret his folly (or perhaps not).

If at any time you are stopped by a Coast Guard Patrol Craft don't, by any means, try to act smart with the officer in charge. He knows all the answers and he is the law. If you see him coming and think you have more speed than he, don't try to run from him, for that little slender rod waving above his cabin top is a radio powerful enough to outdistance any speed that you may have. When ordered to *heave to,* stop at once and allow the officer to board you. If you have everything that the law requires you to have, there is nothing to fear. While some of the youngsters in the service are at times proud of the authority that they wield and become a bit officious, keep your own temper. His is not the attitude of the whole Coast Guard. If you are in trouble at some time or other, it may be this same youngster who will brave hell and high water to help you out.

Be sure that you carry all the equipment that the law calls for and that it is in proper working order. Every piece of it is for your own protection and be sure that you regard it as this and not merely something to get you past the regulations. I know of a case where the fire extinguisher was filled with water to fool the Coast Guard. This was folly in the first place because carbon-tetrachloride and water smell vastly different. The sad part of the affair was that it was more necessary to use the extinguisher than to have it pass inspection. Two people lost their lives and the boat was burned.

If at all possible, equip your boat with electric running lights. Some of these are made with flashlight cells built in, and if the boat does not carry a starting battery, these are the type to use. The old-fashioned oil lamps are forever blowing out and at times refuse to even burn at all.

Be sure that the law requiring your bilges to be ventilated is carried out. Gasoline vapor mixed with the right amount of air is more explosive than dynamite. Get it out of your bilges at all times. *That is the law.* Furthermore be sure that your motor is also equipped with a backfire trap on the carburetor. That, too, is the law.

Check your local C.G. office for the latest rules. They are always in the process of change. Some are *recommendation;* others are law. Be sure to find out which is which.

SAFETY EQUIPMENT

MINIMUM REQUIRED EQUIPMENT

EQUIPMENT	CLASS A (Less than 16 feet)	CLASS 1 (16 feet to less than 26 feet)	CLASS 2 (26 feet to less than 40 feet)	CLASS 3 (40 feet to not more than 65 feet)
BACK-FIRE FLAME ARRESTOR	One approved device on each carburetor of all gasoline engines installed after April 25, 1940, except outboard motors.			
VENTILATION	At least two ventilators fitted with cowls or their equivalent for the purpose of properly and efficiently ventilating the bilges of every engine and fuel-tank compartment of boats constructed or decked over after April 25, 1940, using gasoline or other fuel of a flashpoint less than 110° F.			
BELL	None.*	None.*	One, which when struck, produces a clear, bell-like tone of full round characteristics.	
LIFESAVING DEVICES	One approved life preserver, buoyant vest, ring buoy, or buoyant cushion for each person on board.			One approved life preserver or ring buoy for each person on board.
WHISTLE	None.*	One hand, mouth, or power operated, audible at least ½ mile.	One hand or power operated, audible at least 1 mile.	One power operated, audible at least 1 mile.
FIRE EXTINGUISHER—PORTABLE. When NO fixed fire extinguishing system is installed in machinery space(s).	At least One B-I type approved hand portable fire extinguisher.		At least Two B-I type approved hand portable fire extinguishers; OR At least One B-II type approved hand portable fire extinguisher.	At least Three B-I type approved hand portable fire extinguishers; OR At least One B-I type *Plus* One B-II type approved hand portable fire extinguisher.
When fixed fire extinguishing system is installed in machinery space(s).	None.	None.	At least One B-I type approved hand portable fire extinguisher.	At least Two B-I type approved hand portable fire extinguishers; OR At least One B-II type approved hand portable fire extinguisher.

B-I Type Approved Hand Portable Fire Extinguishers contain: Foam, 1¼ up to 2½ gallons; or Dry Chemical, 2 up to 10 pounds; or Vaporizing Liquid, 1 quart;** or Carbon Dioxide, 4 up to 15 pounds.
B-II Type Approved Hand Portable Fire Extinguishers contain: Foam, 2½ gallons; or Carbon Dioxide, 15 pounds; or Dry Chemical, 10 up to 20 pounds.

*Note.—Not required by the Motorboat Act of 1940; however, the "Rules of the Road" require these vessels to sound proper signals.
**Note.—Toxic vaporizing-liquid type fire extinguishers, such as those containing carbon tetrachloride or chlorobromomethane, will not be accepted after 1 January 1962 as required approved extinguishers on uninspected vessels (private pleasure craft). Existing installations of such extinguishers may be continued until that date if in good and serviceable condition.

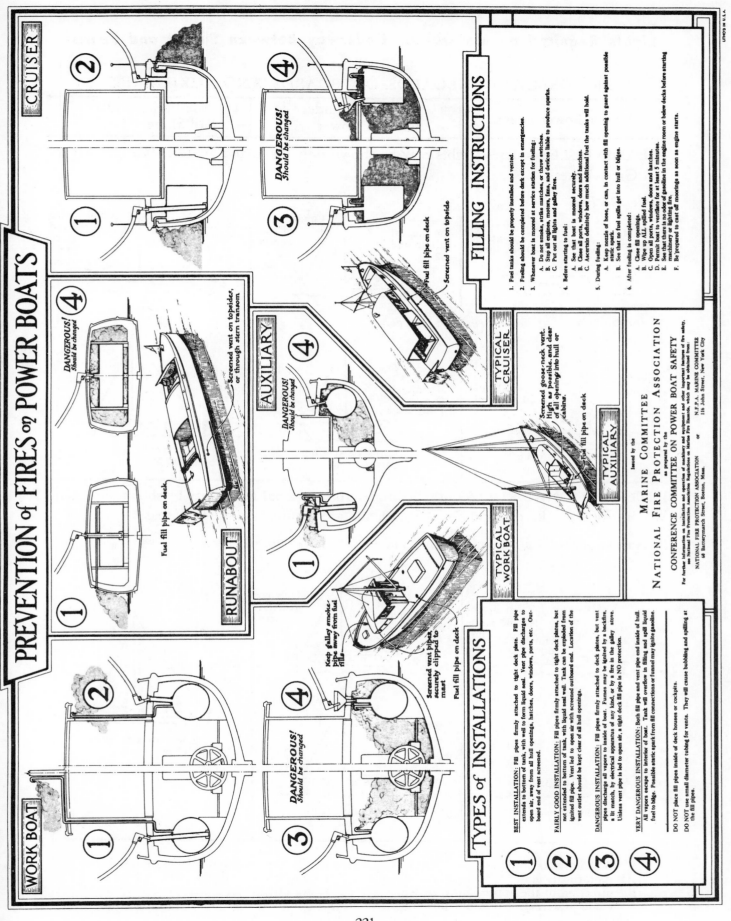

PREVENTION of FIRES on POWER BOATS

CRUISER

WORK BOAT

RUNABOUT

AUXILIARY

DANGEROUS! Should be changed

Fuel fill pipe on deck

Screened vent on topsides, or through stern transom

Fuel fill pipe on deck

Screened goose-neck vent. High as possible, and clear of all openings into hull or cabins.

Fuel fill pipe on deck

Screened vent on topside

Keep galley smoke-pipe away from fuel fill

Screened vent pipe, securely clipped to mast

Fuel fill pipe on deck

TYPICAL CRUISER

TYPICAL AUXILIARY

TYPICAL WORK BOAT

FILLING INSTRUCTIONS

1. Fuel tanks should be properly installed and vented.
2. Fueling should be completed before dark except in emergencies.
3. Whenever boat is moored at service station for fueling:
   A. Do not smoke, strike matches, or throw switches.
   B. Stop all engines, motors, fans, and devices liable to produce sparks.
   C. Put out all lights and galley fires.
4. Before starting to fuel:
   A. See that boat is moored securely.
   B. Close all ports, windows, doors and hatches.
   C. Ascertain definitely how much additional fuel the tanks will hold.
5. During fueling:
   A. Keep nozzle of hose, or can, in contact with fill opening to guard against possible static spark.
   B. See that no fuel spills get into hull or bilges.
6. After fueling is completed:
   A. Close fill openings.
   B. Wipe up all spilled fuel.
   C. Open all ports, windows, doors and hatches.
   D. Permit boat to ventilate for at least 5 minutes.
   E. See that there is no odor of gasoline in the engine room or below decks before starting machinery or lighting fire.
   F. Be prepared to cast off moorings as soon as engine starts.

Issued by the
MARINE COMMITTEE
NATIONAL FIRE PROTECTION ASSOCIATION
as prepared by the
CONFERENCE COMMITTEE ON POWER BOAT SAFETY

For further information on installation and operation of machinery and equipment and other important features of fire safety, see National Fire Protection Association Regulations on Marine Fire Hazards, which may be obtained from:

NATIONAL FIRE PROTECTION ASSOCIATION   or   N.F.P.A. MARINE COMMITTEE
60 Batterymarch Street, Boston, Mass.   116 John Street, New York City

TYPES of INSTALLATIONS

1. **BEST INSTALLATION:** Fill pipes firmly attached to tight deck plate. Fill pipe extends to bottom of tank, with well to form liquid seal. Vent pipe discharges to open air, away from all hull openings, hatches, windows, doors, ports, etc. Outboard end of vent screened.

2. **FAIRLY GOOD INSTALLATION:** Fill pipes firmly attached to tight deck plates, but not extended to bottom of tank, with liquid seal well. Tank can be exploded from ignited fill pipe. Vent led to open air with screened outboard end. Location of the vent outlet should be kept clear of all hull openings.

3. **DANGEROUS INSTALLATION:** Fill pipes firmly attached to deck plates, but vent pipes discharge all vapors to inside of boat. Fumes may be ignited by a backfire, a lit match, by electrical apparatus of any kind, or by a fire in the galley stove. Unless vent pipe is led to open air, a tight deck fill pipe is NO protection.

4. **VERY DANGEROUS INSTALLATION:** Both fill pipe and vent pipe end inside of hull. All vapors escape to interior of boat. Tank will overflow in filling and spill liquid fuel to bilge. Possible static spark from fill connections or funnel may ignite gasoline.

DO NOT place fill pipes inside of deck houses or cockpits.
DO NOT use small diameter tubing for vents. They will cause bubbling and spilling at the fill pipes.

Lights Required on Motorboats Underway Between Sunset and Sunrise

MOTORBOATS: INBOARDS, OUTBOARDS, AND AUXILIARIES

Under Power alone	Auxiliaries under Sail and Power	Auxiliaries under Sail alone

INLAND RULES.—These lights may be shown only on Inland Waters, Western Rivers, and Great Lakes.[1]

Under 26 Feet

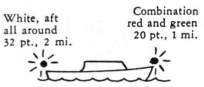

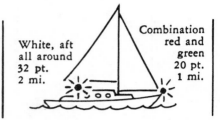

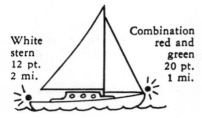

26 feet or over, but not more than 65 feet

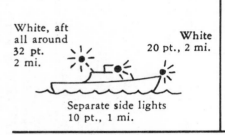

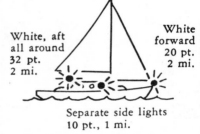

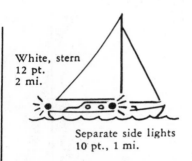

INTERNATIONAL RULES.—Lights under International Rules may be shown on Inland Waters, Western Rivers, and Great Lakes, and are required on the high seas.

Power vessel under 40 gross tons and sail vessels under 20 gross tons [2]

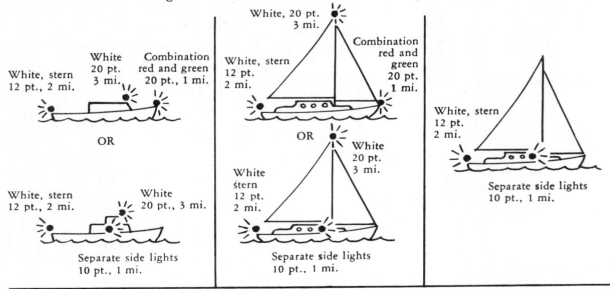

---

[1] A motorboat under sail alone on the Great Lakes is not required to display a stern light. All motorboats under sail alone must on approach of another vessel display a white light in the direction of the approaching vessel.

[2] Under International Rules powerboats of 40 gross tons or over must carry separate sidelights, visible 2 miles, and a 20-point white light visible 5 miles. Sailing boats of 20 gross tons or over must carry separate sidelights, visible 2 miles. Those less than 20 gross tons may use a combination lantern, if under sail alone.

IN RETROSPECT

In the preface it was told how this book came into being. Let us now see how it was ended.

The springtime of another year has once again come to the Chesapeake. The locust tree behind the backhouse in my back yard is covering the ground with its snowlike, scented petals. The last typed word, the last comma, the last period has been struck on the manuscript. The last bit of India ink is dry on the illustrations. Behind all of this there lay thousands of typed words, millions of tiny pen strokes that make up the illustrations, gallons of midnight oil and brain waves beyond enumeration.

Outside the window a bluebird flutters to a landing. He looks at me, his head arched to one side. Slowly his left eyelid closes over a wide open eye and his head jerks quickly in the direction of the Bay. Down on the bar the white perch are slowly scratching themselves behind their ears with their pectoral fins, little catfish are on their bellies contentedly purring, and out in the back yard a faint breeze stirs up the chips beneath my own new boat. Soon the smell of fresh cut wood and paint will mingle with that of the locust blossoms. Soon the white perch will stop scratching and pay attention to some bait. Soon the tommy-catfish will be walking the submarine back fences, breaking the silence of the watery depths with their mating call.

Soon the Bay will be dotted with white sails and outboard motors will be disturbing reveries— It's great to be alive. No more pausing in writing the manuscript to wonder if this or that is plainly written. No more angry tearing up of an illustration (with appropriate words) because a blot mars its surface or because it will not be entirely clear to the reader. No Siree! no more of that. Here's your book, Felix (damya)! Now I'm goin' afishin'.

SAM

SO ENDS

EDITOR'S NOTE:
It has been ages since we last heard from Sam. His new boat has been finished and when last seen he was going down the dock with a lunch basket in one hand and a rod and reel in the other. Recent reports from the Chesapeake Bay indicate a great scarcity of white perch and other small fish. It is our firm belief that he really did go fishing.

TEN YEARS LATER

It has been ten years, almost to the day, since the above was written. Another spring comes to the Chesapeake. There the similarity ends. The son of that bluebird has just cracked the sound barrier and shaken down the petals of the locust blossoms. As he comes in for a landing, there's no sly wink, but a direct "C'mon Pop, let's get this show on the road." In his make-up there is a suggestion of delta wings and after-burners. The tommy catfish no longer purr. Now they are doing Rock and Roll, have snorkels and are atomic-powered.

A new generation of boatbuilders has been born. My little Plains Indian friend, Gordon Adams, dreams not of hunting buffalo, as did his ancestors, but of going to far places in a sailboat. It has been a long up-hill job to complete the revisions and only the nice letter from George Bell of Winterport, Me., spurred me on to the completion. Here again, Felix, is your book. (Note that I haven't said "Damya"; I must be mellowing). Right now I'm a'goin to get me a flock of wood, a couple of gallons of this new stickum, a raft of new power tools and an atomic reactor. I'm going to build me a new boat and feel young again.

So Ends Again,
Sam.

The Following Full-Scale Builder's Blueprints for

Designs in Rabl's BOATBUILDING IN YOUR OWN BACKYARD are available:

SANDPIPER:
  Outboard Utility (5 to 10 H. P.) 15' 0" Long -- 4' 6" Beam. A Modernization
  of Sam Rabl's famous PORPOISE design. (Scale: 1 1/2" = 1')   (3 Sheets) $6.00

OSPREY:
  An outboard runabout in the modern trend, 15' 0" Long -- 6' 0" Beam. (Scale:
  1 1/2" = 1')   (4 Sheets) $8.00

TITMOUSE:
  Sailing Cruiser, (Trailer Sloop) 15' 0" Long -- 6' 0" Beam -- Mainsail Area
  95 Sq. Ft. (Scale: 1 1/2" = 1')   (5 Sheets) $11.50

FISH HAWK:
  Sport Fisherman 18' 0" Long -- 7' 0" Beam -- 20" Draft -- For 25 to 100 H. P.,
  Inboard Power. (Scale: 1" = 1')   (6 Sheets) $13.50

PUFFIN:
  An outboard cruiser designed for trailer operation, 18' 0" Long -- 7' 6" Beam.
  (Scale: 1" = 1')   (3 Sheets) $6.00

PICAROON I:
  A Tabloid Cruiser 18' 3" Long -- 7' 9" Beam -- 2' 9" Draft V-bottomed plywood planked hull. (Scale: 1" = 1') -- Sail Area 200 Sq. Ft.   (8 Sheets) $15.00

PICAROON II:
  A round-bottomed stripped hull built on the same keel as PICAROON I. (Scale:
  1" = 1')   (8 Sheets) $15.00

PICAROON III:
  This additional variation of PICAROON, not included in the book, is available.
  Designed for Auxiliary Power with Universal "Blue Jacket Twin" Model AFT-L,
  Direct Drive.
  Specifications: 23' 0" L. O. A. -- 18' 6" L. W. L. -- 8' 0" (Molded) Beam -- 4' 0"
  Draft -- 5175 Disp. -- Lbs. Per 1" at DWL = 480.0 -- C. B. located 10' 0"
  AFT FP -- Area Lateral Plane 47.6 Sq. Ft. -- Sans Rudder -- C. L. R. located
  12.7 AFT FP -- Area Designed 90.3 Sq. Ft. -- Outside Ballast, total weight,
  1300 lbs. (Scale: 1" = 1')   (7 Sheets) $15.00

KITTIWAKE:
  An inexpensive boat for the water gypsy, 24' 0" Long -- 8' 9" Beam -- 2' 0"
  Draft. (Scale: 1" = 1')   (6 Sheets) $13.50

PELICAN:
  Auxiliary Cruiser 24' Long -- 9' 0" Beam -- 3' 6" Draft -- Sail Area 260 Sq. Ft.
  (Scale: 1" = 1')   (7 Sheets) $14.00

The PLANS described above may be ordered from your bookseller, or:

CORNELL MARITIME PRESS, INC.   Cambridge, Maryland